GW01471585

STUDIES IN THE HISTORY OF THE GREEK TEXT OF THE APOCALYPSE: THE ANCIENT STEMS

TEXT-CRITICAL STUDIES

Michael W. Holmes, General Editor

Number 11

SBL PRESS

STUDIES IN THE HISTORY OF THE GREEK TEXT OF THE APOCALYPSE: THE ANCIENT STEMS

Josef Schmid

Translated and Edited by

Juan Hernández Jr., Garrick V. Allen, and Darius Müller

SBL PRESS

SBL PRESS

Atlanta

Copyright © 2018 by Society of Biblical Literature

All rights reserved. No part of this work may be reproduced or transmitted in any form or by any means, electronic or mechanical, including photocopying and recording, or by means of any information storage or retrieval system, except as may be expressly permitted by the 1976 Copyright Act or in writing from the publisher. Requests for permission should be addressed in writing to the Rights and Permissions Office, SBL Press, 825 Houston Mill Road, Atlanta, GA 30329 USA.

Library of Congress Cataloging-in-Publication Data

Names: Schmid, Josef, 1893–1975, author. |Hernández, Juan, Jr., 1968–, translator.
Title: Studies in the history of the Greek text of the Apocalypse : the ancient stems / by Josef Schmid ; translated and edited by Juan Hernández Jr., Garrick V. Allen, and Darius Müller.
Other titles: Studien zur Geschichte des griechischen Apokalypse-Textes.
Description: Atlanta : SBL Press, 2018. | Series: Text-critical studies ; Number 11 | Includes bibliographical references.
Identifiers: LCCN 2018005081 (print) | LCCN 2018024401 (ebook) | ISBN 9780884142812 (ebk.) | ISBN 9781628372045 (pbk. : alk. paper) | ISBN 9780884142829 (hbk. : alk. paper)
Subjects: LCSH: Bible. Revelation. Greek—Criticism, Textual—History.
Classification: LCC BS2825.52 (ebook) | LCC BS2825.52 .S35813 2018 (print) | DDC 228/.0486—dc23
LC record available at https://lccn.loc.gov/2018005081

Printed on acid-free paper.

Dedicated to our parents:

Juan Hernández Sr. and Margarita Hernández
Julie Grantham, Mark Grantham, and Arthur Garrick Allen
Wilma Müller and Wolfgang Müller

Contents

Second Section

Acknowledgments

This English translation of Josef Schmid's landmark *Die Alten Stämme*, volume 2 of *Studien zur Geschichte des Griechischen Apokalypse-Textes*, is both a labor of love and a fully collaborative project. Passion and diligence are required for any such undertaking, and without expertise and energy, nothing is accomplished. I am very fortunate, therefore, to have been able to conscript two friends—Garrick Allen and Darius Müller—to contribute their considerable gifts to the task.

The project originally began as a literal English translation, undertaken for my personal use during the summer of 2015. It was clear upon completion, however, that additional work could bring the translation to publication standard. I thus approached Garrick and Darius—both of whom were involved with the *Editio Critica Maior* for the Apocalypse—with a preliminary translation and a proposal. We had no publisher. No copyright. No guarantee of success. Only work ahead of us and the conviction that, "if we built it, they would come." That appeared to be enough, and we began to collaborate on this "fool's errand" in January 2016.

The translation work occupied a full fifteen months (January 2016–March 2017). We worked in tandem, independently and interdependently. Schmid's study was broken up into thirds and the editorial labors were divided evenly among us and rotated. Over the course of a month, I would edit a third of the translation, after which Garrick and Darius would review and edit the draft in the month that followed and so forth. The routine was sacrosanct, and we cycled through the entire translation once every three months. By month fifteen, the translation had been examined against Schmid's *Die Alten Stämme* countless times.

The collective effort served a single purpose: to render Schmid's work into clear English for broader consumption. To that end, our collaboration extended to a number of friends who improved the product considerably. Gary A. Long eyed every line of the manuscript and rid it of lingering infelicities. Grace Shull scrubbed the text of typos, omissions, and slips in the Greek. J. K. Elliott, Martin Karrer, James R. Royse, and Moisés Silva offered seasoned judgments on the translation quality and introduction. Peter Malik and Greg Paulson submitted useful reflections on the introductory material.

No project, of course, is possible without moral, material, and institutional support. First in the queue of credits is Mike Holmes, who supported the idea before it had fully materialized. Mike was present throughout the project's entire gestation period—from conception to final product—and shepherded it through the final stages of production. Even as we awaited word on copyright approval (and my confidence threatened to waver!), Mike possessed little doubt as to the outcome. The director of SBL Press, Bob Buller, was instrumental here, tracking down the copyright holder and securing it for the translation. The moment marked the realization of our deepest aspirations.

Time remains our most precious commodity, of course, and the translation of a work like *Die Alten Stämme* demands almost all of it. Everyday responsibilities do not evaporate in the face of such pursuits. The generosity of others, however, makes an enormous difference. My deepest expression of gratitude is therefore reserved for Brannin and Tanya Pitre, who, along with Doris and Terry Looper, underwrote a sabbatical that allowed me to work uninterrupted and to collaborate more fully with Garrick and Darius. The gift bought time for the project's expeditious completion. We could hardly expect more. Our sole petition now is that the expenditures of time and effort have resulted in a translation worthy of the original.

alea iacta est
Juan Hernández Jr.

Sigla and Abbreviations

Text-Critical Sigla

*	reading of the original hand on a manuscript
~	change in word order
+	addition
⌢	homoioteleuton
]	variant reading
[WHort]	a reading in brackets in WHort
λογος[1,2,3]	number indicates which instance(s) of a word repeated within a verse

Ancient Witnesses and Modern Editions

A	Alexandrinus
Aeth.	Ethiopic
Aν	Andreas of Caesarea
Apr	Apringius Pacensis
Aρ	Arethas of Caesarea
Arab.	Arabic
Arm.	Armenian
Beat	Beatus of Liébana
Boh.	Bohairic Coptic
Bousset	Bousset, Wilhelm. *Textkritische Studien zum Neuen Testament.* TU 11.4. Leipzig: Hinrichs, 1894.
C	Ephraemi Rescriptus
Cass	Cassiodorus
Charles	Charles, R. H. *A Critical and Exegetical Commentary on the Revelation of St. John.* 2 vols. Edinburgh: T&T Clark, 1920.
Compl.	Complutensian
Dion	Dionysius of Alexandria

f	*family*
Gig	Codex Gigas
H	von Soden's recension of AC S
Hipp	Hippolytus of Rome
I	von Soden's recension of Aν
Iren	Irenaeus
K	Koine text
Lat.	Vulgate and part of the Old Latin tradition
Latt.	entire Latin tradition
Merk	Merk, Augustinus. *Novum Testamentum Graece et Latine.* Rome: Sumptibus Pontificii Instituti Biblici, 1933.
Meth	Methodius of Olympus
MT	Masoretic Text
Oec	Oecumenius
Ωρ	Greek text of Origen
Orig	Origen
Prim	Primasius
Prisc	Priscillian
Ps-Aug	Pseudo-Augustine
S	Codex Sinaiticus
Sah.	Sahidic Coptic
Slav.	Slavonic
Soden	Soden, Hermann von. *Die Schriften des Neuen Testaments in ihrer ältesten erreichbaren Textgestalt.* 2 vols. Berlin: Duncker, 1902–1913.
Syr.	Syriac
Syr.[1]	Philoxenian Syriac
Syr.[2]	Harkleian Syriac
Tisch	Tischendorf, L. F. C. *Novum Testamentum Graece.* 3 vols. Leipzig: Köhler, 1841.
TR	Textus Receptus
Tyc	Tyconius
Vict	Victorinus of Pettau
Vog	Vogels, Heinrich Joseph. *Novum Testamentum Graece: textum recensuit, apparatum criticum ex editionibus et codicibus manuscriptis collectum addidit Henr. Jos. Vogels.* Düsseldorf: Schwann, 1920.
Vulg.	Vulgate

| Weiss | Weiss, Bernhard. *Die Johannes-Apokalypse: Textkritische Untersuchungen und Textherstellung.* TU 7.1. Leipzig: Hinrichs, 1891 |
| WHort | Westcott, Brooke Foss, and Fenton John Anthony Hort. *The New Testament in the Original Greek.* 2 vols. Cambridge: Cambridge University Press, 1881. |

General Terminology

aliqui	some
ante	before
bis	twice
cod(d).	codex(es)
comm.	*commentarium*, commentary of a manuscript when it differs from the accompanying text
corr.	*corrigendum*, corrected
cum	with
dub.	dubious
edit. rel.	*editiones reliqui*, other editions
errore	error
exc.	*exceptus*, except
fere	approximately
habet	has
hiat	*hiatus*, gap or lacuna
loco	location
mg.	*marginalia*, text in the margin of a manuscript
min.	minuscule
MS	manuscript
non	not
om.	*omittit/-unt*, omit(s)
omn.	*omnes*, all
part.	*partim*, in part
pc.	*pauci*, a few
plur.	*pluralis*, most
post	after
rel.	*reliqui*, rest of the manuscript tradition
sc.	*scilicet*, no doubt, certainly
sed	but
semel	once

sol.   *solum*, alone
ter   thrice
txt.   *textus*, text of a manuscript when it differs from the accom-
                panying commentary
txt-com   *textus-commentarium*, commentary of a manuscript when
                it differs from the accompanying text
ult.   last
var.   variant
vid.   *videtur*, reading apparent but uncertain due to condition of
                the manuscript

Primary Sources and Secondary Works

ABG   Arbeiten zur Bibel und ihrer Geschichte
Ambr.   Ambrose
ANTF   Arbeiten zur neutestamentlichen Textforschung
BETL   Bibliotheca Ephemeridum Theologicarum Lovaniensium
Bib   *Biblica*
BK   Bibliothek der Kirchenväter
BNJ   *Byzantinisch-Neugriechische Jahrbücher*
ByzZ   *Byzantinische Zeitschrift*
BZ   *Biblische Zeitschrift*
Comm. Jo.   Origen, *Commentarii in evangelium Joannis*
CSEL   Corpus Scriptorum Ecclesiasticorum Latinorum
Dem. ev.   Eusebius, *Demonstratio evangelica*
Dion.   Dionysios of Alexandria
EKKNT   Evangelisch-katholischer Kommentar zum Neuen Testa-
                ment
2 Esd   2 Esdras
EstEcl   *Estudios Eclesiásticos*
EvQ   *Evangelical Quarterly*
GCS   Die griechischen christlichen Schriftsteller der ersten drei
                Jahrhunderte
Gn   *Gnomon*
GTW   Grundriss der Theologischen Wissenschaften
HTR   *Harvard Theological Review*
JBL   *Journal of Biblical Literature*
JETS   *Journal of the Evangelical Theological Society*
JTS   *Journal of Theological Studies*

3 Kgdms	3 Kingdoms
4 Kgdms	4 Kingdoms
LXX	Septuagint
4 Macc	4 Maccabees
MThS	Münchener Theologische Studien
NovT	*Novum Testamentum*
NTS	*New Testament Studies*
NTTS	New Testament Tools and Studies
NTTSD	New Testament Tools, Studies, and Documents
OLBT	Old Latin Biblical Texts
P.Oxy.	Grenfell, Bernard P., et al., eds. *The Oxyrhynchus Papyri.* London: Egypt Exploration Fund, 1898–.
Philoc.	Origen, *Philocalia*
Ps.-Ambr.	Pseudo-Ambrose
Pss. Sol.	Psalms of Solomon
RFIC	*Rivista di Filologia e d'Istruzione Classica*
SBAW	Sitzungsberichte der Bayerischen Akademie der Wissenschaften
Sel. Ezech.	Origen, *Selecta in Ezechielem*
Sel. Ps.	Origen, *Selecta in Psalmos*
Sir	Sirach
STR	Studies in Theology and Religion
SVTG	Septuaginta: Vetus Testamentum Graecum
TC	*TC: A Journal of Biblical Textual Criticism*
TCS	Text-Critical Studies
TFBNP	Texte und Forschungen zur Byzantinisch-Neugriechischen Philologie
TLZ	*Theologische Literaturzeitung*
TQ	*Theologische Quartalschrift*
TRu	*Theologische Rundschau*
TU	Texte und Untersuchungen
TWNT	Kittel, Gerhard, and Gerhard Friedrich. *Theologische Wörterbuch zum Neuen Testament.* Stuttgart: Kohlhammer, 1932–1979.
VC	*Vigiliae Christianae*
WUNT	Wissenschaftliche Untersuchungen zum Neuen Testament
ZNW	*Zeitschrift für die neutestamentliche Wissenschaft und die Kunde der älteren Kirche*
ZPE	*Zeitschrift für Papyrologie und Epigraphik*

Translators' Introduction

The Need for an English Translation

Josef Schmid's *Die alten Stämme,* volume 2 of *Studien zur Geschichte des griechischen Apokalypse-Textes,* has stood without an English translation for over sixty years.[1] Published in 1955, the work was hailed as a

---

1. This particular work is isolated for translation because it is the crowning achievement of all of Schmid's labors, which include numerous articles and two additional, preparatory volumes—a critical edition of the Andreas commentary and a study of the commentary and its accompanying manuscript tradition—in addition to the current and final one being translated: Josef Schmid, "Zur Textüberlieferung des Oikumenios-Kommentars zur Apokalypse," *BZ* 19 (1931): 255–56; Schmid, "Der Apokalypsetext des Chester Beatty 𝔓⁴⁷," *BNJ* 11 (1934–1935): 81–108; Schmid, *Der Apokalypsetext des Arethas von Kaisareia und einiger anderer jüngerer Gruppen,* vol. 1 of *Untersuchungen zur Geschichte des griechischen Apokalypsetextes,* TFBNP 17 (Athens: Byzantinische-neugriechischen Jahrbücher, 1936); Schmid, "Untersuchungen zur Geschichte des griechischen Apokalypsetextes: Der K-Text," *Bib* 17 (1936): 11–44, 167–201, 273–93, 429–60; Schmid, "Unbeachtete Apokalypse-Handschriften," *TQ* 117 (1936): 149–87; Schmid, "Der Apokalypse-Text des Kodex 0207 (Papiri della Società Italiana 1166)," *BZ* 23 (1935–1936): 187–89; Schmid, "Die handschriftliche Überlieferung des Apokalypse-Ausleger und Oikumenios der Bischof von Trikka," *BNJ* 14 (1937–1938): 322–30; Schmid, "Die handschriftliche Überlieferung des Apokalypse-Kommentar des Arethas von Kaisareia," *BNJ* 17 (1939–1943): 72–81; Schmid, "Zur Textkritik der Apokalypse," *ZNW* 43 (1950–1951): 112–28; Schmid, *Der Apokalypse-Kommentar des Andreas von Kaisareia: Text,* vol. 1.1 of *Studien zur Geschichte des griechischen Apokalypse-Textes,* MThS 1 (Munich: Zink, 1955); Schmid, *Der Apokalypse-Kommentar des Andreas von Kaisareia: Einleitung,* vol. 1.2 of *Studien zur Geschichte des griechischen Apokalypse-Textes,* MThS 1 (Munich: Zink, 1956); Schmid, *Die alten Stämme,* vol. 2 of *Studien zur Geschichte des griechischen Apokalypse-Textes,* MThS 2 (Munich: Zink, 1955). Subsequent updates also appeared: Schmid, "Der Apokalypse-Text des Oikumenios," *Bib* 40 (1959): 935–42; Schmid, "Unbeachtete und unbekannte griechische Apokalypsehandschriften," *ZNW* 52 (1961): 82–88; Schmid, "Neue griechische Apokalypsehandschriften," *ZNW* 59 (1968): 250–58.

groundbreaking achievement that commanded near universal assent.[2] The situation remains unchanged today; the passing decades have produced no rival.[3] The publication and recognition of the work, however, are accompanied by a notable irony. Despite universal approval, the field of textual criticism has shown little (if any) serious engagement with Schmid's work. Textual critics appear to have restricted themselves to a rehearsal of the book's well-known conclusions; further inquiry was considered unnecessary.[4] Schmid's foundation quickly ossified into orthodoxy. Belief was sufficient.

The dangers of such uncritical trust are obvious.[5] Not only are researchers deprived of a detailed record of the warrants, methods, theories, and material that make such a work possible (and are therefore vulnerable to a faulty understanding of the work's achievement), but the discipline is also left without an obvious standard or measure against which to review further text-critical progress. The availability of the work in German has made little difference; the expectation that scholars would access it never translated into a comprehensive understanding of the

---

2. J. Neville Birdsall, "The Text of the Revelation of Saint John: A Review of Its Materials and Problems with Especial Reference to the Work of Josef Schmid," *EvQ* 33 (1961): 228–37; Ernest C. Colwell, "Method in Establishing the Nature of Text-Types of New Testament Manuscripts," in *Studies in Methodology in Textual Criticism of the New Testament*, NTTS 9 (Grand Rapids: Eerdmans, 1969), 45–55; G. D. Kilpatrick, "Professor J. Schmid on the Greek Text of the Apocalypse," *VC* 13 (1959): 1–13; Bruce M. Metzger, review of *Studien zur Geschichte des griechischen Apokalypse-Textes*, by Josef Schmid, *Gn* 29 (1957): 285–89.

3. See Darius Müller, "Der griechische Text der Johannesapokalypse und seine Überlieferung: Untersucht an der Teststellenkollation und Auswertungslisten in 'Text und Textwert VI. Die Apokalypse'" (PhD diss., Kirchliche Hochschule Wuppertal/Bethel, 2017).

4. This is stated outright by Kurt Aland and Barbara Aland in *The Text of the New Testament: An Introduction to the Critical Editions and to the Theory and Practice of Modern Textual Criticism*, trans. Erroll F. Rhodes, 2nd ed. (Grand Rapids: Eerdmans, 1986), 107.

5. The sole exception here appears to be Colwell's penetrating and prescient review in "Method in Establishing the Nature of Text-Types," 45–55. For a discussion of Colwell's anticipation of problems with Schmid's work that remain relevant even today, see Juan Hernández Jr., "The Creation of a Fourth-Century Witness to the Andreas Text Type: A Misreading in the Apocalypse's Textual History," *NTS* 60 (2014): 106–20.

work.[6] The truncated history of the Apocalypse's text-critical research makes this clear.

The twenty-first century has rendered the need for an English translation of Schmid's *Die alten Stämme* all the more pressing. The field has experienced seismic changes in the years since the book's publication. The discovery of new manuscripts, the rise of the digital humanities, and continued refinements in text-critical terminology and perspectives have ushered in a new era; textual critics face a fully transformed landscape today.[7] The digital humanities, for example, now furnish new and improved images for paleographical and codicological observations, deliver a number of digitization projects, and produce a steady stream of electronic collations with exacting accuracy.[8] The development of the Coherence-Based Genealogical Method (CBGM), itself a part of the digital revolution, offers yet another tool for tracking textual variation, one that plays an increasingly determinative role in the production of critical editions, most notably the *Editio Critica Maior*.[9] The advances, fast and furious as they are, easily

---

6. Martin Karrer has recently highlighted the need to reexamine Schmid's work. See his "Der Text der Johannesapokalypse," in *Die Johannesapokalypse: Kontexte—Konzepte—Rezeption / The Revelation of John: Contexts—Concepts—Reception*, ed. Jörg Frey, James A. Kelhoffer, and Franz Tóth, WUNT 287 (Tübingen: Mohr Siebeck, 2012), 43–78; Karrer, *Johannesoffenbarung (Offb.1,1–5,14)*, EKKNT 24.1 (Göttingen: Vandenhoeck & Ruprecht, 2017), 71–79; Karrer, "Der Text der Apokalypse—Textkritik und Theologiegeschichte," in *Revelation, Colloquium Biblicum Louvaniense*, ed. Adela Yarbro Collins, BETL 291 (Leuven: Peeters, 2017), 207–43.

7. These new manuscripts would include manuscripts such as P[98] (Dieter Hagedorn, "P.IFAO II 31: Johannesappokalypse 1,13–20," *ZPE* 92 [1992]: 243–47; Peter Malik, "Another Look at P.IFAO II 31 [P[98]]: An Updated Transcription and Textual Analysis," *NovT* 58 [2016]: 204–17), P[115] (David C. Parker, "A New Oxyrhynchus Papyrus of Revelation: P[115] (P.Oxy 4499)," *NTS* 46 [2000]: 159–74), and 2846 (Markus Lembke, "Die Apokalypse-Handschrift 2846: Beschreibung, Kollation und Textwertbestimmung eines wichtigen neuen Zeugen," *NovT* 54 [2012]: 369–95). The latter is particularly important in its preservation of readings that, with the exception of 02 and 04, are older than any other manuscript of the Apocalypse.

8. For digitization projects, see, e.g., The Center for the Study of New Testament Manuscripts: http://www.csntm.org/. See the various ECM projects in Münster, Birmingham, and Wuppertal: http://ntvmr.uni-muenster.de/ and http://ntvmr.uni-muenster.de/web/apokalypse-edition/open/-/blogs/final-transcription-of-apoc-104. Note also http://egora.uni-muenster.de/intf/projekte/ecm.shtml and https://tinyurl.com/SBL7011n.

9. Gerd Mink, "Contamination, Coherence, and Coincidence in Textual Transmission: The Coherence-Based Genealogical Method (CBGM) as a Complement and

overwhelm the senses and can distract from the equally important task of understanding the implications of such massive changes. The circumstances warrant a return to the history of the discipline, and Schmid's *Die alten Stämme* offers an opportunity for perspective.

The text of the Apocalypse has only now begun to reap the benefits of the aforementioned material, theoretical, and methodological advances. The newly developed tools and approaches to textual criticism were initially applied almost exclusively to New Testament books *other* than the Apocalypse. The problem with that, of course, is that text-critical approaches are tailored, by necessity, to the extant manuscript tradition; approaches limited to books *other* than the Apocalypse produce yields of limited usefulness *for* the Apocalypse. What works for one textual tradition may not work for another. Now, however, a steady stream of articles and monographs is beginning to address the imbalance. Most (though not all) are associated with the production of a new critical edition of the Apocalypse for the *Editio Critica Maior*.[10] Several volumes have already

---

Corrective to Existing Approaches," in *The Textual History of the Greek New Testament: Changing Views in Contemporary Research*, ed. Klaus Wachtel and Michael W. Holmes, TCSt 8 (Atlanta: Society of Biblical Literature, 2011), 141–216; Mink, "Problems of a Highly Contaminated Tradition: The New Testament; Stemmata of Variants as a Source of Genealogy for Witnesses," in *Studies in Stemmatology II*, ed. Pieter van Reenen, August de Hollander, and Margot van Mulken (Amsterdam: Benjamins, 2004), 13–85; Mink, "Was verändert sich in der Textkritik durch die Beachtung genealogischer Kohärenz?," in *Recent Developments in Textual Criticism: New Testament, Other Early Christian and Jewish Literature; Papers Read at a Noster Conference in Münster, January 4–6, 2001*, ed. Wim Weren and Dietrich-Alex Koch, STR 8 (Assen: Van Gorcum, 2003), 39–68. For a step-by-step introduction to the method, see http://www.uni-muenster.de/INTF/cbgm_presentation/download.html. For further information, see http://intf.uni-muenster.de/cbgm/GenQ.html. See also Peter J. Gurry, "How Your Greek NT Is Changing: A Simple Introduction to the Coherence-Based Genealogical Method (CBGM)," *JETS* 59 (2016): 675–89.

10. The new Greek critical edition of the Apocalypse, the *Editio Critica Maior*, has been under construction at the Institute for Septuagint and Biblical Research (ISBTF) of the Kirchliche Hochschule Wuppertal/Bethel since 2011. The project includes a fresh investigation of the Apocalypse's entire Greek manuscript tradition. As part of this process, a major step forward in textual research is available in the *Text und Textwert* (*TuT*) volume of the Apocalypse; see Markus Lembke et al., *Text und Textwert der griechischen Handschriften des Neuen Testaments VI: Die Apokalypse; Teststellenkollation und Auswertungen*, ANTF 49 (Berlin: de Gruyter, 2017). *TuT* contains the data of 310 Greek manuscripts that are compared at 123 test passages. The volume also includes several useful appendices to support further research, providing a more

appeared, with their findings available for peer review.[11] The availability and proliferation of such research, however, is precisely the reason for another look at Schmid's *Die alten Stämme*. A comprehensive review of the history of research can clarify the warrants, progress, and direction of text-critical projects currently underway. Without it, the production of a critical edition (any critical edition) could be constructed *ex nihilo*—unmoored from the history of text-critical research, unaccountable to prior advances, and vulnerable to text-critical myopia. A return to the history of text-critical research justifies our ongoing projects and contextualizes their production.

It could be argued, of course, that Schmid's *Die alten Stämme* is condemned to obsolescence. Advances in the field have only served to cast the work's shortcomings into bold relief. Misread data, paleographical and codicological inadequacies, the lack of terminological clarity, questionable assumptions and judgments, and other errata threaten to hamper the work's usefulness.[12] The fact that some manuscripts were unknown or

---

comprehensive set of data against which Schmid's conclusions can be evaluated. The *TuT* volume of the Apocalypse is a good starting point from which to investigate the textual development of the Apocalypse and to debate prior findings in a new light.

11. Michael Labahn and Martin Karrer, eds., *Die Johannesoffenbarung: Ihr Text und ihre Auslegung*, ABG 38 (Leipzig: Evangelische Verlagsanstalt, 2012); Marcus Sigismund, Martin Karrer, and Ulrich Schmid, eds., *Studien zum Text der Apokalypse*, ANTF 47 (Berlin: de Gruyter, 2015). See also Garrick V. Allen, "Exegetical Reasoning and Singular Readings in the New Testament Manuscript Tradition: The Apocalypse in Codex Alexandrinus," *JBL* 135 (2016): 859–80. Note also Marcus Sigismund and Darius Müller, eds., *Studien zum Text der Apokalypse II*, ANTF 50 (Berlin: de Gruyter, 2017). See also J. K. Elliott, "Recent Work on the Greek Manuscripts of Revelation and Their Consequences for the *Kurzgefasste Liste*," *JTS* 66 (2015): 574–84.

12. Chief among the misread data is perhaps Schmid mistaking the Apocalypse's postscriptorium corrections in Codex Sinaiticus for corrections contemporaneous with the book's fourth-century transcription. See Hernández, "Creation of a Fourth-Century Text Type," 106–20; Juan Hernández Jr., "The Legacy of Wilhelm Bousset for the Apocalypse's Textual History: The Identification of the Andreas Text," in Sigismund, Karrer, and Schmid, *Studien zum Text der Apokalypse*, 19–32; Hernández, "Nestle-Aland 28 and the Revision of the Apocalypse's Textual History," in *Studies on the Text of the New Testament and Early Christianity: Essays in Honour of Michael W. Holmes*, ed. Daniel M. Gurtner, Juan Hernández Jr., and Paul Foster, NTTSD 50 (Leiden: Brill, 2015), 71–81. See also Peter Malik, "The Earliest Corrections in Codex Sinaiticus: Further Evidence from the Apocalypse," *TC* 20 (2015): 1–12; Malik, "Corrections of Codex Sinaiticus and the Textual Transmission of Revelation: Josef Schmid Revisited," *NTS* 61 (2015): 595–614. Regarding paleographical shortcomings, we

unexamined by Schmid further exacerbates matters.[13] *Die alten Stämme* could justifiably be dismissed as an unreliable exemplar of old research.

The work's undeniable need for revision, however, is not a warrant for its wholesale dismissal. A dismissal would overlook what is irreplaceable about Schmid's magnum opus. Topmost is the fact that Schmid's *Die alten Stämme* is the only work to date to offer a comprehensive history of text-critical research on the Apocalypse from its earliest beginnings to 1955. Strikingly, not a single text-critical manual or commentary today has seriously engaged, let alone superseded, the substance of Schmid's historical review. This includes handbooks on New Testament textual

---

note that 2351 has two different hands, not one, as Schmid states (Schmid, *Die alten Stämme*, 34; see also P. Tzamolikos's recent edition of 2351, a work that has its own shortcomings: *An Ancient Commentary on the Book of Revelation: A Critical Edition of the Scholia in Apocalypsin* [Cambridge: Cambridge University Press, 2013]). In addition, Schmid's claim that "of the correctors who reviewed the Apocalypse's text, C^a corrects the first two leaves" and that "C^c begins with his corrections at 7:16 σκηνωσει" is incorrect. C^a (א^c) made corrections throughout the Apocalypse; C^c (א^{cc}) corrects the first two pages, and C^{c*} (thus א^{cc*}) begins at 7:16, per Tischendorf and Milne and Skeat. (See Schmid, *Die alten Stämme*, 14; see also Constantin von Tischendorf, *Novum Testamentum Sinaiticum cum Epistula Barnabae et Fragmentis Pastoris*, 2 vols. [Leipzig: Brockhaus, 1863]; Tischendorf, *Novum Testamentum Graece*, 3 vols. [Leipzig: Köhler, 1841], 3:346; H. J. M. Milne and T. C. Skeat, *Scribes and Correctors of the Codex Sinaiticus* [London: British Museum, 1938], 50). With respect to codicological shortcomings, we note that Schmid's claim that the Andreas commentary is never included in manuscripts with other NT texts is erroneous. Several manuscripts appear where the Andreas commentary is included with other NT writings (e.g., 82 94 250 254 424 632 743 911 1678 1862). See Ulrich Schmid, "Die Apokalypse, überliefert mit anderen neutestamentlichen Schriften—eapr-Handschriften," in Sigismund, Karrer, and Schmid, *Studien zum Text der Apokalypse*, 421–41; cf. Schmid, *Die alten Stämme*, 39. Schmid's unclear terms are itemized below with respect to his use of labels. Chief among Schmid's questionable assumptions and judgments, according to Colwell, is his treatment of the "old text types" as frozen blocks. See Colwell, "Method in Establishing the Nature of Text-Types," 51. A preliminary listing of errata that pertains to the corrections of Codex Sinaiticus is found in Hernández, "Nestle-Aland 28 and the Revision of the Apocalypse's Textual History," 75 n. 16. A full listing of errata in Schmid's *Die alten Stämme* is included in an appendix in the current volume.

13. 39^a, for example, was unavailable to Schmid and remains missing today. We have no information as to its whereabouts or what happened to it, and one cannot identify this manuscript with any of today's extant manuscripts. Hoskier also cites readings from Vallas's manuscript 5, which is lost or unknown today (Schmid, *Die alten Stämme*, 3 n. 1, 17). The *TuT* volume analyzes twenty-six additional witnesses that were unknown to Schmid.

criticism and major critical commentaries on the Apocalypse. Schmid's broad and comprehensive review of the history of text-critical research, a history that grounds and justifies his *recensio* of the textual tradition, remains unmatched.

But more important, Schmid's historical review is not mere *reportage*. Schmid, rather, offers a critical assessment of every major text-critical work that precedes his own. Schmid's wide-ranging review thus lays the groundwork for his own approach. His magnum opus is a full participant in a complex, extensive, and wide-ranging conversation with the uppermost tier of text-critical practitioners up to his day. Nowhere else will one find as thorough a scrutiny of the text-critical thinking of trailblazers such as Brooke Foss Westcott, Fenton John Anthony Hort, Bernard Weiss, Wilhelm Bousset, Hermann von Soden, and H. C. Hoskier, to name a few. The fact that most of the works reviewed by Schmid *still* exist only in German increases the value of an English edition of *Die alten Stämme* exponentially. Generations of sequestered and overlooked text-critical conversations would instantly become accessible to a broader audience with an English translation. The boon to text-critical knowledge cannot be overstated.

Finally, Schmid's work is noteworthy for its attempt at a systematic *recensio* of the Greek text of the Apocalypse. Every detail is made to fit within a larger scheme of the book's reconstructed textual history, and individual decisions are clarified and justified thereby. To have individual readings cohere within a larger framework, of course, is no guarantee of accuracy or legitimacy. The approach is easily a liability as well as an asset. But the attempt to fit the details into a whole discloses Schmid's larger interpretive framework with its correlating assumptions. Identifying this framework is the first step toward understanding Schmid's individual text-critical decisions, as well as offering fair and informed criticism and advancing the conversation meaningfully. No less important, the translation of the *Die alten Stämme* offers a unique opportunity for English readers to recover a forgotten chapter in the intellectual history of textual scholarship and witness the stunning individual achievement represented by Schmid's landmark work.

Schmid's Textual Groupings

Basic for understanding Schmid's work is his use of textual categories; Schmid's textual groupings and key terms are itemized below with a description of their place in his reconstruction. The description is introductory and no substitute for firsthand engagement with the work.

Stem (*Stamm*), Type (*Typ*), and Text Form (*Textform*)

The terms *stem*, *type*, and *text form* are used interchangeably throughout the work. Schmid identifies four of these: AC, P[47] S, Aν, and K. The terms *major stems* (*Hauptstämme*) or *major branches* (*Hauptäste*) also surface, but these are not predominant.[14] The division of the entire textual tradition into four major text forms is not purely descriptive for Schmid; it is also prescriptive: identifying the Apocalypse's four major text forms guides the reconstruction of the *Urtext*.[15] The groupings allow Schmid to make judgments about individual readings within the context of their particular traditions. The dangers of circularity notwithstanding, the groupings are not unequivocally determinative for the value of a specific reading. No single text form monopolizes the *Urtext* in Schmid's reconstruction; the original may be found in any one of the four stems.[16] The terms for these major textual groupings are not always used consistently, but they offer a fair representation of Schmid's major groupings.

Group (*Gruppe*)

The label *group* is applied to manuscripts whose text belongs to a particular text form but whose affinities with other manuscripts (that also fall under the same text form) are so close that they are assembled under a subordinate grouping. The Aν text, for example, is divided (by Schmid) into twelve subordinate groups of closely related manuscripts, the K text into nineteen.[17] As with Schmid's use of text forms, there is some inconsistency in his application of the term. Schmid, for example, simultaneously calls the Complutensian witnesses a group and a family.[18] In such instances, the witnesses in question should be identified by their placement in Schmid's

---

14. Ibid., viii, 13, 24, 29, 44, 111, 148–49.

15. Ibid., 29.

16. Ibid., 147–48.

17. For the Aν text, see ibid., 26; Schmid, *Einleitung*, 1–78. For the K text, see *Die alten Stämme*, 27; see also Schmid, "Untersuchungen zur Geschichte des griechischen Apokalypsetextes," 11–44, 167–201, 273–93, 429–60.

18. For group, see Schmid, *Die alten Stämme*, 5, 22, 28, 41. For family, see Schmid,

hierarchy of groupings rather than by their labels. By such a standard, the Complutensian group is a family.[19]

Family (*Familie*)

Schmid's term *family* is applied to even smaller groups of witnesses. All families in Schmid's *recensio* appear to be mixed versions of the Av and K texts. Although the term family is not applied consistently to these witnesses, their subordination under the Av and K texts renders them families. Members of this category include the Arethas group, $f^{104/336}$, the Complutensian group, and the O family.[20]

Schmid's Terms for Textual Reconstruction

Text(s)

Text is Schmid's most widely used term, and it is deployed in a variety of ways. The term is applied to the wording of a particular book or books (e.g., the text of the Apocalypse), the wording of a particular manuscript or manuscripts (e.g., the text of Codex Sinaiticus), the wording of a church father (e.g., the text of Hippolytus), the wording of a particular edition (e.g., the text of Souter), and the wording of the *Vorlage(n)*. Perhaps the most prevalent usage of text is for the wording of a particular text form (e.g., the K text). The usage of text in the context of text forms has important implications insofar as such texts are considered identifiable, coherent entities that exist as a whole, although only represented partially (or imperfectly) in the codices in which they appear; the text of a witness is an incomplete representation of the text of a stem, group, or family. The same is true for readings characteristic of particular witnesses. Schmid, for example, distinguishes between the text of S and the text of Codex Sinaiticus. The two may overlap, but they are not always the same thing. Codex

---

Die alten Stämme, 20, 24, n. 64; see also Schmid, *Der Apokalypsetext des Arethas von Kaisareia*.

19. Specifically, Schmid appears to restrict "group" to closely related manuscripts under the umbrella of a predominant text form, while family is used to refer to manuscripts that are mixed versions of existing text forms. As such, the Complutensian witnesses are a family.

20. Schmid, *Die alten Stämme*, 28–29.

Sinaiticus may or *may not* preserve the text of S. Sometimes Codex Sinaiticus preserves the text of AC, Av, K, a mixed reading, or a scribal error.[21]

Urtext/Original Text

Urtext denotes the text produced by the author. The fact that the author's linguistic style can be used to ascertain the *Urtext* confirms the definition. The *Urtext*, however, proves elusive at times. There are instances where the reading that qualifies as the *Urtext* is so problematic that a decision must be made between selecting an inadequate reading and floating a conjecture.[22] There are cases when only secondary readings are attested in the manuscript tradition; here the *Urtext* is not entirely accessible.

Neutral Text

The *neutral text* is the label Schmid assigns to the AC-Oec text form. The label reflects the fact that this particular text form preserves hardly any deliberate corrections.[23] Schmid considers the neutral text form a local text, not an "actual," "proper," or "markedly distinct" recension, as Av and K clearly are.[24] The neutral text is a corrected text, but only modestly so; Av and K, on the other hand, are full-blown recensions characterized by comprehensive editing.[25]

The neutral text overlaps with the *Urtext* but is not identical to it, differing in varying degrees from the *Urtext* at several critical junctures. There are linguistic violations that appear so egregious to Schmid, for example, that they cannot possibly be the *Urtext* in his judgment—irrespective of their support by neutral witnesses (AC Oec).[26] In such instances, the neutral text may preserve secondary readings.

The distinction between the neutral text and *Urtext*, as understood by Schmid, is important; there is a difference between Schmid's understand-

---

21. Ibid., 151 n. 2.

22. Ibid., 87.

23. Ibid., 97, 147.

24. Here Schmid follows Streeter's distinction between local texts and recensions. See B. H. Streeter, "The Caesarean Text of the Gospels," *JTS* 26 (1924–1925): 373–78; see also Schmid, *Die alten Stämme*, 118 n. 1. On Av and K as recensions, see 53, 146.

25. Schmid, *Die alten Stämme*, 250.

26. Ibid., 87, 147; cf. 96–97.

ing of the neutral text and Hort's. For Hort, the neutral text preserves a pure textual stream that flows directly from the original. The authority of the neutral text (AC) was so great for Hort that sometimes he adopts "clear errors" where only a *non liquet* is possible.[27] Thus, while the neutral text represents a separate textual development from the *Urtext* for both Hort and Schmid, Schmid's neutral text deviates from the *Urtext* with greater frequency than Hort's. Schmid concludes that Hort's neutral text is not neutral at all.[28]

Vorlage

Schmid's usage of *Vorlage* appears to conform to general text-critical parlance and denotes the exemplar used for copying a given manuscript. As throughout the rest of the New Testament, the *Vorlage(n)* of the Apocalypse's individual manuscripts must be reconstructed from the copied text in light of the textual tradition and known scribal habits. The only exceptions are cases where both manuscript and exemplar have survived. Schmid labels these manuscripts *Abschriften* and provides a list of eleven.[29] Though considered useless for the goal of *recensio* (and therefore eliminated from further consideration), these manuscripts offer excellent data for examining scribal copying practices. Schmid's itemizing of these thus preserves valuable data for the further study of scribal habits—an objective beyond his original work's concern and well outside the scope of a *recensio*.

Archetype

Archetype is nowhere defined by Schmid, though it does surface throughout the work. His usage of the term is not always clear; it is certainly less clear than the occasional obscurity that accompanies his other terms. The archetype of a textual tradition (in classical usage) refers to the lost exemplar from which subsequent splits in the tradition emerge and is distinct from and subsequent to the *Urtext*. Both the *Urtext* and the archetype are

---

27. Ibid., 244, 251; cf. 101, 108, 246; see also Brooke Foss Westcott and Fenton John Anthony Hort, *Introduction to the New Testament in the Original Greek, with Notes on Selected Readings* (Eugene, OR: Wipf & Stock, 2003), 260–63.

28. Schmid, *Die alten Stämme*, 143.

29. Ibid., 20.

considered lost; both have to be reconstructed.[30] This understanding holds in Schmid's work.

Schmid also appears to distinguish between the *Urtext* and the archetype of the entire textual tradition. The distinction is clearest, for instance, when he concludes that a particular linguistic error goes back "to the original *or at least to the entire tradition's archetype.*"[31] The *Urtext* and the archetype are thus different in this case. It is also clear that the archetype is a subsequent textual development to the *Urtext*.

Several subordinate archetypes also surface alongside the main archetype in Schmid's *recensio*. Schmid, however, makes no terminological distinction between the archetype for the whole tradition and the presumably subordinate archetypes, as classicists traditionally tend to do. The reason for Schmid's apparent reluctance is unclear, but it leads to some confusion. In classical parlance, subordinate archetypes are labeled *hyparchetypes* (or subarchetypes) and their descent from the archetype is unambiguous.[32] Schmid, however, uses no such clarifying labels. The tradition's lines of descent from the archetype to hyparchetypes must be deduced and clarified from the work itself and can only be reconstructed loosely.

The Apocalypse's hyparchetypes (adopting classical usage for illustration) branch off into four major text forms, various groups, and several families. Unlike the hyparchetypes of classical stemmata—which represent lost exemplars for *individual manuscripts*—Schmid's hyparchetypes represent the lost exemplars for *text forms, groups,* and *families.*[33] Schmid also expresses varying degrees of confidence in the possibility of reconstructing the Apocalypse's individual hyparchetypes. The greatest confidence is reserved for the reconstruction of the hyparchetypes of Av and K texts.[34] In fact, Schmid offers a handful of stemmata of hyparchetypes for *actual manuscripts* (as in classical usage) in his reconstruction of the Av text of the Andreas commentary.[35]

---

30. Paul Maas, *Textual Criticism*, trans. Barbara Flower (Oxford: Clarendon, 1958), 1–3.

31. Schmid, *Die alten Stämme*, 245, emphasis added; cf. 96.

32. Maas, *Textual Criticism*, 6.

33. See Schmid, *Die alten Stämme*, 108–9, 127, 135, 138, 147, 151, 251 (text forms); 15 n. 2, 28 (groups); 29 (families).

34. Ibid., 251.

35. Schmid, *Einleitung*, 9, 19, 23, 32, 56.

The reconstructed hierarchy of textual relationships in Schmid's *recensio* appears to be:

1. *Urtext*/original
2. Archetype of the entire Greek textual tradition of the Apocalypse
3. Hyparchetypes of stems/types/text forms, groups, and families
4. The actual stems/types/text forms, groups, and families represented in the manuscript tradition
5. Influence/infiltration from other texts, sometimes in various layers, among the various stems/types/text forms, groups, and families
6. Varying degrees of scribal activity from witness to witness—these occur at every level of the hierarchy following the *Urtext*

Schmid offers no global stemma for the major text forms, groups, and families that make up the Apocalypse's textual history in his *Die alten Stämme*. The reason is straightforward: Schmid considers it impossible to establish the connections of the major text forms of the Apocalypse's Greek textual tradition with complete accuracy and arrange them all in a stemma.[36] This may explain Schmid's reluctance to distinguish between archetypes and hyparchetypes; the labels may imply greater certainty than the data warrant.

The Major Text Forms

Alongside Schmid's major terms and categories, the details of Schmid's four major text forms and their places within the Apocalypse's textual tradition should be clarified. These are itemized and briefly discussed below.

The Two Recensions: Av and K

According to Schmid, the Av and K recensions are the only text forms that can be established with absolute certainty. This is possible through their unique readings, most of which are corrections.[37] Despite the fact that the majority of their unique readings are corrections, Av and K alone

---

36. Schmid, *Die alten Stämme*, 148.
37. Ibid., 44.

preserve the *Urtext* on occasion. Thus, according to Schmid, Av and K are not merely later revised forms of the old text of AC Oec and P[47] S but go back to *Vorlagen* that stand alongside that old text.[38] As such, they have independent value for the reconstruction of the *Urtext* and for tracking the Apocalypse's textual history. And, like the older text forms, their origins can be traced to the fourth century.[39]

The Older Text: AC

While the Av and K readings are for the most part corrections, the vast majority of AC's readings represent the *Urtext*. In fact, the AC text form alone preserves the *Urtext* in some places. Furthermore, AC's common text preserves hardly any corrections, earning it the label neutral.[40] The AC text form is thus considered superior to the other three by Schmid. Furthermore, AC's common inauthentic readings indicate that they form their own stem and are not solely related to each other by the Apocalypse's archetype; A is the more valuable of the AC text form's witnesses.[41] The generally neutral character of the AC text form, however, should not be extended to orthography, as the latter often departs from the *Urtext*.[42]

The Older Text: P[47] S

P[47] S is an old text that stands alongside AC, according to Schmid. The former, however, differs from the latter through a considerable number of corrections. In fact, P[47] S's pattern of corrections sets it apart from the three remaining text forms in opposite ways. P[47] S, for example, has no corrections where Av and K tend to have them. On the other hand, P[47] S does have corrections where the AC text form does not—usually in places where AC preserves the *Urtext* and agrees with Av and K.[43] Strikingly, readings unique to the P[47] S text form preserve the *Urtext* in only one place.[44]

---

38. Ibid., 85.

39. Ibid., 127–29, 135, 150. For problems, see Hernández, "Creation of a Fourth-Century Text Type," 106–20.

40. Schmid, *Die alten Stämme*, 97, 250; cf. 11, 53.

41. Ibid., 96–97, 109.

42. Ibid., 250.

43. Ibid., 109–10.

44. Ibid., 112.

The Western Text?

The characteristic witnesses of the Western Text (as traditionally defined) fail to surface for the Apocalypse, this despite its status as the most widely attested New Testament text form in the second century.[45] Its existence, of course, can be postulated on the basis of analogy for the Apocalypse; the fact remains, however, that no obvious traces of it surface in the extant manuscript tradition.[46] If it were uncovered, it would have to be placed at the head of the tradition, even before the neutral text, according to Schmid.[47]

An Assessment of Schmid's *Recensio, Examinatio*, and *Divinatio* of the Greek Apocalypse

Theory and Method

The theory and method that guide Schmid's text-critical practices in *Die alten Stämme* are never stated in the abstract; their results emerge, fully formed, from the work itself. The work's text-critical principles are therefore to be derived from Schmid's assessment of other projects, his empirical observations, and analyses of the book's peculiar idiom. Text-critical theory appears to follow the data in this particular work; the Apocalypse's idiosyncratic dataset dictates Schmid's text-critical thinking.

No text-critical reconstruction, however, occurs in a vacuum. Every project, irrespective of its empirical grounding, is informed by a shared

---

45. Today textual critics speak of *Western readings* rather than the *Western text*. The nomenclature used above merely reflects the state of the question at the time of Schmid's writing. Where these do surface for the Apocalypse, they fail to behave as Western witnesses. For example, Hippolytus of Rome and Irenaeus, usually cited as Western witnesses, attest to a text that is similar to the neutral text of AC for John's Apocalypse. See ibid., 12 n. 2.

46. Schmid denied that P[47] S could be identified with the Western text because they are not supported by the characteristic witnesses of that text form. Colwell countered, however, that if Western is understood as nonneutral, they could certainly serve as the equivalent of the traditionally Western text. After all, he adds, "Western has long since ceased to be a geographic term." This may be an avenue of promise in future research. See Colwell, "Method in Establishing Text-Types," 52–54; cf. Schmid, *Die alten Stämme*, 12 n. 2.

47. Schmid, *Die alten Stämme*, 149–50.

cultural knowledge. *Die alten Stämme* is no exception; a web of common assumptions binds Schmid's work to others. Furthermore, the disclosure of the web can clarify what otherwise appears obscure about Schmid's text-critical thinking or, better, expose the ways in which Schmid's thinking departs, perhaps even in a pioneering way, from that of his contemporaries.

That Schmid's *Die alten Stämme* is a pioneering work is without question. The ceding of text-critical ground to it for over six decades substantiates the claim. But the work is innovative in a way that has seldom (if ever) been recognized, even by those who have reviewed it. The work is groundbreaking not merely in its oft-rehearsed conclusions but also, and perhaps more importantly, in its status as a transitional project, a liminal project caught between two eras. In particular, *Die alten Stämme* appears to be a project that moves us from the confident reconstruction of a *recensio* typical of the classical works of Schmid's time, which operated on the assumption of an uncontaminated, closed tradition, to a more tentatively reconstructed *recensio* that is beginning to grapple with the vagaries of an open tradition showing signs of contamination. Schmid, of course, does not articulate the problem in such terms; the results of his study, however, speak volumes.

A Transitional Work

Die alten Stämme, here and there, appears to bear the hallmarks of a Lachmannian or Maasian approach to textual criticism, at least initially; the conclusions, however, set it apart. Positing direct dependence upon the works of either Karl Lachmann or Paul Maas is unnecessary; contemporary text-critical practices at the time of Schmid's research disclose a web of assumptions that ground the work in that generation of textual scholarship. *Die alten Stämme*, nonetheless, becomes untethered from the classical approach (and its assured results) and wades into the currents of a turbulent textual tradition.[48] The result is a work that ventures into uncharted terrain with a compass of limited usefulness. The journey discloses the need for a new compass.

The assumptions of *Die alten Stämme* match those of the text-critical studies of the time. First, it is assumed that there are no autographs or

---

48. This is clearest, for example, in Schmid's criticism of his predecessors, many of whom offer text-critical reconstructions he considers far too confident.

copies that have been collated from the originals; it is therefore necessary to reconstruct the *constitutio textus*—that is, the text as close to the original as possible.[49] Three tasks are necessary for the reconstruction: *recensio*, establishing what must be regarded as transmitted; *examinatio*, examining the tradition and considering whether it may be regarded as offering access to the original; and *divinatio*, reconstructing the tradition by conjecture or at least isolating corruption in the textual tradition. *Recensio* is the only term to surface explicitly in Schmid's work; it is nonetheless clear that *Die alten Stämme* executes all three tasks.[50]

Textual traditions must rest either on a single witness or on several.[51] Schmid's cursory statements identify only *one* witness for the Greek text of the Apocalypse—an archetype for the entire textual tradition. Schmid's claim, however, is asserted rather than proven.[52] As noted, hyparchetypes were also theorized by classicists, branches that split from the archetype.[53] These similarly appear in Schmid's work (broadly and in prose rather than in stemmata). The hyparchetype (or subarchetype) label is bypassed, however. He speaks only of archetypes, to be distinguished from one another only by the particular text form, group, or family represented by each. These are subordinate to the archetype of the entire textual tradition and descend from it.

Both the archetype and hyparchetypes are lost and must be reconstructed.[54] Establishing the text of the archetype draws the textual critic closer to establishing the *Urtext*.[55] Schmid's *recensio* offers mixed results. He expresses absolute confidence in the reconstruction of the archetypes (hyparchetypes) of the Av and K texts; he claims to know how these archetypes (hyparchetypes) actually read,[56] a claim he never makes about the arche-

---

49. Schmid, *Die alten Stämme*, 12.

50. Ibid.

51. Maas, *Textual Criticism*, 2.

52. Schmid, *Die alten Stämme*, 96, 245.

53. Maas, *Textual Criticism*, 6.

54. Bousset provided his own reconstruction of the Andreas archetype; indeed, he was the first textual critic to recognize the need for it and attempt it. Schmid offers a close examination and analysis of Bousset's reconstruction before providing his own. See Schmid, *Die alten Stämme*, 66 n. 3; Wilhelm Bousset, "Zur Textkritik der Apokalypse," in *Textkritische Studien zum Neuen Testament*, TU 11.4 (Leipzig: Hinrichs, 1894), 1–44; see also Hernández, "Legacy of Wilhelm Bousset," 19–32.

55. Maas, *Textual Criticism*, 2–3.

56. Schmid, *Die alten Stämme*, 251.

type for the Apocalypse's entire textual tradition. Furthermore, and consistent with the *recensio* phase, Schmid eliminates witnesses that depend exclusively on surviving exemplars. The elimination of these *Abschriften* (or apographs) is part of the *eliminatio codicum descriptorum* phase of *recensio*, another hallmark of the classical approach to textual criticism.[57]

The confident reconstruction of a stemma for the entire textual tradition requires two assumptions in the older classical approach: first, that no contamination has taken place (i.e., no scribe has combined several exemplars); second, that each scribe deviates from his exemplar, whether consciously or unconsciously. These assumptions facilitate the construction of a stemma that (1) "incontestably" demonstrates the interrelationship of all the surviving witnesses (including the number and position of all intermediate splits in the tradition), (2) allows for the certain reconstruction of the archetype everywhere (with some exceptions) that the primary split is into at least *three* branches, and (3) allows for the restoration of the text of the archetype to a point where there are no more than two readings (*variants*) from which to choose, and where the primary split is into *two* branches.[58]

This, however, appears to be where Schmid's project departs from the assured results of the older model. Although there is no explicit discussion of contamination per se in *Die alten Stämme*, Schmid disavows the kind of confident reconstruction of a stemma that *recensio* within an uncontaminated tradition would afford. Schmid concludes his review of the textual tradition by categorically stating "that it is *not* possible to determine the mutual relationships of the old major stems of the Greek text of the Apocalypse tradition completely and to classify them accurately all together in a stemma."[59] This appears to have been due to the presence of *mixture*—the equivalent of the *contamination* of which Maas speaks—that is attested nearly everywhere in the tradition.[60]

---

57. Maas, *Textual Criticism*, 2.
58. Ibid., 3.
59. Schmid, *Die alten Stämme*, 48, emphasis added.
60. Indeed, multiple terms are used in textual criticism to describe this phenomenon: conflation, text bastardy, hybridization, cross-fertilization, contaminated, cross-pollinated, mixed, non-mechanical, or open. See Michael W. Holmes, "Working with an Open Textual Tradition: Challenges in Theory and Practice," in Wachtel and Holmes, *Textual History of the Greek New Testament*, 66.

Some parts of the tradition, however, *are* represented by stemmata, notably a handful of manuscripts within the Av and K groups.[61] But this is a far cry from the entire textual tradition. Further, although it is clear that Schmid regards the reconstruction of the Av and of K archetypes a success, no such claim is made for the archetypes (hyparchetypes) of remaining text forms or for that of the entire textual tradition. Only broad sketches and approximations are possible (albeit fairly confident ones).[62] The data appear sufficiently varied that only parts of the tradition (very few!) can be represented by stemmata with their archetypal readings established.

The manuscript tradition thus appears to have set limits on Schmid's *recensio* project; the tradition turns out to have been neither closed nor free of contamination. (The *examinatio* and *divinatio* phases of the work were more successful for Schmid.)[63] Although he nowhere discusses an *open* tradition per se, the numerous examples of manuscripts that derive from two or more sources are a textbook example of this phenomenon. The same applies to the question of contamination; the frequent examples of mixture, at various levels and junctures of the Apocalypse's textual tradition, appear to point to that very same phenomenon.[64]

Schmid, to be sure, is not entirely free of the old assumptions. The fact that he overrates agreements in readings as evidence of a common lineage and underrates the possibility of coincidental agreement in errors shows it; both operate on the assumption of an uncontaminated tradition.[65] But the older model has been taken to its limits and showcases by trial and error the kind of highly contaminated textual tradition that is widely recognized in the textual tradition today. Furthermore, by abandoning the reconstruction of a stemma of text forms, groups, and families, not to mention of individual manuscripts, Schmid paves the way for an alternative approach to the problem of contamination in the Apocalypse's manuscript tradition, even if he fails to provide an adequate solution for it.

---

61. Schmid, *Einleitung*, 9, 19, 23, 32, 56; Schmid, "Untersuchungen zur Geschichte des griechischen Apokalypsetextes," 34–35, 182, 185, etc.

62. Schmid, *Die alten Stämme*, 146–51, 249–51.

63. To the point that Schmid expressed doubt that future studies will actually improve the text's restoration in any significant manner (ibid., 251)!

64. In one instance, Schmid even describes the kind of scenario that resembles the manner of contamination Maas thought unlikely. Discussing the copying habits of the scribe of f^{2073}, Schmid notes that the scribe "uses a manuscript of group *l* and another from f^{1006} in addition to his Av-*Vorlage*" (ibid., 25).

65. Colwell, "Method in Establishing the Nature of Text-Types," 51.

Facing the Future

The stage is therefore set for newer approaches to the problems disclosed by Schmid's work. The application of the CBGM, for example, a method developed precisely to deal with a highly contaminated tradition, promises to offer a new and innovative approach to the problem of mixture in the Apocalypse's textual tradition. The classical stemmata of manuscripts or text forms (already partially abandoned by Schmid) are replaced by local stemmata of readings at the level of variation units, as well as by a global stemma of texts attested by the manuscript tradition; extant texts rather than extant manuscripts will be linked in order to trace the lineage of particular textual variants back to their *Ausgangstext*, a term that had no text-critical currency in Schmid's day. The method itself is purely text genetic and examines textual relationships apart from their physical trappings. It also presupposes an open and contaminated textual tradition—the very thing that Schmid had encountered. The CBGM will thus begin where Schmid had ended and presupposes what Schmid had found.

The promise of the method, of course, awaits full disclosure; the challenges of the Apocalypse's textual tradition are unlike those of other books. The method itself has undergone refinements in its engagement with different traditions; improvements to the CBGM must continue to run their full course. The introduction of a new text-critical compass for the Apocalypse's difficult textual terrain, however, is much welcomed; more approaches—not fewer—are necessary. Finally, the battery of newer methods, coupled with the translation of Schmid's landmark work into English, promises to broaden the conversation and recontextualize text-critical trends in a period of concentrated and accelerated development. The closure of a longstanding gap in textual scholarship, a gap that has persisted for over six decades, appears imminent.

[x] Foreword

This final part of my investigation into the history of the Apocalypse's Greek text builds upon the results of my prior research. Here the Greek tradition's major ancient stems are placed side by side in order to shed light on their shared relationships, an endeavor that turned out to be far more complicated than it appeared to Hermann von Soden. I have therefore compiled a list of all the manuscripts with which I have become well acquainted in the introduction below, correcting and supplementing the lists of my predecessors, including that of H. C. Hoskier. I do not doubt that one or more of the minuscules preserving the Apocalypse will remain hidden, say, within a collection that includes all sorts of nonbiblical texts. I am nevertheless convinced that such findings will offer no new information about the history of the Apocalypse's Greek text—provided that they are only late minuscules. Of course, Hoskier (d. 8 September 1938) deserves the lion's share of the credit for ensuring that the Apocalypse's Greek textual tradition has been so exhaustively received. His enormous and indefatigable labor of thirty years produced a work that leaves every prior achievement in this field far behind. Hoskier's material forms an essential part of my own studies.

As the title of my work indicates, I limit my study to the Greek textual tradition. Two reasons guide this decision. First, I wanted to live to see the completion of these studies. Second, I believe that the time for a systematic study of the versions has not yet arrived. Only bona fide experts in these languages can use the versions without risk. Further, we lack reliable critical editions and specialized studies for most of the versions. The latter would presumably examine the individual translator's translation technique and tackle [xi] fundamental questions about the degree to which the translator intends to reproduce the Greek *Vorlagen* with accuracy and whether the translator was in fact able to achieve it. For these reasons, it appears to me that we must exercise great caution with Hoskier's statements about versional readings in the apparatus.

Nearly twenty-five years have passed since I began my studies in November 1930. The work was essentially complete in 1942, although I have repeatedly made additions and corrections from manuscripts discovered and made accessible in the meantime. My efforts to find a publisher for this work were long unsuccessful, so much so that I was resigned to the idea that the fruit of several years' labor would never be published. I would have had to come to terms with that fate had I not found a publisher of high idealism and selfless valor in H. K. Zink. I cannot overstate how indebted I am to this publishing house. I would also like to express my gratitude to the Deutsche Forschungsgemeinschaft for the prestigious grant to defray the high cost of printing. It would have been impossible even to consider going to press without their help. I would also like to thank Mr. G. Maldfeld and Mr. P. Elpidius Pax, OFM, for the fact that they so selflessly offered their services and sacrificed their time for me in the arduous editorial work. E. Nestle's keen interest in these studies was a special honor. The final part of this work has especially benefited from his attention.

Munich, June 1955

[1] Introduction

In his *Critique Textuelle*,[1] Marie-Joseph Lagrange draws attention to the contradictory facts he observes in the current state of the text-critical study of the Apocalypse: "There is agreement among editors on a critical text, with divergences, of course, but relatively minor. On the other hand, a radical opposition between critics exists when classifying manuscripts and versions into families." Although the Apocalypse's text is considered "extremely uncertain"[2] and "very poorly transmitted,"[3] modern editions actually differ little from one another, diverging mainly in purely linguistic variants that are irrelevant for interpreting the text. In general, different modern editions select from two (and no more) competing readings of the questionable ones that remain, and only a relatively small number of these readings are significant for understanding the text.[4] If we disregard Constantin von Tischendorf's preference for the text of his foundling, Codex Sinaiticus (S), the cases are indeed rare where one of the modern editions strikes an independent path. In the study that follows, the agreement or

---

1. Marie-Joseph Lagrange, *Critique Textuelle*, vol. 2 of *Introduction à l'étude du Nouveau Testament* (Paris: Gabalda, 1935), 579.

2. Bernhard Weiss, *Die Johannes-Apokalypse: Textkritische Untersuchungen und Textherstellung*, TU 7.1 (Leipzig: Hinrichs, 1891), 1. A Bludau ("Die Apokalypse und Theodotions Danielübersetzung," *TQ* 79 [1897]: 9) also appears to embrace this verdict. Weiss, however, belies his own verdict in the apodictic manner with which he is able to establish the *Urtext* almost entirely on the basis of the Greek tradition alone.

3. Adolf Jülicher, review of *The Armenian Version of Revelation and Cyril of Alexandria's Scholia on the Incarnation and Epistle on Easter*, by Fred C. Conybeare *TLZ* 33 (1908): 79. For Paul Touilleux's much less favorable verdict, see pp. 9–10, below.

4. Thus, for example, there is no agreement as to whether λινον or λιθον is the *Urtext* in 15:6, whether ηκουσα or ηκουσαν should be read in 11:12, or whether εθνων or αιωνων is original in 15:3. The textual problem in 13:10 is of far-reaching and substantial importance, where the text of all modern editions, except for Charles's, is established on general exegetical grounds.

disagreements of the modern editions[5] are repeatedly listed for two reasons: (1) the degree [2] to which the Apocalypse's text remains uncertain thereby becomes clear; (2) the practical effect of the individual researcher's methodological principles emerges. We will repeatedly see that the texts of Brooke Foss Westcott and Fenton John Anthony Hort and of R. H. Charles are on one side and that of Hermann von Soden (with Heinrich Joseph Vogels and Augustinus Merk frequently going against all other editions) is on the other, displaying the greatest distance from the text of the three Englishmen.

Since the goal of the investigation is to research the history of the text of the Apocalypse further than has been done to date, we begin with a historical overview of the modern study and criticism of the Apocalypse's text. Pride of place, of course, belongs to Karl Lachmann,[6] since he was the first to break definitively with the Textus Receptus. Before him, particularly since John Mill and Johann Jakob Wettstein,[7] an ever-increasing collection of variants accompanied the available editions. These variants, however, exerted no influence upon the text's reconstruction. As is commonly known, the manuscript basis of the Textus Receptus consists of the well-known Codex 1^r, a mediocre representative of the Aν text.[8] Not only was this hastily produced transcription very faulty, but Erasmus even ret-

---

5. The texts of Tischendorf, Westcott-Hort, Weiss, Bousset, von Soden, Vogels, Merk, and Charles are taken into account (see the abbreviations list for full citations). I ignore Swete since he usually follows Westcott-Hort. I only acquired Bover as the manuscript of this work was essentially completed. Allo does not claim to offer his own reconstructed text, nor does Nestle. For this reason I ignore their texts.

6. Karl Lachmann, *Novum Testamentum Graece* (Berlin: Reimer, 1831).

7. Caspar René Gregory (*Textkritik des Neuen Testamentes* [Leipzig: Hinrichs, 1900], 946–47, 955) lists the manuscripts first used by Mill and Wettstein (see n. 11 for Mill and Wettstein). These editions have a certain, albeit negligible, value for today's textual criticism because some of the manuscripts they used have been lost, such as 39^a and the now-lost section of 18:7–20:5 from 69 in the Apocalypse.

8. Not a representative of the K text, as E. Bernard Allo (*Saint Jean, L'Apocalypse,* 3rd ed. [Paris: Gabalda, 1933], 187) writes. That the text of the Apocalypse recovered on this basis surpasses the Textus Receptus of the rest of the New Testament books in quality (Brooke Foss Westcott and Fenton John Anthony Hort, *The New Testament in the Original Greek,* 2 vols. [Cambridge: Cambridge University Press, 1881], 2:262–63; Lagrange, *Critique Textuelle,* 597) cannot be granted. The number of unique readings in Aν is not far behind that of the K text. In addition, the Textus Receptus of the Apocalypse suffers from a number of unique errors in 1^r and a mass of errors that were made in the rushed copy.

roverted a section (22:16 from ὁ ἀστήρ to 22:21) into Greek from the Vulgate because a leaf was missing in the manuscript at this location.[9]

Lachmann, as a matter of principle, did not reproduce the [3] *Urtext* because he considered the task impossible. His text stands much closer to that of his successors than to the Textus Receptus, although at that time only A was known of the authoritative manuscripts of the Apocalypse's Greek text.

The editions of Samuel Prideaux Tregelles and Constantin von Tischendorf are the next two significant achievements.[10] The great value of the first (besides the large number of manuscripts Tregelles examined and the reliability of his apparatus) is that Tregelles, for a long time alone in England, fought for the text of the ancient manuscripts and versions and against the dominance of the Textus Receptus. Tregelles is Hort's immediate precursor in this.[11]

---

9. This text, which is bereft of any manuscript support, is also transmitted in the later editions of the Textus Receptus until the nineteenth century.

10. Samuel Prideaux Tregelles, *Book of Revelation in Greek Edited from Ancient Authorities* (London: Bagster, 1844; 2nd ed., 1872); and Constantin von Tischendorf, *Novum Testamentum Graece* (Leipzig: Winter, 1841; 2nd ed., 1849).

11. For the first time since Erasmus, Tregelles compared Codex 1^r (which Franz Delitzsch rediscovered in 1861) and Codex 69 for the Apocalypse. The second edition is changed in 229 places compared to the first (Gregory, *Textkritik des Neuen Testamentes*, 981). Although Tregelles did not know Codex Sinaiticus (S), which Constantin von Tischendorf first discovered, his text is close to Tischendorf's. The following information is important for evaluating the earlier editions: of the four authoritative manuscripts A C P^{47} S, A was used for the first time in the Walton Polyglot (Brian Walton, *Biblia sacra polyglotta* [London: Roycroft, 1657]) and afterwards by John Mill (*Novum Testamentum Graecum* [Oxford: n.p., 1707]), by Johann Jakob Wettstein (*Novum Testamentum Graecum*, vol. 2 [Amsterdam: Dommer, 1752]), and especially by Charles Godfrey Woide (*Novum Testamentum Graecum* [London: Nichols, 1786]). Tischendorf first deciphered C and published it in 1843. Tischendorf also first discovered S and published it in 1863. Frederick G. Kenyon first published P^{47} in 1934 (*The Chester Beatty Biblical Papyri: Descriptions and Texts of Twelve Manuscripts on Papyrus of the Greek Bible* [London: Walker, 1934; facsimile ed., 1936]). Also, Tischendorf was the first to make available the two late majuscules P and Q, which have always been regarded as the authoritative representatives of the Aν and K texts. Q was published in 1846 (*Monumenta sacra inedita* [Leipzig: Tauchnitz, 1846]; previously only some of its readings had stood in Wettstein) and P in 1869 (*Monumenta sacra inedita: Nova collectio*, vol. 6 [Leipzig: Hinrichs, 1869]). The text of all previous editions was therefore reconstructed without these important manuscripts, with the exception of A.

Of Tischendorf's multiple editions, the *Editio Critica Maior Octava* (1869–1872) is important because of the wealth of its apparatus, even to this day.[12] This work was especially significant for the Apocalypse at least until the appearance of Hoskier's collection of material. Like subsequent editions (with the exception of von Soden), Tischendorf prefers the three ancient majuscules A, C, and S for textual reconstruction. Further, as in all other parts of the New Testament, he also asserts his unjustified preference for Codex Sinaiticus's text, which he discovered. Tischendorf adopts unique readings from S into his text of the Apocalypse in thirty-nine places[13] and prefers S's readings in others.

[4] Westcott-Hort's extremely influential edition appeared subsequently in 1881.[14] They dispense with an apparatus as a matter of principle and offer preferred readings only where the text does not appear certain to both editors. The edition is nonetheless extraordinarily important and has been extremely influential because of Hort's introduction. For a while, the edition's methodological principles, established for the text's formation, appeared to be the last word in New Testament textual criticism. Like the text of S B in the rest of the New Testament, Hort considers AC's text in the Apocalypse the authoritative "neutral" text and only abandons it

---

12. Constantin von Tischendorf, *Novum Testamentum Graece: Editio octava critica maior*, 2 vols. (Leipzig: Hinrichs, 1872).

13. A list of the locations where Tregelles, Tischendorf, and Westcott-Hort diverge from one another is in Caspar René Gregory, *Prolegomena*, vol. 3 of Tischendorf, *Novum Testamentum Graece: Editio octava critica maior*, 331–34.

14. Westcott and Hort, *New Testament in the Original Greek*. The value of Frederick Henry Scrivener, who, alongside John William Burgon (*The Revision Revised: Three Articles Reprinted from the Quarterly Review* [London: Murray, 1883]; and H. C. Hoskier, *Concerning the Text of the Apocalypse*, 2 vols. [London: Quaritch, 1929]), was the last stalwart defender of the Textus Receptus (and, as such, an opponent of Tregelles and Westcott-Hort) for the text of the Apocalypse, lies in the initial collation of thirteen minuscules (Scrivener, *A Full and Exact Collation of About Twenty Greek Manuscripts of the Holy Gospels (Hitherto Unexamined)* [Cambridge: Cambridge University Press, 1853]; Scrivener, *An Exact Transcript of the Codex Augiensis: A Graeco-Latin Manuscript of S. Paul's Epistles* [Cambridge: Deighton, Bell, 1859]). I do not have firsthand familiarity with the New Testament editions by Thomas Sheldon Green (*A Course of Developed Criticism on Passages of the New Testament Materially Affected by Various Readings* [London: Bagster, 1856]) and William Kelley (*Revelation of John: Edited in Greek with a New English Version, and a Statement of the Chief Authorities and Various Readings* [London: Williams & Norgate, 1860], Apocalypse only). These have not exerted any influence on further textual research.

where it exhibits obvious error.[15] Unlike Tischendorf, Hort underscores the inferiority of S's text—a text where various text forms are juxtaposed and superimposed and that also teems with idiosyncratic readings and scribal oversights. Because the superior quality of AC's text (especially of A) is undeniable (and was also recognized by the successors of Westcott-Hort), the text of their successors understandably does not differ substantially from that of Westcott-Hort.

Bernhard Weiss's (1891) penetrating investigation of the Apocalypse's Greek text appeared after Hort. Like Westcott-Hort, Weiss rejects Tischendorf's unilateral preference for S. Unlike Westcott-Hort, where the reasons for their decision remain unclear in some cases, Weiss—in a careful and detailed work whose results are laid out before the reader—examines the peculiarity of the individual textual witnesses thereby creating the basis both for their assessment and for the evaluation of variants. Weiss's study uncovers two major text forms: an unrevised "older text" whose witnesses are AC and S, and a heavily corrected "younger text" upon which the two later majuscules P and Q depend. Weiss pursues [5] the relationship of the individual textual witnesses to one another with special care. As testimony to his method, he almost always arrives at a clear decision, having evaluated each reading with apodictic certainty on the basis of the Apocalypse's linguistic style, as well as on the basis of psychological and exegetical considerations. Weiss's text is also very close to Westcott-Hort's, since he also places a high value on AC.

Following a method similar to Weiss's, Wilhelm Bousset also investigated the Apocalypse's textual tradition in a preliminary text-critical study for his commentary on the Apocalypse (1894), as well as in the commentary itself.[16] In these studies, Bousset turns decisively against Weiss's assertion that P and Q depend upon a later revised text and that they are related to each other in this way. Rather, Bousset submits evidence that P and Q (or the two recensions of Aν and K) are two entirely independent, parallel recensions. Their common foundation "is, at least, very narrow"; "it is so far back, and so few traces of it have survived that it defies further investigation."[17] Bousset's judgment that the two majuscules P and Q should not be treated in isolation, as Weiss had done, but in conjunction

---

15. See Westcott and Hort, *New Testament in the Original Greek*, 2:260–63.

16. Wilhelm Bousset, *Textkritische Studien zum Neuen Testament*, TU 11.4 (Leipzig: Hinrichs, 1894).

17. Ibid., 10–11.

with all the minuscules that form a stem of the Apocalypse's textual tradition with P and Q is well founded. Bousset examines the Aν text[18] in his *Textkritische Studien zum Neuen Testament*. However, what he establishes as the Aν text is often wrong because he relies on Tischendorf's material. In particular, Bousset is mistaken—due to gaps in Tischendorf's data—in claiming that the Complutensian group was the most reliable witness for Aν.[19] Bousset's studies nevertheless signal an advance over Weiss's, particularly in their use of the versions alongside Greek manuscripts. Bousset also applies the principle that the author's linguistic style is decisive for reproducing the original text with greater consistency than Weiss. Bousset's text differs at many locations from Weiss's (and Westcott-Hort's) and is founded on the assumption—and here he is the forerunner of von Soden—[6] that Aν and K should be considered two entirely independent text forms and that their common text is usually also the original. Bousset's judgment about AC's value is also necessarily less favorable than that of Westcott-Hort and Weiss.

Of the subsequent critical editions, those of Henry Barclay Swete and Alexander Souter are less important.[20] Swete usually follows Westcott-Hort, and Souter offers the Greek text behind the English Revised Version of 1881. Souter's text is thus not actually his work.

The value of von Soden's work (1910 and 1913) lies primarily in the substantial increase of manuscript material over Tischendorf.[21] Von Soden also believed he could demonstrate the existence of his three recensions H (= AC S), I (= Aν), and K in the Apocalypse, which he assumed were fully independent of one another, as he thought was the case in all of the New Testament's other books.[22] This system results in a significantly lower

---

18. Called K by Bousset.

19. Bousset, *Textkritische Studien*, 12–13.

20. Henry Barclay Swete, *Apocalypse of St. John*; Alexander Souter, *Novum Testamentum Graece*, 2nd ed. (Oxford: Clarendon, 1947).

21. Hermann von Soden, *Die Schriften des Neuen Testaments in ihrer ältesten erreichbaren Textgestalt*, 2 vols. (Berlin: Duncker, 1902–1913)

22. "Just as between Aν and K no relationship likely exists, neither does one between H and one of the other two; the three texts are independent in stature over one another. There is no reason to doubt that a unique reading, represented only by one of these strands, is secondary every time" (von Soden, *Die Schriften des Neuen Testaments*, 1:2075).

Particularly important is §543 (1:2079–84), where von Soden discusses the places where it is difficult to decide on which side the unique reading lies. Here he explains

rating of the text of H (= AC S) for the Apocalypse than his predecessors, including Westcott-Hort and Weiss.

[7] In contrast to his predecessors, Charles's edition (1920) is a completely independent achievement.[23] Charles also collated many manuscripts himself, yet he failed to examine the recensions of Av, K, and the Complutensian. As such, Charles's method is a step back from von Soden and Bousset to Weiss.[24] Like Bousset, however, Charles applies the principle that the author's linguistic style is decisive for reconstructing the text. However, he overemphasizes this correct principle when he dismisses any verses or parts of a verse where a unanimous or mostly attested expression contradicts the author's linguistic style as glosses of a later redactor. By considering the author's linguistic style, Charles concludes that AC are the authoritative textual witnesses for the Apocalypse, and with that he returns to Westcott-Hort.[25]

---

that often the reading offered by two recensions is suspicious because of the parallel. "The idea that reminiscences have coincidentally affected two recensions in the same place is more likely than the argument that the third reading is supported by parallels." This is especially likely if H alone offers the unique reading; K and Av together provide agreements in other places, since Av and K owe most of their unique readings to the influence of reminiscences. Every now and then, however, K or Av alone could have preserved the original reading. These judgments are important because they express that even where two recensions have the same correction, von Soden maintains their mutual independence and because they show that he does not apply the principle cited at the beginning of this note consistently. We should observe, however, that almost all of the decisions von Soden makes in §543 are overturned in the edition. In an extremely high number of places discussed in the mentioned section, one stands before a real riddle.

23. R. H. Charles, *A Critical and Exegetical Commentary on the Revelation of St. John*, 2 vols. (Edinburgh: T&T Clark, 1920).

24. Charles considers P and Q, though not in the same exclusive way as Weiss, for his study without all the corresponding minuscules. According to the total stemma that Charles establishes for the tradition of the Apocalypse's text (*Critical and Exegetical Commentary on the Revelation*, 1:clxxxi), P and Q are not related to each other exclusively by their shared relationship with the original. However, nowhere does Charles come closer to the question of their mutual relationship.

25. The edition of John Oman, *The Text of Revelation: Theory of the Text, Rearranged Text and Translation* (Cambridge: Cambridge University Press, 1923); 2nd rev. ed. under the title *The Text of Revelation: A Revised Theory* (Cambridge: Cambridge University Press, 1928), is irrelevant. This work is an attempt to rearrange the Apocalypse's textual sequence. Oman holds—apart from minor changes and different verses or words that should be removed as interpolations of a redactor—the following textual

The text-critical principles of the hand editions of Heinrich Joseph Vogels (1920, 1949), Augustinus Merk (1933, 1951), and José María Bover (1943, 1953) are not as clear.[26] Their texts stand relatively close to von Soden's.

Hoskier's *Concerning the Text of the Apocalypse* appeared in 1929, a work that took thirty years to complete. Here the most complete collection of material is presented for the Apocalypse's text, [8] a collection that even far surpasses von Soden's. Only a few manuscripts were unknown or inaccessible to Hoskier, and he collated independently and with great accuracy most of the manuscripts that were already known. Therein lies the value of Hoskier's work. However, his data for the patristic citations and versions must be used with caution.[27] Hoskier also did not undertake his own reconstruction of the *Urtext*. This is not a loss for scholarship, however. Hoskier's views concerning the New Testament's textual history deviate radically from what is otherwise considered the reliable results of modern textual criticism.[28] This great work was preceded by the much more prob-

---

arrangement as correct: 1:9–3:21; 10:1–19:21; 4:1–9:21; 21:9–22:20; 20:11–21:6. Oman believes that 1:1–8 and 22:21 are insertions by the editor of the book, which had been left behind by its author in the form of a bundle of imprecisely ordered loose leaves.

26. Heinrich Joseph Vogels, *Novum Testamentum Graece* (Düsseldorf: Schwann, 1920; 3rd ed., 1949); Augustinus Merk, *Novum Testamentum Graece et Latine* (Rome: Sumptibus Pontificii Instituti Biblici, 1933; 7th ed., 1951); José María Bover, *Novi Testamenti Biblia graeca et Latina* (Madrid: Consejo Superior de Investigaciones Científicas, 1943; 3rd ed., 1953). Augustinus Merk outlines his own text-critical principles in "Nova editio Novi Testamenti graece et latine," *Bib* 24 (1943): 182–84; José María Bover outlines his in the prolegomena (*Novi Testamenti Biblia graeca et Latina*, lvi–lxv). Because of these principles, Bover arrives at an unwarranted overestimation of the minuscule 1841, which he describes as "sincerissimi archetypi fidelissima et quasi photographica translatio." Bover deals with it more thoroughly in "¿El códice 1841 (= 127) es el mejor representante del Apocalipsis?," *EstEcl* 18 (1944): 165–85.

27. The data for Hippolytus's text are quite useless. Hoskier ignores Achelis and Bonwetsch's authoritative edition here (*Exegetische und homiletische Schriften*, vol. 1 of *Hippolytus Werke*, GCS 1.2. [Leipzig: Hinrichs, 1897]).

28. See Bousset's judgment ("Neues Testament: Textkritik," *TRu* 17 [1914]: 199–200): "He is a textual critic who charts his own path, working entirely alone and away from the traditional tracks." Also, the first volume of Hoskier's great work (*Concerning the Text of the Apocalypse*, which, alongside some useful material, contains much that is useless) repeatedly delivers new samples of his idiosyncratic opinions. The paleographical description of the manuscripts is quite inadequate.

lematic *Concerning the Date of the Bohairic Version*, which is also limited on the whole to the Apocalypse.[29]

Paul Touilleux outlined his view of the Apocalypse's textual tradition and the contemporary state of its text-critical study in an introductory chapter (pp. 11–24) of his *L'Apocalypse et les Cultes de Domitien et de Cybèle*.[30] Touilleux believes that the textual criticism of the Apocalypse is still very much in its infancy.[31] Everything that has been done to date only serves to demonstrate how the existing problems cannot be solved. Touilleux, however, makes no mention of one of the most unassailable criteria for evaluating textual witnesses: the author's linguistic style. Touilleux believes that the Greek tradition has to be approached with great suspicion, since the majority of its witnesses only produce a text that was standardized in the fourth century. With this approach, however, Touilleux ignores the weighty testimony of the third-century P^{47}. Further, the claim that the Apocalypse's Greek text was standardized in the fourth century not only lacks any compelling evidence but is also extremely unlikely, since from the third century the Apocalypse had been disputed in the Greek Church for hundreds of years. [9] On the contrary, the Greek tradition does not bear witness to an ecclesiastical standard text (= K), which displaces all other text forms on Greek soil, but to four text forms, AC, P^{47} S, Aν, and K, all four of which demonstrably reach back to the fourth century. In line with his perspective, Touilleux considers the versions more reliable witnesses. He nonetheless must concede that the older of the two Syriac versions does not predate the sixth century and that the oldest Armenian version does not precede the fifth. And should the two Coptic versions be considered much older at all? Touilleux then claims that the study of the versions led to the conclusion that a common text type existed for the Latin and Oriental versions.[32] According to Touilleux, the common readings of the versions

---

29. H. C. Hoskier, *Concerning the Date of the Bohairic Version Covering a Detailed Examination of the Text of the Apocalypse and a Review of Some Writings of the Egyptian Monks* (London: Quaritch, 1911).

30. Touilleux, *L'Apocalypse et les Cultes de Domitien et de Cybèle* (Paris: Geunther, 1935), 11–24.

31. If the textual problem in the Gospels and Paul's letters is not yet solved, "it has not been fully discussed, so far as we are aware, for the Apocalypse."

32. Touilleux refers to Charles's judgment (*Critical and Exegetical Commentary on the Revelation*, 1:clxxix): "The presence of a common Latin (?) element in sy[1] arm sa aeth calls for investigation. Most of this element, no doubt, goes back to lost Greek MSS, but there appears to be a residuum of Latin readings which made their way

against the Greek tradition ought to compel this conclusion because of their number, their character, and their constantly changing testimony: "At an early date—just like other texts from the Greek world—the collection of manuscripts included readings that are now found only in versions and accidentally in a few minuscules."[33] Touilleux believes that the disappearance of these very readings from nearly the entire Greek tradition shows that perhaps one ecclesiastical standard text displaced all other text forms in the Greek tradition from the fourth century. Touilleux then points out that the oldest majuscule manuscript, S, stands closest among all Greek manuscripts to the old Latin and Coptic versions.[34] Touilleux overlooks, however, that we now have in P[47] an older sister manuscript to S, which allows us to evaluate S's text with even greater certainty than before and to establish its secondary character vis-à-vis AC, as well as the expressed mixed character of the text of S. Furthermore, Touilleux completely overlooks that many of S's readings can be shown—by exegetical means and by comparison with AC, A𝜈, and K—to be corrections or errors. The minuscules 2329, 1854, and 1611, which he calls witnesses of an old [10] text existing alongside or rather before the "ecclesiastical standard text," are related to P[47] S and AC precisely where they differ from K, and where they agree with the versions against K, there they have the support (setting aside isolated exceptions) of AC or P[47] S or all of these together at the same time. Touilleux then explains that P[47] agrees with those manuscripts that are most closely related to the versions and thereby confirms the great antiquity of this text.[35] But this text is just AC's text, and more recent text critics—perhaps with the exception of Frederick Henry Scrivener and H. C. Hoskier—have never thought to prefer the ecclesiastical text offered "by the majority of the Greek manuscripts." Furthermore, closer examination does not confirm the claim that the citations in Origen, Eusebius (= Dionysius of Alexandria), and Methodius would prove the existence of the Syro-Latin text type in the Greek-speaking region in the third and fourth centuries.[36]

---

into sy[1] and other versions." See also Hoskier, *Concerning the Text of the Apocalypse*, 1:xx–xxi.

33. Touilleux, *L'Apocalypse et les Cultes de Domitien*, 20.

34. Ibid.

35. Ibid., 21.

36. Ibid., 22. The places that Touilleux quotes from Clement of Alexandria turn out, without exception, to be unimportant upon closer inspection.

Lastly, we mention the section that deals with the Apocalypse in Lagrange's *Critique Textuelle* (1935). That section offers a critical presentation of prior research illustrated with various examples. Lagrange grants that Bousset is correct (against Weiss) in claiming that the texts of P and Q are two independent "quasi-recensions" that stand next to each other,[37] but then he identifies—paradoxically—only two major text forms of the Apocalypse: the "great uncials" (AC S), which is also confirmed by P[47] and Hippolytus's citations, and the group that became the ecclesiastical text type. Lagrange also emphasizes: "There is no Greek text that can be said to be Western, either for the Gospels and the Acts or for St. Paul."[38] Lagrange appears to prefer von Soden's text to Westcott-Hort's textual reconstruction, which is closely aligned with AC. Lagrange himself deals most thoroughly with the Latin versions and with the results of Vogels's investigation of them.

The studies of the Apocalypse's versions are these: the critical edition of the Latin commentary of Victorinus in its various forms by Johannis Haussleiter, the edition accompanied by valuable studies of the older of the two Syrian versions of the Apocalypse by John Gwynn, [11] Fred C. Conybeare's *The Armenian Version of Revelation*, the editions (with English translation) of the two Coptic versions (Sahidic and Bohairic) translated by George William Horner), and the studies on the history of the Apocalypse's Latin versions by Heinrich Joseph Vogels, including as a supplement the somewhat unsuccessful critical edition of Beatus's commentary by Henry A. Sanders and the correction of Sanders's important work by Wilhelm Neuss.[39]

---

37. Lagrange, *Critique Textuelle*, 595.

38. Ibid., 589.

39. Johannis Haussleiter, *Victorini Episcopi Petavionensis Opera*, CSEL 49 (Vienna: Tempsky, 1916); John Gwynn, *The Apocalypse of John in a Syriac Version Hitherto Unknown* [Dublin: Academy House, 1897); Fred C. Conybeare, *The Armenian Version of Revelation and Cyril of Alexandria's Scholia on the Incarnation and Epistle on Easter* (London: Text and Translation Society, 1907); George William Horner, *The Coptic Version of the New Testament in the Northern Dialect*, 4 vols. (Oxford: Clarendon, 1898); Horner, *The Coptic Version of the New Testament in the Southern Dialect*, 7 vols. (Oxford: Clarendon, 1911); Heinrich Joseph Vogels, *Novum Testamentum Graece* (Düsseldorf: Schwann, 1920); Henry A. Sanders, *Beati in Apocalipsin libri duodecim* (Rome: American Academy in Rome, 1930); Wilhelm Neuss, *Die Apokalypse des hl. Johannes in der altspanischen und altchristlichen Bibel-Illustration*, 2 vols. (Münster: Aschendorff, 1931).

Here are the goals of the following investigation:

(1) To ascertain and detail the characteristics of the two recensions, Aν and K, by completely enumerating their unique readings. With the material available today, we can improve upon not just the work of Weiss and Bousset but also that of von Soden and Charles. Apart from a few exceptional cases, determining the original K text is a relatively simple task. Determining the Aν text with precision, however, is much more difficult. Here we eliminate the first of several mixed forms of Aν + K, which von Soden classified together under the I stem with the actual text: Compl., $f^{104/336}$, $f^{172/250}$ (= O) and Aρ. Next, we use Andreas's commentary to determine the Andreas text that the ancient commentator actually read. With the help of the commentary, we can generally determine the original Aν text without relying on the kind of subjective criteria von Soden uses. Because this work has already been carried out in a previous part of my studies,[40] those results can be used here. Also, P and Q are no longer isolated from the minuscules and used as the authoritative witnesses of the two text forms Aν and K—which they in no way are, P much less so than Q—but the entire manuscript tradition is taken into account.

(2) We must investigate the relationship between Aν and K (which Weiss and Bousset do not actually complete and their successors only skim) and especially the [12] relationship of each of the individual major text forms to each other with the most complete and accurate representation of the facts.[41]

(3) Bousset had already noticed that the "older text" represented by AC S is not uniform when he observed the close relationship between S and Origen's text. With the discovery of P[47], however, we can now distinguish P[47] S as its own text type opposite AC and the two recensions of Aν and K as well as determine its individual character. P[47] also allows us to

---

40. See Josef Schmid, "Untersuchungen zur Geschichte des griechischen Apokalypsetextes: Der K-Text," *Bib* 17 (1936): 11–14, 167–201, 273–93, 429–40; Schmid, *Der Apokalypsetext des Arethas von Kaisareia und einiger anderer jüngerer Gruppen*, vol. 1 of *Untersuchungen zur Geschichte des griechischen Apokalypsetextes*, TFBNP 17 (Athens: Byzantinische-neugriechischen Jahrbücher, 1936).

41. Von Soden's assumption that the three text types H I K stood alongside each other independently suffers from the outset of internal improbability. If we can observe a strong mutual influence of the different text forms in a later period, then it is hardly imaginable that at the beginning the texts would have been hermetically sealed off from each other for a long time.

capture the well-known character of S as a mixed text with greater accuracy and certainty.

(4) We will also examine the places where AC stand against the rest of the tradition (first of the Greek tradition). Here we will address one of the fundamental questions of the criticism of the Apocalypse's text, namely, whether the assessment of this text form as neutral is entirely correct.

(5) The foundation upon which the two recensions were created should be examined; that is, the relationship of Aν and K to AC and P^{47} S must be studied.

Therefore, the tradition is broken down into its different and demonstrable branches and shoots, and their mutual relationships are examined in the first major section of this study.

(6) The second major section examines the value of this tradition's witnesses and its individual branches by providing data that illustrate the author's linguistic style. The use of the manuscript tradition and the consideration of the author's linguistic style are the two factors that must be used for the *recensio* of each written work (of which the original is no longer available).[42]

---

42. Two more problems no longer belong to the scope of the task that I have set for myself: (1) How did the ancient versions (Lat., Syr.$^{1.2}$, Sah., Boh., old Arm.) relate to those demonstrable text forms in the Greek tradition? Von Soden's contention that they would all represent the same text lying before the recension is in much need of investigation. (2) Does the Apocalypse have a "Western text?" Wilhelm Bousset (*Die Offenbarung Johannis* [Göttingen: Vandenhoeck & Ruprecht, 1896], 156–57) answers this question affirmatively; Lagrange (*Critique Textuelle*, 589, 591–93) denies it, correctly in my view, at least when the Greek textual tradition alone is taken into account. The fact that Hippolytus of Rome, who comes into consideration mainly as a witness to the Western text and from whom we receive extensive citations of the Apocalypse, bears witness to AC's "neutral text" is particularly important. Neither do Irenaeus's citations depart noticeably from this text. See also Hort's judgment on the matter (*New Testament in the Original Greek*, 2:260): "Probable traces of a Western and perhaps an Alexandrian text may be discerned, with analogous relation to the extant uncials which contain other books; but they are not distinct enough to give much help." Must we assume that the Apocalypse's textual history developed differently than that of the other New Testament writings? In any case, this cannot be connected with concerns over the Apocalypse's place in the canon because the fight against it only begins after Origen. The Apocalypse's "Origen text" (P^{47} S), however, cannot be identified with the Western text because the characteristic witnesses of the latter are missing. This most important question can only be based on a careful examination of those versions, if it is to be solved at all.

[13] Before turning to the actual subject matter of this investigation into the history of the Apocalypse's Greek text, that is, to a discussion of the Apocalypse's ancient major stems and linguistic style, I offer (§1.1) a broad overview of the manuscript tradition and then deal with (§1.2) the Apocalypse's place within the New Testament textual tradition. I also relate the citations of the Greek ecclesiastical writers, as well as the ancient papyrus and parchment fragments (except P⁴⁷), to the discussion of the ancient major stems.

1.1. Witnesses for the Greek Text of the Apocalypse

All the material for the witnesses of the Apocalypse's Greek text[43] can be grouped properly into manuscripts (§1.1.1) and patristic citations (§1.1.2).

1.1.1. The Apocalypse's Greek Manuscripts

These are divided into the papyri (§1.1.1.1), the majuscules (§1.1.1.2), and the minuscules (§1.1.1.3)

1.1.1.1. The Papyri

- P¹⁸ = P.Oxy. 1079 (London, Brit. Mus. 2053ᵛ), third/fourth century, contains Rev 1:4–7. See A. S. Hunt, *The Oxyrhynchus Papyri: Part VIII* (London: Egypt Exploration Society, 1911), 13–14.
- [14] P²⁴ = P.Oxy. 1230 (Newton Centre, MA, USA, Andover Newton Theological School), early fourth century, contains Rev 5:5–8; 6:5–8. See Bernard P. Grenfell and A. S. Hunt, eds., *The Oxyrhynchus Papyri: Part X* (London: Egypt Exploration Fund, 1914), 18–19.

The text of both is printed in Charles, *Critical and Exegetical Commentary on the Revelation*, 2:447–51.

- P⁴³ = London, Brit. Mus. pap 2241, contains Rev 2:12–13; 15:8 to 16:2 (seventh century?). See W. E. Crum and H. J. Bell, eds., *Wadi Sarga: Coptic and Greek Texts from the Excavations Undertaken by the Byzantine Research Account*, Coptica 3 (Hauniae: Gyldenalske Boghandel-Nordisk, 1922), 43–45.

---

43. I refer to the texts available in the Greek language. I do not deny that the versions are also indirect witnesses of the Greek texts.

♦ P⁴⁷ = Dublin, Chester Beatty, consists of ten leaves of a third-century papyrus codex, containing Rev 9:10–17:2 with minor gaps. See Kenyon, *Chester Beatty Biblical Papyri*, fasc. 3. P⁴⁷ towers over the rest of the papyri in age and scale. It is the oldest Greek manuscript containing extensive parts of the Apocalypse.

1.1.1.2. The Majuscules[44]

♦ S = London, Brit. Mus. Add. MS 43725, the well-known Codex Sinaiticus, fourth century. Of the three scribes who copy Codex Sinaiticus, D and A transcribe the text of the Apocalypse. D copies 1:1–5 to νεκρων; A copies the rest.[45] The portion copied by A is much more defective than D's. Above all ει and ι are constantly confused, and scribe A frequently writes -αν and -ην (for -α and -η) in the accusative singular of the third declension.[46] Of the correctors who reviewed the Apocalypse's text, Cᵃ corrects the first two leaves; Cᶜ begins with his corrections at 7:16 σκηνωσει.

♦ A = London, Brit. Mus. Reg. I D V–VIII, the well-known Codex Alexandrinus, fifth century.

♦ C = Paris, B. N. Gr. 9, the Codex Ephraemi rescriptus, fifth century. [15] The following portions are missing from the Apocalypse: 1:1; 3:20 init.–5:14 προς [εκυνησαν, 7:14 οι ερχομενοι–7:17 θεος παν, 8:5 init.–9:16 αυτων, 10:11 ε]φαγον αυτο–11:3 ημερας, 16:13 ως βατραχοι–18:2 φυλακη², 19:5 και οι μεγαλοι–22:21.

♦ P (025) = Leningrad, Öff. Bibl. 225, the Codex Porphyrianus, is a palimpsest. The first layer of the palimpsest's text is the Praxa-

---

44. Of the ancient majuscules, B (the Codex Vaticanus) is missing, from which a number of leaves has been lost at the end (from Heb 9:15 onward), as is well known. We may well suspect that the Apocalypse was also once preserved in B. Sixty-six leaves are missing between Mark and last verses preserved in John 3 in Codex Bezae (Dᵉ·ᵃ). John Chapman ("The Original Contents of Codex Bezae," *Expositor*, 6th ser., 12 [1905]: 46–53; Chapman, "The Order of the Gospels in the Parent of Codex Bezae," *ZNW* 6 [1905]: 341 n. 1) tried to demonstrate which lost leaves had preserved the Apocalypse and John's three epistles. The loss of precisely this witness would be especially sensitive to the problem of the Apocalypse's Western text, if Chapman were correct.

45. See the detailed study by H. J. M. Milne and T. C. Skeat, *Scribes and Correctors of the Codex Sinaiticus* (London: British Museum, 1938), 29.

46. See ibid, 54.

postolos and Revelation, tenth (not the eighth or ninth) century.[47]
The Apocalypse is missing the following sections: 16:12 η οδος–
17:1 των επτα, 19:21 αυτων–20:9 αγιων και την, 22:6 ταχει–22:21,
and several words in 5:6–11; 11:13; and 22:2.

P cannot be placed alongside the old majuscules S AC—as has cus-
tomarily been done—since it comes from a time when the minuscule had
long become predominant and the readings that give it its value are only a
secondary layer over the Aν textual foundation.[48]

- ◆ Q (046, Tischendorf and Hoskier mislabel it B) = Vatic. gr. 2066,
  fols. 259–278, is a ninth-century parchment[49] that contains the
  Apocalypse among writings of Basil and Gregory of Nyssa.[50]

- ◆ 051 (Hoskier E) = Athos, Pantokrator 44, is a tenth-century parchment, of which ninety-two leaves are preserved. The manuscript
  contains the Apocalypse with Andreas of Caesarea's commentary, and fols. 89–92 contain John of Damascus, περὶ τῶν ἐν πίστει
  κεκοιμημένων. The text begins in the middle of the commentary to
  Rev 11:14. A leaf is missing between fols. 10 and 11 and between
  fols. 81 and 82. Two leaves are missing between fols. 83 and 84.
  The Apocalypse's text is copied in a majuscule script and the commentary is copied in a minuscule.

- ◆ 052 (Hoskier F) = Athos, Panteleimon 99,2, consists of four
  leaves of a tenth-century parchment that contains Rev 7:11–8:12
  with Andreas of Caesarea's commentary. The Apocalypse's text
  is, exactly as in the previous manuscript, copied in a majuscule
  script. The commentary is copied in a minuscule.

- ◆ 0163 = P.Oxy. 848, University of Chicago, Oriental Institute 9351,
  is a leaf of a fifth-century parchment codex that contains Rev
  16:17–19. [16] See Grenfell and Hunt, The Oxyrhynchus Papyri:
  Part VI, 6.

---

47. The pinax to Arethas of Caesarea's commentary precedes the Apocalypse's
text, providing a clear terminus post quem.

48. Just as in Aν group 052 – 1678 – 1778 – 2020 – 2080, whose archetype is probably older than P. There is therefore no ancient text revised toward Aν in P, as Bousset (Textkritische Studien, 8) considers likely and von Soden (Die Schriften des Neuen
Testaments, 1:2072) claims as certain.

49. Dating according to a personal note from Mons. R. Devreesse.

50. See Gregory, Textkritik des Neuen Testamentes, 120–21; Schmid, "Untersuchungen zur Geschichte des griechischen Apokalypsetextes," 429–30.

- 0169 = P.Oxy. 1080, now Princeton Theological Seminary Pap 5, is a leaf of a fourth-century parchment manuscript that contains Rev 3:19–4:3. See Hunt, *Oxyrhynchus Papyri: Part VIII*, 14–15. See also the illustration of George Milligan, *The New Testament Documents: Their Origin and Early History* (London: Macmillan, 1913), table VIII (at the bottom of p. 196).

The two fragments 0163 and 0169 are printed and discussed in Charles, *Critical and Exegetical Commentary on the Revelation*, 2:448–51 (frags. II and IV).

- 0207 = Florenz, Papiri della Società Italiana 1166, is a leaf of a fourth-century parchment manuscript with Rev 9:2–15, edited by Girolamo Vitelli (*Papiri Greci e Latini*, vol. 10 [Florence: Ariani, 1932], 118–20).[51]

1.1.1.3. The Minuscules

The minuscules that preserve the Apocalypse are now listed, relatively completely, and (with few exceptions) collated in Hoskier's *Concerning the Text of the Apocalypse*, which surpasses all prior compilations. Unfortunately, Hoskier does not keep Caspar René Gregory and Ernst von Dobschütz's "official" recognized numbers for designating manuscripts. Rather, he adopts Scrivener's old numbers and supplements this sequence with his own numbers in order to achieve a consecutive series for the Apocalypse's Greek manuscripts. The compilation here follows Gregory-von Dobschütz's designations, grouping manuscripts according to families, and also makes corrections and additions to Hoskier's edition. The reader should consult my earlier studies for the rationale for the groupings.[52]

First, Hoskier's list, which retains his manuscript designations for now, should be reviewed. Hoskier's list of minuscules includes 252 numbers. But 79 and 230 are used for two manuscripts each, and 155 is used for three, so that the total number initially increases to 256 minuscules. But 230[a] ought to be removed from the list because the manuscript it denotes

---

51. See also Josef Schmid, "Der Apokalypse-Text des Kodex 0207 (Papiri della Societa Italiana 1166)," *BZ* 23 (1935–1936): 187–89.

52. Schmid, *Der Apokalypsetext des Arethas von Kaisareia*; Schmid, "Untersuchungen zur Geschichte des griechischen Apokalypsetextes"; Schmid, *Der Apokalypse-Kommentar des Andreas von Kaisarea: Text*, vol. 1.1 of *Studien zur Geschichte des griechischen Apokalypse-Textes*, MThS 1 (Munich: Zink, 1955).

(Athos, Lawra Ω 177) does not exist; rather, Lawra E 177 is meant. 230ᵃ is therefore identical with 224.⁵³

[17] Similarly, the following three numbers should be omitted because the manuscripts they denote are identical with others:⁵⁴ 183 (allegedly Thessaloniki, Ἑλληνικοῦ γυμνασίου 10) is identical with 052 (Athos, Panteleimon 99,2).⁵⁵ 225 (Athos, Lawra Γ 179) never existed but refers instead to Lawra 138 (formerly B 18); 225 is therefore identical with 222. 2920 (Athos, Batopedi 659, formerly 532, Gregory 2305) is identical with 166. Hoskier reserves 252 on the basis of a statement by Bolides for a manuscript from Elasson, whose existence is questionable. Neither Gregory nor von Soden is aware of a second manuscript from this library (besides Hoskier 245) that contains the Apocalypse.

Hoskier labels the following ten numbers as "vacat": 5 54 60 66 71 76 85 86 105 115. Most stem from lapses in the manuscript lists of Johann Martin Augustin Scholz, Frederick Henry Scrivener, and Caspar René Gregory,⁵⁶ so 54 (= Gregory 263, does not have the Apocalypse); 60 (Paris, suppl. gr. 136, has nothing from the New Testament); 66 (in Scholz and Gregory = 131, which contains only the Gospels); 71 (= Gregory 390, contains the New Testament without Apocalypse); 76 (is identical with 75); 85 (is identical with 142); 86 (is left blank by Hoskier, since in Gregory = Jerusalem, S. Saba 10, which has nothing from the New Testament, by Frederick Henry Scrivener and Edward Miller⁵⁷ = Athens, National Library 490 [= Hoskier 251], or Berlin, MS gr. Quart. 57 = Gregory 1525, which does not have the Apocalypse); 105 (left blank by Hoskier, since in Scrivener = Vallicell. F. 17, which does not contain the Apocalypse, in Scrivener-Miller = Jerusalem, S. Saba 20, which contains nothing from the New Testament). Hoskier left 115 blank because the designated number of leaves (fols. 93–96) of Cod. Vatic. gr. 1182 belong to 39. Finally,

53. See Josef Schmid, "Zur Liste der neutestamentlichen Handschriften," *ZNW* 34 (1935): 309.

54. See ibid, 308–9.

55. See above under the majuscules.

56. Johann Martin Augustin Scholz, *Novum Testamentum Graece: Textum ad fidem Testium Criticorum recensuit, Lectionum Familias subject*, 2 vols. (Leipzig: Fleischer, 1830–1836); Scrivener, *A Plain Introduction to the Criticism of the New Testament* (Cambridge: Deighton, Bell, 1861); Gregory, *Textkritik des Neuen Testamentes*.

57. Frederick Henry Scrivener and Edward Miller, *A Plain Introduction to the Criticism of the New Testament*, 4th ed. (London: Bell, 1894).

manuscript 5 once referred to readings that L. Valla had collected from unknown manuscripts.

The following manuscripts should also be deleted from the list:

- ◆   185 (contains the Praxapostolos without the Apocalypse),
- ◆   249 (also contains Praxapostolos without the Apocalypse),
- ◆   117 (contains the New Testament without the Catholic Epistles and the Apocalypse),
- ◆   116 (contains the Andreas commentary without the Apocalypse's text).

Hoskier designates 3 11 2920 and 230ᵃ as lost.

2920, however, as noted above, is identical with 166, and 230ᵃ is identical to 224. 3 is Estienne ιϛ'.[58] Estienne quotes from [18] its seventy-seven readings, which Wettstein also preserves in his apparatus. That the text of this no longer identifiable manuscript was purely of the K text emerges clearly. The only exception is the coincidence at 3:4 αλλ εχεις ολιγα ονοματα (cum P ƒ²⁰¹⁴ al. pc.[59]). 11 (= von Dobschütz 39ᵃ)[60] must also be considered definitively lost. From Mill, we at least know a number of their readings, which Tischendorf also adds to his apparatus. It shows that their copies of the Apocalypse were of Arethas of Caesarea and therefore the K text (revised toward the Aν text in the last chapters).[61]

---

58. Robert Estienne, *Novum Testamentum*, 2 vols. (Paris: n.p., 1546).

59. Two other unidentifiable manuscripts from French libraries Wettstein named under numbers 21 and 22. R. Bentley used it in his advanced notice of a new edition of the New Testament for Rev 22 (see Gregory, *Prolegomena*, 234ff.).

60. See Ernst von Dobschütz, "Zur Liste der NTlichen Handschriften," *ZNW* 32 (1933): 193; Schmid, *Der Apokalypsetext des Arethas von Kaisareia*, 6.

61. Here we should also mention 1757 (Mytilene, μονὴ τοῦ λειμῶνος 132). According to Gregory, the manuscript also contains the Apocalypse in addition to the Praxapostolos; von Soden says nothing about the latter. Hoskier (*Concerning the Text of the Apocalypse*, 1:435) writes in addition: "The Apc Ms. numbered 132 in that library has disappeared in 1912, torn from the volume." Also considered lost since Frederick Henry Scrivener (*Exact Transcript of Codex Augiensis*, lxiii) is Gregory manuscript 483 (von Soden, *Die Schriften des Neuen Testaments*, δ 376), which Hoskier does not mention, a parchment copied by Theodoros Hagiopetrites in 1295 that contained the entire New Testament including the Apocalypse. Scrivener himself (*A Supplement to the Authorised English Version of the New Testament* [London: Pickering, 1845]) collated the Gospels and the Praxapostolos, as the manuscript was still in the possession of William Pickering's (the London book dealer) complete inventory. In reality it is not lost. It belonged to Lord Vernon for a time. The Chapin library in Willamstown (Massachusetts) acquired it in 1923, and it remains there today. The manuscript contains

83 (Turin B. V. 8) was almost completely destroyed in the fire of the library in 1904.[62] In 1864, Hort collated five chapters of the Apocalypse and explains the text as related to B (= Q) (thus K text).

175 (Athos, Iwiron 661) is described in the catalog of Athos manuscripts by S. Lampros (1895–1903) but has since disappeared.

205 (Sumela 41)[63] disappeared after the Greco-Turkish War of 1922. Of the five manuscripts with the Apocalypse's text from two Macedonian monasteries Kosinitza in Drama (Hoskier 195–197) [19] and Prodromos at Serrai (Hoskier 198 and 199), Hoskier never even saw a photograph.[64] Three of them, however, have now resurfaced: 197 (Kosinitza 124) was purchased by L. Franklin Gruber in Maywood, Illinois (MS no. 152[65]), and after his death (1944) was transferred into the possession of the Theological Seminary of the Evangelical Lutheran Church, Maywood, retaining the old signature.[66] 196 (Kosinitza 53) has now been clearly divided into two

---

the New Testament without the Apocalypse. See the detailed description by Kenneth W. Clark, *A Descriptive Catalogue of Greek New Testament Manuscripts in America* (Chicago: University of Chicago Press, 1937), 17–20.

62. According to Ettore Stampini et al. ("Inventario dei codici superstiti greci e latini antichi della Biblioteca Nazionale di Torino," *RFIC* 32 [1904]: 584), three of the original two hundred leaves of the manuscript containing the entire New Testament are still preserved in severely damaged condition.

63. It is not mentioned in the catalog of manuscripts from Anatolia in Ankara and Izmit of Adolf Deissmann ("Handschriften aus Anatolien in Ankara und Izmit," *ZNW* 34 [1935]: 262–84), so it is really lost.

64. Regarding the fate of these two libraries, see Albert Ehrhard, *Überlieferung und Bestand der hagiographischen und homiletischen Literatur der griechischen Kirche von den Anfangen bis zum Ende des 16. Jahrhunderts*, 3 vols., TU 50–52 (Leipzig: Hinrichs, 1937–1952), 1:xxxix, lii; Marcel Richard, *Répertoire des Bibliothèques et des Catalogues de Manuscrits Grecs* (Paris: Centre national de la recherche scientifique, 1948), 43, 98; L. N. Politis, "Τὰ ἐκ Σερρῶν χειρόγραφα ἐν τῇ Ἐθνικῇ Βιβλιοθήκῃ" [Serbian Manuscripts in the National Library], *Hellēniká* 4 (1931): 525–26. The Bulgarians robbed the manuscripts of the two monasteries in 1916 or 1917, and since then, these manuscripts, especially those from Kosinitza, have partially disappeared. They must have been shipped to Greece in 1924. But only 4 manuscripts of Kosinitza and the majority of the 261 manuscripts of Prodromos have come to Athens. 247 of them are currently in the Greek National Library in Athens, and some are in the Byzantine Museum. Ten of the one hundred parchment manuscripts of Prodromos are missing.

65. See Clark, *Descriptive Catalogue of Greek New Testament Manuscripts*, 104–6.

66. See William H. P. Hatch, *Facsimiles and Descriptions of Minuscule Manuscripts of the New Testament* (Cambridge: Harvard University Press, 1951), 86 (up to table VII) (by personal note from Herr Prof. Aland).

parts. Hoskier himself purchased the second half with Hebrews and the Apocalypse in 1919 and bequeathed it to the Pierpont Morgan Library in New York (now no. M 714 of this library) in 1926. This is no. 129 in Hoskier's list (von Dobschütz-Aland 2349).[67] It forms a family (K text) with 29 – 30 – 98 – 128. The third manuscript of Kosinitza (208, Hoskier 195) is currently lost (perhaps located in Sofia).[68] Of the two manuscripts from Prodromos, one (γ´ 6, Hoskier 198) has come into the possession of the Byzantine Museum in Athens (belonging to the Aν group *i*). The other is missing.

The following also remained inaccessible to Hoskier: 131 (Iwiron 60), 133 and 134 (both Chalki in Istanbul), 213 (contains only Rev 13:14–14:15 with the Andreas commentary), and 248. Of these, von Soden demonstrates that 134 is of the K text. 213 is a sister of 152 and 179. 248 is, at least at the beginning, a copy of the edition of Arethas's commentary, edited by Donatus of Verona, and therefore useless. 131 is [20] a sister of 9 – 27 – 75 (i.e., K text).[69] 133 belongs to the family 153 – 211 – 222 (K text).

The following manuscripts should be withdrawn from the list of witnesses for the Apocalypse's Greek text for various reasons.

57, 141, 235, and 247 are copies of the printed Textus Receptus.[70] The Apocalypse's text in 118 is copied from a printed edition, while its Andreas commentary is copied from a manuscript. 243 is a copy of Aldina in the first four and a half chapters. The rest of it belongs to the large Complutensian family.

The following three manuscripts contain a vernacular Greek translation of Andreas's commentary with a vernacular Greek text of the Apocalypse by Maximos the Peloponnesian: 173, 234, and 239.[71]

---

67. See Kurt Aland, "Zur Liste der griechischen neutestamentliche Handschriften," *TLZ* 78 (1953): 473.

68. A fourth manuscript of Kosinitza (60, Gregory 1780), which also contains the Apocalypse and which remained entirely unknown to Hoskier, will be mentioned below.

69. The Apocalypse's text is not incomplete, as Gregory claims, but fols. 199–206 belong between fols. 214 and 215.

70. It is even certain at 141, despite Hoskier's vacillation.

71. A fourth manuscript with this commentary that von Dobschütz gives the number 2402 is now in Chicago, edited by Harold R. Willoughby and Ernest Cadman Colwell (*The Elizabeth Day McCormick Apocalypse*, 2 vols. [Chicago: University of Chicago Press, 1940]).

The following manuscripts should also be eliminated as completely useless:

- 5 (3:3–4:8, inserted by a late hand in a Gospel manuscript between the text)
- 231 (contains only 1:1–3, Compl. type)
- 236 (contains 1:1–13; 4:4–7; and 19:19–21 with commentary, copied in 1847)
- 237 (contains only 1:1–13 with commentary, copied 1791)
- 238 (contains part of the Apocalypse with commentary, eighteenth or nineteenth century)
- 168 (Apocalypse with commentary, copied in 1798; the text of the Apocalypse appears to be a copy of the Textus Receptus).

Finally, we come to the following eleven numbers, which are useless as copies of manuscripts that are still extant:

- 41 and 53 (copies of 42)
- 63 (copy of 62)
- 73 and 79^a (copies of 79)
- 81 (copy of 204)
- 112 (copy of 103)
- 155^b (copy of 155)
- 176 (copy of 206)
- 216 (copy of 169)
- 217 (copy of 172)[72]

[21] On the basis of the above list, once the currently lost and destroyed number 83 is counted, 52 of the 256 manuscripts Hoskier mentions drop out (or with no. 172: 53), so that the actual number of minuscules useful for textual criticism is 204. In the course of this survey, numerous other manuscripts will be mentioned that are useless for the textual criticism of the Apocalypse. They are inadequate not only for the recovery of the *Urtext* but also for the representation of the Apocalypse's entire textual history.

---

72. 172 itself is a copy of 169 from 11:18 onward. The first half of the text is a copy of a manuscript of the group 51 – 90 – 246. The number of copies, whose *Vorlagen* are still available in the Apocalypse's Greek textual tradition is, on the whole, as low as in the Greek Bible generally, compared to other writings with a richer manuscript tradition.

On the other hand, Hoskier's list should be expanded to include the following manuscripts:[73]

A fragment of an Arethas manuscript—which Hoskier inexplicably did not recognize as such[74]—is Paris, B. N. suppl. gr. 159, fols. 8–11 (von Dobschütz 2419). The manuscript is only valuable as a source for a possible critical edition of the Arethas commentary.

The two following fragments are more trivial: Oxford, Barocc. 48, fol. 18 (Aland 2408), a fourteenth-century leaf of a paper manuscript with the text of Rev 5:1–5—which can be inserted into no other preserved manuscript—and Vatic. gr. 1205, fols. 144–145 with the text of Rev 4:10–5:6 and 6:14–17 together with Andreas's commentary that belongs to it (von Dobschütz 2361).

Also, the three following fragments offer no real enrichment of valuable material for textual criticism:[75] Oxford, Barocc. gr. 212, fols. 108–120. The thirteen leaves that originate from the sixteenth century contain chapters 1–9 of Andreas's commentary without the Apocalypse's text.

[22] Madrid, former Royal Palace Library Cod. 46 (Aland 2435), a paper manuscript copied by Antonio Kalosynas in the sixteenth century with the text of Rev 1:1–8:6 and Andreas's commentary.

A sister manuscript related to 55 and 155ᵃ, which as such is unimportant alongside these, is Madrid, Bibl. Nac. O 2 (4592), a sixteenth-century paper manuscript, which contains Rev 1–3 and 15–22 with Oecumenius's commentary (Aland 2403) among the writings of Pseudo-Dionysius, inter alia, fols. 111–139.

Athos, σκήτη τῶν καυσοκαλυβίων 4 (Aland 2431), is a fourteenth-century paper manuscript (copied in 1332) that contains the Praxapostolos and the Apocalypse, increasing the numerous but useless Complutensian

---

73. See Josef Schmid, "Unbeachtete Apokalypse-Handschriften," *TQ* 117 (1936): 149–87 about some previously unnoticed manuscripts.

74. Hoskier has already collated and published this fragment's text of the Apocalypse (under no. 123). He writes in addition (*Concerning the Text of the Apocalypse*, 1:423): "For a brief space (3:3 to 4:8) another exemplar was used for 123." But this information is not accurate. The leaves taken over from an Arethas manuscript contain Rev 3:1–4:11 with the commentary, while the filled-in gap extends only from 3:3 (ποιαν ωραν) to 4:8 (εσωθεν γεμοντα).

75. Still less useful is Cod. Paris B. N. suppl. gr. 475, a paper manuscript copied in 1643, which (fols. 1–40ʳ) contains the Apocalypse with an excerpt from the Andreas commentary. The manuscript begins in its present condition with the commentary on 16:20. It is a copy of the printed edition of Sylburg.

group by another member. A fifteenth-century paper manuscript, which Professor Adolf Deissmann once owned, containing the entire New Testament including the Apocalypse, also seems to belong to the same group.[76]

I acquired photographs of the three following manuscripts from Professor L. N. Politis: (1) Stadtbibliothek Zagora Cod. 9 (Aland 2433), a paper manuscript copied in 1736 with 134 leaves, which contains the Apocalypse with a catena composed from the commentaries of Andreas and Oecumenius. The Apocalypse's text is usually reproduced only in an abridged form. (2) Stadtbibliothek Zagora Cod. 12 (Aland 2434), a thirteenth-century paper manuscript with 368 leaves, which contains the Apocalypse (fols. 332–368) following the Historia Lausiaca of Palladius and the monastic biographies of Theodoret of Cyrus. The manuscript belongs to the large Complutensian family. (3) Finally, Athens, Byzantine Museum Cod. 117 (5487) (Aland 2377), which is included in leaves 2–10 of a fourteenth-century paper collection with a total of 256 leaves. The leaves measure 12.5 × 9.5 cm and contain various mainly patristic writings.[77] The nine leaves contain the following parts of the Apocalypse: fol. 2: 19:21 ιππου to 20:6 μετ αυτου χιλια; fols. 3–6: 20:14 εβλη]θησαν to 22:6 αληθινοι; fols. 7–8: 13:10 υπομονη to 14:4 ακολουθουντες τ[ω].; fols. 9–10: 22:6 και κυριος to 22:21. Folios 9–10 are accordingly the continuation of fol. 6, and a leaf is missing between fols. 2 and 3. The [23] text in 13:10–14:4 is a pure K text. On the other hand, from 19:21 to the end it is identical with that of 2030 (Hoskier 65, Moscow, Univ.-Bibl. 25, fols. 203–209).[78] 2377, however, cannot be a copy of 2030 because it is missing a few unique readings from 2030. Because 2030 is also incomplete and only contains the text from 16:20 (εφυγεν) to the end, it is uncertain whether 2377 was initially copied from two different *Vorlagen* or from the common *Vorlage* of two manuscripts.

---

76. See Nikos A. Bees, "Χειρόγραφον τῆς μονῆς Πετριτζονιτίσσης-Μπασκόβου: Πρακτικά Χριστιανικῆς Αρχαιολογικῆς Εταιρείας" [Manuscript of the Monastery of Petrizontissis-Mpaskobo: Proceedings of the Christian Archaeological Society] *BNJ* 14 (1937–1938): 457. The manuscript is currently missing, perhaps burned in Leipzig.

77. See the description of Demetrios I. Pallas, "Κατάλογος των χειρογράφων του Βυζαντινού Μουσείου Αθηνών" [Catalog of Manuscripts of the Byzantine Museum of Athens], *BNJ* 11 (1934–1935): λε΄–λζ΄; Aland, "Zur Liste der griechischen neutestamentliche Handschriften," 476 under no. 2377. The manuscript's first two leaves are greatly damaged with a loss of text at the outer edge.

78. See also Hoskier, *Concerning the Text of the Apocalypse*, 1:209–11.

Hoskier overlooks the following three manuscripts (already recorded by Gregory).

Athos, Esphigmenu 67 (Gregory 2922, von Soden α 371), a fourteenth-century parchment manuscript with 230 leaves, which contains the Praxapostolos and the Apocalypse (to 22:19 πολεως) inserted by another hand. The Apocalypse's text is a pure K text.

Kosinitza 60, now Durham, North Carolina, Duke University MS gr. 1 (Gregory 1780), a thirteenth-century parchment manuscript with 198 leaves, which contains the entire New Testament (in the order Gospels, Acts, James, Paul, Catholic Epistles, Apocalypse) with commentary to all parts except the Apocalypse, all copied by one hand. It belongs to the best witnesses of the K text in the Apocalypse.[79]

Athos, Batopedi 17 (Gregory 1773), a very beautifully copied and excellently preserved eleventh-century parchment manuscript with the Apocalypse's text and Andreas's commentary.

New are: Paris, B. N. gr. 746 (Aland 2428), a fifteenth-century paper manuscript with 307 leaves, copied by one hand, which contains the thirty-four homilies of St. John Chrysostom on Hebrews and (fols. 239–307) the Apocalypse with Andreas's commentary. The manuscript breaks off at Rev 17:12.

Paris, B. N. gr. 1002 (Aland 2429), a fourteenth-century paper manuscript with 227 leaves, all copied by the same hand, which contains the fifteen homilies of St. Gregory of Nyssa on the Song of Songs and the eight homilies on Ecclesiastes, a catena on Prov 1:1–9:4, and (fols. 179–227) the Apocalypse with Andreas's commentary. The manuscript breaks off at Rev 12:12.

A sister manuscript to 2065 (Hoskier 159) is Cod. Vatic. Ross. gr. 766 (Aland 2432), which contains Apocalypse with Andreas's commentary.

[24] Paris, B. N. Coisl. gr. 18 (von Dobschütz 2344), is an eleventh-century parchment manuscript with 230 leaves, containing the Praxapostolos and the Apocalypse as well as parts of the Old Testament. The last leaves are in disarray, and the last two are completely destroyed by water. The manuscript provides an excellent text in the Apocalypse and is among the most valuable minuscules to preserve the book.

---

79. See the description of Clark, *Descriptive Catalogue of Greek New Testament Manuscripts*, 51–53. Also, three of the New Testament manuscripts have migrated from Kosinitza to America since 1919 (Gregory 1424, 1780, and the second part from 1795 [now 2349]).

With that the entirety of the currently known manuscript material witnesses for the Apocalypse's Greek text is identified. There are 204 + 8 = 212 minuscules,[80] after the exclusion of utterly useless manuscripts.

A detailed overview of the manuscript tradition of the Apocalypse's Greek text in line with their major stems and families now follows. The useless manuscripts identified above will be ignored.

The Apocalypse's entire Greek textual tradition falls into four major stems.

AC and the text of Oecumenius (2053) form the first and most important.

P[47] and S rank second in importance next to AC and Oecumenius (2053).

A few minuscules belong to these two stems, which stand closer to one another than to the following two, including the degree to which the following two relate to each other. They are:

2053 – 2062 (= Oecumenius). Of these, 2053, next to 2344, is the

---

80. At the last minute, as it were, I was made aware of four other manuscripts. I therefore must be satisfied with a provisional indication of their existence. I owe the reference to the first three of them to Herr Prof. Aland. All three belong to the library of the Great Lawra on Mount Athos and contain the entire Apocalypse among patristic writings. One of them certainly comes with a commentary. There are the following:

(1) Lawra 671 (H 16), copied in 1602 by a Metrophanes, is a paper manuscript with 181 leaves in the small format 15 × 10 cm. The first leaves are lost. The Apocalypse begins after the catalog of Spyridon and Sophronius Eustratiades fol. 82ʳ. It is also missing twenty leaves. There is a misprint in the catalog because the next section ought to begin again on fol. 82ʳ.

(2) Lawra 860 (H 205), a fragmentary fourteenth-century paper manuscript with 137 leaves 31 × 22 cm, in fols. 119ff. has the Apocalypse with a commentary.

(3) Lawra 1564 (Λ 74) is a seventeenth-century paper manuscript copied by the scribe Nikephoros with 369 leaves 27 × 21 cm. Therein fol. 331ʳ begins ἀποκάλυψις τοῦ ἁγίου Ἰωάννου τοῦ ἀποστόλου καὶ εὐαγγελιστοῦ θεολόγου. Because this superscription accurately corresponds to the fifteen manuscripts of the Complutensian family, whose text is included among others in thirteen other manuscripts of the Great Lawra, we ought to presume that the text of the available manuscript also belongs to this late type of the Apocalypse's Greek text.

(4) Regarding a fourth manuscript that to the best of my knowledge is missing from all New Testament manuscript lists, I follow Ehrhard, *Überlieferung und Bestand der hagiographischen und homiletischen Literatur*, 3.2:852, n. 1. It is the Codex Sinaiticus gr. 1692, a paper manuscript of the fourteenth–fifteenth centuries containing a nonmenological collection of hagiographic texts and the Apocalypse to 13:5 (Aland 2493).

most valuable of all the minuscules to preserve the Apocalypse both because of the quality of its text, which is identical to AC's text in all respects, and because Oecumenius's commentary contains the Apocalypse's complete text, which allows for greater controls in establishing its text. [25] Revelation 4–14 and the corresponding parts of the commentary are missing in 2062.

1006 – 1841 – 911. Of these three manuscripts, 911 belongs to this group from 11:9 onward. It corresponds to the K group, f^{920}, from 1:1 to 11:7. 911 can be ignored along with the other two but is of great importance for evaluating Andreas group n.

1611, 1854, 2329, 2050, and 2344 stand on their own. Of these, 2344 is by far the most valuable despite its severe damage.

2351 and 2030 – 2377 are less valuable. A layer of K readings covers the "old" valuable text in 792 almost entirely.

Also, among the groups and manuscripts that belong to Aν and K, there are several that contain a layer of "old" readings in addition to the Aν or K text, especially of Aν: P, 94, f^{2073}, and the two groups l and n; from K: 203 – 506, 61 – 69, and 469.[81] In most of them, however, the immediate *Vorlagen* from which these "old" readings were taken are still clearly visible, and for this reason, the dependent groups and manuscripts (in addition to their *Vorlagen*) are useless. The scribe of f^{2073} uses a manuscript of group l and another from f^{1006} in addition to his Aν *Vorlage*.[82] The details are analogous in the Aν group n. The layer of old readings in n comes from a manuscript with an identical *Vorlage* to the text type of 911, therefore, again from f^{1006}. The K group 203 – 506 also adopts some old readings from a manuscript of f^{1006}. The influence of f^{1006} is significantly stronger in 469.

[26] The vast majority of minuscules belong to one of the two other stems, Aν and K, or to one of the various mixed texts from Aν and K. Approximately eighty manuscripts belong to Aν and K.

Aν (i.e., the text of the Apocalypse upon which Andreas of Caesarea's commentary is based) includes the following, arranged here according to groups of manuscripts.[83]

---

81. For 203 – 506, see Schmid, "Untersuchungen zur Geschichte des griechischen Apokalypsetextes," 177–79; for 61 – 69, see 284–93; for 469, see 433–36.

82. A portion of these ancient readings from f^{2073} are passed on to 2017 (and from 2017 to its copy 2258).

83. Manuscripts that are expendable, and therefore useless for reconstructing the text, and closely related to the others of their group are provided in parentheses.

- $a = 2814 - 2186 - 2428$
- $b = 2059 - 2081 (- 2259)$
- $c = 2028 (- 2029 - 2033) - 2044 (- 2052 - 2054 - 2068) - 2069$ $(- 2083 - 2361)$
- $d = (743 -)2051 (- 2055) - 2064 (-2067 - 2435)$
- $e = 2026 - 2057 (- 2091)$
- $f = (051^{84}) (- 35 - 2023) - 2031 - 2056 - 2073 (- 2254)$ (also 2063 and Barocc. 212, which only contain the commentary without the Apocalypse's text)
- $g = 205 - 2886 - 2920 - 2045 (- 2071)$ (also 632, which contains Andreas's commentary in the margins, but the Apocalypse's text belongs to K)
- $h = 2060 - 2286 - 2302$
- $i = (88 - 1384) - 1685 (- 1732 - 1876 - 2014 - 2015 - 2034) - 2036$ $- (2891 -) - 2042 - 2043 (- 2047) - 2074 (- 2082)$ (also 2066, of which the Apocalypse's text is a copy of the printed Textus Receptus)
- $l = (052^{85}) - 1678 - 1778 (- 2020) - 2080 (- 2433)$
- $m = 2037 - 2046$
- $n = 2065 - 2429 - 2432$

The following stand-alone manuscripts can be added to this list: 94 2919 254 2595 (with its copy 2038) 1773 (with 911[comm.], which does not belong to Av in the text of the Apocalypse) 2019 and P, of which 2919 and 254 are useless.

All of the groups presented are important for reconstructing the Av text, with the exception of m, which is nothing but a mixed text of c and i. Within each group, however, especially in c and i, some of their members can be ignored, so that in the end only thirty-nine out of a total of seventy-five manuscripts remain valuable.

The K text's witnesses are discussed in my article "Untersuchungen zur Geschichte des griechischen Apokalypsetextes." [27] 2922, 1424 (related to 141 – 1719), 2923 (related to 325 – 456 – 517), and 1780, of which I have now received photographs, have not yet been added to the eighty-three manuscripts mentioned. The compilation and groupings above are repeated here in order to present the entirety of the manuscript material.

---

84. See above regarding the majuscules.
85. See above regarding the majuscules.

- 920 – 1859 – 1872 – 2027 – 2256 – (– 911)
- 18 – 2039 – 2138 919 2004 2200
- 385 – 2921 – 522 – 1849 – 1955 – 2349
- 141 – 1424 – 1719
- 808 – 1893
- 218 – 2824
- 2024 – 2079
- 177 – 2918 – 337
- 203 – 452 – 467 – 506 – 2021
- 935 – 1728 – 1734 – 1870
- 149 – 201 – 368 – 386 – 1597 – 1948 – 2025
- 110 – 627 – 2048
- 498 – 1704 – 2058
- 325 – 456 – 517 – 2923
- 42 – 367 – 468
- 61 – 69 Q
- 82, 93, 699, 2922, 1780, 1852, 469, 632, 241, 2436 – 2078 (and 3, 83[86])
- 91 – 175 – 242 – 256 – 617 – 1934 – 2017 } Arethas Text
- 39A – 314 – 664 – 1094 – 2016 – 2075 – 2077 – 2419

This list includes eighty-seven manuscripts (without 911, 3, and 83).

In light of the K tradition's exceptional and extensive unity, a large part of it may be ignored (in addition to 467 and 2021, which are copies of 452 and 2078, which is a copy of 2436), especially 469, 632, 241, 2436, and the double group 325 – 456 – 517 – 2923 and 42 – 367 – 468, all of which offer the K text in a low level of purity. We can also ignore the fifteen manuscripts of the Arethas group since their text is revised toward Aν in the last five chapters and the group as a whole is sufficiently closed.[87] 61 – 69 are of far less interest as witnesses for K than for their relationships with P[47] S, AC, and 2351. The remaining groups and individual manuscripts [28] are roughly equivalent to each other in terms of value.[88] Yet 110, 627, 2048, as well as 82 and 1780, deserve special mention because of the purity of their text, while Q, the only majuscule among the K witnesses, is considerably less valuable. The first five groups of the above list (f^{920} 920 to 808 – 1893)

---

86. Both lost; see pp. 19–20.

87. See Schmid, *Der Apokalypsetext des Arethas von Kaisareia*, 4–26.

88. See also the observation in Schmid, "Untersuchungen zur Geschichte des griechischen Apokalypsetextes," 444 n. 2.

also form a close family within the K stem, whose common archetype is later than K. In the groups that consist of several manuscripts (similar to the Aν tradition), two or three are sufficient to determine the archetype in each case.

Regarding mixed texts from Aν and K, four groups should be mentioned:

1. The Arethas group; see above under K.

2. The $f^{104/336}$ group consists of the following ten manuscripts:
- 104 – 459 – 680 – 922 – 2493
- 336 – 582 – 620 – 628 – 1918

The second series of five manuscripts within these ten is once more revised toward a K manuscript.[89] Since the text of the whole group is nothing but a mixture of Aν and K, it is completely useless beside Aν and K.[90]

3. The Complutensian group of Hoskier,[91] so-called because its text is identical to the Complutensian polyglot's Greek text of the Apocalypse, includes thirty-six manuscripts,[92] most of which are on Mount Athos or come from there, and only a few of which offer the family's text impurely. They are the following:
- 35, 60, 432, 757, 824, 986, 1072, 1075, 1248, 1328, 1384, 1503, 1551, 1617, 1637, 1652, 1732, 1733, 1740, 1745, 1746, 1771, 1774, 1864, 1865, 2926, 1903, 1957, 2023, 2035, 2041, 2061, 2196, 2352, 2431, 2434

The text of 35 and 2023 is composed of f^{051} (Aν) and Compl., where Compl. is the later layer. 1384 and 1732 provide the text of the f^{2036} (Aν), heavily revised toward Compl. [29] 1903 is a copy of the Aldina edition from the year 1518 in 1:1–5:11 and a Compl. text from 5:12 onward. The Compl. text is itself a mixed text from Aν and K and has very few unique readings.

(4) The O family. The following thirteen manuscripts make up the O family:

---

89. Regarding this group, see Schmid, *Der Apokalypsetext des Arethas von Kaisareia*, 59–78.

90. The fact that very occasionally an "old" reading appears in it that is not from Aν or K, as οι πλυναντες τας στολας αυτων instead of the spurious οι ποιουντες τας εντολας αυτου in 22:14, does not annul this judgment.

91. Hoskier's f^{10}.

92. Probably Lawra 1564 (see 26 n. 80) and a manuscript Prof. Adolf Deissman once owned but that is now lost (probably burned) belong to this group also.

- 250 – 424 – 616 – 2084
- 172 – 1828 – 1862 – 1888 – 2018 – 2032
- 2070 – 2305 2022

2070 and 2305 are heavily revised toward the K group, f^{920}. And this text is again revised toward K in 2305. The subgroup 172 – 1828 – 1862 – 1888 – 2018 – 2032 has been heavily revised from 17:3 to the end toward an Arethas manuscript. 250 – 424 – 616 – 2084, on the other hand, provides the text of the O archetype unchanged. Also, as mentioned, O is a mixed text from Aν and K. But the Aν *Vorlage* of O belongs to group *l* (f^{052}), and O has kept this text type more faithfully in some places than the manuscripts of the group itself. There is also a thick layer of "old" readings, which is otherwise present only in AC or P^{47} S and the few minuscules related to these under the components of the text of *l*.[93]

In this collection of the Apocalypse's Greek manuscripts, the entire database of witnesses, comprising over two hundred manuscripts, leads back to a relatively small number of groups[94] *that can be summarized again in four chief branches. In this way, the entire manuscript tradition can be used for the Urtext's reconstruction and what is useless can be eliminated.*

1.1.2. Citations of the Apocalypse in Early Christian Writers

Only five Greek authors offer citations that are useful for textual criticism: Irenaeus, Origen, Hippolytus of Rome, Eusebius (= Dionysius of Alexandria), and [30] Methodius. The citations of Hippolytus and Origen are the most important. Irenaeus's citations survive almost without exception only in the Latin and Armenian versions and should therefore be used with caution. Some citations in Clement of Alexandria are completely useless for textual criticism. Oecumenius's later commentary is extremely important because of the quality of the text of the Apocalypse he uses and

---

93. See also in Schmid, *Der Apokalypse-Kommentar des Andreas von Kaisarea: Einleitung*, vol. 1.2 of *Studien zur Geschichte des griechischen Apokalypse-Textes*, MThS 1 (Munich: Zink, 1956), §2.2.6.

94. Of course, Hoskier observes these smallest subgroups and correctly establishes them. His larger groups ("Egyptian family," "Coptic family," etc.), however, are quite fantastic and lie outside the realm of possibility. The major determining factor is his polyglot theory. Examining more closely this weakest side of his great contribution is unnecessary. Indeed, Hoskier's idiosyncratic opinions do not damage the immense value of the second volume of his gigantic work.

because he reproduces that text, for the most part, literally in the commentary.

[31] 1.2. The Place of the Apocalypse within
the Tradition of the New Testament

The Apocalypse's peculiar fate in the Greek Church is well known. None of the great Greek exegetes—neither Alexandrian nor Antiochene—wrote a commentary on it. The book was also excluded from liturgical usage.[95] The manuscript tradition reflects this fate. The number of manuscripts that preserve the Apocalypse lags behind that of the rest of the New Testament significantly. Only six ancient majuscules from the fourth and fifth centuries (S, A, C, 0163, 0169, 0207) hand it down to us alongside some third- and fourth-century papyri (P[18], P[24], P[43], P[47]).[96] Then, after a lapse of about four centuries (at the frontier of the transition from majuscule to minuscule script), the next witness, Codex Q, surfaces in the ninth century, preserving the Apocalypse's text among the writings of the Cappadocian brothers Basil and Gregory of Nyssa. The three majuscules P, 051, and 052 belong to the tenth century, alongside some minuscules (93, 456, 627, 1424, 1841, 1870, 2004, 2074, 2329, 2351). The eleventh century is represented by thirty-one manuscripts, the eleventh/twelfth centuries by eight, the twelfth century by twenty-three, the thirteenth century by twenty, the thirteenth/fourteenth centuries by thirteen, the fourteenth century by twenty-eight, the fourteenth/fifteenth centuries by sixteen, the fifteenth century by thirty-eight, fifteenth/sixteenth centuries by eight, and the sixteenth century by twenty-eight. This means that the number of manuscripts for the Apocalypse increases exponentially from the eleventh century onward.[97]

The combinations in which the Apocalypse surfaces in the manuscript tradition are also instructive and worth considering. According to von

---

95. Apart from Cappadocia and Coptic Egypt, the Apocalypse remained under suspicion in the East until the time of Palaiologos. See Adolf Jülicher, *Einleitung in das Neue Testament*, 7th ed., GTW 3.1 (Tübingen: Mohr, 1931), 53–36; Eugène Jacquier, *Le Nouveau Testament dans l'Eglise chrétienne*, 2nd ed., 2 vols. (Paris: Gabalda, 1911), 1:735–44.

96. Whether B preserved it cannot be determined.

97. It should also be noted, however, that in the following centuries (until the sixteenth century) the number of διαθήκη and Praxapostolos manuscripts without the Apocalypse still surpasses significantly those with the Apocalypse, as von Soden's and von Dobschütz's lists make clear (see 33 nn. 98–99).

Soden's collection,[98] [32] we have 167 διαθήκη manuscripts, 50 of which preserve the Apocalypse. Only 62 of 279 Paraxapostolos (Acts, Catholic Epistles, Pauline Epistles) manuscripts also contain the Apocalypse.[99] The numerical ratio is therefore even less favorable for the Apocalypse in the Praxapostolos manuscripts (approximately 1:4.65) than in the διαθήκη manuscripts (1:3.34). In other words, the Apocalypse is present in only one out of four Praxapostolos manuscripts, while it is present in only one out of three διαθήκη manuscripts.

Nine manuscripts preserve the Gospels and the Apocalypse (without the Praxapostolos):

*   60 (Gregory, 10 Hoskier). The Apocalypse inserted by a later hand?
*   792 (113) the Apocalypse supplemented in this manuscript according to von Soden
*   1006 (215)
*   1328 (140) bound together
*   1551 (212) from a single hand
*   1685 (198) from a single hand

In 2087 (15), a fifteenth-century scribe crammed Rev 3:3–4:8 into two separate locations between the text of an eighth-century Gospel majuscule.

In 866 (115), a bookbinder bound a few leaves with the Apocalypse's text to Matt 7:24–10:40 and other texts. The leaves of the Apocalypse (fols. 93–96) belong to 1918 (39).[100]

In 2595 (204), an excerpt from the St. Luke catena of Nicetas and the Apocalypse with Andreas's commentary stand among various patristic

---

98. Von Soden, *Die Schriften des Neuen Testaments*, 1:289–90 with supplement 2141–47.

99. The numbers, which Ernst von Dobschütz mentions (von Dobschütz, ed., *Eberhard Nestle's Einführung in das griechische Neue Testament*, 4th ed. [Göttingen: Vandenhoeck & Ruprecht 1923], 103), are higher by a trifle: fifty-five διαθήκη manuscripts with the Apocalypse, of which two (920 and 1859) are without Paul. Praxapostolos manuscripts with Rev sixty-seven, Acts-Catholic Epistles (without Pauline Epistles) with Rev three, Paul-Rev seven, Gospels and Rev nine. 1704 and a manuscript in the possession of Deissmann should supplement von Soden's fifty διαθήκη manuscripts. 39ª, 2922, 1864, 1903, 2344, 2349, and 2431 should supplement the sixty-two Praxapostolos manuscripts with the Apocalypse.

100. In the meantime, the library administration removed leaves 93–96 from 866 (Cod. Vatic. gr. 1882) and inserted them into 1918 (Cod. Vatic. gr. 1136).

writings. Here the main interest is the commentary in the transcription of both books.

Six manuscripts contain Paul and the Apocalypse, that is, the last part of the New Testament or the Praxapostolos: 1771 (227), 1918 (39), 1934 (64, with commentary for both), 1948 (78), 1955 (93), and 2349 (129, Hebrews and Apocalypse).[101]

Other combinations are exceptions:

+ 325 (9): 3 John, Revelation, Pauline Epistles (eleventh century). A thirteenth-century hand supplemented it with Acts 15:29–2 John.
+ [33] 2926 (187): Revelation and, inserted by another hand, Paul and Catholic Epistles.
+ 743 (123): Revelation with Andreas commentary, 1–3 John attached without commentary, John with Nicetas's catena.
+ 368 (84): John, Revelation, 1–3 John, so again a Johannine corpus.

The total number of previously mentioned manuscripts that contain the Apocalypse along with the rest of New Testament or parts of it is 141, that is, less than three-fifths of the total stock of the Apocalypse's manuscripts.

Many manuscripts contain only the Apocalypse with the commentary of Oecumenius, Andreas, or Arethas: 1^r, 1773, 1678 (catena from Andreas and Oecumenius), 2026, 2028, 2029, 2031 – 2034, 2035 (translation of the Italian commentary of Federigo da Venezia), 2036, 2891, 2037, 2043, 2044, 2046, 2047, 2053, 2058 (catena from Andreas and Oecumenius in a collection compiled by the bookbinder), 2065, 2066 – 2068, 2072, 2075, 2077, 2081, 2302; further, 052 (fragment), 2361 (two leaves from the Andreas commentary, inserted by the bookbinder in a collection), 2432, 2435, and 2433 (catena from Andreas and Oecumenius).

In many other cases, the Apocalypse with commentary is combined with a variety of other writings, either with homilies to other biblical books to form a volume (thus 2060, 2083, 2186, 2259, 2286, 2428) or with other texts (thus 051, 2595, 1775, 1776, 1777, 2018, 2022, 2023, 2026, 2038, 2042, 2045, 2051, 2054, 2056, 2059, 2062, 2064, 2069, 2070, 2073, 2074, 2082, 2091, 2116, 2254, 2305, 2350, 2403, 2428, 2429).

The main interest is the commentary rather than the Apocalypse's text in these two classes of manuscripts.[102]

---

101. See also p. 21.

102. This is particularly clear in 2063 and Barocc. 212, fols. 108–120. Both contain the Andreas commentary without the Apocalypse's text (similar also in 2433).

The observation that the Apocalypse frequently appears (without commentary) in the midst of all sorts of nonbiblical writings is particularly revealing for the evaluation of the Apocalypse in the Byzantine Church.[103] This is the case in the following manuscripts:

- Q: preserves the Apocalypse's text along with the writings of Basil and Gregory of Nyssa.
- 920 (61): the Apocalypse precedes the writings of Basil, Theodoret and Maximos.
- [34] 1774 (232): the Apocalypse is followed by treatises against the Paulicians and against the Messalians; after these, a text entitled: ἄνθος τῶν χαριτῶν.
- 2076 (172): the Apocalypse is in the first position; patristic writings follow.
- 2258 (217): the Apocalypse is together with patristic writings (a copy of 2076 in the Apocalypse).
- 1806 (205): the Apocalypse precedes the writings of Theodore of Gaza.
- 2015 (28): the Apocalypse is among the writings of the fathers.
- 2016 (31): preceding the writings of Pseudo-Dionysius Aeropagite
- 2017 (32): a *Logos of Theodore Prodromos on the Mother of God* inserted by a later hand
- 2024 (50): the Apocalypse among the Lives of the Saints
- 2025 (58): preceding the book of Job and Justin's *Cohortatio ad Graecos*
- 2048 (140): the Apocalypse appended to the Panadect of Antiochus, etc.
- 2049 (141): the Apocalypse (copy of the Textus Receptus) among the Lives of the Saints and other theological writings
- 2050 (143): the Apocalypse among biographies and writings of the holy fathers
- 2057 (121): the Apocalypse among liturgical, homiletical, and dogmatic texts
- 2061 (154): the Apocalypse (in a three-volume codex) amidst a collection of hagiographic texts for the entire church year
- 2079 (177): the Apocalypse preceding the Psalms

103. In addition to the aforementioned fact that it is missing in the majority of Bible manuscripts.

- 2084 (188): the Apocalypse among the writings of the fathers
- 2196 (233): the Apocalypse in a collection copied by one hand with the writings of John of Damascus, Ephraem, Andrew of Crete, John Chrysostom, Theodore the Studite, et al. μέθοδος περὶ τοῦ κύκλου τῆς σελήνης follows after the Apocalypse as a last text.
- 2329 (200): and 2351 (201) are in immediate succession (2351 with a commentary) in a codex that contains twenty-four different writings, all of which are copied by the same hand.
- 2436: the Apocalypse among the homilies of John Chrysostom, Gregory of Nyssa, Gregory Palamas, John of Damascus, et al. (total of thirty-four works)
- [35] 2078 (176): the Apocalypse is among the writings of John Chrysostom and John of Damascus (a copy of the previous manuscript in the Apocalypse; the remaining content of the two manuscripts is not identical).
- 2377: patristic writings follow the Apocalypse.
- 2434: the Apocalypse precedes the monastic lives of Palladius and Theodoret.

This situation, witnessed in these twenty manuscripts,[104] is rarely operative for other New Testament books.

Manuscripts that contain the Apocalypse alone are rare and are sometimes fragments of manuscripts that were originally larger.[105] The following are singled out:

- 911 (95): the Apocalypse with Andreas's commentary in the margins; originally formed one manuscript with 911 (Praxapostolos)
- 2017 (32): seems originally to have contained only the Apocalypse.
- 2256 (218): also seems to have contained no more than the Apocalypse, but this claim needs to be examined more closely.
- 2039 (90): was stolen by Matthaei in the Moscow Synodal Libray and sold in 1788 to the Dresden library. He probably took these leaves from a larger manuscript.
- 2021 (41): copied by Georgios Hermonymos from 452 (42); contains only the Apocalypse
- 2352 (202): lacks an accurate description.

---

104. Also, the four manuscripts mentioned here are classified on p. 26 n. 80.
105. The oldest papyrus fragments are disregarded here.

- 2408 is a single leaf of a lost manuscript, which was inserted into 1215 (28).

In some manuscripts, mainly Codices Vaticani, the Apocalypse was bound together with other texts by the bookbinder. This is the case in 2020 (38), 2361 (two leaves of an Andreas codex), 866 (115) (see p. 33), and 2030 (65, here is a quaternio of a manuscript of the Apocalypse inserted in a volume with the writings of the fathers). In 2419, four leaves of an Arethas manuscript were used to fill a gap in an Andreas codex (743). Also, in 2259 (213), 2022 (43), 2032 (68), 2004 (142), 1328 (190), and apparently also in 792 (113), the bookbinder combines the Apocalypse with other writings.

[36] We can summarize the findings as follows: fifty-two manuscripts contain the entire New Testament including the Apocalypse; seventy manuscripts contain the Praxapostolos and the Apocalypse; and six manuscripts contain Paul and the Apocalypse. Only a few manuscripts contain the Apocalypse alone. In twenty-three cases, the Apocalypse surfaces among nonbiblical writings. Seventy-one manuscripts contain the Apocalypse with a commentary, combined for the most part with nonbiblical material. In a way, these two latter classes of manuscripts do not belong to the New Testament's manuscript tradition.

If only a much smaller portion of New Testament manuscripts also contains the Apocalypse, then we can make another observation (which diminishes the ratio of the Apocalypse to the rest of the New Testament books even further): even where the Apocalypse is included in manuscripts with the rest of New Testament or its second half (the Praxapostolos), the book is simply treated as a kind of appendix. We repeatedly find clear traces of this. In a number of manuscripts, the Apocalypse was added only subsequently by a later hand. This is the case in the following manuscripts:

- 2919 (12): the Praxapostolos is from the eleventh century, and the Apocalypse appears on the remaining empty leaves from a fifteenth-century hand, attached from a *Vorlage* with the Andreas commentary.
- 35 (17): a homily of John Chrysostom lies between Paul and the Apocalypse, evidence that Paul was placed at the end of the New Testament in the *Vorlage*.
- 61 (92): with the infamous Codex Montfortianus, the fourth of the manuscript's four scribes added the Apocalypse in 1580, after a great interval of time from the three former ones.
- 632 (22): two scribes (twelfth and thirteenth centuries) copied the

Praxapostolos; a third scribe added the Apocalypse's text in the fourteenth century, and a fourth scribe added the marginal scholia in the sixteenth century.

- 2920 (46): again, someone added the Apocalypse later, but soon after the preceding New Testament parts.
- 1957 (91): a fifteenth-century scribe restored the lost leaves of this most famous of all the Greek Bible manuscripts (B), Heb 9:14 to the end and the Apocalypse in minuscule script.
- [37] 385 (29): a later hand added the Apocalypse to the Praxapostolos; some of John Chrysostom's writings are between Hebrews and the Apocalypse.
- Also in 88, (99) a later scribe appeared to add the Apocalypse.
- 2921 (30): a fifteenth-century hand added the Apocalypse to the Praxapostolos (fourteenth century) on different paper; there are again all sorts of additions to the Apostolos at the end of Hebrews.
- 2923 (131): a fifteenth-century scribe added the Apocalypse on paper to a thirteenth-century parchment manuscript with the Praxapostolos.
- 172 (87): three hands copied the Praxapostolos and the Apocalypse; the third hand copied the Apocalypse.
- 1728 (211): the Praxapostolos and the Apocalypse; the Erotapokriseis lies between Hebrews and the Apocalypse (fols. 353^v–356^r).
- 2926 (187): the scribe of the Apocalypse (sixteenth century) inserted the book at the beginning of a manuscript containing the Praxapostolos (eleventh century).
- 757 (150): contains the entire New Testament, the Apocalypse by a later hand (von Soden)
- 2922 (missing in Hoskier): the Praxapostolos and, inserted by a later hand, the Apocalypse

The fact that this situation surfaces so frequently suggests that the same circumstances persist in other cases, going back only one or a few stages in the textual transmission. It is also not difficult to see in a few cases. For instance, the Martyrdoms of Peter and Paul are between Paul and the Apocalypse in P. The Apocalypse's text, moreover, comes from a *Vorlage* with the Andreas commentary. In 1780 (missing in Hoskier), there is "a short account of ecumenical councils" between the end of the Catholic Epistles and the Apocalypse (fols. 170^r–191^r).[106]

---

106. Clark, *Descriptive Catalogue of Greek New Testament Manuscripts*.

An examination of the text forms discloses the same phenomenon in a number of other manuscripts. In the more than eighty manuscripts that comprise the K group, sister manuscripts in the text of the Apocalypse are rarely ever sisters in the Praxapostolos,[107] and sister manuscripts in the Praxapostolos are almost never immediate sisters in the [38] Apocalypse. Thus, for example, 61 – 69 are related to each other only in the Apocalypse. Of the family 177 – 2918 – 337, 177 forms a closer group in the Praxapostolos with 460 – 1245, two manuscripts without the Apocalypse. Indeed, 337 in the Praxapostolos belongs, as 177, to von Soden's I^a Text. However, there it is not a direct sister to 177 as in the Apocalypse. Of the group 935 – 1728 – 1734 – 1870, 935 in the text of Paul is closely related to 216 and 440, two manuscripts without the Apocalypse. Of the group 920 – 1859 – 1872 – 2027 – 2256, 920 in the Praxapostolos belongs to von Soden's I^a text. On the other hand, 1872 belongs to I^b and is closely related to 1149, which contains the New Testament without the Apocalypse. 1859 has not been investigated yet in other New Testament books, only 2027 and 2256, however, contain the Apocalypse. 1611 is part of the I^c text in the Praxapostolos and a sister to 1108, 1518, and 2138, of which 1108 and 1518 only have the Praxapostolos; 2138 also preserves the Apocalypse but contains a different text than 1611. 2344 is of the I^{a3} type in the Praxapostolos, most closely related with 69 – 492 and 436, of which only 69 contains the Apocalypse, but again in line with another text type.

The fact that often only one of the numerous sister manuscripts in the Praxapostolos preserves the Apocalypse shows that the latter was copied from another *Vorlage*. This observation confirms that manuscripts that only contain the Apocalypse are related in this way with those that contain either the Praxapostolos or the rest of the New Testament.[108] That is to say, the Apocalypse is always copied from another *Vorlage*.

We can place these findings on an even broader foundation if all manuscripts, whose text of the Apocalypse is known, were also examined for the rest of their New Testament books. The nearly identical observations that can be made about the manuscripts investigated in all the New Testa-

---

107. 919, 2004 form one of the very rare exceptions. However, although manuscripts 18 and 2138 belong to the same group in their text of the Apocalypse, they belong to quite different groups in the Praxapostolos. In the Praxapostolos, 2138 is closely related to 1611 1108 and 1518, of which only 1611 also contains the Apocalypse.

108. See also the comments in Schmid, "Untersuchungen zur Geschichte des griechischen Apokalypsetextes," 174, 186–87, 192–93, and 194–95, especially 167.

ment books allow us to extend the conclusions reached here to the entire manuscript material.

Therefore, all of the Apocalypse's Greek manuscripts are examined and grouped from the perspective of the combinations in which the book occurs. We can now relate the above grouping of the Apocalypse's textual tradition according to text families with the list given here and ask: In what kind of manuscripts do the various text forms occur? Moreover, we need to establish whether or not certain text forms also have a peculiar kind of tradition. I begin with that class [39] of manuscripts where the Apocalypse's text only forms a part of the commentary and for which the primary interest (i.e., the reason the manuscripts in question were really copied) was the commentary.

By far, *Andreas of Caesarea's commentary* on the Apocalypse is the one most frequently handed down in manuscripts. It is present in fifty-four manuscripts in its original form.[109] These fifty-four manuscripts contain (1) the same type of text of the Apocalypse, virtually without exception.[110] This text might often be more or less heavily influenced by other text forms, especially the K text. (2) This commentary is never included in any manuscript with other New Testament texts.

The Andreas Text was rarely copied without the commentary and therefore rarely surfaces in διαθήκη or Praxapostolos manuscripts. The following are exceptions:

- P: the Praxapostolos and the Apocalypse
- 35 (17): the Apocalypse added only by a later hand to the Praxapostolos
- 205 – 2886 – 2920 (46 – 88 – 101): three copied on the order of Bessarion, identical manuscripts of the whole New Testament in the text
- 88 (99): the Praxapostolos and the Apocalypse (Apocalypse by a later hand?)
- 2919 (12): the Apocalypse appended by a later hand in the Praxapostolos

---

109. In addition, 2063, 2433, and Barocc. 212 contain the commentary without the Apocalypse, as well as the now-lost manuscript 175 (old number Iwiron = 661).

110. In 2066, the Apocalypse's appended text was copied from the printed Textus Receptus. In 82, 911, and 632 the Andreas commentary was added only in the margins (in 632 by a much later hand). These three manuscripts do not belong to Aν in the text of the Apocalypse.

- 1384 (191): the whole New Testament with the Apocalypse
- 1732 (220): the Praxapostolos with the Apocalypse
- 1876 (135): the Praxapostolos and the Apocalypse by one hand
- 2080 (178): the Praxapostolos and the Apocalypse

1678 (240) contains (in addition to liturgical writings) the whole New Testament with a commentary to all parts and a catena from Andreas and Oecumenius in the Apocalypse.

This list clearly shows that manuscripts used to supplement the New Testament or the Praxapostolos with the Apocalypse preserved the Andreas text several times. It is still evident in the majority of these manuscripts that their text of the Apocalypse comes from a *Vorlage* with the commentary. [40] The tradition of the A*v* text forms only a part of the tradition of the Andreas commentary. The minor influence of the A*v* text on the other forms of the Apocalypse's text, as well as the rare instances where this text was used to supplement Bible manuscripts (a text first lifted from the commentary), explains this influence.

An abridged form of this commentary, which J. A. Cramer edited according to the Cod. Paris. Coisl. 224,[111] resides in a group of manuscripts that also forms a special textual family (O) in the Apocalypse's text. These are 250, 424, 1862, 1888, 2018, 2032, 2070, 2305, and 2022. The same text of the Apocalypse is available but without commentary in several other manuscripts, namely, 172, 616, 1828, and 2084. In 172, 616, and 1828, this text is appended to the Praxapostolos. In 2084, it is in the midst of a collection of nonbiblical writings. In 250, 424, 1862, and 1888, this commentary supplements the Praxapostolos, which is likewise accompanied by a commentary. In 2018, 2070, and 2305, it stands in the midst of nonbiblical writings. 2022 and 2032 are collections assembled by the bookbinder. It is therefore no longer possible to discern in what combination this commentary originally stood. The impression is that this excerpt of Andreas's commentary was created because someone wanted to complete the Praxapostolos manuscripts (which were supplemented with a commentary or a catena) in the same manner that the Apocalypse was completed. None of these manuscripts predates the eleventh century.

Oecumenius's commentary, which has a very narrow tradition, stands once (2053) on its own. In four other closely related manuscripts (2062,

---

111. John Anthony Cramer, *In Epistolas Catholicas et Apocalypsin*, vol. 8 of *Catenae Graecorum Patrum in Novum Testamentum* (Oxford: Typographeo Academico, 1844), 498–582. See also p. 30–31.

2062^A, 2062^B, and 2403), it stands in a collection of manuscripts with Pseudo-Dionysius Aeropagite, as well as in three[112] catena manuscripts, only one of which (Codex 1678 mentioned above) contains other New Testament texts. The Apocalypse's text never surfaces outside of this combination with the commentary and has exerted no influence on the other forms of the Apocalypse's text.

The Arethas commentary tradition is slightly broader. It surfaces in seven manuscripts, one of which (2419) is a small [41] but extensive fragment of four leaves. Four times (91, 314, 617, 1934) the Arethas commentary is combined with the Pseudo-Oecumenius commentary to the Praxapostolos (in 1934 with Paul). It stands alone in the two sister manuscripts, 2075 and 2077. Also noteworthy is the fact that 314 is the only manuscript to provide this commentary in its complete form. In 91, 617, and 1934, however, we encounter an abridged version by mechanical omissions, which forms a counterpart to the previously mentioned abridged form of the Andreas commentary. One of these two abridged commentaries was used to supplement the annotated Praxapostolos.

Eight manuscripts contain the Arethas text of the Apocalypse without the commentary, and six of them are combined with the rest of the New Testament (175, 242, 664, 1094) or the Praxapostolos (256, 39^a). The Arethas text bound with nonbiblical writings (Pseudo-Dionysius Aeropagite) surfaces only in 2016. In 2017, the Apocalypse originally stood alone.

Eight of the ten manuscripts of $f^{104/336}$ contain either the whole New Testament or the Praxapostolos. Of the other two that remain, one is a nonbiblical writing, and one is preserved fragmentarily.

Of the thirty-six manuscripts of the Complutensian group, fourteen contain the entire New Testament, ten contain the Praxapostolos, two (60 and 1551) contain the Gospels and the Apocalypse, one (1771) contains Paul and the Apocalypse, and one (2041)—and probably also a second (2352)—contains the Apocalypse alone. 1957 is the well-known supplement of Cod. Vatic. gr. 1209 (B). The Apocalypse is bound with nonbiblical writings in five manuscripts (1328, 1774, 2061, 2196, 2434). Only in two is this text combined with a commentary (2023, Aν text revised toward the Compl.; 2035, a Compl. text bound with the Greek translation of the Italian commentary of Federigo da Venezia).

---

112. 1678, 1778, 2433.

Twenty-six of the seventy-two K text manuscripts[113] contain the entire New Testament, twenty-seven contain the Praxapostolos (920 and 1859 without Paul), and three (1948, 1955, 2349 [Hebrews and the Apocalypse]) contain Paul and the Apocalypse. 325 contains (all from one hand) 3 John, Paul, and the Apocalypse, and 368 contains John, 1–3 John, and the Apocalypse. Three (2021, 2039,[114] and 2256) contain only the Apocalypse. Finally, the Apocalypse surfaces nine times (2027, 2076, 2258, 2024, 2025, 2048, 2079, 2436, Q) in the midst of nonbiblical writings. 2058 [42] is a collection compiled by the bookbinder that also contains the Apocalypse with a catena.

Of the few minuscules that provide an old, valuable text, 1006, 1611, 1841, 1854, and 2344 contain the Apocalypse with the Praxapostolos. 2329 and 2351 are juxtaposed in the same collection. Also, the fragment 2050 is in a collection with nonbiblical writings, and 2030 was inserted by the bookbinder in a similar collection.

This statistical compilation leads to clear results.

(1) To supplement the New Testament or the Praxapostolos, some readily available and arbitrary manuscript of the Apocalypse was usually copied. This emerges with perfect clarity from the fact that manuscripts, which in other parts of the New Testament are sisters, are also almost never sisters in the Apocalypse and that these same manuscripts are not sisters in the text of the Apocalypse with the books that precede it.[115] Different text forms of the Apocalypse stand side by side arbitrarily in the διαθήκη and Praxapostolos manuscripts—if they contain the Apocalypse at all. Only Oecumenius's text is completely missing from actual Bible manuscripts. The same is almost as true for the Aν text, despite its rich manuscript tradition. The reason for this—and one only has to look for this fact—is that scribes avoided the necessary effort to extract the Apocalypse's text from a commentary. Without question, an actual barrier stands between the two forms of tradition.[116] This emerges from the fact that the Aν text was heavily influenced by the K text (and in a few cases by

---

113. After the elimination of the fifteen Arethas manuscripts. Contrarily, 2076 and its copy 2258 belong to K up to 1:13.

114. Probably originally a part of a more extensive manuscript; see p. 34.

115. See p. 34.

116. Against Hoskier (*Die Schriften des Neuen Testaments*, 1:xi). See, in addition, already Schmid, "Untersuchungen zur Geschichte des griechischen Apokalypsetextes," 459–60; von Dobschütz, "Zur Liste der NTlichen Handschriften," 198–99.

the Compl. text; in one case—subgroup f^{205} of the Av text—by the type of f^{336}) and also that several forms of mixed texts were created for the most part without commentary, which then have also been introduced into the actual Bible manuscripts. That the clear influence of the Av text upon the K text tradition is limited to two cases ($f^{42/325}$ and 2436) is not due to an aversion to texts considered "noncanonical" but for the same practical reason that explains why the Av text is rarely found in the manuscripts of the Bible.

[43] (2) The Andreas text forms a branch of the Apocalypse's textual tradition that departs from the ecclesiastical tradition as seldom as those manuscripts that appear to preserve the Apocalypse in the midst of non-biblical texts. For here again, only text forms represented in the actual "biblical" tradition appear.

(3) In some cases, the Apocalypse, accompanied by a commentary, is added to the Praxapostolos, which already had a commentary. Just as the so-called Oecumenius commentary appears in the Praxapostolos, so also are the abridged Andreas commentary or the similarly abridged Arethas commentary used for the Apocalypse. Only in three exceptional cases (82, 632, 911) is the original Andreas commentary appended, but again, in an independent, abridged form. And only once (1678) was a catenae for the Apocalypse with the complete commentaries of Andreas and Oecumenius used in order to produce a completely annotated New Testament.

First Section
2. The Major Stems of the Greek Text of the Apocalypse and Their Interrelationships

All the minuscules that preserve the Apocalypse[1] were examined on the basis of their text form in previous studies. The bulk of these minuscules can be traced back to the two recensions Av and K or are texts that demonstrably emanate from these. These studies have led to the elimination of many useless manuscripts, as well as to the classification of the Apocalypse's entire Greek tradition into four ancient major stems. We now place these stems alongside each other and examine their interrelationships.

We can establish the entirety of the text of the Av and K recensions with absolute certainty. In the first place, the recensions are presented by listing each of their unique readings.[2] Their special readings will be cited by chapter and verse in order to demonstrate clearly the degree to which their respective texts of the Apocalypse are revised. We bypass grouping these readings according to kind (e.g., error, linguistic corrections, clarifications, parallel influence, etc.), since Weiss, Bousset, and von Soden already classify them accordingly. Clearly, most of these unique readings are corrections.

2.1. The Text of the Apocalypse of Andreas of Caesarea (= Av)

1:2   ειδε] + και ατινα εισι και ατινα χρη γενεσθαι μετα ταυτα (influenced by 1:19) cum Arm.a^2

1:4   α] + εστιν (likewise 5:13 for των S A)

---

1. Only the currently lost manuscripts, 1760, 1785, and 1806, and the three named manuscripts of the Great Lawra (26 n. 80) have not been investigated yet.

2. The Textus Receptus, as it is reprinted in Hoskier, was chosen as the *Vorlage* of the collation.

[45] 1:5   + εχ ante των νεκρων (influenced by Col 1:18) cum Syr.[1.2] Sah. Boh. Arm.

αγαπωντι] αγαπησαντι (harmonization to the following λυσαντι)

1:6   βασιλειαν] βασιλεις χαι (see 5:10) cum Arm.a[-2.3**]

1:9   + εν τη ante βασιλεια (stylistic improvement) cum Syr.[1] h εν

ιησου] ιησου χριστου

1:11   + εγω ειμι το αλφα χαι το ω ο πρωτος χαι ο εσχατος χαι ante ο βλεπεις (harmonization to 1:8; see 21:6; 22:13) cum Arm.a

1:12   ελαλει] ελαλησε (stylistic improvement; likewise 2:14 K)

1:17   αυτου[2] + χειρα (clarification) cum Syr.[1.2] Sah. Boh.

1:18   ~ αδου ... θανατου

1:20   αι λυχνιαι αι επτα] αι επτα λυχνιαι ας ειδες cum Syr.[1] Boh.

2:2   βαστασαι] -ξαι

2:3   ~ εβαστασας χαι υπομονην εχεις (correction "since εβαστασας is influenced by 2:2 for the improvement of the tense and mood": Bousset)

2:5   πεπτωχας] εχπεπτωχας cum Syr.[1.2] Sah.

2:7   τω παραδεισω] μεσω του παραδεισου (see Gen 3:3)

2:9   om. εχ (likewise 13:3; 21:9)

2:13   ημεραις] + εν αις (correction of the anacoluthon)

πιστος] + οτι πας μαρτυς πιστος cum Syr.[1] (perhaps originally a marginal note)

2:14   τω βαλαχ] εν τω βαλααμ τον βαλαχ

2:15   ομοιως] + ο μισω cum Arm.a (see 2:6)

2:17   + φαγειν απο ante του μαννα cum Gig. Ambr. Tyc.[2] Arm.a

2:20   η λεγουσα] την λεγουσαν

3:2   om. μου cum Arm.a[-1.3]

3:4   om. αλλα Av[plur.] cum Apr. Arm.a

α] οι (*constructio ad sensum*; qualifies as the *Urtext*, as Bousset also recognized; see p. 250)

3:7   χλειν] χλειδα (see 20:1 and K to 1:18)[3]

χλεισει] χλειει (harmonization to ανοιγει)

3:9   ιδου[2]] χαι (stylistic improvement)

3:18   εγχρισαι] -σον

4:1   λεγων] λεγουσα cum S[a] (correction relating to φωνη; likewise 9:14 P[47]Av)

---

3. Av is not consistent here; see 1:18 χλεις (accusative plural) and 20:1 χλειν.

4:2 + και ante ευθεως cum Vulg. Beat. Ps.-Ambr. Syr.[1] Boh. Arm. Aeth.

(επι) τον θρονον] του θρονου

[46] 4:7 ως ανθρωπου] ως ανθρωπος

4:11 ησαν] εισι

5:2 om. εν ante φωνη (likewise 18:2 S Aν K; vice versa + εν 19:17 S K; 21:16 Aν)

5:3 ουδε ter

5:4 ανοιξαι] + και αναγνωναι cum Arm.*a*

5:6 απεσταλμενοι] τα -να

5:8 κιθαραν] -ας (see 11:9)

5:13 ο] + εστιν et + α ante εστιν[(2)]

6:1 om. επτα (likewise 15:8; 16:1; 5:6 A Aν; 10:4 P[47] C)

φωνη] φωνης

6:8 ηκολουθει] ακολουθει

6:10 εκραξαν] εκραζον (likewise 18:18, 19 Aν K)

εκ] απο (likewise 1:5 K; on the other hand, 19:2 εκ all)

6:11 εως] + οὖ (analogue 7:3 K)

6:12 + και ante οτε (harmonization to 6:3, 5, 7, 9; however, see also 19:1; 20:3; 21:19; 22:12, 16; also 3:9)

om. ολη cum Latt.[part.]

6:13 ~ μεγαλου ανεμου (von Soden[txt.]; however, μεγας always follows nouns in the Apocalypse)

6:15 ~ οι πλουσιοι και οι χιλιαρχοι

om. και οι ισχυροι Aν[part.] (whether this is true for Aν itself is questionable)

+ πας ante ελευθερος

7:1 τουτο] ταυτα (harmonization to other usage in the Apocalypse)

7:4 χιλιαδες] -ας Aν[part.] (whether this is true for Aν itself is questionable)

7:9 περιβεβλημενους] -οι cum S[a]

7:16 om. ετι[2] (stylistic improvement)

8:5 ~ φωναι και βρονται και αστραπαι

8:7 πρωτος] + αγγελος cum Gig. Vulg. Boh. Sah.[2/3] Arm.[exc. 4] (see 8:8)

om. εν ante αιματι

8:11 εγενετο] γινεται (harmonization to the previous λεγεται)

8:12 φανη] φαινη (analogue 20:3 K)

8:13 αετου] αγγελου cum Vict. Arm.*a* Arab.

9:4 om. του θεου cum Arm.*a*

9:10 om. και post κεντρα et + και ante η εξουσια (misunderstands text)

9:11 + και ante εχουσι Aν^part. (see 9:10 and 6:12 above)

9:12 ερχεται] ερχονται cum S^a 0207 (correction; ουαι is feminine; see 19:14)
om. ετι

[47] 9:18 om. πληγων Aν^plur. (whether this is correct for Aν itself cannot be established)

9:19 om. και εν ταις ουραις αυτων (homoioteleuton)

10:1 om. η ante ιρις (see the omission of the article before ιρις in the entire tradition of 4:3)

10:2 εχων] ειχεν or εχει (original Aν reading cannot be established)

10:4 μη αυτα γραψης] μετα ταυτα γραφεις cum Aeth. (misunderstanding)

10:7 ετελεσθη] τελεσθῆ (misunderstanding of the syntax)

10:9 δουναι] δος (easing of the syntax)

10:11 λεγουσιν] λεγει cum Latt. Syr.^1.2 Arm. Aeth. (harmonization to λεγει μοι 10:9).

11:4 κυριου] θεου
εστωτες] εστωσαι (see 4:1 and 9:14 above; likewise 11:15 P^47 S C Aν)

11:5 ~ αυτους θελει^2 Aν^plur. (probably Aν)

11:6 om. αυτα Aν^plur. (whether it is the original Aν text cannot be established)

11:7 om. και αποκτενει αυτους (homoioteleuton)

11:9 το πτωμα] τα πτωματα (harmonization to 11:9b; the same correction 11:8 P^47 S Aν; see also 5:8 above, as well as 13:16 το μετωπον] των μετωπων P^47 Aν and 17:8 το ονομα] τα ονοματα S Aν)

11:18 om. και ante τοις φοβουμενοις Aν^part. (alters the meaning)
διαφθειροντας] φθειροντας

12:1 om. η ante σεληνη Aν^part. (whether this is an original Aν text is doubtful)

12:5 om. εν (non C, errat Hoskier)
om. προς ante τον θρονον (stylistic improvement)

12:8 ουδε] ουτε (see 20:4 below)

12:9 om. μετ αυτου (homoioteleuton)

12:10 εβληθη] κατεβληθη
om. ημων^3 Aν^part.

12:14 πετηται] πεταται (See on the other hand 4:7; 8:13; 14:16; 19:17; scribal error? πέταται, not πετᾶται is to be read.)

12:15 αυτην] ταυτην (likewise 14:8 K)

13:3 om. εκ (likewise 2:9; 21:9)

ολη η γη] εν ολη τη γη (correction)

13:4 θηριω¹⌒²

13:6 + και ante τοις cum Sᵃ Syr.² Sah. Boh. Latt. Arab.

14:2 η φωνη ἡν] φωνην (φωνην et ως] + φωνην P⁴⁷ 2053)

om. ως ante κιθαρωδων (see 19:1, 6 below)

[48] 14:6 καθημενους] + τους κατοικουντας (mixed text; καθημ.] κατοικουντας A al. pc.)

om. επι ante παν (επι¹ om. Aν K; only Aν has completed the correction)

14:12 + ωδε ante οι τηρουντες (missed the correction of the misunderstood apposition)

14:13 λεγουσης] + μοι (see 17:1 and 18:6 below)

om. αυτων²

14:14 καθημενον ομοιον] -ος bis (-ος ... ον P⁴⁷)

14:15 ναου] ουρανου cum Arm.a·¹·² (correction or reading error?)

ηλθε] + σου

15:2 αυτου¹] + εκ του χαραγματος αυτου και

15:8 om. επτα² (see 6:1 above)

16:1 om. και² (correction)

om. επτα ante φιαλας

om. του θεου Aνᵖᵃʳᵗ· (whether this reading is original to Aν cannot be established)

16:2 εις την γην ... επι τους ανθρωπους] επι την γην ... εις τους ανθρωπους⁴

16:4 τριτος] + αγγελος cum Arm.a·¹·² (see 16:10, 12, 17 below; likewise 16:3 Aν K; 16:8 S Aν)

16:10 πεμπτος] + αγγελος cum Arm.a·¹·²

16:12 εκτος] + αγγελος cum Latt.

om. αυτου²

ανατολης] -λων (on the other hand, 7:2; 21:13; however, 21:13 K)

---

4. In this passage and in 16:17, Bousset (*Textkritische Studien*, 28) remarks well: "In each of the three cases the changing of the preposition presupposes deliberate thought. In fact, επι fits better in the first variant, in the other two, εις."

16:14 δαιμονιων] -νων (likewise 18:2 Aν K)

16:17 εβδομος] + αγγελος cum Sᵃ multiple versions

       επι] εις

       om. του ναου

17:1   λεγων] + μοι (see 14:13 above; 18:6 below)

17:3   ονοματα] ονοματων (correction)

17:4   πορφυρουν] -αν

       ~ χρυσουν ποτηριον

17:6   om. ιησου Aνᵖᵃʳᵗ· (whether this belongs to Aν itself cannot be established with certainty)

17:16 om. και γυμνην (homoioteleuton)

18:1   + και ante μετα cum Arm.a⁻² (see 6:12 above)

[49] 18:2   φωνη] + μεγαλη

18:3   ~ του θυμου του οινου

       πεπτωκαν] πεπωκε (*Urtext*?; on account of the neuter plural, the singular must be a correction)[5]

18:4   εξελθατε] -θετε

       εξ αυτης om. Aνᵖᵃʳᵗ· (questionable, whether a true Aν reading)

       ο ante λαος om. Aνᵖᵃʳᵗ· (likewise)

       om. και εκ των πληγων αυτης

18:6   απεδωκεν] + υμιν (see 14:13 above)

       διπλωσατε] + αυτη

18:7   αυτην] εαυτην cum Sᵃ (Weiss[6] maintains αὐτήν as similarly impossible as with 8:6; see also under Aν K below)

       om. και πενθος¹

       om. οτι ante εν

       18:9 κλαυσονται] + αυτην

18:11 επ αυτην] εφ εαυτους

       ουκετι iungit cum sequentibus

18:12 βυσσινου] βυσσου (likewise 18:16 K)

18:14 απωλετο] απηλθεν (harmonization to the previous απηλθεν)

       ~ ου μη ευρ. αυτα

       ευρησουσιν] ευρησεις

18:16 om. και λεγοντες Aνᵖˡᵘʳ·

       om. και ante κεχρυσωμενη Aνᵖˡᵘʳ· (likewise 17:4 Aν K)

---

5. See Weiss, *Die Johannes-Apokalypse*, 14.

6. Ibid., 138.

18:17 om. ο post πας² (likewise 22:18 below)
τοπον] των πλοιων (correction)

18:19 om. τα ante πλοια

18:20 αυτη] αυτην (likewise 18:9, 11 *Urtext*, while all modern editions read αυτη here)

19:1 + και ante μετα (see 6:12 above)
om. ως (see 14:2; 19:6; likewise 6:6 K; 14:3 P⁴⁷ S K)
om. μεγαλην

19:2 + της ante χειρος

19:3 om. αυτης Aν^part.

19:5 om. λεγουσα (see 18:16 and 19:17)

19:6 om. ως ante φωνην¹ (see 14:2 and 19:6)
λεγοντων] λεγοντας
om. κυριος

19:8 ~ καθαρον λαμπρον

19:10 προσκυνησαι] και προσεκυνησα

[50] 19:13 κεκληται] καλειται

19:14 ηκολουθει ... εφ ιπποις λευκοις] ηκολουθουν ... εφιπποι πολλοι

19:15 + και ante της οργης

19:17 om. λεγων (see 19:5)
om. και συναχθητε
τον μεγαν του] του μεγαλου cum Arm.*a*·²

19:19 om. τον ante πολεμον (see 9:7, 9; likewise 16:14 P⁴⁷ Aν; see further 18:19; 20:3, 8; labeled a *Wahllesart* by von Soden)

19:20 μετ αυτου] μετα τουτου
εβληθησαν] βληθησονται
+ τω ante θειω

20:2 om. ο ante σατανας (likewise 12:9 P⁴⁷ K)

20:3 εκλεισεν] εδησε cum Apr Arm.⁴
om. ετι
om. τα ante χιλια (see 19:19)
+ και ante μετα (see 18:1)

20:4 το θηριον] τω θηριω
ουδε] ουτε (see 12:8)
την εικονα] τη εικονι
μετωπον] + αυτων cum Syr.¹ Sah. Boh. Arm. Arab. Aeth.
om. του ante χριστου

20:5 + και ante οι

20:6 ~ ο θανατος ο δευτερος

20:8　om. τον ante πολεμον (see 19:19 above)
　　　om. αυτων (see 13:8)
20:11　~ λευκον μεγαν
20:13　~ τους εν αυτη νεκρους
　　　~ τους εν αυτοις νεκρους
20:14　πυρος$^{1}\frown{}^{2}$
21:1　απηλθαν] παρηλθε (misguided correction)
21:2　~ απο του θεου εκ του ουρανου cum Arm.*a* (see 20:9 K below)
21:3　~ θεος αυτων
21:4　απηλθαν] -ον
21:5　καινα ποιω] καινοποιω
　　　~ αληθινοι και πιστοι cum Arm.*a*
21:7　αυτος εσται ... υιος] αυτοι εσονται ... υιοι
21:8　om. και ante εβδελυγμενοις
　　　~ ο δευτερος θανατος
[51] 21:9　om. εκ (likewise 2:9 and 13:3 above; on the other hand, 5:6; 6:1
　　　[bis] 7:13; 15:7; 17:1)
　　　~ την νυμφην του αρνιου την γυναικα
21:10　πολιν την] + μεγαλην και
21:11　om. ως λιθω (correction)
21:13　om. και ter
21:15　om. μετρον
21:16　+ εν ante τω καλαμω (conversely, 5:2 above)
21:18　ομοιον] -α (misguided correction)
21:20　σαρδιον] -ος
　　　βηρυλλος] -λλιος
　　　ενατος] εννατος
21:27　[ο] ποιων] ποιουν
22:1　ποταμον] + καθαρον cum Arm.*a*
22:2　εκειθεν] εντευθεν
　　　+ ενα ante εκαστον
22:3　ετι] εκει (harmonization to 21:25)
22:5　ετι] εκει (likewise)
　　　~ χρειαν ουκ εχουσι
22:6　πνευματων των] αγιων cum Arm.*a*
22:7　om. και ante ιδου
22:8　καγω] και εγω
22:9　om. και^{3}
22:10　ο καιρος γαρ] οτι ο καιρος

22:12   + και ante ιδου (see 6:12)
        ~ αυτου εσται
22:13   ~ αρχη και τελος ο πρωτος και ο εσχατος
        om. η ante αρχη et το ante τελος
22:15   + ο ante φιλων (conversely, 18:17 and 22:18)
22:16   om. επι
        + και ante ο αστηρ
22:18   om. τω ante ακουοντι
        + επτα ante πληγας (influenced by 21:9; explained as a chosen
        reading in von Soden)
22:20   ιησου] + χριστε cum Sᵃ

There are also some orthographic forms:

3:7   κλειν] κλειδα, see p. 46
6:11   αποκτεννεσθαι] αποκτεινεσθαι
6:14   ελισσομενον] ειλισσομενον
[52] 9:11   αβαδδων] αββαδων Αν Kᵖᵃʳᵗ.
18:13   κινναμωμον] κιναμωμον (κιναμωμου K)

The majority of Αν witnesses have the form of δυναμαι with η in the imperfect tense in all passages (5:3; 7:9; 14:3; 15:8).

For πυλων, the majority of witnesses have the uncontracted dative plural form πυλεωσι (21:12; 22:14).

All of the Αν text's distinctive readings are listed here.[7] In some places, the original Αν reading is doubtful. If we include these doubtful cases, the total number of distinctive Αν text readings is 243. Summing up the individual readings by their kind, simple errors are clearly very rare. Parallel influences are probably present[8] but not in the majority, as von Soden assumed. The great majority of the Αν text's own readings are independent

---

7. I count only the unique readings of Αν (or K) in this list and ignore the corrections that Αν (or K) share with P⁴⁷, S, or C, since for the time being it is only necessary to lay out the defining characteristics of the text type of Αν (and K). The total extent of the corrections (or errors) existing in Αν (or K) is not yet recorded but, as it turns out, it goes beyond the nonhereditary readings in the list above, so that the list already gives a true overall picture of this text form.

8. See 1:2, 5, 11; 18:14; 21:2; 22:3, 5, 20.

corrections.[9] There is no strict consistency, however, as in the case of the K text. This can be said, for example, in such a simple case as the consistent addition of αγγελος in 16:3–17.[10] The instrumental εν, however, is attached one time (21:16) and is removed elsewhere (5:2). A more precise examination is necessary for the strikingly few common insertions of και (see 6:12). We wonder here whether Andreas first attached it, at least a few times, especially in those places where a section of text resumes after a commentary portion. In fact, this και surfaces several times precisely at the [53] beginning of a new κείμενον section in the Αν text (4:2; 18:1; 19:1; 22:16).[11] However, this assumption loses its foundation together with its major implication[12] because και is occasionally added within a section of lemma text (9:11; 20:3; 21:19 [with S*]; 22:12).[13] We will discuss later whether readings that may reflect the *Urtext* also surface among the unique readings of Αν.[14] The secondary character of the vast majority of these unique readings is obvious. And their great number shows that Αν is a recension in the proper sense, that is, the work of someone who corrected the text in all its chapters, although the recensor may have already adopted a (small) part of the corrections. But this also illustrates the inferiority of the Αν text form compared to the more "neutral" text of AC Oecumenius. By no means does it follow, however, that the Αν text is of no independent value for reconstructing the *Urtext* alongside AC Oec and P[47] S. Furthermore, in keeping with its

---

9. Bousset attempts a classification of the various corrections (*Textkritische Studien*, 3–35). However, a strict definition of the different classes is not feasible in practice. Many of the readings Bousset presents are also to be discussed in Αν.

10. Generally similar cases are also: 11:9; 13:16 (plural instead of singular); complement of μοι or ημιν (14:13; 17:1; 18:6); omission of the article, when no specific object or subject is meant (18:19; 19:19; 20:3, 8); omission of εκ (2:9; 13:3; 21:9).

11. As one could explain conversely at 22:7 that a newly prepared segment of text begins at λεγων where και is omitted before ιδου in Αν.

12. The possibility that Andreas himself first omitted the και in 22:7 and that he inserted it in a few other places at the beginning of a section of text is certainly not out of the question. What we should reject as an unfounded inference is that Andreas of Caesarea first created the Αν text on the whole, since the text is demonstrably older than him. However, because all our witnesses for this text go back to the Andreas commentary we can say nothing certain about it, namely, whether or not Andreas also edited the text that he encountered with one or another minor change.

13. There is a harmonization to 6:3, 5, 7, 9 at 6:12, as von Soden correctly noted.

14. Only the following readings should be considered: 3:4 α] οι and 18:3 πεπωκεν and 4:4 (see p. 76 Αν K) and 5:13 (see p. 250), but not 19:19 and 22:18, also not 18:7 εαυτην.

age, the Aν text certainly reaches back beyond the randomly received major witnesses of the "neutral" text, AC Oec.

2.2. The K Text

1:4	+ θεου ante ο ων
1:5	λυσαντι] λουσαντι
	εκ ante των αμαρτιων] απο (likewise below, 3:12; 9:18; 16:17; Aν in 6:10; Aν K in 21:4; vice versa 21:10)
1:9	συγκοινωνος] κοινωνος
	+ χριστω ante ιησου[1] cum *h* Vulg. Prim.
	ιησου[2]] + χριστου (likewise 22:21 Aν K; see also Aν in 22:20)
1:10	~ φωνην οπισω μου μεγαλην
1:11	φιλαδελφειαν (-φιαν S AC, dub. Aν; likewise 3:7)
[54] 1:12	και[1]] + εκει
1:14[15]	+ και ante ως[1]
1:20	ους] ων (attraction to αστερων)
2:7	θεου] + μου
2:8	om. ος (haplography)
2:10	πασχειν] παθειν
	ιδου] + δη
	βαλλειν] βαλειν
	ημερων] -ας
2:13	ημεραις] + αις (see also p. 91)
2:14	αλλ] αλλα (likewise 2:4 S K; 2:20 A K; 10:9 S 1611; conversely, 3:4 K; see also below 19:14 εφ] επι)
	εδιδασκε] -ξε (likewise 1:12 Aν)
	τω βαλακ] τον βαλακ (εν τω βαλααμ τον βαλακ Aν)
	+ και ante φαγειν
2:20	η λεγουσα] η λεγει (see 3:12 below)
2:25	αν ηξω] ανοιξω
3:1	οτι ζης] και ζης
3:2	στηρισον] τηρησον K[part.], στηρισον rel.
	εμελλον αποθανειν] εμελλες αποβαλλειν
3:3	και[1]⌒3

---

15. See Schmid, "Untersuchungen zur Geschichte des griechischen Apokalypse-textes," 446.

3:4 αλλα] αλλ (see 2:14 above)
~ ολιγα εχεις ονοματα

3:7 φιλαδελφεια (see 1:11 above)
ουδεις κλεισει αυτην ει μη ο ανοιγων και ουδεις ανοιξει (= και κλειων] ει μη ο ανοιγων)

3:9 om. εγω

3:12 η καταβαινουσα] η καταβαινει (see 2:20 above)
εκ ante του ουρανου] απο (see 1:5 above)
om. μου[ult.]

3:16 ουτε[1]] ου

3:18 ~ χρυσιον παρ εμου
εγχρισαι] ινα εγχριση

4:3 ομοιος ορασει σμαραγδινω] ομοιως ορασις σμαραγδινων

4:4 om. και[1]
θρονους[2]] + τους

4:5 θρονου[2]] + αυτου (see 7:11 and 9:4 below)
α] αι
om. τα (article with the predicate noun; likewise below, 21:12; 5:8 S* K)

[55] 4:7 το προσωπον ως ανθρωπου] προσωπον ανθρωπου
om. ζωον[ult.] (stylistic improvement)

4:8 om. αυτων
εχων] εχον cum Αν[part.] (correction; according to Weiss,[16] it is also *Urtext*)

4:9 δωσουσιν] δωσιν

4:11 ημων] + ο αγιος ([von Soden])
om. τα ante παντα

5:2 αξιος] + εστιν (see 14:4 below)

5:3 ουρανω] + ανω (see Exod 20:4)

5:4 και[1]] + εγω (om. S Αν, hiant AC, *Urtext*)

5:5 ανοιξαι] ο ανοιγων

5:6 οι] α
απεσταλμενοι] αποστελλομενα (Bousset 1st loco)[17]

5:8 προσευχαι] -ων Κ[plur.]

5:12 + τον ante πλουτον (harmonization to την δυναμιν)

---

16. Weiss, *Die Johannes-Apokalypse*, 54, 103.
17. See the detailed discussion in Bousset, *Die Offenbarung Johannis*, 258.

5:13   παντα] παντας
5:14   ελεγον] λεγοντα το
6:1   οτε] οτι
6:2   om. και ειδον (but 6:1 + και ιδε S K)
6:3   ~ την δευτεραν σφραγιδα
6:4   om. και ante ινα
6:5   om. και ειδον (on the other hand, + και ιδε S K)
6:6   om. ως
        κριθων] κριθης (harmonization to σιτου)
6:8   om. και ειδον (on the other hand, 6:7 + και ιδε S K)
        αυτοις] αυτω
6:9   μαρτυριαν] + του αρνιου cum Syr.[2] Arm.[3]
6:10   φωνη μεγαλη] φωνην μεγαλην
6:11   om. εκαστω
        om. μικρον
        + και ante οι μελλοντες
7:3   αχρι] αχρις οὗ (analogue 6:11 εως] + οὗ Αν)
7:4   εσφραγισμενοι] -ων
7:5, 8 εσφραγισμενοι] -αι
7:9   om. αυτον
        εστωτες] -ας (harmonization to the following περιβεβλημενους)
7:11   θρονου[2]] + αυτου (see 4:5 above)
[56] 7:14   ειρηκα] ειπον
        επλυναν] επλατυναν
        om. αυτας
7:15   του θρονου[2]] τω θρονω
7:16   ουδε[2]] ουδ ου
7:17   ποιμανει ... οδηγηγσει] ποιμαινει ... οδηγει
8:8   om. πυρι
8:9   om. των[2]
        διεθφαρησαν] -ρη (harmonization to απεθανε)
8:12   ~ και το τριτον αυτης μη φανη η ημερα
9:2   μεγαλης] καιομενης ("because in comparison with the smoke, it did not matter that the furnace was large but that it was on fire")[18]

---

18. Weiss, *Die Johannes-Apokalypse*, 10.

9:4   μετωπων] + αυτων (see 4:5 and 7:11 above; influenced here by 7:3)

9:5   αυτοις] αυταις cum Aν[part.] (WHort[txt.] Vog Charles; however, probably a correction to 9:3 and 9:4)

       βασανισθησονται] -σθωσι (labeled *Wahllesart* by von Soden; but the subjunctive is a harmonization to αποκτεινωσιν)

9:6   ζητησουσιν] ζητουσιν

       φευγει] φευξεται

       ~ απ αυτων ο θανατος

9:7   ομοιοι χρυσω] χρυσοι (correction; see 4:4; 14:14)

9:10   και η εξουσια αυτων] εξουσιαν εχουσι

       + του ante αδικησαι

9:11   εχουσι] -σαι

       ~ βασιλεα επ αυτων

       om. τον ante αγγελον

       και εν] εν δε

9:12–13   μετα ταυτα iungit cum sequentibus

9:14   λεγοντα] -τος

9:15   + εις την ante ημεραν (similar to 10:11 below)

9:16   ιππικου] ιππου

       om. δις

9:18   εκ[1]] απο (see 1:5 and 3:12 above)

9:19   οφεσιν] οφεων

9:20   om. και τα χαλκα

10:1   om. αλλον

10:7   εαυτου δουλους] δουλους αυτου

10:8   λαλουσαν ... λεγουσαν] -σα bis (chosen reading in Bousset and von Soden)

[57]   βιβλιον] βιβλιδαριον cum Aν[part.]

10:9   βιβλαριδιον] βιβλιδαριον cum Aν[part.]

10:11   + επι ante εθνεσι (see 9:15 above)

11:6   ~ τον ουρανον εξουσιαν κλεισαι

       ~ οσακις εαν θελησωσιν εν παση πληγη

11:9   αφιουσι] αφησουσι cum S[a]

11:10   ευφραινονται] ευφρανθησονται (harmonization to the following δωσουσιν)

       πεμψουσι] δωσουσι

11:13   om. και[1]

ωρα] ημερα ("because in v. 11 a certain day, but not a specific hour, is mentioned")[19]

11:14 ~ η ουαι η τριτη ιδου

11:16 + του θρονου ante του θεου (influenced by 7:15)

11:19 ηνοιγη] ηνοιχθη
        om. και σεισμος

12:6 απο] υπο
        τρεφωσιν] εκτρεφωσιν (on the other hand, 12:14)

12:8 αυτων] αυτω (related to ο δρακων; thus also ισχυσαν] -σεν A K)

12:14 οπου τρεφεται] οπως τρεφηται

13:3 ως] ωσει (likewise 1:14 C Αν; 16:3 S; 16:13 P[47] S)

13:4 οτι εδωκεν] τω δεδωκοτι
        om. και ante τις[2]
        δυναται] δυνατος (harmonization to the previous ομοιος)

13:5 + πολεμον ante ποιησαι (influenced by 13:7)

13:6 om. το[1] K[part.]

13:10 εις[1]] εχει (scribal error?)
        om. αποκτενει
        om. εν μαχαιρα[2]

13:11 om. δυο

13:12 ποιει[2]] εποιει

13:13 ινα — ουρανου] και πυρ ινα εκ του ουρανου καταβαινη

13:14 + τους εμους ante τους κατοικουντας
        εχει] ειχεν
        om. την ante πληγην (πληης sine της S)
        ~ και εζησεν απο της μαχαιρας

13:15 ~ πνευμα δουναι

13:16 δωσιν] δωσωσιν
        om. της ante χειρος

[58] 13:18 om. και

14:1 εστος] εστηκος (see 5:6)
        + αριθμος ante εκατον

14:3 ουδεις] ουδε εις

14:4 ουτοι[2]] + εισιν (see 5:2 above)
        αν] εαν
        + υπο ιησου ante ηγορασθησαν

---

19. Weiss, *Die Johannes-Apokalypse*, 18.

14:5   ~ ουχ ευρεθη εν τω στοματι αυτων
14:7   θεον] κυριον
       τω ποιησαντι] αυτον τον ποιησαντα
14:8   αυτης] ταυτης
14:10   αγγελων αγιων] των αγιων αγγελων (Weiss)[20]
14:13   ~ λεγει ναι
       (ινα) αναπαησονται] -παυσωνται
14:16   την νεφελην] τη νεφελη
14:18   + εν ante φωνη (likewise 21:16 Αν)
       ηκμασαν αι σταφυλαι αυτης] ηκμασεν η σταφυλη της γης
14:19   εβαλεν] εξεβαλεν
15:2   ~ εκ της εικονος και εκ του θηριου αυτου
       + τας ante κιθαρας (according to Weiss,[21] Urtext)
15:4   φοβηθη] + σε
       οσιος] αγιος
       παντα τα εθνη] παντες
15:6   om. εκ του ναου (likewise 16:1 below)
       + οι ησαν ante ενδεδυμενοι (on the other hand, 19:4)
16:1   om. εκ του ναου (see 15:6 above)
16:3   om. ζωης
16:4   + εις ante τας πηγας
16:8   ~ εν πυρι τους ανθρωπους
16:9   εβλασφημησαν] + οι ανθρωποι (from 16:21)
16:12   ~ αυτου την φιαλην (has the language in 16:2ff., 17 against it)
16:13   ~ ακαθαρτα τρια
16:16   αρμαγεδων] μαγεδων
16:17   εκ] απο (see 1:5 above)
[59] 16:18 om. εγενετο[1]
       + οι ante ανθρωποι
16:21   αυτης] αὕτη
17:1   υδατων πολλων] των υδατων των πολλων
17:3   om. εν ante πνευματι (on the other hand, 21:10)

---

20. Weiss (*Die Johannes-Apokalypse*, 127) thinks that the K reading must therefore be the *Urtext* because it alone explains the reading of A (των αγγελων cum Boh. Aeth., also WHort[mg.] Charles[txt.]). But on this condition, the emergence of the reading of P[47] S Αν remains incomprehensible, and the A text is, exactly like the K reading, merely an idiosyncratic correction of the singular due to the anarthrous αγγελων αγιων.

21. Weiss, *Die Johannes-Apokalypse*, 138.

+ το ante κοκκινον

17:4 αυτης²] της γης (see 14:18 above; *Urtext* according to von Soden)

17:6 om. εκ ante του αιματος¹ (labeled a *Wahllesart* by von Soden; however, the status of εκ¹ as the original follows from εκ² and from 17:2)

om. και²

17:8 επι της γης] την γην (influenced by 17:2? Otherwise, always επι της γης; see 3:10; 6:10; 11:10 [bis]; 13:8, 14; 14:6)

το βιβλιον] του βιβλιου

~ οτι ην το θηριον

17:8–9 και παρεσται ωδε iungit cum sequentibus K[part.]

17:9 ~ εισιν επτα[(2)]

17:10 ~ δει αυτον (perhaps influenced by 11:5; 13:10)

17:13 ~ εχουσι γνωμην

17:16 γυμνην] + ποιησουσιν αυτην

17:17 ~ γνωμην μιαν (see, on the other hand, 17:13)

τελεσθησονται] -σθωσιν (see 15:8; 20:3, 5)

17:18 + επι ante της γης

18:5 εμνημονευσεν] + αυτης

18:6 + ως και αυτη και ante κατα τα εργα αυτης

18:7 καθημαι] καθως

18:8 om. και¹

18:11 κλαιουσι και πενθουσι] κλαυσουσι και πενθησουσι

επ αυτην] επ αυτη

18:13 om. και αμωμον cum Aν[part. 22]

om. και οινον

~ προβατα και κτηνη

18:14 ευρησουσιν] ευρης (*Urtext* according to Bousset, because otherwise the aorist subjunctive almost always follows ου μη; but this reason is not really conclusive, and the second-person singular is a harmonization to the three occurrences of σου)

18:15 + και ante κλαιοντες

18:16 om. ουαι²

βυσσινον] βυσσον (likewise 18:12 Aν)

---

22. Likewise Bousset (*Die Offenbarung Johannis*, 422); according to Heinrich Joseph Vogels, "with good reasons" (*Untersuchungen zur Geschichte der lateinischen Apokalypse-Übersetzung* [Düsseldorf: Schwann, 1920], 10).

18:23 om. οτι[1]
[60] 19:1 ~ η δυναμις και η δοξα
19:2 εφθειρε] διεφθειρε
19:3 ειρηκαν] -κεν (to φωνη taken from 19:1 [Weiss])[23]
19:6 λεγοντων] λεγοντες (WHort[mg.]; Weiss;[24] λεγοντων in the text by accident, Bousset, Charles;[25] on the other hand, in the commentary; see p. 253)
19:7 αγαλλιωμεν] -ωμεθα (thus otherwise always in the New Testament)
19:8 + και ante καθαρον
19:10 + του ante ιησου[2]
19:11 + καλουμενος ante πιστος (Tisch; must be the *Urtext*)
        ~ πιστος καλουμενος S (Weiss, om. A Αν. Weiss[26] thinks that K only makes the change to avoid breaking the connection of πιστος with αληθινος)
19:12 + ονοματα γεγραμμενα και ante ονομα (influenced by 21:12?)
19:14 στρατευματα] + τα (see 11:19; 20:8; so correctly all modern editions except Tisch Sod)
        εφ] επι
19:15 + διστομος ante οξεια (from 1:16)
19:17 om. ενα (correction)
19:18 μικρων] + τε
19:20 ~ ο μετ αυτου (Sod)
20:2 σατανας] + ο πλανων την οικουμενην ολην (from 12:9)
20:3 πλανηση] πλανα (likewise 8:12 Αν)
20:4 + τα ante χιλια
20:6 μετ αυτου] μετα ταυτα
20:7 οταν τελεσθη] μετα (simplification of the expression)
20:8 + τον ante μαγωγ cum S[a]
        ως η] ωσει
20:9 εκ του ουρανου απο του θεου (see 21:2 Αν)
20:12 om. τους μεγαλους και τους μικρους
        ηνοιχθησαν] ηνοιξαν

---

23. Weiss, *Die Johannes-Apokalypse*, 14.
24. Weiss, *Die Johannes-Apokalypse*, 136 and the observation at this location.
25. R. H. Charles, *Studies in the Apocalypse*, 2nd ed. (Edinburgh: T&T Clark, 1915).
26. Weiss, *Die Johannes-Apokalypse*, 39.

20:13 αυτων] αυτου

20:15 τη βιβλω] τω βιβλιω (see 13:8)

21:1   απηλθαν] -ον (Sod)

21:3   λαοι] λαος cum P *f*[1006] 1611 1854 2050 2053 – 2062[txt.] 2329
       multiple versions (WHort[mg.] Weiss Bousset Charles; according
       to Weiss[27] and Bousset, λαοι is a thoughtless harmonization to
       ουτοι)[28]

[61] 21:4 εξαλειψει] + απ αυτων

21:5   om. και[1]
       ~ παντα καινα ποιω
       αληθινοι] + του θεου (from 19:9)

21:6   om. εγω[1]
       + και ante η αρχη
       δωσω] + αυτω (Tisch Bousset)

21:7   κληρονομησει] δωσω αυτω (because the influence of 3:21 is clear
       here, the same can be assumed in 21:6. Therefore, αυτω is not
       original there).

21:8   απιστοις] + και αμαρτωλοις

21:9   των γεμοντων των] γεμουσας (τας γεμουσας Weiss,[29] Bousset 2nd
       loco)
       ~ την γυναικα την νυμφην του αρνιου

21:10 απο] εκ (K text, otherwise vice versa; see 1:5 above; a thought-
       less harmonization here to εκ του ουρανου [Weiss])[30]

21:12 δωδεκα[2]] δεκαδυο (see 21:16 below)
       om. τα ante ονοματα[2] (om. τα ονοματα S Αν; see 4:5 above)

21:13 ανατολης] -λων (likewise 16:12 Αν; on the other hand, 7:2; 16:12)

21:15 αυτης[1⌒2]

21:16 δωδεκα] δεκαδυο (see 21:12 above)
       χιλιαδων] + δωδεκα (mixed text?)

---

27. Weiss, *Die Johannes-Apokalypse*, 101.

28. More important is Charles's argument (*Critical and Exegetical Commentary
on the Revelation*, 2:377): "In the New Jerusalem God has only one λαος." Also the Old
Testament passages that inspire the text each offer the word in the singular (Jer 38:33
[31:33 MT]; Ezek 37:27; Zech 8:8).

29. Weiss (*Die Johannes-Apokalypse*, 137) rejects the genitive as a completely
meaningless and thoughtless harmonization that has no analogue in any of the Apocalypse's other linguistic inaccuracies.

30. Weiss, *Die Johannes-Apokalypse*, 24.

21:17 om. εμετρησεν
21:23 αυτῇ· η γαρ δοξα] αὐτὴ γαρ η δοξα
21:24 την δοξαν αυτων] αυτω δοξαν και τιμην των εθνων
21:26 αυτην] + ινα εισελθωσιν
22:2   ~ αποδιδους εκαστον (sive εκαστος)
22:5   om. ετι
       χρειαν ουκ εχουσι] ου χρεια (Bousset)
       om. ηλιου
22:6   ειπεν] λεγει
       αυτου¹⌢²
22:8   και⁴] + οτε
       εβλεψα] ειδον
[62] 22:18 επιθησει] -σαι
       ~ ο θεος επ αυτον (against S Aν, hiant AC; *Urtext* according to
       WHort, Weiss,[31] Charles, Merk)
22:19 αφελει] -οι
22:20 αμην] + ναι

In addition, the following variants are related to linguistic style. First, αποκτενεσθαι in 6:11. Second, the aorist form of επεσον in the singular and plural—despite some variation in the tradition—will have to be designated as the K text. Finally, regarding υαλος — υελος and υαλινος — υελινος, the tradition varies in such a way that even though the reading is υελος in 21:21, the majority of textual witnesses have the form with α in 4:6; 15:2; and 21:18.

The total number of the K text's unique readings is 290. The number surpasses that of the Aν readings by about one-fifth. The vast majority stems from corrections, as with Aν. Errors are also very rare here (see 2:8, 25; 3:3; 9:16; 18:13; 21:15, 23; 22:6). Von Soden heavily emphasizes the influence of parallels as the main factor in textual chaos,[32] and he is probably correct here and there, and perhaps a little more often than with Aν. In actuality, however, parallel influences only occur infrequently in the K text.[33]

---

31. Weiss, *Die Johannes-Apokalypse*, 89, 103.

32. Von Soden, *Die Schriften des Neuen Testaments*, 1:2075: "In Aν and K [the unique readings] are parallel influences in the vast majority."

33. In addition to the thesis that the text forms H, Aν, and K stand opposite each other and are completely independent of one another is the thesis that requires that

The unsystematic nature of the textual editing is clear in both recensions. This shows that grammatical transgressions in the Apocalypse's original Greek text are nowhere improved evenly and consistently.

[63] We will provide a complete overview of all the facts in the section on the Apocalypse's linguistic style (pp. 183–263). This discussion will show that the creators of the two recensions Aν and K proceeded on a case-by-case basis, alternating between correcting major solecisms and clarifying the text's meaning. The observation that the same correction carried out in one location by Aν is also carried out in a different one by K is of methodological importance for this discussion. It is therefore wrong in principle to conclude with Weiss that the similarity of these corrections means that they stem from a single corrector, whose recension is the source of corrections partially taken over by Aν and K, respectively. Apart from the hypothetical nature of this "younger text," it is unclear why Aν, as well as K, should have been limited to a selection in their adoption of these corrections and that only one of them—as a rule—would have taken over a given correction. Bousset had already objected to Weiss, "Nonetheless, one could reply that, once it has been revised, various revisors could proceed on similar principles."[34] In what follows, a number of convincing examples support Bousset's objection. The two lists of unique readings in Aν and K (which in the course of these studies will be shown to be irrefutable) will show that Aν and K are two adjacent forms of the Apocalypse's text, each of which is based on a particular textual recension. With this finding, however, the question of the genealogical relationship of these

---

parallel influences cause a very large part of the corrections. Practically speaking, this is the second pillar in von Soden's text-critical system. And both theses hang together internally. Von Soden considers it more likely that two recensions are influenced by reminiscences than that the third one replaces a reading taken from a parallel with a unique reading. In such cases, von Soden opts for the reading of the third recension as the *Urtext*, while he lets the majority (two out of the three) decide on the textual reconstruction in the rest. But even here a fundamental defect emerges in his system. Thus, the undeniable tendency toward textual alignment is present. Yet, this is by no means the extent of von Soden's case. The investigation of the Apocalypse's linguistic style proves the opposite regarding parallel readings (i.e., readings that deviate from the author's linguistic style, usually unique readings from Aν or K): they should be rejected as corrections. For the same reason, however, in contrast to von Soden, the larger part of the Aν-K readings should be rejected, and their readings are only valuable for examining the problem of the relationship between Aν and K.

34. Bousset, *Textkritische Studien*, 1.

two text forms to one another remains and has yet to be described completely and accurately. This is because, in addition to the 240 unique readings of Aν and the nearly 300 unique readings of K and a number of other errors and corrections (in which either Aν or K agrees with P⁴⁷ S), there are a significantly smaller though not an insignificant number of readings that Aν and K share with each other and that can be observed only in the smallest part of the *Urtext*. The investigation must now turn to this problem, which Weiss and Bousset solve in different ways.

[64] We must also evaluate critically how Weiss and Bousset handle these problems because of the important methodological issues they raise.

2.3. The Relationship of Aν to K

According to Weiss, P (= Aν) and Q (= K) go back to a common foundation, which would have already included a number of corrections compared to the representatives of the oldest text (S AC). In addition, P and Q would still have been revised independently of each other toward a "younger revised text." Weiss[35] surmises the existence of the "younger revised text" from the similar corrections of P and Q. However, he infers the common foundation of the two from orthographic peculiarities and scribal errors, some of which P and Q share, some of which occur only in one of them. The juxtaposition of clear errors and deliberate corrections proves to Weiss that the text of P and of Q is based on two different *Vorlagen*.

The value of Weiss's explanation lies in his careful and comprehensive presentation of the facts. But Bousset correctly objects to Weiss's interpretation of the data. In the first place, Bousset points to the fact that "according to Weiss's count, P has 130 unique readings and Q has 350, while P and Q are in agreement only in some 50 cases over against S A (C)."[36] The disparity between the great number of corrections that only P or Q is said to have adopted from that "younger revised text" and the far fewer corrections that P and Q share is striking indeed. Likewise, Bousset's aforementioned second objection is valid in opposing Weiss's principle that the corrections in P and Q must have come from one and the same corrector, namely, the redactor of the "younger revised text," on account of their similarities. In reality, these corrections are exactly the same kind found in the other

---

35. Weiss, *Die Johannes-Apokalypse*, 9.
36. Bousset, *Textkritische Studien*, 1.

New Testament books and in other Greek authors, who have a rich and highly differentiated textual tradition. Furthermore, Weiss's [65] emphatic argument,[37] distinguishing between two different foundations for the texts of P and Q, lacks probative value, especially his assertion that the superior character of the revisions over the shared foundation text precludes carelessness throughout. On the contrary, the text of P, and especially of Q, is thoroughly defaced with all kinds of transmissional negligence. First of all, in contrast to Weiss's approach, P and Q should not be examined in isolation from the rest of their textual families, a point we will reemphasize below. When these manuscripts are examined in the context of their families, the scribal oversights come into focus, oversights that are invariably lost when P and Q are examined in isolation.[38] However, the juxtaposition of repeated errors and corrections also surface even in the most carefully revised recension. The redactor either does not recognize the errors as such or was unable to improve them because the entire manuscript tradition of the text under consideration was unavailable to him.[39] The evidence for Weiss's thesis that the text of P and Q is based on two common foundations is therefore invalid. The assumption of a "revised younger text" from which the bulk of the corrections—from P as from Q—ought to have originated is groundless. It is also contrary to Bousset's correct judgment, since the genealogical relationship of both to one another also has to be established: "The families Aν and K have obtained their particular character because each has emerged from a particular textual recension."[40] With full justification, then, Bousset criticizes,[41] as a further defect of Weiss's investigation, that Weiss uses the two majuscules P and Q respectively as the authoritative representatives of their families because they happen to be the oldest.[42] In fact, [66]

---

37. Weiss, *Die Johannes-Apokalypse*, 42.

38. See p. 87, where it is noted that Aν and K have only two errors in common.

39. A nice example, well illustrated by what is important here, is demonstrated by Albert Severyn's *Le codex 239 de Photius*, vol. 1 of *Recherches sur Chrestomathie de Proclos* (Liège: Faculté de Philosophie et Lettres, 1938), 279–95, 342–57. Even such a careful and learned man such as Arethas of Caesarea introduces many careless errors when he takes the trouble to correct a manuscript of the "library" of his teacher by Photios. Even orthographic mistakes undermine him.

40. Bousset, *Textkritische Studien*, 41.

41. Ibid., 5.

42. The same complaint is even to be made against Charles, who, in his introduction (*Critical and Exegetical Commentary on the Revelation*, 1:clxiii–clxiv), presents P and Q alongside AC and S simply because they happen to be majuscules and makes

this applies neither to P nor to Q. Q is not a particularly faithful witness of the K text.[43] This applies far more to P for Aν.[44] P, whose age has been significantly overestimated since Tischendorf, is a markedly mixed text from Aν and an old text similar to C. The two families Aν and K must replace P and Q, as has already been done in the listing of the unique readings of these text forms above. Bousset had already consulted the minuscules. But his attempt to reconstruct the Aν text with their use failed due to the fragmentary nature of the material available to him.[45]

---

no attempt to actually reconstruct the Aν and K text on the basis of the entire tradition. At 19:14, for example, where according to Charles P has the *Urtext* (+ τα post στρατευματα), K also has τα (but against Q).

43. See Schmid, "Untersuchungen zur Geschichte des griechischen Apokalypsetextes," 429–30. Even in age, Q does not surpass the oldest minuscules in any significant way, once one bears in mind the same distance from the original or from the common archtype K. Q is at most a century older than the oldest minuscule of K. Not only does Q deviate from the generally very closed tradition of type K in markedly unique readings, as every manuscript, but Q is also slightly revised against another type, namely, the eclectic text of 61 – 69. That the relationship between Q and 61 – 69, which I point to in "Untersuchungen zur Geschichte des griechischen Apokalypsetextes" (429), is best understood as one in which Q is dependent upon 61 – 69 has become clear to me. Q goes wrong in a number of other places where it deviates from K, following other text forms (429–30).

44. Thus, for example P 17:8 with A (hiat C) 1611 reads θαυμασθησονται against S Aν K θαυμασονται. At 2:9, P alone omits with AC and a few minuscules against S Aν K τα εργα και before την θλιψιν. At 11:6, only P has (against S Aν K) with P[47] AC the article before εξουσιαν[1]. At 11:2, only P reads εσωθεν, not Aν. At 17:3, only P reads with A S* against Aν K γεμοντα and with S alone εχοντα. At 11:10, only P has with P[47] S* *f*[2014] 2595 2019 – 2429 πεμψουσιν] πεμπουσιν. At 2:22, only P Q with S and a pair of minuscules read βαλω (instead of βαλλω), not however Aν and K, and likewise, only P Q with 1611 and *f*[2014] have inserted ως before εξ ενος at 21:21, not however Aν and K. Analogously, many readings of Q are not those of K. Many readings Weiss cites are, as I mentioned, only unique readings of P or Q, sometimes with a few minuscules together. At 2:20, προφητιν] -την is witnessed only by P Q and a few minuscules. No value is to be placed on itacistic errors, such as σαπφιρος in 21:19 (P Q min. pc.), nor on the spelling Θυατηρ- in 2:18, 24. Even less value is to be placed on errors, such as χρυσταλιζοντι (with a λ) in 21:11 in P Q and many minuscules, nor on ωφελον (instead of οφελον) in 3:15, nor in the numerous minuscules that write ιδον. Here and in many other places a tradition cannot cannot be spoken of. On the other hand, Weiss overlooks many Aν readings because they are not in P, as well as K readings missing in Q. Consequently, his portrayal of the two later text forms Aν and K is unusable.

45. Bousset did not recognize the entirely useless character of the Complutensian text for textual criticism and argues that it is the most reliable witness for Aν (*Textkri-*

Even if Weiss's previous explanations about the shared textual founda-tion of Aν and K, from which the text of both Aν as of K should be recon-structed, [67] were proven, the problem of the relationship between Aν and K would remain unsolved.

According to Weiss, the common errors of the two text forms dem-onstrate that the two also go back to a common foundation. Bousset, on the basis of his own investigation, also opposes Weiss on this point and explains that the common foundation of Aν and K, if it exists at all, is a very narrow one.[46] Where P and Q stand together with their allies, they allegedly also preserve the original wording in more than half of the cases in question. The common foundation of S AC is at least as great as that of P Q. That foundation, however, lies so far back and so few traces of it are pre-served that it eludes further investigation. Inexplicably, recent researchers have not examined this important question more closely. Von Soden is content to conclude that Aν and K had no original relationship.[47] Charles makes no attempt to reconstruct the recensions Aν and K on the basis of the entire manuscript tradition and limits himself to the observation that P and Q are related.[48] Since Weiss and Bousset—the only two researchers to study this issue—arrive at conflicting results, and because their recon-structions of the two text forms are wrong to a considerable extent, the question needs to be reexamined. Anticipating what lies ahead, we will see that the shared common errors of the two text forms, which provide the basis of Weiss's argument, are almost nonexistent.

In a number of places, as Bousset points out,[49] Aν and K correct the original text—or the text of their common *Vorlage*—in various ways.

[68] The list of these locations inaugurates the following investigation.

1:9   εν ιησου S C P f^{1678} 1611 2050

     εν χριστω A

---

tische Studien, 12–13). His reconstruction of the archetype Aν (K in Bousset) differs substantially from what I have described above.

46. Bousset, *Textkritische Studien*, 40–41.

47. Von Soden, *Die Schriften des Neuen Testaments*, 1:2075. Hoskier also has the same view (*Concerning the Text of the Apocalypse*, 1:287), "The P revision was almost entirely independent of the B [= Q] recension."

48. Charles, *Critical and Exegetical Commentary on the Revelation*, 1:clxxxii. The highly inaccurate characteristics of the two manuscripts that Charles gives there are only mentioned here.

49. Bousset, *Textkritische Studien*, 3–5. The following list does not coincide with the one in Bousset.

εν χριστω ιησου Κ
ιησου χριστου Αν

2:20   (την γυναικα) η λεγουσα ΑC S
                    την λεγουσαν Αν
                    η λεγει (likewise 3:12; see p. 55) Κ

3:18   εγχρισαι ΑC S
        εγχρισον Αν
        ινα εγχριση Κ

4:7   το προσωπον ως ανθρωπου Α (hiat C)
        το προσωπον ως ανθρωπος Αν
            προσωπον ανθρωπου Κ

4:9   (οταν) δωσουσιν Α (hiat C)
                    δωσωσιν Αν S
                    δωσιν Κ (see 12:6 below; also 14:13)

5:6   (πνευματα) απεσταλμενοι Α (hiat C) Oec
                    τα απεσταλμενα Αν, απεσταλμενα S
                    αποστελλομενα Κ

7:9   εστωτες … περιβεβλημενους … φοινικες Α
        εστωτων … περιβεβλημενους … φοινικες C
        εστωτες … περιβεβλημενους … φοινικας S
        εστωτες … περιβεβλημενοι … φοινικες Αν
        εστωτας … περιβεβλημενους … φοινικας Κ

9:10   και κεντρα, και εν ταις ουραις αυτων η εξουσια αυτων αδικησαι Α
        (hiat C) S
        και κεντρα εν ταις ουραις αυτων, και η εξουσια αυτων αδικησαι Αν
        και κεντρα, και εν ταις ουραις αυτων εξουσιαν εχουσι του αδικησαι
        Κ

9:11   εχουσι Α (hiat C) S
        και εχουσι Αν[part.]
        εχουσαι Κ

9:14   (φωνην) λεγοντα Α (hiat C) S*
                    λεγουσαν Αν (see 11:4, 15)
                    λεγοντος Κ

11:11   (εισηλθεν) εν αυτοις Α *f*[1006] 1854 2329 al. pc.
                    αυτοις C Αν 1611 2053
                    εις αυτους P[47] S K

[69] 12:6   (ινα) τρεφουσιν C S 2329 al. pc.
                    τρεφωσιν Α Αν
                    εκτρεφωσιν Κ (see 4:9 above; 14:13 below)

13:3 εθαυμασθη ολη η γη AC P⁴⁷ (see 17:8 θαυμασθησονται A P 1611)
εθαυμασθη εν ολη τη γη Αν
εθαυμασεν ολη η γη S K

13:13 ινα και πυρ ποιη εκ του ουρανου καταβαινειν AC P⁴⁷ ƒ¹⁰⁰⁶ 1611 ƒ¹⁶⁷⁸
~ ινα και πυρ ποιη καταβαινειν εκ του ουρανου Αν
~ και πυρ ινα εκ του ουρανου καταβαινη K

14:13 (ινα) αναπαησονται A P⁴⁷ S
αναπαυσονται C Ανᵖᵃʳᵗ·
αναπαυσωνται K
(see 4:9 and 12:6 above)

14:16 (επι) της νεφελης A P⁴⁷ S al. pc.
την νεφελην C Αν (WHortᵐᵍ· Bousset)
τη νεφελη K

16:3 ψυχη ζωης AC ƒ¹⁰⁰⁶ 1611
ψυχη ζωσα P⁴⁷ S Αν
ψυχη K

17:3 (θηριον) γεμοντα ονοματα A (hiat C) S* P Oec
γεμον ονοματων Αν
γεμον ονοματα K

18:3 πεπτωκαν AC
πεπωκεν Αν (*Urtext* πεπωκαν?)
πεπτωκασιν S K

18:4 εξελθατε A S
εξελθετε Αν
εξελθε C K
ο λαος μου εξ αυτης C S P ƒ¹⁶⁷⁸
ο λαος μου Αν
~ εξ αυτης ο λαος μου A K

18:6 διπλωσατε τα (om. A) διπλα κατα τα εργα αυτης AC S
διπλωσατε αυτη διπλα κατα τα εργα αυτης Αν
διπλωσατε τα διπλα ως και αυτη και κατα τα εργα αυτης K

18:11 επ αυτην C S P (εν αυτη A 2329)
εφ εαυτους Αν
επ αυτη K (likewise 18:9 Αν)

18:14 ευρησουσιν AC S P 1611 ƒ¹⁶⁷⁸ ƒ¹⁷²
[70] ευρησεις (-σης) Αν
ευρης K

Aν and K eliminate the impersonal plural and apply the verb to the addressed "Babylon."

19:8   λαμπρον καθαρον A (hiat C) S P f^{1006} 1611 f^{1678} f^{104}
        ~ καθαρον λαμπρον Aν
        λαμπρον και καθαρον K

21:1   απηλθαν A (hiat C) S 2329
        παρηλθεν Aν
        απηλθον K

21:5   πιστοι και αληθινοι A (hiat C) S f^{1006} 1611 f^{1678} 2050 2053 – 2062 2329
        ~ αληθινοι και πιστοι Aν
        πιστοι και αληθινοι του θεου K

21:8   απιστοις και εβδελυγμενοις A (hiat C) S. f^{1006} 1611 2050 2053
        απιστοις   εβδελυγμενοις Aν
        απιστοις και αμαρτωλοις και εβδελυγμενοις K

21:9   την νυμφην την γυναικα του αρνιου A (hiat C) S P f^{1006} 1611 f^{1678} 1854 $f^{172/250}$
        ~ την νυμφην του αρνιου την γυναικα Aν
        ~ την γυναικα την νυμφην του αρνιου K

21:27   ποιων A (hiat C) S^c f^{1006} 2050 (Weiss Sod Charles)
        ποιουν Aν
        ο ποιων S* K (Tisch Vog Merk; [ο] ποιων WHort Bousset)

22:5   ετι A (hiat C) S P f^{1006} 2050 2053 – 2062 2329 f^{172}
        εχει Aν
        om. K
        ουκ εχουσι (ουχ εξουσι A 2050 2329) χρειαν A (hiat C) S f^{1006} 2050 2053 – 2062 2329
        ~ χρειαν ουκ εχουσι Aν
        ου χρεια K (Bousset)
        φωτος λυχνου και φως ηλιου A (hiat C) (WHort Charles)
        φωτος λυχνου και φωτος ηλιου S (edit. rel.; [φωτος^1] Sod)
            λυχνου και φως (sive φωτος) ηλιου Aν
            λυχνου και φωτος K

22:12   εστιν αυτου A (hiat C) S 2030 (2050)
        ~ αυτου εσται Aν
        εσται αυτου K

[71] What clearly emerges from this list is that Αν and K correct the text offered by the ancient textual witnesses independently of one another in all these places. Here we find exactly what we have come to expect in a great number of corrections in Αν and K. If Αν, like K, has 240 or 300 corrections in a text of 405 verses, it is only natural to expect them to often have coincidental corrections in the same place. The distinctive quality of the enumerated places in this list demonstrates that Αν and K each make corrections in the same place but always in different ways. We can conclude from this that the creators of the two recensions Αν and K make these corrections themselves (or possibly found them already in their *Vorlagen*, in which case the emergence of the two recensions spreads across two or more generations rather than depending upon a single agent for each).

The following list offers a complete collection of places where the readings of Αν and K agree against those of other ancient text forms. The list is designed not only to represent the facts completely and accurately but also to evaluate the individual passages and provide their assessment by the more recent textual editions.[50]

1:11   λαοδικειαν Αν K contra λαοδικιαν AC S min. pc.

3:14   λαοδικεια Αν K contra λαοδικια AC S min. pc.

Only von Soden and Merk write λαοδικεια. Not only do the inscriptions demonstrate that the form λαοδικια is incorrect, but the testimony of AC S is less valuable here because these witnesses display so many itacistic errors where the tendency to avoid diphthongs prevails (as in θυατειρα, see pp. 200–201).[51] Αν K offer the original reading.

1:13   χρυσαν] χρυσην Αν K min. omn. contra AC S* (Sod)

Almost all modern editions consider the increasingly common form with α[52] in Koine Greek as the *Urtext*. But the correction in Αν and K is also easily understandable.

---

50. Tisch(endorf), W(estcott-)Hort, Weiss, Bousset, (Herman von) Sod(en) Vog(els), Charles, Merk.

51. The same applies for Col 2:1; 4:13, 15–16.

52. Harmonization to αργυρα; see Friedrich Blass, *Grammatik des neutestamentlichen Griechisch*, ed. Albert Debrunner, 9th ed. (Göttingen: Vandenhoeck & Ruprecht, 1954), §45.

[72] 1:15 πεπυρωμενης AC (WHort[txt.] Weiss Charles)

πεπυρωμενω S 2050 2053 – 2062[txt.] f^{336} (Tisch Bousset)

πεπυρωμενοι Αν K (WHort[mg.] Sod Vog Merk)

Modern textual critics judge the textual tradition quite differently here (see especially Weiss, Bousset, and Charles at this location). It cannot be denied, however, that AC's text is linguistically incorrect and that only S's text is satisfactory. In spite of that, S's text can only be a subsequent correction.[53] That does not mean that the reading of Αν K should be understood as the *Urtext*. If AC's unconstructable reading is not the *Urtext*, then it can only be understood as a senseless mistake. An unequivocal judgment is not possible here, but it is very likely that the text of Αν and K is a later, but misguided, correction.[54]

1:18 αιωνων] + αμην Αν K S[a] 2329

The same entirely thoughtless addition surfaces in other places; see 4:9 S 2351 2017 2057 Syr.[1]; 4:10 S f^{205} 2329 Syr.[1]; 5:13 Αν K (see below); 11:15 S f^{1678}.

2:2 αποστολους] + ειναι Αν K S[c] and almost all minuscules against AC S* P 2053[txt.-comm.] 2329 ([Sod]).

The ειναι is correctly considered a later correction. It is missing in the same construction in 2:20, where only S* 2019 2050 include it. On the other hand, ειναι is unanimously attested in 2:9 and 3:9.

2:5 ερχομαι σοι] + ταχυ Αν K against AC S P 1854 2050 2053[txt.-comm.] 2329 and most of the versions (Bousset [Sod])

Most of the versions decide against ταχυ as original here. 2:16 and 3:11 are not parallels that confirm authenticity but cause the addition.

2:13 + τα εργα σου και ante που κατοικεις (after 2:2) Αν K against AC S P 1854 2050 2053 2329 Syr.[1] Sah. Boh. Latt. ([Sod]).

Αν K preserve the same words with S against AC P 1611 1854 Oec 2329 Syr.[1] Sah. Boh. Latt. also at 2:9 (+ τα εργα και ante την θλιψιν), a passage where only von Soden considers their authenticity possible. 2:9 and 2:13 should be evaluated in the same way despite the mixed testimony, for

---

53. So Charles correctly.

54. Weiss properly evaluates the location 1:15. See further p. 257.

their status as original seems difficult, [73] if not crucial, to the matter that these words are present in all five remaining letters to the seven churches (2:1, 19; 3:1, 8, 15). For this very reason, however, they could have been inserted later, while their subsequent omission is difficult to explain. And that S preserves it in the first of the two passages in question (2:9), and only there, proves that S is influenced by the later text, as is often the case. The absence of these words in the second passage (2:13) in S proves that no error is peculiar to the AC type here.

2:25   αχρι] αχρις Αν Κ
The sigma was included in order to eliminate the hiatus (οὖ follows it). A (εως οὖ) also makes a correction here.

2:27   συντριβεται] -βησεται Αν Κ
This "insufficient correction" (Bousset) is correctly rejected by all modern critical editions (a thoughtless harmonization to the following future ποιμανει) because the verb συντριβησεται lacks the subject.[55]

3:5   ουτως] ουτος Αν Κ Sᵃ
Bousset, and more decisively von Soden, consider this reading the *Urtext* because ουτως appears superfluous, while ουτος corresponds to the Apocalypse's linguistic style (see 17:10) (Bousset). But the testimony of the versions probably decides in favor of ουτως.[56]

3:9   (ινα) ηξουσι και προσκυνησουσι] ηξωσι και προσκυνησωσι Αν Κ
      against AC S P 792 2050 2329 (Sod)
This is an obvious correction. See the analogous cases that follow, where a part of the textual witnesses also regularly produces the subjunctive: 6:4, 11; 8:3; 9:4, 5, 20; 13:12; 14:13; 22:14.

4:3   om. και ο καθημενος (homoioteleuton) Αν Κ against A (hiat C) S
      P 1611 2050 2329 versions
We must ask here whether the homoioteleuton error of Αν and Κ was made independently.

---

55. It is ως — συντριβησεται, taken as a parallel set to ποιμανει – σιδηρα (Weiss).

56. Weiss (4:6) explains that ουτως was corrected to ουτος because it was not understood, but this might even be a simple scribal error.

4:3   ιερεις A (hiat C) S f^{2014} 2329 Arm.[exc. 4] Aeth.

         ιρις Αν K

ιερεις is a mere scribal error, and Αν K preserve the original text.

[74] 4:4   θρονους] θρονοι Αν K against A (hiat C) S f^{1678} 2053 $f^{172/250}$

(WHort[txt.] Bousset Sod Vog Merk against WHort[mg.] Tisch Weiss. Swete and Charles read θρονους … τεσσαρες and understand τεσσαρες as an accusative form.)[57] Weiss says that Αν K changed the anacolouthonic θρονους into θρονοι.[58] Von Soden, on the other hand, explains θρονους as a harmonization to 4:2b. In any case there is a break in the sentence structure, whether θρονους is read or the transition from the nominative to the accusative surfaces only at $\overline{κδ}$ πρεσβυτερους. The accusative form εικοσι τεσσαρας that immediately follows precludes understanding εικοσι τεσσαρες after θρονοι (or θρονους) as an accusative. But in that case, this nominative εικοσι τεσσαρες supports the nominative θρονοι, so the text of Αν K represents the *Urtext*.[59]

4:4   επι τους θρονους [+ τους K] εικοσι τεσσαρας πρεσβυτερους Αν K
         Syr.[1.2] Boh. Gig. Prim. Arm.

         ~ επι τους εικοσι τεσσαρας θρονους πρεσβυτερους A (hiat C) 1854
         εικοσι τεσσαρας$^{1 \frown 2}$ S

The versions confirm the text of Αν K, or more precisely, the text of Αν. The homoioteleuton error of S also presupposes this text form. A preserves the numeral before the noun as in some other locations.

4:8   om. τα ante τεσσαρα Αν K contra A (hiat C) S P $f^{104/336}$ $f^{172/250}$
         Compl. al. pc. is correctly rejected by the modern critical editions. 4:6 lacks the article because the four living creatures are first introduced in this passage. In 5:8, however, the article is present because the creatures are already known.[60]

---

57. Likewise, Westcott and Hort, *New Testament in the Original Greek*, 2:138.

58. Weiss, *Die Johannes-Apokalypse*, 4.

59. See again p. 257.

60. See also p. 206.

4:9   (τω καθημενω) επι τω θρονω] επι του θρονου Αν K against A (hiat
        C) S 1854 2050 (WHort[mg.] Sod Vog) is a harmonization to 4:10
        (Weiss)[61] and has the Apocalypse's linguistic style against it.[62]

5:1   εσωθεν και οπισθεν A (hiat C) Αν[part.] 61 – 69 2329
        εμπροσθεν και οπισθεν S
        εσωθεν και εξωθεν Αν[rel.] K (Bousset)[63] Charles[mg.] (correction)

[75] 5:10   βασιλειαν] βασιλεις Αν K against A (hiat C) S 1611* 1854 f^{1678}
        2050 2329 Sah. Boh. Latt. Arm. 4 (Sod)

The fact that only Αν preserves the correction at 1:6, and here it is in
both Αν K, proves that the text of A S is original.

5:13   αιωνων] + αμην Αν K Compl. f^{336} against A (hiat C) S f^{1006} 1611
        1854 2050 2053 2329 2351 f^{104} $f^{172/250}$ Sah. Boh., see 1:18 above.

6:8   ο θανατος Αν K (WHort Weiss Sod [Vog] Merk)
        θανατος C S f^{1006} 1854 2053
        ο αθανατος A

A's error confirms that the text of Αν K is original here.

8:3   (ινα) δωσει] δωση Αν K (Bousset Sod)
See 3:9 above.

8:6   αυτους] εαυτους Αν K against A (hiat C) S* 2351 (αὐτους Tisch,
        Bousset;[64] αὐτους WHort, Bousset,[65] Charles; εαυτους Weiss
        Sod Vog Merk).

We must choose either αὐτους or εαυτους, since the contracted form
αὐτ- is no longer in use by New Testament times.[66] Although only Αν S[a]

---

61. Weiss, *Die Johannes-Apokalypse*, 5.

62. See also p. 222.

63. Bousset (*Textkritische Studien*, 387; *Die Offenbarung Johannis*, 254 n. 1)
understands the text of A and S to be a correction toward Ezek 2:10 LXX (εμπροσθεν
και τα οπισω). But the agreement with the LXX is not literal and proves the very reason
that the Αν-K reading is a subsequent improvement. Also, S confirms that A's reading
is original.

64. Bousset, *Die Offenbarung Johannis*, 105 n. 1.

65. Ibid, ad. loc.

66. See Blass, *Grammatik des neutestamentlichen Griechisch*, §64.1. According

change αυτην into εαυτην in 18:7 and K reads αυτου in the place of εαυτου in 10:7, we must consider εαυτους a correction here.

9:7   ομοιοι S 792 (Tisch WHort[mg.] Weiss Charles[mg.])
        ομοιωματα A (hiat C)
        ομοια Αν K (WHort[txt.] Bousset Sod Vog Merk Charles[txt.])

A final decision is not possible here for two reasons. First, S's defective and poorly attested text is possibly still the *Urtext*. Second, the correct ομοια could be a subsequent improvement of Αν K.[67] It is very likely that ομοιοι is a simple scribal error stemming from S's careless scribe.

9:10   ομοιοις A (hiat C) S al. pc. (WHort[mg.])
        ομοιας Αν K

[76] ομοιοις is a thoughtless harmonization to the following σκορπιοις, which all modern critical editions correctly reject. In contrast, some editions adopt the same error in 1:15 (see p. 74); 11:3 (see p. 108); 19:20 (της καιομενης A [hiat C] S P); and 21:9 (των γεμοντων A [hiat C] S Αν against K). On the other hand, the analogous error in 2:9 των … ιουδαιων (C S* 2050 2329) has not been appreciated at all. The reason for the inconsistent evaluation of the same phenomenon is obviously related to the different groupings of the tradition adopted by each scholar. No one dares to reject a reading supported by the entire Greek tradition except for K at 21:9. This is an important fundamental and methodological problem for evaluating AC and especially for assessing the Apocalypse's language. We shall return to this point in the discussion of the Apocalypse's linguistic style (pp. 256–61). But we must recognize here that Αν and K could also have corrected the difficult linguistic errors independently of each other.

9:13   + τεσσαρων ante κερατων Αν K Syr.[1] it against A (hiat C) P[47] S
        0207 1611 Oec 94 *f*[1678] Syr.[2] Sah. Boh. Latt.[plur]

All modern critical editions except WHort and Charles adopt τεσσαρων, even though the "old" text here is preserved in P[47] and 0207,

---

to Edwin Mayser (*Grammatik der Griechischen Papyri aus der Ptolemäerzeit*, 2 vols. [Berlin: de Gruyter, 1923–1938], 1:2, 65; 2:2, 71ff.) αὐτ- is no longer found in the first century BCE on papyrus. For this reason, the spelling in 2:20 of αὐτην in some modern critical editions should be rejected. See the matter again pp. 216–18.

67. According Weiss (*Die Johannes-Apokalypse*, 4), ομοιοι is related to αυτοις (9:3–5) and is therefore the *Urtext*, a very unlikely assertion.

two weighty witnesses. Von Soden explains: "Insertion is not explicable, but omission is probable." The passage is very important for the evaluation of the entire tradition.

9:20   (ινα) προσκυνησουσιν] -σωσιν Αν K against AC P[47] S
Only von Soden explains the reading of Αν K as the *Urtext* in line with his general evaluation of the Apocalypse's textual tradition. The passage should also be assessed in a manner similar to 3:9 and 8:3 (see 3:9 above).

11:9   om. και ante ημισυ Αν K (the reading chosen by von Soden)

11:12   αναβατε] -βητε Αν K against A C P[47] S P 792 2329 2351 (Sod)
Αν K eliminate the unusual form.[68]

11:18   τους φοβουμενους ... τους μικρους και τους μεγαλους A P[47] 2351
         τοις φοβουμενοις ... τους μικρους και τους μεγαλους C S* 2329
         τοις φοβουμενοις ... τοις μικροις και τοις μεγαλοις Αν K
This passage should be evaluated analogously to 9:10 (see above); 11:3 (see p. 108); 19:20; and 21:9 (see also the judgment of [77] Weiss, 103 at this location). The text of Αν K has to be recognized as the *Urtext*.

12:2   om. και ante κραζει Αν K against C P[47] S (A) f[1006] Oec multiple
         versions (WHort[mg.] [Bousset] Sod [Vog])
This is an obvious correction.

12:18   εσταθη] -θην Αν K against AC P[47] S (Tisch Sod Vog)
εσταθην should be understood as a harmonization to the following και ειδον with Weiss[69] and Bousset. However, εσταθη should not to be taken as a thoughtless harmonization to ωργισθη.[70] A similar correction surfaces at 11:12 (ηκουσα[ν]) in P[47] Αν K.

13:5   βλασφημα A Αν[b-d-i-2019] 2329 f[172/250] (Weiss)
         βλασφημιας C P[47] S (most modern editions)
         βλασφημιαν Αν K (Bousset Sod 1st loco)

---

68. See Blass, *Grammatik des neutestamentlichen Griechisch*, §95.3.
69. Weiss, *Die Johannes-Apokalypse*, 5.
70. So von Soden, *Die Schriften des Neuen Testaments*, 1:2076.

Bousset's opinion that the former two readings are each a harmonization to the previous μεγαλα may be true for A's text but not for βλασφημιας.

13:6 βλασφημιας] -αν Aν K
This variant belongs with the previous one. Consequently, Bousset and von Soden consider them the *Urtext*.

13:8 οὗ ... αυτου (A) C Oec (f¹⁶⁷⁸) 1854 2053 (so most modern editions)
      ὧν ... αυτων P⁴⁷ S* f¹⁰⁰⁶ 1611 2329 (Charles^mg·)
      ὧν Aν K (Sod Vog; Merk ὧν ... [αυτων])

Aν K again have an obvious correction, and indeed a correction of the text of P⁴⁷ S*. S has the same correction in 3:8, K alone in 7:9, C Aν in 12:6, P 2329 at 13:12, and Aν alone at 20:8. See also the correction of K in 12:14.

13:12 (ινα) προσκυνησουσιν] -σωσιν Aν K (Sod Vog)
See 9:20 above.
Quite inconsistently, Vogels goes with von Soden here but not in 9:20.

13:14 μαχαιρης] -ας Aν K (Sod)
Likewise 13:10 μαχαιρη] -ρα Aν K with S (Sod)

13:17 (ινα) δυνηται] δυναται Aν K against AC P⁴⁷ S 792 f¹⁰⁰⁶ 1611 1854 2329 (WHort^mg· Weiss)

Weiss[71] explains δυναται as the *Urtext* and δυνηται as a harmonization to the previous δωσιν because, "otherwise the formation of δυναται remains unexplained." Since elsewhere Aν K [78] regularly change the indicative to the subjunctive after ινα (see 3:9 above), the reverse trend is surprising here. But in 12:14, Aν alone reads the present indicative (ινα πεταται). And since the present indicative following ινα is uncharacteristic of the Apocalypse's linguistic style,[72] we cannot consider it the *Urtext* here. Thus, its origin may remain inexplicable.

---

71. Weiss, *Die Johannes-Apokalypse*, 103. Likewise von Soden, *Die Schriften des Neuen Testaments*, 1:2083. He nonetheless reads δυνηται in his critical edition.

72. All modern editions except Tisch WHort^mg· Charles^txt· discard the reading of C S ινα τρεφουσιν as a scribal error in 12:6.

14:6   om. επι ante τους καθημενους Αν K
       om. επι ante παν Αν

Bousset is inclined to delete the first επι. But the later correction is clear: the simple accusative, i.e., the transitive use, is also the usual construction of ευαγγελιζειν in the Apocalypse (see 10:7). Only Αν also consequently eliminates επι before to παν. The K text's partial correction, however, proves that the absence of the first επι is actually a correction.

14:13   γαρ] δε Αν K against AC P⁴⁷ S P 792 *f*¹⁰⁰⁶ 1611 *f*¹⁶⁷⁸ 2053 2329
      and most versions as well as modern critical editions.[73]

Taking γαρ as the original (and most sensible) reading is far more illuminating than the reason for which δε presumably replaces it.

16:1   εκχεετε] -χεατε Αν K (correction)

16:3   δευτερος] + αγγελος Αν K

This is a clear correction. Only Αν and K add αγγελος here. Αν alone adds it in the third to seventh angels.

16:14   της μεγαλης ημερας A (hiat C) P⁴⁷ *f*¹⁰⁰⁶ 1611 (WHort^mg.
      Charles^mg.)
      της ημερας της μεγαλης S 61 – 69 *f*¹⁶⁷⁸ 2053 – 2062 2329 (so
      almost all modern critical editions)
      της ημερας εκεινης της μεγαλης Αν K Syr.¹·² Prim. ([Bousset]
      [Sod])

P⁴⁷'s discovery has weakened the authority of the nearly unanimously preferred reading of S by modern editions. Apparently, this reading is preferred because it appears to be presupposed by Αν K. The reading of A P⁴⁷ is at odds with [79] the Apocalypse's linguistic style, where μεγας otherwise never appears before the noun. However, the reading of Αν K is often attributed to the influence of the common designation for Judgment Day, ἡ ἡμέρα ἐκείνη.[74] An unequivocal decision is hardly possible here, since the

---

73. Also, von Soden, who originally decided on δε as the *Urtext* (*Die Schriften des Neuen Testaments*, 1:2076) because of the agreement of Αν and K, overturns this decision once again.

74. See Weiss, *Die Johannes-Apokalypse*, 34; von Soden (*Die Schriften des Neuen Testaments*, 1:2080) explains: "The addition to Mt 24:36, etc. is more likely than the omission of such a solemn word. Or should have Jud 6 and 12 influenced the reading?"

deletion of εκεινης can also be explained from the opacity of the Αν-K reading, which is also supported by two other weighty witnesses, Syr.[1] Prim.

> 16:17 εκ του ναου A (hiat C) P[47] S
>   εκ του ουρανου Αν 792 1854
>   εκ του ναου του ουρανου K (Sod [Merk])

Αν has the same correction (or simple scribal error?) in 14:15 as here. K, however, has an obvious mixed reading and is influenced by Αν.[75]

> 17:3 (θηριον) γεμοντα ονοματα A (hiat C) S* P Oec 2329 (Tisch WHort Bousset Charles)
>   γεμον ονοματα K (Sod Vog Merk)
>   γεμον ονοματων Αν

The correction of the masculine participle[76] by Αν and K is reasonable since γεμοντα is related to θηριον (see 13:14; 17:11).

> 17:3 εχοντα S P Oec[com.] (Tisch WHort[mg.] Bousset 2nd loco)
>   εχων A (hiat C) (WHort[txt.] Bousset 1st loco Charles[txt.])
>   εχον Αν K (Weiss Sod Vog Merk)

Whether εχοντα or εχων represents the Urtext is not discussed here.[77] The reading of Αν K is logical because it follows γεμον.

> 17:4 om. και ante κεχρυσωμενη Αν K against A (hiat C) S 1611 f[1678] 1854 2030 2053 2329 f[104/336] al. pc. ([Sod])

The omission of και before κεχρυσωμενη is an attempt to improve the sentence construction. The rest of the sentence, however, retains the καις.[78]

> 17:12 αλλα A (hiat C) S f[1006] 61 – 69 Hipp
>   αλλ Αν K

[80] The Αν-K reading eliminates the hiatus (see 21:10 below).

---

75. Bousset also recognizes this (Textkritische Studien, 35 n. 3).

76. The following εχοντα shows that γεμον τα should not be read with Weiss.

77. See also p. 248.

78. On the other hand, in 18:16, where no other clause without και exists, only the majority of Αν omits the και. 18:16 does not speak against it but for και as the original in 17:4.

17:16 γυμνην] + ποιησουσιν αυτην K

και γυμνην om. Αν

The omission in Αν is best understood as a homoioteleuton error (αυτην$^{1⌒2}$) and presupposes K's text.

18:2 δαιμονιων A (hiat C) S Q f^{1006} 1611 Oec 2329

δαιμονων Αν K (Sod Vog)

Αν also has the same correction in 16:14. On the other hand, δαιμονιον is almost unanimously attested in 9:20. It has also been shown to be the *Urtext* in 18:2 because it corresponds to the Apocalypse's linguistic style (and to that of the entire New Testament except Mark 5:12 and parallels).

18:12 μαργαριτων S 792 f^{1006} 1611 f^{1678} Syr.$^{1.2}$ (Tisch WHort$^{txt.}$ Weiss Merk Charles)

μαργαριτας C P (WHort$^{mg.}$)

μαργαριταις A sol.

μαργαριτου Αν K (Bousset Sod Vog)

18:16 μαργαριτη] -ταις Αν K against AC S P f^{1006} 1611 2053 – 2062 2329 al. pc. (Weiss)

These two passages should be discussed together and compared with 17:4, where all textual witnesses read μαργαριταις. The word is in the midst of many singular readings in all three passages. In 18:16, which repeats 17:4, the plural μαργαριταις may be a harmonization to 17:4. That the plural is attested in 17:4 (the old textual witnesses have the singular in the repetition of the sentence at 18:16), however, proves that a decision cannot be made on the basis of the Apocalypse's linguistic style. The reading of C P in 18:12 is undermined by the fact that the same two manuscripts also read χρυσουν, αργυρουν, and λιθους τιμιους, which is weakened in S by the fact that S (with f^{1678}) also has βυσσινων. However, Αν and K also correct the reading here, a fact which will be discussed shortly. And with this correction, the explanation that the singular μαργαριτου is also a harmonization to the context (i.e., a correction) gains acceptance.

18:12 πορφυρας C (om. A) S f^{1006} 1611 f^{1678} 1854 2053 – 2062 2329 $f^{104/336}$ $f^{172/250}$ al. pc.

πορφυρου Αν K (Sod)

Although Αν changes πορφυρουν to πορφυραν in 17:4 (like a few groups of Αν with $f^{172/250}$ in 18:16), here πορφυρου seems to be a harmonization in the numerous masculine genitives to -ου, among which stands the feminine πορφυρας.

[81] 18:14 σου της επιθυμιας της ψυχης AC S P f^1006 1854 (and all modern editions)
       ~ της επιθυμιας της ψυχης σου Αν K
This is an improvement of the pronoun's unusual placement (see 2:19).

18:19 + και ante λεγοντες Αν K
This is an obvious stylistic improvement (see 18:16).

18:21 μυλινον A 2053 – 2062 (WHort Charles)
       μυλικον C (Weiss)
       μυλον Αν K (Tisch Bousset Sod Vog Merk)
Bousset explains μυλινον (μυλικον) as a simple mistake. But μυλινον is not meaningless and μυλον is again an obvious correction.

18:24 αιμα] αιματα Αν K f^1006 1611 1854 (Tisch Vog)
The plural is contrary to the Apocalypse's linguistic style; see especially 16:6 (where S f^336 has the plural).

19:5 τω θεω] τον θεον Αν K (contra all modern editions)
The accusative corresponds to the LXX and New Testament's usual linguistic style; therefore, it is a correction.

19:6 θεος] + ημων Αν K S^a (S* + ημων post κυριος)
This contradicts the Apocalypse's linguistic style and, especially, the usual rendering of God's name.[79]

19:18 (των καθημενων) επ αυτους A (hiat C) 61 – 69 (WHort^txt.)
            επ αυτοις S
            επ αυτων Αν K and almost all the rest.
The Apocalypse's linguistic style shows that Αν K preserve the original reading.

---

79. See Charles, *Critical and Exegetical Commentary on the Revelation*, 1:cxlvii, clxii.

19:20 (την λιμνην) της καιομενης A (hiat C) S P al. pc.

την καιομενην Aν K (Bousset Sod Vog)

See 1:15 and 9:10 above.

20:9 εκ του ουρανου A (hiant C S) 94 f^{1678} f^{2014} Prim. (Tisch WHort-txt. Weiss Sod Charles^txt.)

εκ του ουρανου απο του θεου K (WHort^mg. [Bousset])

εκ [του] θεου απο του ουρανου Aν

(απο του θεου εκ του ουρ. Vog; [απο του θεου] εκ του ουρ. Merk Charles^mg. with S^a P)

See 21:2 εκ του ουρ. απο του θεου A (hiat C) S K

~ απο του θεου εκ του ουρ. Aν

21:10 εκ του ουρ. απο [εκ K] του θεου

[82] Since Vulg. Syr. also confirm the Aν reading, this reading (or the K text) has a greater claim to being original. And because Aν also adapts the reading in 21:2, we may give preference to the K text, which agrees with 21:2, 10. It is more likely that απο του θεου was omitted by an oversight in A than that Aν and K have inserted it in line with 21:2, 10 (so Weiss 7).[80]

20:11 (τον καθημενον) επ αυτου A (hiat C) f^{1006} 1611 2053 2329 (WHort^txt. Charles[81] Merk)

επανω αυτου S (likewise 9:17 P^47 S)

επ αυτον Aν K (Tisch WHort^mg. Weiss Bousset Sod Vog)

επ αυτον has to be considered the *Urtext* because it corresponds to the Apocalypse's linguistic style.

20:11 om. του ante προσωπου Aν K against A (hiat C) S P 792 f^{1006} 1611 2050 2329 and all modern editions except [Sod].

The omission of the article corresponds to the Apocalypse's linguistic style elsewhere (see 6:16; 12:14), as well as to that of the New Testament and the LXX.[82] The previous relative pronoun οὗ may have influenced its insertion at this location. Aν K thus have the corrected text by harmonizing it to a common expression.

---

80. See further p. 226.

81. The redactor's mistake, according to Charles.

82. There are only a few times, among many dozens of examples, where the article is included, and it is omitted in some witnesses. Cf. 4 Kgdms 17:18; 23:27; 24:3; Job 13:20; Pss 50:11; 138:7; Jer 4:1.

21:3   θρονου A (hiat C) S 94 Vulg.

ουρανου Αν K and all the rest ([Bousset] Sod)

The exegesis of the passage weighs in favor of θρονου. ουρανου may be a simple reading error or introduced from 21:2.[83]

21:4   εκ A (hiat C) S (likewise 7:17 and all others except S with some allies, including most modern critical editions).

απο Αν K (WHort[mg.] Sod Charles[mg.])

A subsequent harmonization to 7:17 in the older text (thus von Soden) is less likely than a correction by Αν K (perhaps under the influence of Isa 25:8).

21:10   επι A (hiat C) S f[1006] 1611 2050 Oec 2329 f[172]

επ Αν K (likewise LXX Ezek 40:2; Sod Vog)

It is not possible to have complete certainty here, but the elision that eliminates the hiatus is more likely a later correction.[84]

[83] 21:22   επι τους πυλωνας S (hiat C, om. A)

επι τοις πυλωσιν Αν K (and all modern editions)

21:20   αμεθυστος A (hiat C) P 1611 f[1678] 2030 f[172] 2595 f[2060] al. pc. (and all modern editions)

αμεθυσος Αν K S[a] f[1006] 1854

αμεθυστινος S*

22:5   om. φωτος ante λυχνου Αν K against A (hiat C) S f[1006] f[1678] al. pc. ([Sod] [Vog])

The omission of φωτος is a clear correction. It is easier to explain K rather than Αν as the *Urtext* here in the the readings that remain.

om. επ ante αυτους Αν K against A (hiat C) S f[1006] f[1678] 2050 2329 94 f[172/250] ([WHort] [Bousset] [Sod] [Vog])

This is a harmonization with the usual transitive use of φωτιζειν (see John 1:9; 1 Cor 4:5; Eph 3:9).

---

83. Not the opposite of θρονου from 19:5 (von Soden, *Die Schriften des Neuen Testaments*).

84. See ibid., 1:1379, and 17:12 above.

22:6   om. ο ante κυριος Αν K (WHort^mg·) against A (hiat C) S 1611
2053 – 2062 2329 61

This is a harmonization to 1:8; 4:8; 18:8; 19:6; 22:5.[85]

22:11   ρυπανθητω S 94 792 1854 (hiant AC)
ρυπαρευθητω Αν K f^1006 f^1678 2053 – 2062 2329 (WHort^mg·
Bousset)

The testimony of the important minuscules does not favor the reading
accepted by almost all modern critical editions, which adopt S's reading. It
is notable that the form ρυπαρευω is not attested before this reading in the
text of Αν K. Is this an argument for or against ρυπαρευω as the original?
Probably the latter.

22:12   εστιν] εσται Αν K (Vog) against A (hiat C) S f^205 f^1678 2030 (but
different word order in Αν and K)

This is a misguided correction.

22:14   πλυνοντες (πλυναντες f^104 2050) τας στολας αυτων A (hiat C) S
f^1006 2053 – 2062 Sah. Vulg.
ποιουντες τας εντολας αυτου Αν K (Sod^txt·)

Modern editions correctly and almost unanimously reject the Αν-K
reading, despite its strong support by some of the versions. ποιειν (instead
of τηρειν; see 12:17; 14:12) τας εντολας runs counter to the Apocalypse's
linguistic style. It probably presents an old reading error (Bousset), rather
than a conscious correction (Weiss).[86]

[84] 22:21   ιησου] + χριστου Αν K against A (hiat C) S 1611 2053 – 2062
([WHort] Sod)
μετα παντων A (hiat C) (Tisch Weiss)
μετα των αγιων S 2329 (WHort)
μετα παντων των αγιων Αν K (Bousset Sod Vog Merk Charles)

This list is profoundly important. Of the seventy passages that it
encompasses, the Αν-K reading is an obvious error in only a few exceptional cases (4:3; 22:14). The majority of these cases are significant cor-

---

85. But the genitive των πνευματων shows that God's Old Testament name is not
meant (Weiss, *Die Johannes-Apokalypse*, 7).
86. Ibid., 10.

rections. In several locations, the text of Aν K must be recognized as the *Urtext* (certainly in 4:4; 6:8; 9:10; 19:18; 20:11; 21:12; probably also 13:17). In a number of other cases, a decision about what the *Urtext* is—at least preliminarily—is not possible with the desired certainty. Among the passages where Aν K clearly have a corrected text, several instances with a correction are so close that Aν and K could have made them completely independent of each other (see 1:13; 3:9; 4:4; 8:3, 6; 9:20; 11:12; 13:12, 14; 14:6; 17:3; 18:14, 21; 19:20; likewise also 1:15; 5:1; 16:3; 18:12, 16; 21:10; 22:5). Also, the fact that both Aν and K happen to have a homoioteleuton error in 4:3 may be purely coincidental. After removing the twenty-nine passages where Aν K have either the *Urtext* or the same obvious correction or the same error, forty-three cases remain where their agreement against the witnesses of the "old" text cannot be understood without assuming a close relationship between Aν and K.[87] In one passage (16:17), K has an obvious mixed reading of the text of A P[47] S and the text of Aν, indicating thereby its dependence upon the Aν text. It is questionable, however, to infer from this mixed reading alone that all of K's common corrections with Aν, which cannot be explained from a random coinciding of the two text forms, have been taken over directly from Aν.[88] But this reading also raises concerns against the assumption that Aν and K go back to a common *Vorlage*. Since—as will be [85] demonstrated—Aν shares errors with A, it must go back to a text related to (but not identical with) A. The places, however, where Aν K alone preserve the *Urtext* show that they are not only later revised forms of the old text of AC Oec and P[47] S but go back to *Vorlagen* that stand alongside that old text. For this reason, the facts, when fully considered, are complicated, ruling out a simple explanation. It is very clear and certain that Aν and K are not related to each other only by their shared connection to the original text, as Bousset and von Soden allege.[89]

---

87. See the particularly compelling example in 22:14. Bousset underestimates the number of examples or readings common to Aν and K that represent the *Urtext*.

88. Also, another explanation of the facts is not precluded in 16:17: K could probably have corrected an Aν reading preserved in its primary *Vorlage* in line with a manuscript with an "old" text.

89. It is the practical outworking of this principle that Bousset and particularly von Soden usually explain the common readings of Aν K as the *Urtext*, as the list above clearly shows.

2.4. The Two Older Text Forms

The investigation now turns to the evidence that relates to two text forms that can be sharply distinguished from each other in the "old" text: AC Oec, on the one hand, and P⁴⁷ S, on the other. The aforementioned[90] minuscules that preserve the old text sometimes agree with AC Oec and sometimes with P⁴⁷ S. 2329 f^{1678} and 1854 are closer to P⁴⁷ S than AC Oec.

2.4.1. The Text of AC Oec

C is missing about a third of its text.[91] And Oecumenius's text cannot be established with absolute certainty everywhere. To ascertain the text of AC Oec, then, the following measures are taken. First, all the readings are listed and, as far as possible, evaluated to determine which ones are distinct to the AC Oec type.[92] Where C's text is lacunose, A's testimony has to be supported by the few valuable minuscules in addition to Oec in order to belong to the AC Oec type. P also contains a layer of readings of the type AC Oec. Finally, in some places, A's text alone serves as the representative of this text type, based on the data gathered from the list itself about the value of A.

[86] 1:9   δια ante την μαρτυριαν om. AC Oec f^{1006} 1611 f^{1678} 2344 f^{2014} $f^{172/250}$ al. pc. (see 6:9, where only A 1854 are against C and all the rest do not have δια²)

All modern editions except Tisch Bousset Sod consider the reading of AC Oec the *Urtext*.

1:11   θυατειρα] -αν AC (θυατιραν AC) Q 1611 f^{1678} 1854 2050 $f^{172/250}$ al. pc. (Charles)

In contrast, 2:18 correctly preserves θυατειροις with all others against θυατειρη K$^{plur.}$ $f^{104/336}$. The feminine ending in 1:11 is a thoughtless harmo-

---

90. Pp. 26–27.

91. It is missing in: 1:1; 3:20–5:14; 7:14–17; 8:5–9:16; 10:10–11:3; 16:13–18:2; 19:5–21:21.

92. Charles counts thirty-eight (+ thirteen orthographic) distinctive readings of AC Oec, only two of which appear to be faulty.

nization to the other feminine place names,[93] as the neuter plural in 2:18, 24 demonstrates.

1:15   πεπυρωμενης AC
         -νω S
         -νοι Aν K
See, in addition, p. 74.

2:1   της] τω AC 1854, της τω 2019, 2429; likewise 2:18 A, om. C
See also pp. 208–9.

2:2   σου post κοπον om. AC Oec P f^{205} f^{2014} f^{051} 1611 2595 Compl.
         (thus also all modern editions except Sod[94] Vog Merk)
The addition of σου is a misguided correction after κοπον since "κοπος and υπομονη are the two types of intended εργα" (Bousset).

2:3   κεκοπιακες AC (and all modern editions; Bousset and Merk
         κεκοπιακας)
         εκοπιασας S Aν K (a harmonization to εβαστασας)
See 16:6 below.

2:7   + επτα ante εκκλησιαις A
         + ταις επτα post εκκλησιαις C
The addition is a harmonization to 1:11, 20. The following conclusions to the letters to the churches (2:11, 17, 29) demonstrate that επτα was not in the original text.

2:9   om. τα εργα και ante την θλιψιν AC P Oec 1611 1854 2329 2344
         ([Sod])
See pp. 74–75 in 2:13.

2:10   μη AC Q f^{1678} 2050 al. pc. (WHort$^{\text{txt.}}$ Weiss Merk Charles)
         μηδεν S Aν K (Tisch WHort$^{\text{txt.}}$ Bousset Sod Vog)
Bousset opts for μηδεν as the more difficult reading.[95] [87] μηδεν could

---

93. Thus also Weiss, *Die Johannes-Apokalypse*, 135.

94. Different yet, von Soden, *Die Schriften des Neuen Testaments*, 1:2081.

95. Weiss's contrary choices (*Die Johannes-Apokalypse*, 125) have no weight despite the certainty of his tone.

have been eliminated because it fails to accord with the plural α that follows. However, there is no explanation for the opposite scenario (i.e., if μηδεν is the original reading).

2:13   habent και ante εν ταις AC 1611 *f*[1678] 2050 2053 2329 2344 versions (except Arm. Arab.)
        om. S Aν K (Tisch WHort[mg.] Sod)
The omission of και is a correction.[96]

2:13   ημεραις AC Oec *f*[1678] 2329 (Tisch WHort[txt.] Merk Charles)
        + αις K (WHort[mg.1] Weiss Bousset Vog)
        + εν αις Aν S (WHort[mg.2] [Sod])
        + εν ταις S*

Lachmann, Swete, Charles, Zahn attempt to establish Αντιπα through conjecture.[97] We could argue with Weiss and Bousset that the K reading is the *Urtext* and that the omission of αις stems from haplography (Weiss).[98] This proposal does not solve the text's problems, however, because the relative pronoun ος that follows would compete with αις and produce an anacolouthon.[99] The K reading (and likewise the Aν text) should therefore be rejected as an inadequate correction, leaving only a choice between Lachmann's conjecture and the assumption of an egregious grammatical break in the *Urtext*, which then AC Oec must have received. See further p. 251.

2:13   πιστος] + μου AC 61 – 69 2050 2053 (om. [WHort] Bousset [Sod]).
Omitted from S Aν K because the reading is troublesome and superfluous.[100]

2:17   νικωντι] νικουντι AC
All modern editions correctly reject this reading as an error.

---

96. A few analogous cases are recorded in Weiss, *Die Johannes-Apokalypse*, 107.
97. See also Westcott and Hort, *New Testament in the Original Greek*, 2:137–38.
98. Analogous to the omission of ος in 2:8 in the K text.
99. Aρ and *f*[172/250] have omitted ος.
100. Weiss, *Die Johannes-Apokalypse*, 107.

3:2   om. τα ante εργα AC (WHort[txt.] Weiss Charles[txt.]).
The omission is doubtlessly a mistake here, despite the certainty with which Weiss[101] explains the article as a later harmonization to 3:1.

3:7   om. του ante δαυιδ AC Oec 1611 f^{1678} 1854 (likewise WHort[txt.]
       Weiss Bousset Charles Merk against Tisch WHort[mg.] Sod Vog)
AC's text has to be considered the *Urtext* in 3:7 because proper names in the Apocalypse are normally anarthrous, even in the *casus obliqui* (see 5:5; 15:3; 22:16; except 2:14). The article's subsequent [88] addition makes sense after the noun την κλειν, which is governed by an article. A subsequent deletion would be inexplicable.[102]

3:9   διδωμι] διδω AC (and all modern editions except Sod)
The change of the unusual διδω[103] into the usual διδωμι is a clear correction, as 22:2 (αποδιδουν) shows.

3:17   habent οτι ante πλουσιος AC 1611 f^{1678} 2329 A𝜈[pc.] $f^{172/250}$ (likewise all modern editions)
The omission of οτι *recitativum* in S A𝜈 K is a clarifying correction.

3:17   ουδεν AC 1854 2053 A𝜈[pc.]
       ουδενος S A𝜈 K (Sod Vog)
ουδενος is a stylistic correction prompted by χρειαν εχω.[104]

3:17   ελεεινος] ελεινος AC al. pc. (WHort)
The ει of ελεινος displays one of the frequent itacistic errors in AC.

4:4   om. εν ante ιματιοις A (hiat C) P 1854 f^{2014} (WHort[txt.] Charles)
Error (see 3:5).

---

101. Ibid., 108, 165.
102. Also, at least a portion of the witnesses always insert the article in other places.
103. = διδοω.
104. See Ludwig Radermacher (*Neutestamentliche Grammatik: Das griechisch des Neuen Testaments im Zusammenhang mit der Volkssprache dargestellt*, 2nd. ed. [Tübingen: Mohr, 1925], 32) at this location: ουδεν instead of ου is also frequently in Dionysius of Halicarnassus.

4:9   (οταν) δωσουσι A (hiat C) P *f*[1678] al. pc.
        δωσωσι S Aν (Bousset)
        δωσι K

Later texts regularly correct verbs linked to οταν with the present or future indicative[105] (see 6:4 below).

5:6   (πνευματα) απεσταλμενοι A (hiat C) Oec (and all modern editions)
        τα (om. S) απεσταλμενα S Aν
        αποστελλομενα K

5:9   om. ημας A Aeth. (hiat C) (likewise all modern editions except Sod Vog [Merk])

Exegesis makes clear that A alone preserves the *Urtext* here against the rest of the Greek tradition and all the versions except Aeth. The object that the corrector misses is included in εκ πασης φυλης, and αυτους in 5:10 proves that ημας is spurious.

[89] 6:4   (ινα) σφαξουσι AC 792 2329 al. pc. (and all modern editions)
        σφαξωσι S Aν K

See 4:9 above and 8:1 below; also Aν K in 3:9; 9:20; 13:12

6:11   πληρωθωσι AC 2344
        πληρωσωσι S Aν K (Tisch WHort[mg.] Sod)

7:1   + και ante μετα S Aν K Syr. Arm.[3] Aeth. Beat. against AC *f*[1006] 1854 2053 2351 (WHort[txt.] Weiss [Bousset] Charles[txt.] Merk)

και is missing in the same expression found in 4:1; 7:9; 9:12 (+ K); 18:1. 15:5 stands against. This finding precludes a firm decision.

7:9   om. και ιδου A Meth. Syr.[1] Boh. Sah.[2/3] Latt.[plur.] (Weiss)
        om. ιδου C 1611*

Despite Weiss's resolute defense of A's reading (where οχλος πολυς is consequently corrected to οχλον πολυν), the reading must be rejected as an error or a correction.[106]

---

105. On this, see Blass, *Grammatik des neutestamentlichen Griechisch*, §382.4.
106. Weiss, *Die Johannes-Apokalypse*, 110–11.

8:1   οταν AC *f*[1006] 1611
       οτε S Aν K (Bousset)

Bousset's argument against οταν—that this particle always accompanies the subjunctive in the Apocalypse—is incorrect (see 4:9 above). The fact that οτε ηνοιξε occurs six times in chapter 6 cannot similarly decide in favor of οτε in 8:1, since οταν can hardly be understood as a simple scribal error.

8:1   ημιωρον AC 2053[txt.] (contra the commentary)
       ημιωριον S Aν K (Weiss Sod Vog Merk)

The form ημιωρον is otherwise unattested. Does this mean that it is a simple scribal error (Weiss),[107] or that it was precisely for this reason that S Aν K corrected it? The former is decidedly more likely.

9:2   εσκοτωθη A (hiat C) 0207 61 – 69 *f*[1006]
       εσκοτισθη S Aν K (Bousset Sod Vog)

10:1   επι την κεφαλην AC
       επι της κεφαλης P[47] S Aν K (Sod Vog Merk)

10:8   βιβλιον AC 61 – 69 *f*[1006] 1611 1854 2053 (dub. P[47])
       βιβλαριδιον S Aν[part.] (Tisch Bousset Sod Vog)
       βιβλιδαριον Aν[rel.] K

11:19 θεου] + ο AC *f*[1006] *f*[1678] 2329 2351 61 – 69 *f*[172/250] ([Sod] [Vog])

The article corresponds to the Apocalypse's linguistic style (see p. 207) and is therefore the *Urtext*.

[90] 12:5 αρσεν AC
           αρσενα Aν *f*[1006] 1611 Hipp (Weiss Bousset)
           αρρενα P[47] S K (Sod Vog)

αρσεν is not a simple scribal error, as Weiss says, but the *Urtext*, as the Old Testament *Vorlage* shows (Isa 66:7; see Jer 20:15). αρσενα and αρρενα are obvious corrections. αρσεν should not be understood in apposition to υιον but as an attribute of it.

---

107. Ibid., 98.

12:7   om. του ante πολεμησαι P[47] S Αν K contra AC P f[1006] 1611 f[051]
    Compl. (and all modern editions except Tisch)

Although του does not occur elsewhere in the Apocalypse before the infinitive (10:9 + K; 14:15 in some minuscule groups), it is original here.[108]

13:8   οὗ οὐ γεγραπται το ονομα αυτου C Oec 1854 2344
    ουαι γεγραπται το ονομα αυτου A
    ουαι ουαι οὗ οὐ γεγραπται το ονομα αυτου f[1678]
    ὧν οὐ (ου om. S) γεγραπται τα ονοματα αυτων P[47] S f[1006] 1611
    2329 f[2060] f[2065] (Charles[txt.])
    ὧν οὐ γεγραπται το ονομα K (Sod [Merk])
    ὧν οὐ γεγραπται τα ονοματα Αν

We can establish the three developmental stages of the textual history of these readings here. C Oec preserve the original text, which A and f[1678] also presuppose. The error ουαι only emerged because οὗ οὐ was misunderstood. f[1678] combined the error from A (doubled) with the original text. All the other readings are obvious corrections: the replacement of the singular οὗ … αυτου (after παντες οι κατοικουντες) by the plural ὧν … αυτων, as well as the plural τα ονοματα in the place of the singular το ονομα,[109] and finally the omission of the many demonstratives.

13:15   αυτη AC[110] (WHort[txt.] Charles[txt.])[111]
    αυτω P[47] S Αν K (and all modern editions except WHort[txt.] Charles[txt.])

[91] Almost all modern critical editions correctly abandon AC's reading. It can only be explained as a thoughtless scribal error (influenced by μαχαιρα?).[112]

---

108. R. V. G. Tasker ("The Chester Beatty Papyrus of the Apocalypse of John," *JTS* 50 [1949]: 62–63) considers, however: "As τοῦ with the infinitive was tending to disappear in Hellenistic Greek, we perhaps ought to allow for the possibility that the presence of τοῦ after αὐτοῦ may be due to dittography, rather than to assume that its absence is due to a correction."

109. The same correction is found in 11:8 P[47] S Αν (το πτωμα] τα πτωματα); 17:8 S Αν; 18:24 (αιματα) Αν K.

110. Charles and Hoskier erroneously also name P*.

111. Charles reads αυτω in the commentary; he reads αυτη in the introduction (*Critical and Exegetical Commentary on the Revelation*, 1:cxlvi).

112. See also Westcott and Hort, *New Testament in the Original Greek*, 2:138. Weiss (*Die Johannes-Apokalypse*, 136) offers a complicated explanation.

13:15 habent ινα ante οσοι A P f^{1006} 2329 2344 2019 f^{2065} (hiant C P^{47} Oec: θηριου$^{1⌢3}$) (Weiss Bousset Charles) contra S Aν K (Tisch [WHort] [Sod] [Vog] [Merk]

ινα is indispensable here and therefore cannot simply be a later correction. Aν inserts it before αποκτανθωσι.

13:15 την εικονα A (hiant C P^{47} Oec) Aν$^{pc.}$
τη εικονι S Aν$^{plur.}$ K

The study of the Apocalypse's linguistic style will demonstrate that A makes a correction in this case.

14:4 (οπου αν) υπαγει AC 2329 $f^{104/336}$ (WHort Charles)
υπαγη S Aν K (hiat P^{47})

In light of the frequent itacistic error in A and C, a scribal error in AC is more probable in 14:4 than that the indicative is original, which would then be explained analogously to οταν with the indicative (see 4:9).

14:6 habent αλλον AC S^c f^{1006} 1611 2053 2329 2344 f^{051} versions (and all modern editions)
om. P^{47} S Aν K

Again, AC preserve the *Urtext*.

14:7 om. την ante θαλασσαν AC Aν$^{part.}$ f^{1006} (likewise all modern editions except Tisch [Bousset]).

The article is correctly rejected as a subsequent correction. The following και πηγας υδατων forms a pair with και θαλασσαν and speaks against its authenticity.

14:8 habent ἡ AC f^{1006} f^{1678} 2053 2344 $f^{172/250}$ Syr.$^{1.2}$ Latt. (and all modern editions) against P^{47} S^a (hiat S*) Aν K

ἡ could have fallen out behind μεγαλη by simple haplography.

14:18 + ο ante εχων AC 2329 ([WHort] Weiss [Bousset] Charles Merk against Tisch Sod Vog)

Here also AC's text must be explained as the original on exegetical grounds (it is spoken by the angel, which has power over the water). It is quite unlikely that this proper text form is simply a later correction.

[92] 15:6   λιθον AC Oec 1778[mg.] 2020[mg.] Latt.[part.] (WHort Charles)
             λινον Αν K, λινουν P[47] al. pc., λινους S

Despite the fact that WHort, Charles, and Lagrange consider λιθον the *Urtext*,[113] λιθον cannot be original because καθαρον fits well as an attribute of λινον but badly as an attribute of λιθον.[114] Αν K preserve the *Urtext* here.

   16:3   ζωης AC f^{1006} 1611
           ζωσα P[47] S Αν (Sod)[115]
           om. K

Again, AC's text preserves the original. The other text forms eliminate the Hebraism ψυχη ζωης.

   16:3   απεθανεν] + τα AC 1611 2344 Αν[pc]
                       + των f^{1006} 2019 f^{2065}
           om. P[47] S Αν K (and [Bousset] Sod Vog)

The remaining text forms eliminate the article because it generates an incongruity.

   16:6   δεδωκας AC 1611 2329 (WHort[txt.] Weiss Charles[txt.] Merk)
           εδωκας P[47] S Αν K (Tisch WHort[mg.] Bousset Sod Vog Charles[mg.])

The aorist is a harmonization to εξεχεαν. See the analogous correction in 2:3 above.

   16:18   ανθρωπος εγενετο A (hiat C) 254 (~ f^{1678}) Boh.[part.] (Tisch
           WHort[mg.] Weiss Bousset 2nd loco Charles[txt.])
           ανθρωπος εγενοντο P[47] (so)
           ανθρωποι εγενοντο S Αν f^{1006} 1611 1854 2053 2329 (WHort[txt.])
           οι ανθρωποι εγενοντο K

The fluctuation of the modern editions is well established. A's text only receives partial and late support from P[47].

---

113. Lagrange, *Critique Textuelle*, 582.

114. Charles (*Critical and Exegetical Commentary on the Revelation*, 2:38) correctly rejects WHort's note (*New Testament in the Original Greek*, 2:139) on Ezek 28:13 (παν λιθον χρηστον ενδεδεσαι) for the authenticity of λιθον as inconclusive. For Charles, λιθον is not only the more strongly attested text form but above all also the *lectio difficilior*. He acknowledges, however, that it is also too difficult to be correct. That is why he decides to accept a translation error.

115. Von Soden (*Die Schriften des Neuen Testaments*, 1:2083) declares ζωης the *Urtext*. Bousset considers ζωσα to be more likely.

17:8   υπαγει A (hiat C) 1611 2053 – 2062 *f* [205] 2814 Syr.[1] Boh.

υπαγειν S (hiat P[47]) Aν K (Tisch WHort[mg.] [Bousset] Sod Vog Charles[mg.])

It is far more likely that υπαγειν is a later harmonization to the previous (μελλει) αναβαινειν [93] than the opposite correction (or a simple scribal error?) in A. A therefore has the *Urtext*.

17:8   θαυμασθησονται A (hiat C) P 1611

θαυμασονται S (hiat P[47]) Aν K (Tisch Sod Vog Merk)

13:3 confirms that A's text is original.

18:3   om. του οινου AC Oec 1611 ([WHort])

The omission is simply a careless error. The Aν text also presupposes this error (~ του θυμου του οινου).

18:12   μαργαριτας C P (WHort[mg.])

μαργαριταις A

μαργαριτων S *f* [1006] 1611 *f* [1678] Syr.[1.2]

μαργαριτου Aν K

A's text is a simple scribal error, presupposed by the reading of C P. Modern critical editions correctly reject it (see p. 83).

18:18   εκραξαν AC P *f* [1006] 1611 1678 – 2080 2329 Hipp (WHort Bousset Charles)

εκραζον S Aν K (Tisch Weiss Sod Vog Merk)

18:19   εκραξαν AC 2329 Hipp (WHort Bousset Charles)

εκραζον S Aν K

A firm decision is hardly possible here (likewise 7:2; see p. 107). While Bousset[116] explains that the seer does not appear to have used the imperfect of κραζειν and that the aorist in all three places was the probable *Urtext*, Weiss[117] maintains that the aorist in 18:18 is a thoughtless harmonization to the previous εστησαν and that the aorist in 18:19 is a harmonization to εβαλον. The imperfect's subsequent harmonization to the aorist εστησαν is in fact more difficult to understand than the opposite development.

. Bousset, *Textkritische Studien*, 169.

117. Weiss, *Die Johannes-Apokalypse*, 121, 136.

19:9   + οι ante αληθινοι A (hiat C) al. pc. (WHort^{mg.} Weiss [Bousset] Charles)

   om. S Aν K

A firm decision is also hardly possible here. However, οι before αληθινοι appears to be indispensable because the following του θεου probably cannot be removed as a gloss.

19:12   habent ως ante φλοξ A (hiat C) *f*¹⁰⁰⁶ *f*¹⁶⁷⁸ *f*²⁰²⁸ versions (WHort^{mg.} [Bousset] Charles)

   om. S Aν K (and most modern editions)

In the case of 1:14 (see 2:18), one can argue both for and against the authenticity of ως because a subsequent harmonization is possible. [94] Although the subsequent loss is difficult to explain, the testimony of A and the versions is very strong (ως is removed in 14:3 in P⁴⁷ S K, 19:6 in Aν).

19:19   αυτων] αυτου A (hiat C) Aρ (Weiss)

Weiss's argument[118] that the kings aligned with the beast had the supreme command over their armies transferred to the beast, leading to αυτου as the original text, is unnecessary.

20:2   (τον δρακοντα) ο οφις ο αρχαιος A (hiat C) *f*¹⁶⁷⁸ (Tisch WHort^{txt.} Weiss Charles)

   τον οφιν τον αρχαιον S Aν K (WHort^{mg.} Bousset Sod Vog Merk)

A *f*¹⁶⁷⁸ clearly offer the original text since the word in apposition to a noun in the nominative case stands in a *casus obliquus*. This is in line with the Apocalypse's linguistic style.

21:6   γεγοναν A (hiat C) S^a 1678, 1778

   γεγονασιν Oec *f*¹⁰⁰⁶ 2020, 2080 *f*²⁰⁶⁵ Boh. Gig. Vulg. Tyc. Prim. Ir.

   γεγονα S* Aν K (Sod Vog)

21:6   ειμι A (hiat C) *f*¹⁰⁰⁶ *f*¹⁶⁷⁸ 2053 *f*²⁰⁶⁵

   om. S Aν K (and all modern editions except Weiss Charles[119])

These two variants belong together. In particular, we note that ειμι is missing precisely in those text forms that read γεγονα (S* Aν K). This is

---

118. Ibid., 106.

119. Charles would like to remove this reading as a gloss in 21:6a (*Critical and Exegetical Commentary on the Revelation*, 2:204).

because these forms have incorrectly drawn γεγονα to what follows in the sense of ειμι.[120] This does not establish the authenticity of ειμι in and of itself. 1:8 can be cited in support of the authenticity of ειμι in 21:6. 22:13, however, is against it, where only a few meaningless and related minuscules offer ειμι. The emergence of γεγονα appears to presuppose that ειμι was missing. This is due to the fact that the relationship of γεγονα to what follows is readily understandable and does not require the assumption that ειμι was only removed because of the emergence of γεγονα. Even if the omission of ειμι is older than the emergence of γεγονα, it does not explain whether ειμι was also missing in the original text and inserted first from the A text form (probably under the influence of 1:8). The judgment about this depends especially on how the AC text is evaluated.[121]

[95] 21:16 οσον και A (hiat C) *f*[1006] 1611 2050 al. pc. (Weiss Charles [Bousset])

οσον om. Aν

και om. S K (Tisch WHort Sod Vog Merk)

The deliberate removal of και (also in Aν) is much more easily understandable than a later insertion.

21:18 και[1]] + ην S* [om. ἡ] Aν K (Bousset Sod [om. ἡ] Vog [Merk]) against A (hiat C) S[a] P Oec 1611 *f*[2044] Syr.[1]

Since the copula is also consistently missing in 21:19–20, ην should be considered a later addition.

21:18 ενδωμησις A (hiat C) S[a] 1854 2329 al. pc. (and all modern editions except Sod)

ενδομησις S* Aν K

The possibility that the unusual ενδωμησις is a simple scribal error cannot be ruled out.

21:22 ο ναος A (hiat C) 1678 2080 469 1773 (Weiss Charles)[122]

om. ο S Aν K (and most modern editions)

---

120. See the text form in Origen.

121. That the testimony of the versions cannot be used to support the authenticity of ειμι emerges from 22:13, where the versions contradict the Greek tradition.

122. Likewise Bousset, *Die Offenbarung Johannis*, 175; on the contrary, 451.

The article corresponds to the Apocalypse's linguistic style and is therefore the *Urtext*. The article was subsequently omitted because ναος is a predicate noun.

22:2   αποδιδουν A (hiat C) 2053 – 2062 Αν^{part.}
        αποδιδους S Αν^{plur.} K (Tisch WHort^{mg.} Bousset 1st loco Sod Charles^{mg.})

The unusual word form (from -διδοω), which also surfaces in 3:9, confirms the authenticity of the reading of A 2053 – 2062.

22:5   φωτισει A (hiat C) P *f*¹⁰⁰⁶ 2050 2329 al. pc.
        φωτιει S Αν K (Tisch Bousset Sod Vog Merk)
        φωτιει is again a correction.

There are still the following orthographic variants as well.[123]

2:1   χρυσων] χρυσεων AC (rejected by all modern editions)
This uncontracted form surfaces only in a few locations in the LXX.[124]

[96] 16:6   πειν A, πιν C
             πιειν P⁴⁷ S Αν K

The non-Attic contracted form, which the modern editions of Tisch WHort Weiss Charles (against Bousset Sod Vog Merk) adopt, also surfaces in the LXX and frequently in various different manuscripts.[125] The tradition also varies between the two forms in the other New Testament writings, and the modern editions disagree over them.[126] Therefore, it remains an open question whether we can speak of an actual tradition here and for many of the other forms to be discussed. This applies above all to the assimilation of consonants or their absence in the forms τεσσερα — τεσσαρα, τεσσερακοντα — τεσσαρακοντα, and ερευναω] εραυναω AC (as

---

123. See also already 3:17 and 8:1 (ημιωρ[ι]ον) above.

124. See Henry St. John Thackeray, *Introduction, Orthography and Accidence*, vol. 1 of *A Grammar of the Old Testament in Greek: According to the Septuagint* (Cambridge: Cambridge University Press, 1909), 172–73. See also p. 188 in the discussion of the Apocalypse's linguistic style.

125. See ibid., 64.

126. Von Soden (*Die Schriften des Neuen Testaments*, 1:1377) rejects πειν as an error.

well as the modern editions except Sod Vog) in 2:23. We should also mention that the consistent spelling εμμεσω instead of εν μεσω, which Weiss views as the *Urtext*, is characteristic in AC: 1:13 AC 2060$^{com.}$; 2:1 AC 2060; 4:6 A (hiat C) 1854 2329 2060; 5:6 bis A (hiat C) 2329, 1st loco 1854; 6:6 AC 2329; 22:2 A (hiat C) 2050. All these and some other morphological phenomena in question will be discussed in greater detail in the study of the Apocalypse's linguistic style.

With this, the facts of the case are laid bare, and we can deduce several important findings from them. The number of the distinctive readings[127] that belong to the AC type is not much smaller than that of Aν-K readings. There is, however, an essential difference in the character of their shared readings. The Aν-K readings are for the most part corrections, while the vast majority of AC's readings are certainly, or at least probably, representative of the *Urtext*. As such, they demonstrate the superior quality of the AC text form. As far as they are the *Urtext*, they do not prove that A and C also form a close pair within the Apocalypse's tradition. There are some places where the authenticity of AC's text is highly questionable (see 1:11; 2:7, 17; 3:2; 4:4; 7:9; 13:15; 14:4 [?]; 15:6; 18:3, 12). These examples offer the first compelling evidence that AC are not related to one another merely by the archetype of the Apocalypse's entire Greek textual tradition but [97] that they also form their own stem. It is, however, a very remarkable fact that only a single correction (2:7) surfaces among these apparently secondary readings. This means that we have a stem of the Apocalypse's textual tradition in AC Oec that hardly contains corrections and, as such, deserves the predicate "neutral text" with some justification. What will be confirmed again and again in what follows emerges clearly at this juncture: the AC Oec text type significantly towers over the other text forms in terms of value. In the majority of the passages discussed, AC certainly or at least probably bear witness to the original text. Most of the AC Oec text, however, simultaneously differs from the rest of tradition (P^{47} S Aν K). By establishing these facts, we readily identify a new problem: How should the mutual relationship of the three other text forms P^{47} S, Aν, and K be determined? Some of the corrections may be so obvious that several correctors could have made them independently, such as the use of the subjunctive in place of the future indicative with ινα (see 6:4), διδω] διδωμι (3:9), or μαχαιρη] -ρα (13:10, 14).

---

127. At least within the Greek tradition.

This justifiable assumption, however, does not completely solve the problem of the relationships of the three text forms to each other.

A and C differ in a number of places. Moreover, all those places should be disregarded where either A or C has a unique reading that is easily recognizable as a scribal error.[128] Of primary interest in this context are those places where A and C each agree with various other text forms, as well as the question of their possible interference from other text types. That C is copied far more carefully than A and contains far fewer thoughtless and orthographic errors than A is known.[129] And its unique readings are therefore harmless in nature, as they are easily recognizable as errors of the scribe (or his *Vorlage*).[130] A is indeed more carelessly copied than C.[131] Among [98] its circa 210 unique readings,[132] there are no less than 56, if not 63, that represent the *Urtext* in Charles's judgment.[133] This means that A is the more valuable of the two manuscripts.[134] C is less valuable than A not merely because it is lacunose but also because it exhibits traces of external influence.

The passages where we should consider this influence are enumerated as completely as possible in the following list.

1:4   των A S *f*[2014] (WHort[mg.] Charles)
        α C K 1611 1854 2050 2329 2344
        α εστιν Aν

---

128. Compilations of unique readings including the error in Weiss, *Die Johannes-Apokalypse*, 49–95; and von Soden, *Die Schriften des Neuen Testaments*, 1:2069–71.

129. See the statistic in Weiss, *Die Johannes-Apokalypse*, 90. Weiss counts 110 unique readings from C (bearing in mind that a third of C's text is lost). Charles (*Critical and Exegetical Commentary on the Revelation*, 1:clxxi) counts only about 67.

130. C alone has the *Urtext* (but with Oec 1854 2344) in 13:8 οὗ οὐ γεγραπται το ονομα αυτου. A, however, also has no correction here but an error based on a misunderstanding. See p. 95.

131. But not nearly as neglectful as S.

132. Weiss, *Die Johannes-Apokalypse*, 90; Charles counts 229 (+ 27 orthographic).

133. This statistical data that illuminate the value of C and A now undergoes a change insofar as many of their unique readings are also in the minuscules, which do not belong to Aν or K or offer mixed texts of these. Undoubtedly, the number of A's unique readings would also decrease if C were complete.

134. A remains the Apocalypse's most valuable manuscript by far, even after P[47]'s discovery. This is not a new insight. It explains why modern editions differ relatively little from each other even though they were created on the basis of different principles.

Almost all modern editions correctly adopt reading 2, which explains the rise of readings 1 and 3. των is a harmonization to the previous απο των πνευματων (Weiss),[135] and 2 cannot be explained as deriving from 1.

1:14   ως[1]] ωσει C Αν
This reading contradicts the Apocalypse's linguistic style elsewhere.[136]

1:19   μελλει] δει μελλει(ν) C S 2329
This reading can be explained from the influence of 1:11; 4:1; 22:6.

1:19   γενεσθαι C S* K (Tisch Weiss Merk)
          γινεσθαι A Sᵃ Αν (WHort Bousset Vog Sod Charles)
The fact that the present infinitive is the more common tense following μελλειν,[137] as in the whole of the New Testament (yet compare 3:2, 16; 12:4), gives the reading of γινεσθαι a certain ascendancy.

2:9   ιουδαιους] -ων C S* 2050 2329 2344
This reading is a thoughtless harmonization to των λεγοντων. On the other hand, see 3:9.

2:10   εξετε S K (Tisch WHort^mg.1 Weiss Bousset Sod Vog Merk)
          εχετε C Ανᵖˡᵘʳ· (WHort^mg.2)
          εχητε A 1854 Αν ᵖᶜ· (WHort^txt· Charles)
[99] Weiss[138] and Bousset correctly judge εχητε as a misguided harmonization to the previous πειρασθητε. εχετε, however, may have originated from εχητε.

2:20   αλλα] αλλ C S Αν (Tisch)
αλλ is a correction to eliminate the hiatus.

2:20   γυναικα] + σου A K (WHort^mg·) contra C S Αν

---

135. Weiss, *Die Johannes-Apokalypse*, 101.

136. The same form is a correction also in 1:17 and 16:3 in S; 16:13 in P^47 S; 13:3 in K.

137. Blass, *Grammatik des neutestamentlichen Griechisch*, §338.3.

138. Weiss, *Die Johannes-Apokalypse*, 136.

2:22   (εαν) μετανοησουσιν A S
                  -σωσιν C Aν K (Weiss Bousset Sod Vog)
Since no clear example of εαν with the future indicative surfaces in the New Testament,[139] the reading of A S, which also has 2:5 (εαν μη μετανοησης) against it, is probably a scribal error.

2:22   αυτης C S K
       αυτων A Aν (WHort[mg.]) 1854 2329 2344
       αυτων is a correction of the misunderstood αυτης.

2:25   αχρι οὗ C S 1611 2053 2329 2351
       αχρις οὗ Aν K
       εως οὗ A sol.
A's reading is an obvious correction.

3:7   ~ ο αληθινος ο αγιος A S sol. (WHort[mg.])
On the other hand, see 6:10.

3:14   + ο ante αληθινος C S al. pc. ([WHort])
       και αληθινος] ο αληθινος f[104/336] 61 – 69 f[2014] 2050 2053 2351

3:16   ~ ουτε ψυχρος ουτε ζεστος A P f[205] Syr.[1] Vulg. (Charles[txt.])
This reading is a harmonization to 3:15

3:17   om. ο ante ελεεινος C S Aν
       habent A K (WHort[mg.] Charles)
The article must be assessed as a thoughtless harmonization to the first part of the list. It is missing from the following members of the list.

3:18   κολλουριον A Aν
       κολλυριον C S K (Tisch Bousset Sod)
This is a correction to the usual form.

6:4   αυτω[1] om. A S[a] (correction)
       εκ της γης C S Aν[part.] K
       εκ om. A Aν[plur.] ([WHort])
The omission is clearly a correction.

---

139. Blass, *Grammatik des neutestamentlichen Griechisch*, §373.2.

6:7   φωνην του τεταρτου ζωου A S Aν
[100]   του τεταρτου ζωου K P
        το τεταρτον ζωον C Oec

6:8   om. αυτου[1] C Aν 1611 Oec ([WHort])

This reading can only be understood as an error, not as a correction (Weiss).[140]

6:8   om. ο ante θανατος C S Oec f^{1006} 1854 Compl. (Tisch [WHort] [Vog])

This reading is probably the result of an old scribal error.[141] The article is original since it corresponds to the Apocalypse's linguistic style.

6:9   om. δια[2] A 1854 Sah.[1/2] Boh. Latt.[part.] (Weiss)
        habent C Aν K

6:16   πεσατε A P 2329 al. pc. (WHort Weiss Charles)
        πεσετε C S Aν K al. pc. (Tisch Bousset Sod Vog Merk)

A firm decision is not possible since the aorist imperative occurs only here in the Apocalypse. Otherwise, the aorist form επεσον belongs to the later manuscripts.

6:17   αυτου] αυτων C S Oec 1611 1854 2329 f^{1678} Syr.[1.2] Latt. (Tisch WHort Sod Vog Merk against Weiss Bousset Charles)

The exegesis of the text weighs in favor of αυτου's authenticity in 6:17. As 6:16 shows, the speech is from the wrath of the Lamb appearing as a judge (= Christ).

7:1   παν δενδρον S Aν
        τι δενδρον C K (WHort[mg.] [τι] Weiss Sod Charles[txt.])
            δενδρου A

All modern editions correctly reject A's reading, but opinions are divided over the assessment of the other two readings. The examples in 7:16; 9:4; 18:22; 21:27; and 22:3, where each πας occurs in a negative sentence, speak for παν as the *Urtext* rather than against it (against Weiss).[142]

---

140. Weiss, *Die Johannes-Apokalypse*, 129.
141. Ibid., 100.
142. Ibid., 125.

It is clear that επι δενδρου is not an error in A but rather a conscious correction. It is not a reading that presupposes the reading in C K (Weiss). A already omits the article in επι της θαλασσης (it completely omits επι της γης due to homoioteleuton). It aligns επι δενδρου to the case of επι θαλασσης and also makes it indefinite. However, the testimony of παν, which Bousset[143] advances as a real objection to this reading, is not so decisive. The versions cannot be used to establish the original reading, as the analogous passages 9:4 and 21:27 show.

7:2   ανατολης] -λων A f[18] 1778[corr.*] (WHort[mg.] Weiss Charles[mg.])
See 16:12 below.

[101]7:2   εκραξεν C S 1854 2329 2344 Aν K
            εκραζεν A P (WHort[mg.] Weiss Bousset 2nd loco Charles[mg.])
See also p. 98 with AC in 18:18–19.

7:4   εκατον] + και C K
All modern critical editions reject the addition.

7:9   εστωτες] εστωτων C f[1678] f[2028] (correction)

9:18   + εκ ante του καπνου C
        + εκ ante του καπνου et του θειου P[47] Aν

9:20   ουτε[1] A Aν (WHort[mg.1] Bousset 2nd loco Sod Vog Charles[mg.1])
        ουδε P[47] S Q f[1678] 2053 (Tisch WHort[mg.2] Weiss Bousset Charles[txt.])
        ου C K 2344 (WHort[txt.] Charles[mg.2] Merk)
ου is a clarifying correction, since the other two readings could be accepted as the *Urtext*.

9:21   φαρμακ[ε]ιων   A Aν
        φαρμακων C P[47] S K (WHort[txt.] Sod)
        πορνειας C P[47] Aν K
        πονηριας A S* f[1678]
Despite the fact that πονηριας is a simple scribal error, the agreement between A and S* can hardly be coincidental. Is it possible that C produces the original reading only by a correction?

---

143. Bousset, *Textkritische Studien*, 280 n. 1.

10:2   βιβλαριδιον] βιβλιδαριον C* Aν$^{part.}$ Compl. f^{104}

10:4   om. επτα^2 C Sah.$^{1/3}$ Gig., superlinear addition in P^{47}
The omission could be coincidental.

10:6   και την γην — αυτη^1 om. A Aν
        και την θαλασσαν — αυτη^2 om. A S* f^{1678} f^{205} ([WHort])

11:3   περιβεβλημενους] -οι C Aν$^{plur.}$ K Hipp
Only the staunchest adherents of the "neutral text," WHort^{144} and
Charles (see also p. 78 on 9:10), trace the obvious senseless reading -ους of
A S* Aν$^{part.}$ (a thoughtless harmonization to σακχους) to the original.

11:5   θελησῃ A S
        θελησει P^{47} (WHort$^{mg.2}$)
        θελει C Aν K (WHort$^{mg.1}$ Sod as the selected reading)
θελει is a harmonization to the previous θελει.

11:11   εν αυτοις A Aν$^{part.}$ f^{1006} 1854 2344 2351 (Tisch WHort [εν] Weiss
         Bousset Charles Merk)
         αυτοις C Aν $^{rel.}$ (Sod Vog)
         εις αυτους P^{47} S K
[102] εν could have fallen out by haplography after εισηλθεν (likewise
10:6 P^{47} S K).

11:12   φωνην μεγαλην ... λεγουσαν A K (WHort$^{txt.}$ Bousset 2nd loco
         Sod Vog Charles$^{mg.}$ Merk)
         φωνης μεγαλης ... λεγουσης C P^{47} S Aν (Tisch WHort$^{mg.}$ Weiss
         Bousset 1st loco Charles$^{txt.}$)
No firm decision is possible here.

11:15   (φωναι) λεγοντες A K
                     λεγουσαι C P^{47} S Aν (Sod^{145} Vog)
An obvious correction (likewise 4:1; 9:13–14; and 11:4 Aν)

---

144. On this text, see Westcott and Hort, *New Testament in the Original Greek*, 2:138.
145. Von Soden, *Die Schriften des Neuen Testaments*, 1:2082, still evaluated correctly.

11:16 οι [om. A] πρεσβυτεροι ενωπιον του θεου καθημενοι A Aν
        οι πρεσβυτεροι οἳ [om. P⁴⁷] ενωπιον του θεου καθηνται C P⁴⁷ Sᵃ
        f¹⁰⁰⁶ 1611 2053 2344 (WHortᵐᵍ·)
        οι [om. S] πρεσβυτεροι οι ενωπιον [+ του θρονου K] του θεου οἳ
        καθηνται S* K (Tisch Sod)
[WHort] Weiss Bousset Vog Charles Merk read οι ενωπιον του θεου
καθημενοι with P Compl. and a few others (WHort places οι in brackets).
This is a very weakly attested text because P's authority is very minimal.
The omission of οι before πρεσβυτεροι in A S* is certainly an error, as is the
absence of οι before ενωπιον. In the end, P's text is still the *Urtext* and C's
reading is a correction,[146] perhaps under external influence.[147]

11:17 + και ante οτι C P⁴⁷ S* (Tisch WHortᵐᵍ·)
The addition cannot be original; it is a thoughtless mistake.

11:18 καιρος] κληρος C Oec (*expresse*) f²⁰⁶⁵
κληρος is a scribal error.

11:18 τοις φοβουμενοις] τους φοβουμενους A P⁴⁷
The error of A P⁴⁷ is easy to understand here, much like its subsequent
correction in C.

12:2   εχουσα] + και C P⁴⁷ S Oec f¹⁰⁰⁶ 2344 2020 – 2080 versions
        ~ κραζει και A (see p. 79)
A assumes the text of C P⁴⁷ S.

12:2   κραζει] εκραζεν (al. εκραξεν) C K (correction)

12:3   ~ πυρρος μεγας C P⁴⁷ S K against A Aν (Tisch WHortᵐᵍ· Bousset
        2nd loco Sod Vog Charlesᵐᵍ· Merk)
[103] In 20:11 (μεγαν λευκον), the word order of A Aν is preferable
(Weiss).[148]

---

146. The same replacement of the participle by a relative clause in K also occurs
at 2:20; 3:12; see also 5:13.
147. Weiss (*Die Johannes-Apokalypse*, 121–22) could be right in his assessment of
the location of the external influence.
148. Weiss, *Die Johannes-Apokalypse*, 122.

12:6   om. εχει C Aν (correction)

12:6   (ινα) τρεφουσιν C S (hiat P⁴⁷) 2329 al. pc. (Tisch WHort^mg.
       Charles^txt.)
          τρεφωσιν A Aν
          εκτρεφωσιν K
The present indicative after ινα should be rejected because it contradicts the Apocalypse's linguistic style.

12:8   ισχυσεν A K (WHort^txt. Weiss Bousset 1st loco Charles^txt.)
       ισχυσαν C P⁴⁷ S Aν
The reason why ισχυσεν is more probable lies solely in the fact that the plural can be understood as a correction but not the singular.[149] This is true, since the subsequent αυτων would have offered strong support for the plural ισχυσαν.

12:10 κατηγωρ A sol.
       κατηγορος C rel. (Sod Vog Merk)
Most modern critical editions regard κατηγωρ the *Urtext* because it surfaces as a loanword in rabbinic literature and because the usual κατηγορος can be understood as a correction.[150]

12:10 αυτους A P⁴⁷ Aν
       αυτων C S K f¹⁰⁰⁶ 1611 1854 2053 2329 2344 2351 (Sod Merk)
The genitive corresponds to the New Testament's predominant linguistic style elsewhere. The fact that this reading is not changed anywhere else speaks for αυτους as the *Urtext*.

12:12 om. οι ante ουρανοι C S P K 1854 2053 2329 f¹⁰⁴/³³⁶ f¹⁷²/²⁵⁰
       (Tisch WHort^txt. Weiss Sod Vog Merk) contra A Aν f¹⁰⁰⁶ 1611
       2344 2351 (WHort^mg. Bousset Charles)
That the nominative replaces the vocative in the Apocalypse speaks almost entirely for the article's authenticity. Compared to this weighty

---

149. In some other passages where A changes the number of the verb (see 8:2; 15:6; 16:4; 20:13), it is solely a matter of thoughtless harmonizations, which would not be the case here.

150. See, on the other hand, Tasker, "Chester Beatty Papyrus," 65.

argument, Weiss's assumption (111) that the article was thoughtlessly harmonized with οι κατοικουντες is hardly convincing.

[104] 12:12 σκηνουντες] κατοικουντες S al. pc.
    κατασκηνουντες C sol. (mixed text?)

12:17 om. επι C P^{47} (correction)

13:1 ονομα C P^{47} S Aν f^{1006} 2329
    ονοματα A K (Tisch WHort$^{txt.}$ Weiss Bousset 1st loco Charles$^{txt.}$
    Merk)
17:3 proves the plural's authenticity.[151]

13:5 βλασφημα A f^{1678} 2329 f^{2014} f$^{172/250}$ (Weiss)
    βλασφημιας C P^{47} S f^{1006} 1611 2053 2344
    βλασφημιαν Aν K (Bousset Sod)
βλασφημα is not the *Urtext* but a harmonization to the previous
μεγαλα. Conversely, βλασφημιας is not a harmonization to 13:6 but the
Urtext.

13:5 om. και ante δυο C P^{47} S Aν
    habent A f^{1006} 1854 f^{336} ([WHort] Weiss Charles)
Likewise 11:2 om. και P^{47} S Aν contra A (hiat C) K.
A probably preserves the original text in both cases.

13:10 om. εις αιχμαλωσιαν^2 C P^{47} S Aν K ([Sod])
The omission is an error based on haplography, despite the overwhelmingly strong testimony.

13:15 θηριου$^{1⌢3}$ C P^{47} 2053$^{txt.}$
    om. ινα ante οσοι C P^{47} S Aν K (Tisch [WHort] [Sod] [Vog]
    [Merk] contra A P f^{1006} 2329 f^{104} al. pc. (Weiss Bousset Charles)
ινα must be original because it is indispensable for the sentence construction.

---

151. Weiss (*Die Johannes-Apokalypse*, 129–30) explains the singular as a breakdown in the final syllable. It is, however, probably a deliberate correction.

13:17 om. και C S* 1611 f^{2014} f^{2044} Sah. Boh. Syr.[1.2] (Tisch [WHort] [Bousset])

The omission of και is probably due to a misunderstanding of the relationship between 13:16 and 13:17. The omission is therefore secondary.

13:17 η το ονομα] του ονοματος C 792 1773 f^{2044} Syr.[1.2] Latt.[plur.] Arm.[2] Aeth.

13:18 αυτου] + εστιν C Αν f^{1006} 1611 1854 2053 2329 (WHort[mg.] Sod)
The same addition occurs in Αν at 1:4 and in K at 5:6 and 14:4.
εξακοσιοι] -αι C S (WHort[mg.])

14:8 ~ αλλος αγγελος δευτερος (-ον C) C S[a] Αν (Tisch Weiss)
αγγελος is missing in P[47] S*, which, if αγγελος is genuine, appears to presuppose the word order of C Αν, since αγγελος [105] could more easily fall away right after the similar αλλος than after δευτερος. If this is the case, then A K have secondary readings, similar to the reading in A in 19:4. Also, 14:9 speaks for the authenticity of the word order in C Αν.
    om. επεσεν[2] C S[a] (hiat S*) K (likewise 18:2 S K)

14:10 βασανισθησεται C (hiat P[47]) S Αν K
    βασανισθησονται A f^{1006} 2019 61 – 69 (Weiss Bousset)
The transition from the singular (14:10 αυτος πιεται) to the plural (14:11 ο καπνος … αυτων) already takes place here in A, as in the text of the other later witnesses—a transition that is possible in light of the Apocalypse's style. βασανισθησονται can be understood as a harmonization to the continuation of the phrase in 14:11, just as βασανισθησεται can be a subsequent harmonization to the preceding πιεται (Weiss). The value of C S Αν K gives the singular βασανισθησεται the weight of probability, but there is no other evidence.

14:13 (ινα) αναπαησονται A P[47] S
    αναπαυσονται C Αν (Bousset 2nd loco)
    αναπαυσωνται K (Sod)
Readings 2 and 3 are both corrections of 1.

14:14 υιον A S K
    υιω C P[47] Αν (Weiss)
A correction, like 1:13 A C Αν against S K.

14:14 της κεφαλης] την κεφαλην A 1611 f^{1678} 1854 2344 f^{2014} (Bousset Charles)

The accusative corresponds to the Apocalypse's attested linguistic style (with the exception of 12:1). It should thus be considered the *Urtext*.

14:16 (ο καθημενος) επι της νεφελης A S 1611 f^{1678} al. pc.
    επι την νεφελην C Αν (WHort$^{mg.}$ Bousset)
    επι τη νεφελη K, dub. P^{47}

The C-Αν reading corresponds to other instances of the Apocalypse's linguistic style.

The idea that the genitive is preserved here because ειδον no longer exerts influence (Weiss) is implausible.

14:18 om. εξηλθεν A P^{47} Oec 1611 al. pc. ([WHort]) against C S Αν K

The omission must belong to the older text, and C and S made a correction, since A P^{47} Oec could not have the same mistake by coincidence.

14:18 φωνη A S* f^{1006} f^{1678} 2053 (most modern editions)
    κραυγη C P^{47} Αν K 1611 1854 2329 (Sod Vog)

[106] A convincing argument for the authenticity of one of these readings can hardly be identified. Most modern critical editions prefer φωνη because it corresponds to similar formulations in the Apocalypse. But even this detail renders the reading suspicious, whereas parallel influences cannot explain the presence κραυγη. We should nonetheless note that εκραξε φωνη μεγαλη is always used in other locations (6:10; 7:2, 10; 10:3; 14:15; 18:2; 19:17), whereas εφωνησε φωνη (or κραυγη) μεγαλη occurs here. The argument that an original εφωνησε φωνη was changed into εφωνησε κραυγη to avoid repetition (Weiss),[152] however, is less obvious than the argument that a secondary φωνη goes back to the influence of 14:15 (Sod).[153]

15:3 εθνων A Αν K
    αιωνων C P^{47} S* f^{1006} 1611 94 1778$^{txt.}$ Sah.$^{2/3}$ Syr.$^{1.2}$ Vulg. (WHort$^{txt.}$) Charles$^{mg.}$)

The authenticity of εθνων is certain in 15:3, as is the fact that the agreement between C and P^{47} S cannot be coincidental.

---

152. Weiss, *Die Johannes-Apokalypse*, 61.
153. The correction of κραυγη into φωνη surfaces in Luke 1:42 in D K.

16:4   εγενετο C S Aν K
εγενοντο A P⁴⁷ f¹⁰⁰⁶ 1611 1854 2053 – 2062 2329 Sah. Boh.
Syr.¹·² (WHort^mg· Charles)

The obviously spurious text from A P⁴⁷ is due to a misunderstanding
of the meaning.

16:12   ανατολης C P⁴⁷ S K
ανατολων A Aν (WHort^mg· Weiss Charles^mg·)

ανατολης corresponds to the Apocalypse's linguistic style. A also has
the same correction in 7:2 (see above) and K in 21:13.

16:13   στοματος¹⌢² C
στοματος¹⌢³ S*

A coincidental agreement (a similar case is found in 10:6 above).

18:4   εξελθατε A S, εξελθετε Aν
εξελθε C K Oec 1611

A correction to remove the *constructio ad sensum*.

18:4   ο λαος μου εξ αυτης C S P f¹⁶⁷⁸
~ εξ αυτης ο λαος μου A K (WHort^mg· Charles^mg·)
εξ αυτης om. Aν^part·

The change in A K serves to improve the word order. C corrects the
text with K (εξελθε) in one part, while A corrects it with K (~ εξ αυτης ο
λαος μου) in another (i.e., they are both influenced by K in different clauses
of this verse). [107] S alone preserves the original text.

18:6   + τα ante διπλα C S K ([WHort] [Bousset], om. Charles)
The omission in A Aν is either a correction or a careless error.

18:8   om. κυριος A f¹⁰⁰⁶ Vulg. Aeth. ([WHort] [Bousset] Charles)
~ ο θεος ο κυριος S (a later addition?)

18:9   κλαυσουσι C Aν K
κλαυσονται A S f¹⁰⁰⁶ 2053 Hipp (Tisch WHort^mg· Sod Merk)

κλαυσονται is not a harmonization to the και κοψονται that follows
(Weiss) but a correction of the unusual future active tense.

18:9   επ αυτην C S K
        επ αυτη A Αν f[1006] 1611 2053 – 2062 2329 (WHort[mg.] Bousset
        Charles[txt.])
and again in 18:11:
        επ αυτην C S P 1854 f[336]
        εν αυτη A 2329 (likewise in 18:20 A 2030)
        επ αυτη K, εφ εαυτους Αν
C S preserve the original reading here every time.

18:10   μιᾷ ωρα] μιαν ωραν A Oec f[1006] 1611 (WHort[mg.])
18:17 and 18:19 demonstrate that A changes the text here.

18:14   om. τα[2] C S 1611 2053 – 2062 2329 al. pc.
The omission is a stylistic improvement.

18:16   εν χρυσ[ι]ω C S Αν
        εν om. A P K f[1006] 2053 – 2062 2329 ([WHort] [Bousset] Charles)

18:18   πολει] + ταυτη C 2329 Sah.[plur.] Boh. Latt.[(exc. Prim.)] Syr.[2] Arm. Arab.

18:19   εβαλαν C
        εβαλον S Αν K
        επεβαλον A 469 2429 (WHort[mg.] Charles[mg.])
        επεβαλλον f[1006] 2065 2432
The occurrence of the compound verb is due to the influence of the
επι τας κεφαλας that follows (analogous corrections include: 1:17 εθηκεν]
επεθηκεν S Αν; 2:5 πεπτωκας] εκπεπτωκας Αν).

18:20   om. και οι[1] C Αν Latt.
A misunderstanding.

18:22   om. πασης τεχνης A S Boh. ([WHort])

18:23   + φωνη ante νυμφης C 2329 Hipp Syr.[1] al. pc.
The addition is a correction in the form of a harmonization to the Old
Testament *Vorlage* Jer 25:10; 7:34; 16:9.
[108] 19:3   ειρηκαν A S Αν, ειρηκεν K
        ειπαν C, ειπον f[1678]
The same correction is found in 7:14 K.

19:5   om. και ante οι φοβουμενοι C S P Sah. contra A Aν K

Of the modern editions, Tisch WHort omit the word and Bousset Sod Merk place it in brackets. Only Weiss Vog Charles adopt it. It is unclear who the "Godfearers" are and how they relate to God's servants.

Where P departs from Aν, it agrees with the old text a few times, in particular with C; see

11:11   τους θεωρουντας] των θεωρουντων C P 2057 f^{2060}
14:13   κυριω] χριστω C P 792 1854
18:12   χρυσου ... αργυριου ... λιθου τιμιου ... μαργαριτου] χρυσουν ... αργυρουν ... λιθους τιμιους ... μαργαριτας C P

The readings are obvious errors in all of these cases. Also, Oecumenius's text, which usually belongs to the AC type, agrees with C against A several times; see

1:7   μετα] επι C Oec
2:14   om. οτι C Oec 1611 f^{1678} 1854
6:7   φωνην του τεταρτου ζωου] το τεταρτον ζωον C Oec
6:8   om. και^1 C 2053 (silet comm.)
11:18   καιρος] κληρος C Oec
12:4   αστερων] αστρων C Oec
18:12   om. εκ C 2053 – 2062 94 1611 792

None of these readings belong to the *Urtext*.

Occasionally Oec agrees with A against C; see

1:6   ημας] ημιν A 2053, ημων C
14:18   om. εξηλθεν A P^{47} 2053 al. pc.
18:10   μιᾷ ωρα] μιαν ωραν A Oec

Of the sections where C is missing and P agrees with A against Aν, the following variant should be mentioned:

4:4   om. εν ante ιματιοις A P f^{2014} f^{2031} f^{2065} 1854 (on the other hand, 3:5)

Despite the fact that WHort$^{txt.}$ and Charles regard this reading as the *Urtext*, it should certainly be rejected. Furthermore, this reading should not be attributed to AC's archetype since A deletes the instrumental εν in a few other places, something which AC do not do.

[109] The list above demonstrates that C does not provide a pure text of the AC Oec type. At least in some of C's readings, which are obvious corrections, the agreements with other text types should not to be understood as coincidental (see 6:17; 9:20; 11:5, 15; 12:2, 10 [bis]; 13:1, 17, 18; 14:14, 18; 15:3; 18:23; 19:3). The finding regarding A, however, differs from C.

Although a secondary set of readings in A (even more than in C) mars the AC archetype, none of A's readings are an obvious correction arising from the influence of another text.[154] For this reason, A must be considered the more valuable of the witnesses of the AC type. What is striking, however, is that A shares repeated errors with other text forms. S, in particular, agrees with A against C in obvious secondary readings.[155] The same is true of Aν, about which more will be said below.

2.4.2. The Text of P[47] S and Origen

Alongside the "neutral" text of AC, another "old text" is found in P[47] S, which differs from AC (Oec) with a considerable number of corrections.

For the evidence that P[47] S constitute a separate stem of the Apocalypse's textual tradition, it would be necessary, once again, to place all the passages where Aν and K share the same corrections with each other (that are not in AC P[47] S) beside the list of unique readings of AC and its textual allies. The text of P[47] S is initially defined negatively by the other stems in these two lists. This is because the two lists show that P[47] S do not have many corrections that are in Aν and K and that they have corrections in many places where AC likely bear witness to the *Urtext* [110] and usually agree with the later text forms Aν K. The following list of unique readings that P[47] S share positively describes and discloses the P[47] S stem in its distinctive features. Bousset was the first to recognize that Sinaiticus's text is closely related to Origen's.[156] It is possible for him "to almost say that the immediate textual foundation of S was identical to the *Vorlage* of Origen." As long as Codex Sinaiticus (a manuscript that was copied very carelessly and contains a plethora of unique readings,[157] as well as obvious

---

154. By the way, it is repeatedly observable in the list above that WHort and Charles explain, or at least take into account, readings that A almost alone provides against C rel. as the *Urtext* (see in 2:10 [εχητε]; 2:22; 3:7, 17; 6:4, 16; 11:3; 12:8; 13:5; 14:18; 16:4, 12; 18:4, 6, 8, 9, 10, 16). They not only regard AC as the authoritative text form, almost never to be betrayed, but they also consider A the authoritative witness of this text.

155. As a further, albeit insignificant example of this, 11:11 ημισυ] ημισου A S* (likewise 12:14 P[47] S) should be mentioned.

156. Bousset, *Die Offenbarung Johannis*, 157–58.

157. S's text is teeming not only with harmless orthographic violations but also with all kinds of other careless errors. Weiss (*Die Johannes-Apokalypse*, 90) counts 515 (in 405 verses for the entire Apocalypse); Charles only counts 472. I do not give the

mixed readings)[158] was the only complete witness of this text type, it was impossible to identify the text type accurately. This was due to the fact that no stable criterion was available to distinguish between unique readings stemming from the scribe of Codex S (or perhaps its immediate *Vorlage*) and readings that are earlier. The number of verses where Origen's text can be placed alongside S is not very high. There are only enough to allow us to recognize the close relationship between his text and the text of S. With the text of P[47], however, we acquire a new witness to this text, which controls assumptions about the character of Codex S by comparison to the extant text of P[47].

Apart from minor lacunae from the loss of some lines, P[47] preserves the text of Rev 9:10–17:2. P[47] also contains many errors and idiosyncratic corrections but is still significantly better than S in its scribal performance.[159] Furthermore, P[47] was transcribed at a time when Origen was probably still alive. P[47] and S provide controls for each other, just like A and C, and make it possible to distinguish which readings belong to the P[47] S text type, which readings S takes over from another [III] text,[160] and which readings stem from the scribe's own arbitrariness or carelessness. P[47]'s unique readings, as far as they are not insignificant scribal errors, are listed in my "Der Apokalypsetext des Chester Beatty 𝔓[47]," 81–86. The list below provides a compilation of readings that P[47] S share with one another against the remaining major stems of the Apocalypse's tradition: AC, Aν, and K.

9:11   ονομα αυτω A (hiat C) Aν K
          ω ονομα P[47] 94 2344
          ω ονομα αυτω S

---

exact number here, since only a general characteristic of the text needs to be provided. Since the discovery of P[47] and of minuscules with an "old" text, the number of unique readings (listed in Weiss and Charles) has decreased, but the characteristics of this text as a whole have not changed.

158. All researchers who have dealt closely with the Apocalypse's text agree that S is the least reliable of the old majuscules. See the judgment of Westcott and Hort, *New Testament in the Original Greek*, 2:206–7; Weiss, *Die Johannes-Apokalypse*, 148–49; Bousset, *Textkritische Studien*, 157; von Soden, *Die Schriften des Neuen Testaments*, 1:2067–68; Charles, *Critical and Exegetical Commentary on the Revelation*, 1:clxxii, also clx–clxvi.

159. See also Josef Schmid, "Der Apokalypsetext des Chester Beatty 𝔓[47]," *BNJ* 11 (1934–1935): 81–108.

160. S has long been recognized as a mixed text.

9:11   ~ εχει ονομα P⁴⁷ S 582 2019 2344

9:12   η ουαι η μια] om. η¹ P⁴⁷ S 1678 – 1778 2023

9:13   om. και¹ P⁴⁷ S Q 61 – 69 2344 al. pc. Sah. Boh. Syr.¹

9:16   δισμυριαδες] δυο μυριαδες (-ας S) P⁴⁷ S f²⁰¹⁴

9:17   επ] επανω P⁴⁷ S

9:20   + αυτων ante ταυταις P⁴⁷ S

       ουδε ante μετενοησαν P⁴⁷ S Q 61 – 69 f¹⁶⁷⁸ 2053 (Tisch WHortᵐᵍ·²
       Weiss Charlesᵗˣᵗ·)

       ουτε A Αν 1611 2329 (WHortᵐᵍ·¹ Sod Vog)

       ου C K (WHortᵗˣᵗ· Merk)

       χρυσα] χρυσεα P⁴⁷ S 2351

       χαλκα] χαλκεα P⁴⁷ S

10:4   οτε] οσα P⁴⁷ S f²⁰¹⁴ Boh. Gig. Prim. Tyc.¹

       α] οσα P⁴⁷ S 2344 Syr.²

10:7   ~ του αγγελου του εβδομου P⁴⁷ S 2344

       + και ante τους προφητας P⁴⁷ S 2329 2344

10:9   βιβλαριδιον] βιβλιον P⁴⁷ S f¹⁰⁰⁶ f¹⁶⁷⁸ 1854 2053

       ~ λαβε αυτο και καταφαγε P⁴⁷ S 2344

11:2   εδοθη] + και P⁴⁷ S*

11:5   ~ αδικησαι αυτους² P⁴⁷ S

11:7   + τοτε ante το θηριον P⁴⁷ 2344 Sah. Boh.ᶜᵒᵈᵈ·

       + τοτε post θηριον et om. το² S*

11:8   om. αυτων P⁴⁷ S* 367

11:10 ~ οι προφηται οι δυο P⁴⁷ S 2344 (see 10:7 above)

11:14 ~ ερχεται η ουαι η τριτη P⁴⁷ S 2019 2344
       (harmonization to 9:12; see also 10:7; 11:10 above)

11:17 κυριε] ο κυριος P⁴⁷

       κυριος S

[112] 11:18 ωργισθησαν] ωργισθη (with neuter plural) P⁴⁷ S

12:9   ο δρακων ο μεγας, ο οφις AC rel. plur.

       ο δρακων   ο οφις ο μεγας P⁴⁷ f¹⁰⁰⁶ f²⁰²⁷ S

       ο δρακων, ο μεγας οφις S f²⁸⁴¹ 2081 Sah. Prim.

13:8   οὗ … αυτου (A)C 2053 2344 (f¹⁶⁷⁸)

       ὧν … αυτων P⁴⁷ S f¹⁰⁰⁶ f²⁰⁶⁰

       ὧν Αν K

       τω βιβλιω] τη [om. S] βιβλω P⁴⁷ S 1611 1854 f²⁰⁶¹ 2019 2026

14:8   om. αγγελος P⁴⁷ S* 792 f¹⁰⁰⁶ 1854 2344

14:13 om. ναι P⁴⁷ S* f³³⁶ Boh. Vulg.

14:14 εχων] εχοντα P⁴⁷ S* f¹⁰⁰⁶ f¹⁶⁷⁸ f²⁰¹⁴ al. pc.

15:2   om. εκ² P⁴⁷ S 2329 *f*¹⁰⁴/³³⁶

15:3   εθνων] αιωνων P⁴⁷ S* C *f*¹⁰⁰⁶ 1611 94 2344 Sah.¹/³ Syr.¹·² Vulg.
       Ps.-Ambr.

15:4   τις] + σε P⁴⁷ S *f*¹⁰⁰⁶ *f*¹⁶⁷⁸ 1854 2329
           (+ σε post φοβηθη K [Bousset])

15:6   om. οι ante εχοντες P⁴⁷ S P 2595 1854 *f*²⁰¹⁴ *f*²⁰⁵¹ 2053 – 2062

16:2   ~ πονηρον και κακον P⁴⁷ S* *f*¹⁶⁷⁸
       ~ πονηρον κακον Sah.¹/³

16:4   εις] επι P⁴⁷ S* 94 792 2042

16:13 ως βατραχοι] ωσει βατραχους P⁴⁷ S*

Thirty-six times P⁴⁷ S agree with one another against AC, Aν, and K. The number of places would increase to around 110 if P⁴⁷ were preserved completely. The number is much smaller than that of the unique readings of Aν and K but (importantly) surpasses the number of readings in AC. With this, the text of P⁴⁷ S emerges as a separate stem within the Apocalypse's textual tradition. In only one place (9:20 ουδε) does the P⁴⁷ S stem preserve the *Urtext*. The majority of the readings presented above do not consist of errors but of conscious corrections. This text thus differs significantly from the mainly "neutral" text of AC Oec. On the other hand, this text does not display the same deliberate linguistic improvements we find in Aν and K. The P⁴⁷ S text form can only be established with precision for that part of the Apocalypse's text that is extant in P⁴⁷. For the rest (about two-thirds of the whole text), we only have S as a witness—a witness whose unreliability is evident compared to P⁴⁷. Origen's citations from the missing chapters in P⁴⁷ only allow for comparison with some verses. But it is clear from the data above [113] that P⁴⁷ S is accompanied by a group of minuscules (which fluctuates minimally, namely, *f*¹⁰⁰⁶, 2344, often also *f*¹⁶⁷⁸, 1611, and 1854), as well as by the two Coptic versions. These second- and third-tier witnesses appear to offer the possibility of establishing the "Origen text" in those parts of the text that are lost in P⁴⁷. This promising path, at least as it initially seems, becomes problematic because the aforementioned minuscules and versions also often agree with S when it provides a revised text and departs from the text of P⁴⁷.[161] In these cases, it is always important to observe that those minuscules partly agree with P⁴⁷ and partly with S. In such instances, the common readings between the

---

161. See the collection of readings in Schmid, "Der Apokalypsetext des Chester Beatty 𝔓⁴⁷," 94–97.

minuscules and P⁴⁷ are less conclusive because they represent the *Urtext* almost without exception. We can draw two conclusions from this finding:

(1) In places where P⁴⁷ is missing, the unique readings of S with their textual allies partly represent the P⁴⁷ S type. There is, however, no reliable criterion for distinguishing between the readings that represent the P⁴⁷-S text and those that represent a later layer in S.

(2) Since we cannot assume that the minuscules related to S and the Coptic versions all depend upon the one majuscule S, their relationship with S against P⁴⁷ means that a large part of S's corrections were not simply created by the scribe of this manuscript. This text—a later stage of the development of the P⁴⁷ S type—must have enjoyed a wide manuscript dissemination. The text of the aforementioned minuscules and the Coptic versions go back to this later stage.

We return again to the older stage of this text, as far as we can establish it through the common witness of P⁴⁷ and S. The previously listed corrections are not the only deviations of this text form from the *Urtext*. There are, in addition, three more groups of readings, those in which: (1) P⁴⁷ S have common readings with the two later recensions Aν and K, (2) P⁴⁷ shares readings with AC (or AC K or AC Aν), or (3) S shares readings with AC (or AC K or AC Aν).

(1) The first of these three groups comprises all those places where AC alone stands opposite the rest of the text forms; [114] their list is thus identical to that of AC's unique readings.¹⁶²

Only the following few places are to be mentioned:

10:1   την κεφαλην AC
      της κεφαλης P⁴⁷ S Aν K
11:19 om. ο post θεου P⁴⁷ S Aν K
12:5   αρσεν AC
      αρρενα P⁴⁷ S K, αρσενα Aν
12:7   om. του ante πολεμησαι P⁴⁷ S Aν K
13:8   οὔ] ὧν P⁴⁷ S Aν K
14:18 om. ο ante εχων P⁴⁷ S Aν K
16:3   ζωης] ζωσα P⁴⁷ S Aν, om. K

---

162. See pp. 89–101.

The degree to which we have the original form of the P[47] S type before us must remain an open question where S is the only ancient witness for this text form.[163]

Since P[47] goes against S with AC in some places and usually preserves the *Urtext* in those cases,[164] the same situation should be assumed for the nonextant portions of P[47]. The details of this first group of readings from P[47] S are of great importance. The remaining Greek textual tradition stands opposite to the "neutral" text in a number of places with a text that is clearly secondary. From this secondary text, it is possible to isolate the foundation for Aν and K (=Aν K) in a number of other places. The Aν and K recensions were produced[165] by means of comprehensive editing in this third stage of the text.

---

163. P[47]'s incompleteness represents an unfillable lacuna for the study because of the heavily revised and wild character of S's text. C's incompleteness is much easier to bear. For one thing, the relationship between A and C is much closer than the relationship between P[47] and S. Moreover, A, the most valuable witness of the AC type, is extant in its entirety, while the situation is reversed in the P[47] S type.

164. See Schmid, "Der Apokalypsetext des Chester Beatty 𝔓[47]," 94–97.

165. P[47] S preserve the *Urtext* against the rest of the tradition only in 9:20 (ουδε). P[47] never preserves the *Urtext* by itself, and S alone preserves the *Urtext* in 2:5 (πεπτωκες); 9:3–4 (αυτοις); 9:7 (ομοιοι); 18:12 (μαργαριτων); 19:20 (μετ αυτου ο ψευδοπροφητης); and probably also 22:11 (ρυπανθητω). See also p. 114 in 18:4. P[47] is lacunose in all these places. 19:13 needs a more detailed discussion, where the text tradition is as follows:

βεβαμμενον A (hiat C) Aν K Sah. Syr.[1] (and most modern editions)
περιρεραμμενον S* (Tisch) περιρερανισμενον S[a]
ρεραντισμενον P 2019 2329 Hipp Orig. (WHort[txt.] Charles[mg.])
ρεραμμενον 1611
ερραντισμενον f[1006] 792 1678 – 1778[mg.] 2053 f[2065] f[172] Ir. Latt.[omn.] Boh. Syr.[2]
    Arm.[2.3] Aeth.

The testimony of S's reading is, if one disregards only the substantial and important differences in word form in the second line (either from ραινω or from ραντιζω), very strong in spite of the counterweight of A Aν K Sah. Syr.[1], since also Boh. Latt. have it—traditions that otherwise agree with AC Oecumenius and the two oldest Greek Fathers, Hippolytus, and Origen. The value of the Latin version of Irenaeus is diminished in that all Latin forms have the same reading. Westcott and Hort (*New Testament in the Original Greek*, 2:139–40) also advance the connection in favor of the second reading. Apart from the fact that ρεραμμενον is the worst attested form, it is clear that ρεραμμενον is not simply a scribal error for βεβαμμενον (Bousset) because Mark 7:4 also shows that the tradition varies between βαπτισωνται and ραντισωνται, where ραντισωνται has the stronger claim to authenticity. Contrary to Charles's claim,

[115] (2) P⁴⁷ S agrees with Aν against AC K in the following places:

11:2   om. και post τεσσαρακοντα

11:8   το πτωμα] τα πτωματα (likewise 11:9 Aν)
       om. και$^{ult.}$ P⁴⁷ Sᵃ Aν

11:12 φωνην μεγαλην … λεγουσαν] -ης P⁴⁷ S C Aν (likewise all modern
       editions except Tisch WHort$^{txt.}$ Bousset 1st loco Charles$^{txt.}$)

12:8   ισχυσεν] -σαν P⁴⁷ S C Aν (see also p. 110)

13:1   ονοματα] ονομα P⁴⁷ S C Aν (see also p. 111)

13:8   το ονομα] τα ονοματα (likewise 17:8 S Aν)

15:7   om. ἐν

16:3   ζωης] ζωσα (om. K)

16:14 α εκπορευεται] εκπορευεσθαι

(3) There are only a few readings that P⁴⁷ S share with K:

10:6   om. εν ante τω ζωντι (haplography; likewise 11:11 C Aν^{part}; see
       p. 108)

11:2   εξωθεν²] εξω P⁴⁷ K (Weiss), εσω S*
       εσω in S is a harmonization to εσωθεν in place of εξωθεν¹, but
       it presupposes the reading of P⁴⁷ K. Therefore, this reading is
       classified here.

11:11 εν αυτοις A Aν$^{part.}$ (om. εν C Aν$^{rel.}$)
       εις αυτους P⁴⁷ S K
       επεπεσεν] επεσεν (Sod)

11:19 αυτου¹] του κυριου P⁴⁷ K
                 του θεου S
       S's correction presupposes the text of P⁴⁷ K once again.

[116] 12:5 αρσεν] αρρενα (αρσενα Aν)

12:14 om. αι ante δυο

14:3   om. ως ante ωδην¹ (Tisch Weiss [Sod])

14:5   αμωμοι] + γαρ (Tisch [Bousset] Charles$^{txt.}$)
       γαρ is added to establish the relationship between the two sen-
       tences (see 14:4).

14:7   + την ante θαλασσαν P⁴⁷ S K Aν ^{part} (Tisch [Bousset]) See also p.
       96.

15:4   τις] + σε P⁴⁷ S
       + σε post φοβηθη K

Isa 63:3 did not influence the text's development. Just which reading is the *Urtext*
remains unclear.

C also goes with P⁴⁷ S in two passages:

9:21   φαρμακειων] -κων

12:3   ~ πυρρος μεγας

See further 11:16 (p. 109)

These readings are corrections, almost without exception.

We will now examine the passages where P⁴⁷ and S diverge and correspond to various other text types.[166]

P⁴⁷ goes with C a few times.

10:4   om. επτα² C P⁴⁷ Sah.^{1/3} Gig.

12:17   om. επι C P⁴⁷ Sah. Boh.^{pc.} Prim.

13:15   θηριου¹⌒³ C P⁴⁷ 2053

14:14   υιον] υιω C P⁴⁷ Aν

14:18   φωνη] κραυγη C P⁴⁷ Aν K 792 1611 1854 2329 Boh. Syr.²

Only the last two readings are remarkable. Of these, 14:14 is an obvious correction of a serious grammatical violation, and 14:18 is probably the *Urtext* (see already p. 113).

P⁴⁷ shares the following readings with Aν against AC S (K):

9:14   (φωνην) λεγοντα] λεγουσαν

9:18   + εκ ante του καπνου et ante του θειου (+ εκ ante του καπνου C 2053)

11:7   ~ πολεμον μετ αυτων (see 12:17; 13:7; 19:19)

11:8   om. και post οπου P⁴⁷ Aν Sᵃ

11:12   ηκουσαν] -σα P⁴⁷ Sᵃ Aν K (Sod)

       The error should not be explained from the distant influence of 14:13 (Weiss)[167] but is caused by the seer repeatedly speaking what he heard.

12:13   αρσενα] αρρενα

       [117] The same correction in P⁴⁷ S K occurs in 12:5 (see p. 123).

13:2   om. ην

13:7   om. και λαον

13:16   το μετωπον] των μετωπων

14:1   om. το ante αρνιον

       εστος] εστως (a simple scribal error, hardly the *Urtext*)

14:2   η φωνη ην] φωνην

---

166. The unique readings of P⁴⁷ and of S are disregarded.

167. Weiss, *Die Johannes-Apokalypse*, 126.

16:14   om. τον ante πολεμον

16:15   (ινα) βλεπωσι] βλεπουσι

This reading is an error because the present indicative is anomalous after ινα in the Apocalypse (the same error in 12:6 C S, dub. P⁴⁷). The error appears to stem from a misunderstanding of the sentence construction.

16:18   ουτω] ουτως

See the correction above in 14:14 υιον] υιω C P⁴⁷ Aν.

Despite the fact that almost all of these readings consist of corrections (which have their analogies in the purely unique readings of P⁴⁷ and Aν), the agreement of P⁴⁷ and Aν cannot be understood as coincidental in every case. See 11:12 especially. Also, the number of P⁴⁷-Aν readings exceeds that of the common errors or corrections of P⁴⁷ S Aν.

The number of readings P⁴⁷ shares with K against S AC Aν is approximately the same.

9:20   δυνανται] δυναται (neuter plural)

10:2   βιβλαριδιον] βιβλιον P⁴⁷vid. (likewise 10:9 P⁴⁷ S)

10:8   ηνεωγμενον] ανεωγμενον (against 10:2)

(11:6   om. εν ante παση P⁴⁷ Q al. pc., non K; likewise 14:15 P⁴⁷ 2329)

12:9   om. ο ante σατανας (likewise 20:2 Aν)

12:12   την γην και την θαλασσαν] τη γη και τη θαλασση (the same correction occurs in 8:13 A [hiat C] Aν)

13:13   εις] επι

13:16   χαραγμα] χαραγματα

15:8   + εκ του ante καπνου (see 9:18 above in P⁴⁷ A)

16:5   ο ην και ο οσιος] και ος ην και [om. K] οσιος

16:18   ~ αστραπαι και βρονται και φωναι

Because P⁴⁷ preserves only about a third of the Apocalypse's text, the number of unique readings of P⁴⁷ Aν and P⁴⁷ K would increase if P⁴⁷ were complete. In this review, we acquire a number of readings attested in the later recensions, Aν and K, that should not be ignored. P⁴⁷'s testimony makes clear that these readings reach into the third century and—barring some [118] chance occurrence—must have already been recovered by the two recensions. Accordingly the number of purely unique readings of Aν and K would be diminished. However, if the agreement of P⁴⁷ Aν and P⁴⁷ K is not accidental—in at least a portion of the readings presented—then S regularly preserves the *Urtext*. If this is the case, then the question must be posed from those places where S has the better, original text. Since it will become clear below that S is a patently identifiable mixed text, it is natural to assume that S once again eliminates the erroneous readings presented above. But this is not the only possibility. The text represented by P⁴⁷ S must not have been a strictly self-contained unit, as the "neutral" appears to be, whose representatives have come down to us coincidentally and no longer give us a true picture of the differences that may have existed between the different witnesses of this text form at one time.¹⁶⁸ S could therefore have preserved the original reading in some places, where the branch of this text type represented by P⁴⁷ was influenced by another text. The idea that the various, distinguishable text forms of the Apocalypse's tradition were somehow hermetically sealed off from each other and that they only experienced cross-pollination in their subsequent history (as von Soden appears to accept) is as unlikely or as impossible in the Apocalypse as in any other New Testament book.

We must turn our attention now to those places where P⁴⁷ and S diverge and where S provides a secondary text. We will disregard the many idiosyncratic corrections and errors that S alone (or accompanied by a few minuscules) preserves. Only those variants that S shares either with Aν K against AC P⁴⁷ or with Aν or finally with K alone will be mentioned.

(1) AC P⁴⁷ against S Aν K:

   11:6   + την ante εξουσιαν¹ AC P⁴⁷ P 1611 1841 f^{1678} 2053 2351 Syr.¹
          om. S Aν K (Tisch Bousset)
          [119] Although εξουσιαν εχειν, δουναι, and so on followed by the infinitive otherwise always surfaces without the article, the article must be original here because its subsequent omission is easy to understand. The same is not true for a later addition.

   13:10 μαχαιρη to AC P⁴⁷ 2351
          μαχαιρα S Aν K

   (13:14 μαχαιρης AC S, dub. P⁴⁷)

   16:12 τον ευφρατην AC P⁴⁷ f^{1006} 1611 2329 $f^{172/250}$ f^{2014} ([WHort] Sod [Charles])
          om. τον S Aν K (Tisch Weiss Bousset Vog Merk)
          We cannot be certain which reading is original here. The fact that the article is otherwise missing not only for proper names in general but especially in the same phrase in 9:14 (as here in

---

168. We surely have to think of both text forms, the "neutral" and P⁴⁷ S Orig., as local texts, not as actual recensions. See this distinction in B. H. Streeter, "The Four Gospels: A Study of Origins," *JTS* 26 (1925): 374–75.

16:12) speaks against its authenticity. But in favor of its authenticity are the following: the weightiest witnesses preserve it, and its subsequent omission in the most fully edited text forms can probably be explained, whereas its subsequent addition cannot.[169]

The yield is practically zero here because the correction μαχαιρα in 13:10 requires no explanation and because it is clear that there are no obvious traces of another text's influence in the other two places in S (assuming P[47] actually has the *Urtext*).

P[47] agrees with A alone versus all others at a few places:

10:9   απηλθα A P[47] (*Urtext*)
        απηλθον C S Aν K

11:18   τοις φοβουμενοις] τους φοβουμενους A P[47], harmonized toward
        τους μικρους και τους μεγαλους AC P[47] S*

14:18   om. εξηλθεν A P[47] al. pc. (error)
        habent C S Aν K (see p. 113)

16:4   εγενοντο A P[47] min. pc. (error)
        εγενετο C S Aν K See also p. 114

16:14   της μεγαλης ημερας A (hiat C) P[47] f[1006] 1611
        της ημερας της μεγαλης S 61 – 69 f[1678] 2053 2329 (and all modern editions)
        της ημερας εκεινης της μεγαλης Aν K (Sod[txt.])

[120] There is an obvious correction again at 10:9 in C S Aν K. S has the better text in 11:18; 14:18; 16:4, 14. P[47] has an error with A.[170]

(2) AC P[47] K against S Aν:

11:2   εξωθεν[1]] εσωθεν S Aν[part.] f[172/250] 2329 Syr.[1]

11:11   om. τας ante τρεις S Aν 1854 (Tisch [WHort])
        The authenticity of τας should not be doubted because "the anaphoric article corresponds to the Apocalypse's linguistic style."[171]

13:8   αυτον] αυτω S Aν

13:13   ~ καταβαινειν εκ του ουρανου S Aν (Tisch)

14:20   εξωθεν] εξω S Aν (see p. 123, 11:2)

---

169. The addition of την before ιεζαβελ in 2:20 in A (against C), to which Weiss (*Die Johannes-Apokalypse*, 97) refers as an analogy, is not really a conclusive parallel.

170. The reverse case: A S contra P[47] C Aν K surfaces only twice: 9:21 πορνειας] πονηριας A S*; 11:16 om. οι ante εικοσι A S. Both are obvious errors.

171. Bousset; likewise Weiss, *Die Johannes-Apokalypse*, 125.

16:5   + ο ante οσιος S Aν Oec (likewise, correctly, all modern editions
        except [WHort] and Charles)
        και ος ην και οσιος P⁴⁷ presupposes the absence of the article
        before οσιος.

16:8   τεταρτος] + αγγελος S Aν
        Aν consistently adds αγγελος in the second to seventh angels.
        K adds it in the second. And only *f*¹⁷²/²⁵⁰ and some late groups
        added it in the first.

All of these readings are clear corrections with the exception of 16:5.

3. AC P⁴⁷ Aν against S K:

   10:10   βιβλαριδιον] βιβλιον S K, βιβλιδιον P⁴⁷
   11:16   + οἳ ante καθηνται S* K (Tisch Bousset varia lectio Sod) (see p.
           109)
   12:10   αυτων S K C (*Urtext*)
           αυτους A P⁴⁷ Aν (see p. 110)
   13:3   εθαυμασθη (P⁴⁷ᵛⁱᵈ·)] εθαυμασεν S K (Tisch Sod Vog Merk)
           This reading is a correction despite 17:6–7 (see the analogous
           correction in S Aν K in 17:8).
   13:7   και εδοθη¹⌒² AC P⁴⁷ Aν contra S K
   13:14   (θηριω) ος] ο S K
           την πληγην] πληγην K
                      πληγης S
   15:4   δοξασει] -ση S K (Sod)
           δοξαση is harmonization to the preceding φοβηθη.

Of these places, 13:7 is by far the most important; [121] S K alone preserve the *Urtext* there. However, if the agreement of AC P⁴⁷ and Aν in the
omission of a whole sentence is not a coincidence, then S cannot provide
the original form of the P⁴⁷ S type here against P⁴⁷. S must have made a
correction in the direction of K. Also, the rest of the common readings of
P⁴⁷ K (except 13:14) can hardly be coincidental. This is far more likely at
least in the few unique readings of S Aν.

When we survey the facts stated in their details regarding the P⁴⁷ S
type, we come to the following results:

(1) A sufficient number of unique readings demonstrate the existence
of this text type.

(2) Although the two witnesses of this text are older than the rest of
the Apocalypse's extant Greek manuscripts, the text itself, quite obviously,

contains many corrections and is further away from the original than the text of AC Oec as a consequence. In some places, P⁴⁷ S have common corrections with the later text forms Aν and K: seven times with Aν K together, ten times with Aν, and eleven times with K.

(3) The two manuscripts repeatedly diverge and combine with several of the other text forms as expected. But the number of these readings is small compared to the length of the sections of text preserved in P⁴⁷ and S:

P⁴⁷ Aν 14 times

P⁴⁷ K 10 times

P⁴⁷ AC against S Aν K 3 times

P⁴⁷ A against C S Aν K 5 times

P⁴⁷ AC K against S Aν 6 times

P⁴⁷ AC Aν against S K 7 times

Although these different groupings cannot be explained as simply coincidental, the extensive unity of the tradition of P⁴⁷ S emerges from the small number of locations. In the vast majority of places where the two manuscripts diverge, one of them, usually S, has a unique reading.

We must now examine the relationship between S and the two later text forms, Aν and K, for the Apocalypse's entire text. In this respect, we must establish [122] how the total number of these readings (S Aν and S K) relates to the number of readings that P⁴⁷ S share with Aν and K, as well as to the number of the readings that S shares with Aν or K against P⁴⁷. Our assessment of the character of S's text depends upon this result.

First, the S-Aν readings:

1:7   οψεται] οψονται S Aν 2351 Sah. Boh. Syr.¹˒² Arm.⁴ Vict.

οψονται is a harmonization with the following κοψονται.

1:8   ω] + αρχη και τελος S* Aν 1854 2050 2351 ƒ¹⁷²/²⁵⁰ Boh. Gig.

+ η αρχη και το τελος ƒ²⁰¹⁴ 2329 al. pc. (see 21:6; 22:13)

1:17   εθηκεν] επεθηκεν S Aν 2050 2329 Compl.

1:20   ~ αι επτα λυχνιαι Aν 1611 1854 2053 – 2062 2329 2351 Compl. ƒ¹⁷²/²⁵⁰

επτα λυχνιαι S

2:15   + των ante Νικολαιτων S Aν (likewise all modern editions except WHort Bousset Charles)

As Weiss notes, 2:6 appears to guarantee the article.[172] To argue that the omission is a thoughtless harmonization to 2:14

---

172. Ibid., 135.

την διδαχην Βαλααμ, however, is unconvincing. See again p. 202.

2:16   om. ουν S Aν 2053 – 2062 2329 2351 Compl. Syr.[2] Latt. (Tisch [Bousset])

The omission is possibly a purely thoughtless error (influenced by μετανοησον).[173]

2:20   σου] + πολυ S Aν 2050 Syr.[1] Gig.[174]

(2:21   om. και ου θελει μετανοησαι [homoioteleuton] S* Aν)

The words are missing in most Aν witnesses. The commentary, however, shows that it belongs to the Aν tradition.

2:24   βαθεα] βαθη S Aν 2050 2053 2329

3:2   στηρισον] στηριξον S Aν Q al. pc.

3:7   και κλειων S Aν, και om. A

κλειων] κλειει C, K others (S Aν Urtext)

3:19   ζηλευε] ζηλωσον S Aν 0169[c] 2053

This is the usual New Testament form and is simultaneously a harmonization to the following aorist imperative.

[123]   4:9   (οταν) δωσουσιν A (hiat C)

δωσωσιν S Aν (Bousset)

δωσιν K

Bousset explains the S Aν reading as the Urtext because the subjunctive always accompanies οταν in the Apocalypse. On the other hand, see p. 230.

4:10   βαλουσι] βαλλουσι S* Aν

4:11   ο κυριος και] κυριε Aν

κυριε ο κυριος S (a mixed reading)

5:4   om. εγω S Aν (hiant AC) contra K (likewise Tisch [WHort] Weiss Sod Charles against Bousset Vog Merk)

The omission of εγω[1] in K 3:9 and 21:6 speaks for its authenticity.

5:6   απεσταλμενοι] τα [om. S] απεσταλμενα S Aν

5:10   βασιλευσουσι S Aν (Urtext)

βασιλευουσι A (hiat C) K (WHort Charles[txt.])

The same error occurs also in A 20:6.

---

173. Ibid., 126.

174. Of the modern editions, von Soden appears to regard πολυ as original. See von Soden, Die Schriften des Neuen Testaments, 1:2081 and the apparatus at the location, which presupposes that it is in the text. But this is missing in the main text, apparently by mistake.

5:13 (τω καθημενω επι) τω θρονω] του θρονου S Αν
      This reading contradicts the Apocalypse's linguistic style.
6:9   + των ανθρωπων ante των εσφαγμενων S Αν
7:1   παν S Αν (WHort[txt.])
      τι C K, om. A 1611 2329
      See also p. 106.
8:7   μεμιγμενα] -ον S Αν (Tisch)
      A misguided correction: the neuter plural occurs here because
      the participle refers to two nouns of different gender.
8:11 om. ο ante αψινθος Αν
      αψινθιον sine articulum S*

The following passages where P[47]'s text is lacunose (from 9:10 to 17:2;
see above) should be mentioned.
10:8 βιβλαριδιον S Αν[plur.] (Tisch Bousset Sod Vog)
      βιβλιδαριον K Αν[part.], βιβλιον AC
      It is not possible to tell whether βιβλαριδιον or βιβλιδαριον is the
      original Αν reading (see p. 241) here, as well as in 10:2.
13:8 αυτον] αυτω S Αν
13:15 εαν] αν S Αν (dub. P[47], hiat C) (likewise 3:19 S; 11:6 C)
16:1 ~ φωνης μεγαλης S Αν (Bousset)
      The reading corresponds to the Apocalypse's fixed word order
      in this expression. [124] Thus one must consider it (with Weiss)[175]
      a secondary harmonization to the usual word order.[176]
17:4 χρυσιω] χρυσω S Αν (likewise Tisch WHort[mg.] Sod Charles[mg.])
      in a way similar to
18:16 χρυσιω] χρυσω S Αν (likewise Tisch WHort[mg.])
      (In contrast, 9:7 χρυσω all, 18:12 almost all; on the other hand,
      3:18; 21:18, 21, all of which read χρυσιον.)
      Only the weight of the witnesses, rather than the author's lin-
      guistic style, can tip the scales here because the author uses[177]
      both forms indiscriminately, side by side.[178]

---

175. Weiss, *Die Johannes-Apokalypse*, 126.

176. Also, μεγαλη is always in front of πολις without exception in the reading of 18:21 (η μεγαλη πολις).

177. The juxtaposition of 18:12 and 17:4 with 18:16 rebuts Weiss's overly confident distinction (*Die Johannes-Apokalypse*, 123).

178. Likewise as το βιβλιον (thus usually) and η βιβλος (3:5; 20:15).

17:7	~ σοι ερω S Aν (Tisch WHort^{mg.} Sod Charles^{mg.})

The reading should be rejected because, as Bousset noted, σοι always occurs after the verb in the Apocalypse.

17:8	το ονομα] τα ονοματα S Aν (likewise 13:8 P⁴⁷ S Aν; analogue 13:16 χαραγματα K, 11:8

το πτωμα] τα πτωματα P⁴⁷ S Aν)

17:13	+ την ante εξουσιαν S Aν (Tisch WHort^{txt.} Bousset Sod [Merk] against WHort^{txt.} Weiss Vog Charles)

Examples of the article's repetition and nonrepetition are cited in lists below (see p. 205). Here we cannot make a clear decision. The article before εξουσιαν, however, is probably spurious because δυναμις and εξουσια form a hendiadys in 17:13.

19:5	απο] εκ S Aν (Tisch)

Although απο otherwise repeatedly replaces εκ, here εκ is "simply the preposition conformed into the verbum compositum."[179]

19:6	om. κυριος Aν sol.

~ ο θεος ο κυριος S*

The reading is likely a later addition; see 19:11 p. 137 in S K.

19:9	om. του γαμου S* Aν (a careless error)

~ εισι του θεου S* Aν (a correction)

19:20	μετ αυτου [μετα τουτου Aν] ο ψευδοπροφητης S Aν (*Urtext*)

οι μετ αυτου, ο ψευδοπροφητης A (an error)

ο μετ αυτου ψευδοπροφητης K (a correction)

[125] 20:3	~ αυτον λυθηναι S Aν (Tisch Bousset Sod)

The same simplification of word order occurs in 17:8 K.

20:8	+ και ante συναγαγειν S Aν Aρ (a correction)

20:9	εκυκλευσαν] εκυκλωσαν S Aν

The reading is the more common word.[180]

20:10	om. και post οπου S Aν

Analogous to 11:8 P⁴⁷ Aν Sᵃ.

21:3	μετ αυτων εσται αυτων θεος A (hiat C) 2053 2329 Syr.^{1.2} Vulg. (WHort^{mg.} Weiss)

μετ αυτων εσται K (WHort^{txt.} Vog Merk)

εσται μετ αυτων θεος αυτων Aν Aρ

εσται μετ αυτων S (Tisch Bousset Sod)

---

179. Weiss, *Die Johannes-Apokalypse*, 125.

180. κυκλευω surfaces in the New Testament only in John 10:24 B, but κυκλοω surfaces a number of times.

Charles rejects the shorter text of S and K due to insufficient testimony. For him, the parallelism speaks against it, and he considers the sentence a superfluous repetition of 21:3b–c. Of the two longer forms, A's form is problematic insofar as the word order of αυτων θεος contradicts the author's linguistic style. The form of Aν Aρ, which one would prefer as the best reading, is quite insufficiently attested according to Charles. Charles therefore considers the text corrupt. He also believes that ο θεος μετ αυτων must be removed as a marginal gloss and that the text should read: αυτων θεος εσται or εσται θεος αυτων. Conversely, Bousset considers θεος αυτων a later addition from the Old Testament parallels. He therefore sides with S's shorter text. Weiss[181] finally sees a later correction in the missing αυτων θεος. He believes these words were removed because they were considered superfluous. A has the original text. In my opinion, either θεος αυτων or αυτων θεος should certainly be considered original on the basis of the Old Testament parallels (Ezek 37:27; Jer 31:33; Zech 8:8). One would like, however, to give preference to the word order attested only by Aν (θεος αυτων), since it corresponds to the Apocalypse's linguistic style. μετ αυτων εσται (A K) is probably also original and S Aν have made a change. If this is correct, then A's text is still the best even considering the word order αυτων θεος. If εσται μετ αυτων is a correction, the θεος αυτων has also been changed in connection with it in order to avoid the collision of two αυτωνs.

21:5   λεγει] + μοι S Aν (likewise 14:13 and 17:1 Aν alone, on the contrary 19:9 all) (WHort[mg.])

[126] 21:12   om. τα ονοματα S Aν (likewise all modern editions except Bousset and Charles, om. τα K)

In addition to the Apocalypse's linguistic style, the unanimous testimony of the versions here speaks for the authenticity of τα ονοματα.

21:16   σταδιους] -ων S* Aν (likewise the modern editions except WHort[mg.] Weiss Bousset Charles[txt.])

However, σταδιων is simply a thoughtless harmonization to χιλιαδων.

21:19   + και ante οι θεμελιοι S* Aν ([Bousset] Charles[mg.])

Likewise 9:11 Aν.

22:8   ~ βλεπων και ακουων S Aν (Tisch Bousset Sod[txt.])

ακουων και βλεπων is not (with Bousset) a subsequent harmo-

---

181. Weiss, *Die Johannes-Apokalypse*, 195.

nization to the following οτε ηκουσα και εβλεψα but, on the contrary, should be considered evidence that S Αν changed the word order because the author is in the first place a seer.

22:8   εβλεπον A (hiat C) Oec (WHort^mg· Weiss)
εβλεψα S Αν (Tisch WHort^txt· Sod Vog Charles^mg· Merk)
ειδον K

The aorist must be regarded a correction because the Apocalypse otherwise avoids the aorist of βλεπω and because the subsequent formation of the imperfect tense would be inexplicable.

22:18   ~ επ αυτον ο θεος S Αν (Tisch Bousset Sod Vog)
επ αυτον om. A* (hiat C)

The list includes forty-five readings,[182] of which only 2:15; 3:7; 5:10; 7:1; 19:20 represent the *Urtext*. The vast majority are obvious corrections and as such prove that S has a closer relationship to Αν, since it is clear that most of these agreements could not occur by chance. Bousset defines the relationship between S and Αν as one in which S was dependent upon Αν.[183] Only 4:11, where S preserves one of its frequent mixed readings,[184] actually confirms Bousset's thesis. But it is methodologically inadmissible to conclude from this one reading that [127] S takes over all the readings from Αν that they share against any other old text forms. On the contrary, in the extant portions of P^47, P^47 S agree with Αν against AC K eight times; P^47 S and C agree with Αν against K two times;[185] and P^47 agrees with Αν against S AC K fifteen times. If we consider the relative quantity of text preserved in P^47, these figures correspond to the relative number of S-Αν readings. It appears then that at least some of these readings—indeed most of them—go back to the archetype of the P^47 S text form. Furthermore, Αν probably influences S in some places. However, separating this secondary layer from the older P^47-S-Αν readings is impossible. All we can do here, as in other cases, is identify the problem and concede its insolubility.

---

182. Bousset (*Textkritische Studien*, 35) also gives a list of the S-Αν readings. But 2:7, 10; 6:8; 7:15, 17; 10:2; 11:15; 13:8; 14:6, 9; 15:4, 7; 16:3, 17; 17:17; 20:10; 21:6 should be removed from it.

183. Bousset, *Textkritische Studien*, 35: "S perhaps dependent on Αν"; yet more certain in his commentary (158): that "S shows the influence of Αν."

184. 17:4, on the contrary, does not belong here and should be mentioned only in the S-K readings.

185. See p. 128.

This is the appropriate place to discuss the corrections that are present in S. According to Milne and Skeat's careful study,[186] which provides a corrective to the studies of Tischendorf and K. Lake, the corrections of S[c187] stem from two scribes, A and D, who were involved in the manuscript's production and who also copied the text of the Apocalypse.[188] Because these corrections stem from the fourth century and are demonstrably as old as Codex S, they represent a separate manuscript of the Apocalypse contemporaneous with S. The corrections of S[c] are similarly from the two hands dated to the seventh century by Tischendorf. The first of them corrects the first two leaves of the Apocalypse. The second, which Milne and Skeat relegate to the eighth century, undertakes all the S[c] corrections from 7:15 (σκηνωσει) onward. Bousset,[189] for his part, made a list of the most important corrections of S[a] and S[c] and arrives at the clear and certain conclusion that at least the majority of the fourth-century corrections (= S[a]) were taken from a manuscript belonging to Aν.[190] Also, a [128] number of readings where Aν K agree against the older text forms surfaces among the corrections of S[a].[191] And only occasionally do readings from other groupings surface,[192] some of which may stem from pure chance. An Aν

---

186. Milne and Skeat, *Scribes and Correctors of the Codex Sinaiticus*, 40–50.

187. I write S[a] for S[c] (and S[c] for S[cc]).

188. From D comes 1:1–5 (bis νεκρων); the rest comes from A, a much more careless scribe.

189. Bousset, *Textkritische Studien*, 42–44.

190. I do not need to repeat Bousset's evidence, but I am satisfied to report that I reexamined all the corrections in Hoskier's critical edition. The number of distinct Aν readings is strikingly large. Of course, there are also many others where S[a] corrects a unique error of S* and where AC P[47] K agree with Aν. These are unimportant in the present context.

191. See Bousset, *Textkritische Studien*, 43.

192. Only the following should be mentioned:

5:13: om. και ante τω αρνιω S[a] A (hiat C) 1611

6:4: om. αυτω ante λαβειν S[a] A (von C) Latt.

9:13: om. τεσσαρων S[a] A (hiat C) P[47] 1611 f^{1678} 2053 94 versions

15:7: + ἐν ante εκ S[a] AC K contra S* P[47] Aν

16:2: εις την γην S[a] AC K contra Aν (hiat S*)

16:3: om. αγγελος S[a] P[47] AC P f^{1006} 1611 1854 2053 2329 94 contra Aν K

19:9: om. του γαμου S* Aν, + S[a] (hiat C) K

19:13: κεκληται S[a] A (hiat C) K, καλειται Aν

κεκλητο S*

21:27: ο ποιων S* K, ποιων S[a] A (hiat C) f^{1006} 2030 2050 2329 61 94 al. pc., ποιουν Aν

manuscript was probably also used for the seventh or eighth-century corrections (S^c), as Bousset demonstrates (44). We should [129] note, however, that all these readings, with the exception of 11:8 (+ εσται S^c Boh.), 12:8 (om. ετι S^c P[47] f[104] f[2014] 2053), and 16:10 (εσκοτωμενη] εσκοτισμενη S^c f[2014] f[2051] al.) are also in Compl., and 11:1 (+ και ειστηκει ο αγγελος) is only in S^c Compl. f[172/250] 61 – 69 1854 2329 al. pc. (against Aν and all the rest). S's later corrections are irrelevant for determining Aν's age since they are later than Andreas's commentary. The corrections of S^a, however, clearly prove that the Aν type is at least as old as Codex S, i.e., it reaches into the fourth century.

The results in K S are exactly analogous to the S-Aν readings, But here there is a difference insofar as S depends upon K, a relationship disclosed in several locations with absolute clarity. We begin with the decisive locations:

6:1–2 ερχου. και ειδον και ιδου AC Aν

   ερχου και ιδε. και ιδου K

22:3: ετι (om. S*) S^a A (hiat C) K, εχει Aν

S^a agrees with K a few times:

4:3–4: ομοιως ορασει σμαραγδινω και κυκλοθεν του θρονου S^a (S* omission): inaccurate correction with the harmonization to adjacent lines, ομοιως with K, ορασει with the rest.

1:18: αιωνων] + αμην S^a K

2:14: τω βαλακ] τον β. S^a K (om. S*)

11:9: αφιουσι] αφησουσι S^a K

17:6: om. εκ ante του αιματος[1] S^a K (τω αιματι S*)

20:8: + τον ante μαγωγ S^a K

20:12: ηνοιχθη] ηνεωχθη S^a K

See also 19:12 ονοματα γεγραμμενα και ονομα γεγραμμενον K, ονοματα γεγραμμενα S^a f[336] f[42/325]

Other groupings:

6:9: ~ σφραγιδα την πεμπτην (πεμπτην om. S*) S^a 61 – 69 1611 1854

10:10: επικρανθη η κοιλια μου] εγεμισθη η κοιλια μου S* 1854 2329, + πικριας S^a 1854 2329

11:16: om. οι ante καθηνται S^a P[47] C f[1006] 1854 2053

14:8: πεποτικεν] πεπτωκαν S^a (hiat S*) P[47] 1854 (πεπτωκεν)

19:9: ~ του θεου αληθινοι εισιν S^a f[1006] f[2065] 2329

18:8: κρινας] κρινων S^a f[250] f[2014] Aρ f[2814]

13:16: ποιει] ποιησει S^a 2329 1854 (-ση)

20:1: + αλλον ante αγγελον S^a 792 2017 2050 Syr.[1] versions al.

14:3: om. αι S^a f[104/336] f[2014] 792 2053

21:15: καλαμον] -μου S^a Aρ[1] 2050

12:6: εξηκοντα] + πεντε S^a Arm.[1.2.3.4]

ερχου και ιδε. και ειδον και ιδου S

6:3–4 ερχου. και εξηλθεν AC Aν K

ερχου. και ειδον και ιδου εξηλθεν S

6:5 ερχου. και ειδον και ιδου AC Aν

ερχου και ιδε. και ιδου K

ερχου και ιδε. και ειδον και ιδου S

6:7–8 ερχου. και ειδον και ιδου AC Aν

ερχου και ιδε. και ιδου K

ερχου και ιδε. και ειδον και ιδου S

The facts in the first, third, and fourth passages allow for only one interpretation. K replaces και ειδον with και ιδε and draws it to the previous sentence instead of to the subsequent one. In each instance, S conflates the original and the K reading. Additionally, S 6:3–4 harmonizes the occurrence of the second rider with the other three.[193] Because the senseless και ιδε of the K text can only be understood as a competing reading to και ειδον—which is why it is missing from the second rider—the combination of the two readings in S must represent the latest stage of textual development, suggesting that S depends upon K.[194] The facts are also clear in the two following locations:

[130]2:10 βαλλειν] βαλειν K

+ βαλειν S*

17:4 αυτης²] της γης K

+ και της γης S

S constantly displays a mixed text influenced by K. In the same vein, the following location likely shows a mixed text as well.

19:11 καλουμενος πιστος και αληθινος K Orig. (Tisch [Bousset] Vog [Charles] Merk)

πιστος και αληθινος A (hiat C) Aν (Sod)

πιστος καλουμενος και αληθινος S ([WHort] Weiss)

In this reading, K is not a later change designed to produce the usual combination πιστος και αληθινος (3:14; 21:5; 22:6), but rather, S adds καλουμενος, which is missing in A Aν, in line with K.

The remaining readings that S K share with each another against the rest of the old textual witnesses now follow.

---

193. Significantly, και ιδε is missing here.

194. Bousset (*Die Offenbarung Johannis*, 264 n. 2) and Charles (*Critical and Exegetical Commentary on the Revelation*, 1:clxii) also interpret the facts this way. Weiss (*Die Johannes-Apokalypse*, 119–20) evaluates it incorrectly.

1:6   ημας βασιλειαν S K (*Urtext*)
       ημας] ημιν A, ημων C
       βασιλειαν] βασιλεις και Aν

1:13   + επτα ante λυχνιων S K

This reading is probably the *Urtext*, according to Bousset. The grouping of witnesses is in fact the same as in 5:6, where also A (hiat C) Aν omit επτα before πνευματα. While only WHort, of the modern editions, places it in brackets, the rest keep it. Nevertheless, it can only be a later addition (from 1:12).

1:13   υιω] υιον S K

All modern editions except WHort^mg.. Weiss correctly explain this reading as the *Urtext*—a reading that the other text forms correct (likewise 14:14 A S K against C P^47 Aν).

1:18   κλεις] κλειδας S K (likewise 3:7 Aν; 20:1 only in some late groups κλειδα)

2:4   αλλ] αλλα S K (likewise 2:14 K; 2:20 A K; 20:6 S 1854 2053; so also the modern editions except Weiss Bousset Charles)

2:10   εξετε S K (likewise all modern editions except WHort^txt. and Charles)
       εχετε C Aν (WHort^mg.2)
       εχητε A (WHort^txt. Charles)

See also p. 104.

[131] 3:3   ηξω] + επι σε S K

This reading stems from the second half of the verse. Only Bousset appears to keep these words as original (see comment on 3:3).[195]

3:3   γνως] γνωση S K (likewise Tisch WHort^mg. Charles^mg.)

Because the aorist subjunctive regularly occurs after ου μη in the Apocalypse (in fourteen places), the text of S K (here and below in 9:6) is

---

195. See also Bousset, *Textkritische Studien*, 156 n. 1.

probably a correction, caused by the future ηξω. Otherwise, the future ηξω appears only in 18:14, where only K offers the aorist subjunctive (ευρη).

3:7   ανοιγει] -ξει S K (Tisch)
Apparently, this reading is a harmonization necessitated by the previous κλεισει.

3:20   + και ante εισελευσομαι S K (likewise Tisch WHort[mg.] Bousset
       Charles against WHort[txt.] Weiss Sod Vog Merk)
That the reading is a Hebraism (= *waw consecutivum*) weighs in favor of the S-K reading's authenticity, which also surfaces and is unanimously (or almost unanimously) attested in 10:7 and 14:10.[196]

4:8   αγιος ter] novies K
       octies S* (is only a byproduct of the carelessness of S's negligent
       scribe, who naturally intended to write αγιος 9x)

5:3   ουδε] ουτε ter K
       ουτε[1.3] S (in between omission due to homoioteleuton γης[1⌢2])
       ουτε[3] A (hiat C)
The tradition is very confused here, which is also why the modern critical editions differ. Tisch WHort[mg.] Sod read ουτε three times with K, WHort[txt.] Weiss Vog Merk read ουδε — ουδε — ουτε with A, Bousset and Charles[txt.] read ουδε three times with Aν (which, linguistically speaking, is the least flawed text), and Charles[mg.] reads ουτε — ουτε — ουδε. See the location once more below (p. 237).

5:6   + επτα ante πνευματα S K (likewise all modern editions except
       [WHort])
See 1:13 above.

---

196. To explain the και partially as a thoughtless harmonization with the previous ανοιξη is impossible insofar as the future indicative rather than the aorist subjunctive stands with εισελευσομαι. When Weiss (*Die Johannes-Apokalypse*, 116), in support of this view of the facts of the case, points out that S already reads ανοιξω instead of ανοιξη and that it is therefore possible to begin the following sentence with και ανοιξω, he begins with the unproven assumption that S offers the older text against K here, a reading which was only half corrected in K.

[132] 5:8   om. αι ante προσευχαι S* K
Predicate noun; the same correction surfaces in 4:5 in K alone.

5:11   + ως ante φωνην S K (likewise Tisch WHort[mg.] Bousset)
The decision as to whether ως is original or a later addition finds no firm foundation in the study of the use of ως in the Apocalypse. The general tendency is to remove ως (reversed only in A al. pc. in 19:12), which would also speak for its authenticity in our passage. But A does not remove ως in other locations. Weiss[197] and Charles[198] attempt to solve the problem exegetically: "Since both ειδον, as κυκλω του θρονου, indicate the actual existence of angels." Thus, ως would be inappropriate, a reminiscence of passages such as 6:6; 19:1. This argument carries some weight, and ως is then probably a later addition.

6:8   μετ αυτου] αυτω S K
This is an obvious correction (see 14:13).

6:12   ~ μελας εγενετο S K (Tisch)
The transposition is a harmonization to the previous μεγας εγενετο.

6:13   βαλλει] βαλουσα K
            βαλουσα S 1611 1854 f[172/250] f[336] al. pc. (Tisch)

6:14   ελισσομενον] -ος S K (WHort[mg.] Charles[mg.])
A misguided correction. This is by no means the easier reading, but all the versions are against it in addition to AC Aν.

6:16   (του καθημενου επι) του θρονου] τω θρονω S K (Tisch)
Likewise 7:15 K. This reading contradicts the Apocalypse's linguistic style.

7:9   φοινικες] -ας S* K (Tisch)
This is a harmonization to περιβεβλημενους. K alone also already writes εστωτες] -ας (likewise Weiss).

---

197. Ibid., 78.
198. Charles, *Critical and Exegetical Commentary on the Revelation*, 1:36.

8:3   (επι) το θυσιαστηριον¹] του θυσιαστηριου S K (Tisch WHort[txt.] Bousset Sod Vog Charles[mg.] Merk against WHort[mg.] Weiss Charles[txt.])

8:5   ~ βρονται και φωναι και αστραπαι S K (likewise most modern editions against WHort[mg.] Weiss Charles)

8:13   (ουαι) τοις κατοικουσι] τους κατοικουντας S K (likewise all modern editions except WHort[mg.] Charles)

S K preserve the original text here, and A (hiat C) Aν make a correction, since the accusative is undeniably the more difficult reading. The dative is the classic construction (note that in 12:12 K produces the dative). [133]9:1–2 αβυσσου¹⌢² S K

9:6   ευρωσι] ευρησουσι S K 0207 (likewise modern editions except WHort[mg.] Weiss Bousset Charles[mg.])

The Apocalypse's linguistic style supports the aorist subjunctive as the *Urtext* (see 3:3 above). ευρησουσι is thus a harmonization to the two future-tense verbs that come before and after it, which makes the aorist subjunctive's subsequent placement difficult to understand.

9:10–17:2 of P[47] will not be mentioned further in light of the P[47]-S-K and S-K readings listed on pp. 123 and 127–28.

17:11   αυτος] ουτος S K (a correction)

18:2   om. εν ante ισχυρα S K (dub. Aν) (*Urtext*)
Conversely, see 19:17 below.

18:2   om. επεσεν² S* K (likewise 14:8 C K, hiat S)

18:3   πεπτωκαν] -κασιν S K
πεπτωκασιν is a correction of AC's reading and, therefore, even less original than πεπτωκαν.

18:6   ποτηριω] + αυτης S K
This is certainly a secondary reading.

18:13 κιν[ν]αμωμον] -ου S K

This is a harmonization to the preceding genitive.

19:7 δωμεν S K (and most modern editions)
        δωσομεν A (hiat C) (WHort^txt. Weiss Charles)
        δωσωμεν Aν

δωσομεν in A should be described as a scribal error;[199] it makes no grammatical sense after the two hortatory subjunctives.

19:17 + εν ante φωνη S K

The modern editions vary here. Only Tisch Weiss Vog Merk opt for εν without reservation. WHort and Bousset place it in brackets, while von Soden and Charles reject it. In fact, we encounter places with εν φωνη μεγαλη (5:2; 14:7, 9, 15; 16:17), as well as others without εν (6:10; 7:10; 8:13; 10:3). Consequently, we cannot establish the authenticity of εν in 18:2 from parallels to this passage. What is decisive, however, is the discovery that εν is present when λεγων precedes it but missing after κραζειν (6:10; 7:2, 10; 10:3) and φωνειν (14:18). It must therefore be rejected here and at 18:2.

20:4–5   ετη^1⌒2 S K

[134] 21:3 om. θεος αυτων S K
        See p. 132.

21:4 απηλθαν] -εν (neuter plural) S K (WHort^mg. Vog)

21:16 οσον και A (hiat C) al. pc.
              και Aν
        οσον S K
See also p. 100.

21:27 ο ποιων S* K (Tisch [WHort] Bousset Vog Merk)
            ποιων A (hiat C) S^a f^1006 2030 2050 2329 61 94 (Weiss Sod Charles)
            ποιουν Aν

The article corresponds to the Apocalypse's linguistic style and is therefore the *Urtext*.

---

199. Weiss's defense (*Die Johannes-Apokalypse*, 116) is overly subtle.

(22:2 αποδιδουν] -διδους S K Aν[plur.]; Tisch WHort[mg.] Bousset[txt.] Sod Charles[mg.]. This passage does not belong here because Aν probably also reads -διδους).

22:8 δεικνυοντος] δεικνυντος S K (Tisch Sod)
δεικνυντος is the classical rather than the Hellenistic form.

22:16 επι S K (likewise all modern editions except WHort[mg.] Weiss Charles[txt.])
εν A (hiat C) f^{1006} f^{1678} 2329, om. Aν

Also, the correction of Aν assumes επι, proving that A makes a correction.[200]

22:21 αγιων] + αμην S K (Sod Vog Charles Merk)

Among the total of forty-three readings in this list, there are several (1:13; 2:4, 10; 3:10; 8:3, 5, 13; 18:2; 19:7, 21:27; 22:16) where S K preserve the *Urtext*. The rest consist almost entirely of corrections, as in S Aν. The two homoioteleuton errors in 9:17 and 20:4–5 could be a coincidence, a conclusion that cannot be accepted in most cases of common corrections.[201] It follows that some kind of relationship exists between S and K, as well as between S and Aν. It is clear from 2:10; 6:1–8; and 17:4 that S depends upon K. We cannot say, however, that S also takes over all the other readings listed above from K unless they are based on a coincidence.[202] We must [135] note again, as in S Aν, that P[47] S also agree[203] with K eleven times in P[47]'s extant portion, and only in seven other cases does S agree with K against P[47] AC Aν. We must conclude that some of the unique readings of S K, which parallel P[47]'s lost portions, were probably part of the archetype of P[47] S.[204] However, we lack the necessary criteria to separate this older layer of P[47]-S-K readings from those readings that only infiltrate S later from K. Because the facts of the case in the relationship between P[47] S and K are

---

200. Weiss's defense of the reading of A (ibid.) is ineffective.

201. See especially 3:3; 18:6.

202. 2:9 (+ τα εργα σου και ante την θλιψιν) must also definitely be seen as insertion from K or Aν. See pp. 74–75 at 2:13.

203. Likewise, often P[47] alone agrees with K; see pp. 123 and 124–25.

204. Also Hoskier, *Concerning the Text of the Apocalypse*, 1:146ff., whose authority is of course equal to zero here, assumes a common foundation for S and K.

analogous to the relationship between P⁴⁷ S and Aν, the same judgment applies in both cases. In both cases we remain without a comprehensive solution to the underlying problem. It nonetheless follows—from those passages where it is clear that S depends upon K—that K (like Aν) is older than S and reaches at least into the fourth century.[205]

S shares a number of erroneous readings at various locations with A. The more important of these are those where C is also available. Because the individual locations were already discussed above, simply listing them below is sufficient.

1:4   α] των A S (a correction)

2:22   εαν μετανοησωσιν] -σουσιν A S

3:7   ~ ο αληθινος ο αγιος A S

4:3   ιρις] ιερεις A S (hiat C)

9:5   παιση] πεση A S (hiat C) al. pc.

9:10   ομοιας] -οις A S (hiat C)

9:21   πορνειας] πονηριας A S*

11:11   ημισυ] -σου A S* (likewise 11:9 ημιου A*, ημισου A**; 12:14 ημισου P⁴⁷ S*)

11:16   om. οι¹ A S* 2053

14:18   κραυγη] φωνη A S al. pc.

18:8   om. κυριος A., ~ ο θεος ο κυριος S (a misguided addition?)

[136] 18:9   κλαυσουσι] κλαυσονται A S

18:21   om. ισχυρος A S

        λιθον] + ισχυρον S (erroneously added?)

18:22   om. πασης τεχνης A S

Common mistakes of A P⁴⁷ are very rare.

11:18   τοις φοβουμενοις] τους φοβουμενους A P⁴⁷

14:18   om. εξηλθεν A P⁴⁷

16:4   εγενετο] εγενοντο A P⁴⁷

---

205. Also, the fragment 0207 (containing 9:2–15), which belongs to the fourth century along with S, contains some K readings, confirming the age of the K text; see:

    9:4: μετωπων] + αυτων

    9:5: αυτοις] αυταις

    9:6: ευρωσιν] ευρησουσιν 0207 S K

    9:7: ομοιοι χρυσω] χρυσοι

    9:12–13: μετα ταυτα iungunt cum sequentibus

We can also observe a number of common errors in C S.

1:19   μελλει] δει μελλει(ν) C S
2:9   ιουδαιους] -ων C S*
3:14   + ο ante αληθινος C S
6:8   om. ο ante θανατος C S
6:17   αυτου] αυτων C S
12:6   (ινα) τρεφωσιν] τρεφουσιν C S (dub. P[47])
13:17 om. και C S*
13:18 εξακοσιοι] -αι C S
18:14 om. τα[2] C S

Also, P[47] or P[47] S together share various readings with C, where A has the older text.

9:21   φαρμακειων] -κων C P[47] S K
11:15 (φωναι) λεγοντες] λεγουσαι C P[47] S Αν
12:3   ~ πυρρος μεγας C P[47] S K
12:8   ισχυσεν] -σαν C P[47] S Αν
13:1   ονοματα] ονομα C P[47] S Αν
13:5   om. και ante δυο C P[47] S Αν
13:15 om. ινα ante οσοι C P[47] S Αν K
14:14 υιον] υιω C P[47] Αν
15:3   εθνων] αιωνων C P[47] S

As Bousset[206] already notes, Αν is also related to AC, or more precisely to A. The foundation upon which the Αν recension was created stood near A's text. The following errors and corrections make this clear.

1:13   om. επτα AC Αν, likewise 5:6 om. επτα[3] A (hiat C) Αν ([WHort])
1:13   υιον] υιω AC Αν (likewise 14:14 C P[47] Αν)
1:19   γενεσθαι] γινεσθαι A Αν
2:10   εξετε] εχετε C Αν, εχητε A (see p. 104)
[137] 2:22   αυτης] αυτων A Αν
3:20   om. και ante εισελευσομαι A (hiat C) Αν (see p. 139)
6:4   om. εκ ante της γης A Αν ([WHort] [Charles])
8:13   (ουαι) τους κατοικουντας] τοις κατοικουσι A (hiat C) Αν (WHort[mg.] Sod variant 1 Charles)

---

206. Bousset, *Textkritische Studien*, 36; Bousset, *Die Offenbarung Johannis*, 156 n. 1.

9:6   (ου μη) ευρωσι A (hiat C) Aν, ευρησουσι S K
         A Aν probably preserve the *Urtext* here; see p. 141.

9:20   ουδε] ουτε A Aν, ου C K

10:5   om. την δεξιαν A Aν

12:3   ~ μεγας πυρρος A Aν. Perhaps the *Urtext*; see p. 109.

13:3   εθαυμασθη (εθαυμαστωθη C) ολη η γη AC P[47]
         εθαυμασεν ολη η γη S K
         εθαυμασθη εν ολη τη γη Aν
         Aν presupposes the AC reading, which is also the *Urtext*.

14:3   + ως ante ωδην AC Aν (WHort Bousset Vog Charles Merk
         against Tisch Weiss [Sod]). This is probably the *Urtext*.

14:6   τους καθημενους C P[47] S K
         τους κατοικουντας A al. pc.
         τους καθημενους τους κατοικουντας Aν
         Aν offers a mixed reading from the *Urtext* and that of A.

16:12   ανατολης] -λων A Aν
         Likewise 7:2 A; 21:13 K.

16:17   om. μεγαλη A (hiat C) Aν

18:2   + εν ante ισχυρα A (hiat C) Aν
         See p. 142 at 19:17.

18:3   om. του οινου AC Oec 1611
         ~ του θυμου του οινου Aν
         The Aν reading is a misplaced addition that presupposes AC's
         text.

18:6   om. τα ante διπλα A Aν (non C)

18:9   επ αυτην] επ αυτη A Aν (non C) (WHort[mg.] Bousset Charles[txt.])

19:7   δωμεν] δωσωμεν Aν
         δωσομεν A (hiat C)
         The A text is probably simply a scribal error in the place of
         δωσωμεν.

19:11   om. καλουμενος A (hiat C) Aν
         See p. 137.

21:4   om. οτι A (hiat C) Aν (WHort[txt.] Charles)
         οτι is omitted by mistake after ετι.

21:7   αυτω] αυτων A (hiat C) Aν

[138]21:27   ο ποιων] ποιων A (hiat C), ποιουν Aν
         Aν is probably a correction of A's text.

22:5   φωτος[2]] φως A (hiat C) Aν (WHort Charles)
         Aν also shares the homoioteleuton error in 13:7a with AC P[47].

The evidential value of this list lies in the fact that it includes errors and corrections almost exclusively and that these are for the most part preserved only in A, not in C. However, we cannot determine whether the reading in question goes back to the AC archetype where C is missing.

Notably common errors or corrections in C Aν do not occur often (6:8 om. αυτου[1] is an isolated example).

Common errors in AC K or A K (where C is missing) are rare, if not almost entirely missing. It is at least probable that the article's omission before Νικολαιτων in 2:15 AC K is not original. It is even more certain that the omission of the article ο before οσιος in 16:5 is spurious. A K (against C S Aν) have an obvious, misguided common correction in 2:20 την γυναικα] + σου.

See also: 3:17 + ο ante ελεεινος A K.

5:10   βασιλευσουσιν] βασιλευουσιν A K (hiat C) (WHort Charles[txt.])

11:12   φωνης μεγαλης] φωνην μεγαλην A K
        See also p. 108.

12:8   ισχυσεν A K, ισχυσαν rel. See p. 110.

14:8   ~ αλλος δευτερος αγγελος A K. See p. 112.

18:4   εξ αυτης ο λαος μου A K. See p. 114.

18:16   om. εν ante χρυσ[ι]ω A K

To conclude this presentation of the various forms of the Apocalypse's Greek text and their mutual relationships, three places should be discussed where the tradition is particularly confused and the original text is more or less problematic. The first of these is by far the most important because understanding the text correctly depends upon the recovery of the correct reading here.

13:10. For the sake of clarity, the textual tradition of the two halves of the verse should be displayed separately.

10a   ει τις εις αιχμαλωσιαν εις αιχμαλωσιαν υπαγει A 2344 Vulg.[afm]

       ει τις εις αιχμαλωσιαν υπαγει C P[47] S Aν f[1006] 1611 1854 2053 Q Arm.[4]

       ει τις εχει αιχμαλωσιαν υπαγει K f[336]

[139]   ει τις αιχμαλωτιζει εις αιχμαλωσιαν υπαγει f[104] Sah.

       ει τις εις αιχμαλωσιαν απαγει εις αιχμαλωσιαν υπαγει f[172/250] 2351 Syr.[1.2] Prim. Gig. Vulg. (Bousset)

All modern editions and commentaries except Bousset opt for reading 1. Von Soden places εις αιχμαλωσιαν[2] in brackets. The fact that reading 2 can be explained from reading 1 speaks for its authenticity, despite the fact that reading 2 enjoys the broadest attestation in the Greek textual tradition. The omission of one of the two immediately repeated instances of εις αιχμαλωσιαν—due either to haplography or deliberate deletion—is far more likely than their addition. Moreover, Jer 15:2 confirms reading 1 decisively. Furthermore, readings 4 and 5 presuppose the text of 1 and are no more than misguided clarifications of 1. Reading 3, which can hardly be translated, should be understood as nothing more than a simple scribal error (εχει instead of εις) that emerges from the series of witnesses for reading 2.

10b (1) ει τις εν μαχαιρη (-ρα) αποκτενει δει αυτον εν μαχαιρη (-ρα) αποκτανθηναι C P⁴⁷ S f¹⁰⁰⁶ Αν Compl. f¹⁰⁴/³³⁶ f¹⁷²/²⁵⁰ versions omn. (S reads with a few minuscules αποκτεινει, f¹⁰⁰⁶ f¹⁷²/²⁵⁰ αποκτεννει)

(2) ει τις εν μαχαιρα δει αυτον αποκτανθηναι K

(3) ει τις εν μαχαιρη αποκτανθηναι αυτον εν μαχαιρη αποκτανθηναι A

Reading 1 of 13:10b has, on the whole, the same witnesses for it as reading 2 in 13:10a. Moreover, it also has the unanimous testimony of the versions this time. At the same time, the K text, which cannot be understood as a simple textual corruption, is difficult and important. At first glance, it is clear that the thought of retribution is expressed neither in 13:10a nor in 13:10b in K. It would be incomprehensible, however, that K should have deliberately deleted or mistakenly omitted any examples of αποκτενει. Such an omission is easier to understand if K had used the linguistically difficult language from A (αποκτανθηναι[1]). The reason why the K text is not considered original is because the second εν μαχαιρη (-ρα), which both the text forms and the Jeremiah *Vorlage* establish, is missing here. Text 3, which A alone attests, differs from 1 and 2 by the ungrammatical infinitive in the antecedent and the absence of the δει in postscript. The δει, [140] however, also does not appear to surface in some of the versions. They read, namely,

gladio interficietur Gig.
occident eum in gladio Sah. Boh.
(in) gladio occidetur Syr.[1]

A's text (with the infinitive occurring twice instead of an expected finite verb in each case) is entirely un-Greek. Should we then conclude that this text is corrupt? From an exegetical perspective, the text cannot have the principle of *lex talionis* in view; rather, it communicates the idea that Christians ought to know God's will in whatever fate they encounter. With this in mind, the active αποκτενει (or αποκτεινει), which the entire textual tradition except A provides, cannot possibly be the *Urtext*. A's text, if not original, must nonetheless represent a level of textual development closer to the original than that of all other textual witnesses.

This can be proved first for the concluding clause's δει, which A lacks. The idea of divine predestination fits in the antecedent but not in the concluding clause, which intends to express the notion that what God has determined will occur with unavoidable certainty. But the αποκτανθηναι in the antecedent must also stand closer to the *Urtext* than the factually impossible αποκτενει (or αποκτεινει) of C P⁴⁷ S Aν. Charles, who alone among modern editors of the Apocalypse's text rejects the text of the majority of the witnesses, has, in principle, correctly identified a blatant Hebraism here, whose only analogy in all of the New Testament is in Rev 12:7 (ο Μιχαηλ και οι αγγελοι αυτου του πολεμησαι μετα του δρακοντος). This explanation works, however, only for the antecedent, not, as it would seem, for the concluding clause where αυτον εν μαχαιρη αποκτανθηναι is expected: εν μαχαιρη αποκτανθησεται. Nevertheless, the fact that the δει αυτον εν μαχαιρη αποκτανθηναι, which is not attested in the rest of the tradition except in A, is preserved, instead of the smooth αποκτανθησεται, weighs in its favor. A's text remains difficult, even if one recognizes it as a Hebraism. Furthermore, it remains an open question whether A's text—exegetically and in light of the Jeremiah *Vorbild*—comes closest to the *Urtext* within the whole textual tradition, even if it is not the *Urtext* itself.

[141] This location is of fundamental importance for assessing the Apocalypse's textual tradition. Not only is A's surpassing value proven as quintessentially the best of the Apocalypse's manuscripts, but C is also shown to have been influenced by another text.

In addition, virtually the entire tradition is corrupted in the following location.

18:3   εκ του οινου της πορνειας αυτης πεπτωκαν παντα τα εθνη AC 2031
(πεπτωκαν also WHort^txt.)

In the place of πεπτωκαν, other witnesses read:

πεπτωκασιν S K *f*¹⁰⁰⁶ 1611 *f*¹⁰⁴/³³⁶ Hipp

πεπτωκε 1854 Oec al. pc. (because of the neuter plural)

Both are corrections of the uncommon aorist form πεπτωκαν.[207]

πεπωκεν (πεποκεν) Aν^plur.

---

207. See the exact same correction in 21:6 γεγοναν A (hiat C) 1678 – 1778, γεγονασιν *f*¹⁰⁰⁶ 2020 – 2080 Oec (γεγονα S* Aν K).

πεπωχαν 2329 (Tisch WHort[mg.] Weiss Sod Vog Charles[mg.] Merk)
πεπωχασιν *f*[1678] *f*[250] Aρ (Bousset)
πεποτιχεν *f*[2014(-2074)] 2026 – 2057 2065 – 2432 94 Syr.[1]

The original Aν reading is somewhat uncertain because of the tradition's fragmentation. The commentary, however, clearly establishes it. Andreas writes: πῶς δὲ τοῦ οἴνου τῆς ἰδίας πορνείας ἐπότισεν ἡ παροῦσα Βαβυλών. In light of this, πεπωχεν appears to be the original Aν reading to which πεποχεν is simply an orthographically bad variant. The Arethas text reads πεπωχασι (a mixed text of Aν and K) along with its dependent *f*[250] and some other manuscripts. Only a few groups of the Aν text, as well as Syr.[1], read πεποτιχεν. Of the versions, Sah. Boh. Arm.[1/2] Aeth. read "have fallen"; Gig. Vulg. Tyc.[2] Beat. Syr.[2] "have become drunk." Despite the fact that the reading πεπτωχαν (AC), of which πεπτωχασιν (S K) is a correction, surpasses other readings on the basis of its attestation in the textual tradition, all modern editions (except WHort[txt.]) abandon πεπτωχαν and consider it a thoughtless reading or a scribal error for πεπωχαν. Consequently, modern editions adopt a reading that is virtually unattested in the tradition and preserved only in Aν. It has been correctly pointed out that 14:8 and 17:2 are parallel passages, which disclose how incorrect the most strongly attested reading is within the tradition.

[142] 14:8   οτι εκ του οινου του θυμου της πορνειας αυτης πεποτιχε παντα τα
            εθνη

17:2   εμεθυσθησαν οι κατοικουντες την γην εκ του οινου της πορνειας
            αυτης.

14:8 is on the whole identical with 18:3, and the harmonization to Jer 25:15 is also clear here. It is important to present the textual tradition exactly.

πεποτιχεν AC Aν K versions
πεπτωχαν S[a] (hiat S*), πεπτωχεν 1854
πεπτω[..]ν P[47]

The patently original reading πεποτιχεν (confirmed by Jer 25:15) is also to be expected in 18:3. Nevertheless, if almost all modern editions adopt the most poorly attested πεπωχαν into their text rather than πεποτιχεν, this is because they consider the overwhelmingly and strongly attested πεπτωχαν a scribal or reading error, presupposed by πεπωχαν. Naturally, no one will regard the testimony of *f*[2014] 2065 – 2432 94 for πεποτιχεν as going back to an actual old tradition. Rather, πεποτιχεν is a mere (although admittedly excellent) conjecture and nothing more. However, we need to consider whether we should adopt this conjecture. That the parallels, the Jeremiah

Vorlage, and the context[208] require the conjecture in the same way and that πεπωχαν is not really a satisfactory reading cannot be seriously denied. It is indeed an obvious assumption, at first glance, that πεπτωχαν was simply a scribal or reading error for πεπωχαν. Yet, this hypothesis is not compelling. It is also possible that πεπωχεν, which the majority of Aν manuscripts attest, is a subsequent correction prompted by the memory of 14:8, just like πεποτιχεν. Of course, we can and must still ask whether the text's free paraphrase in Andreas's commentary above actually presupposes πεπωχεν rather than πεποτιχεν. Admittedly, Andreas's εποτισεν can also be understood in the textual reading πεπωχεν since the text of 14:8 also had to be in Andreas's memory.

That Sᵃ and P⁴⁷ also read πεπτωχαν (or possibly πεπτωχεν) in 14:8, which no one considers the *Urtext*, [143] suggests another explanation of the passage's textual history—an explanation as convincing as the conventional one. Furthermore, επεσεν επεσεν Βαβυλων precedes πεπτωχαν in 14:8 (as in 18:3) and explains the development of the P⁴⁷-Sᵃ reading. It is clearer here that the reading πεπωχαν could have arisen from πεπτωχαν by what was read, although the Greek textual tradition does not bear witness to πεπωχαν—a reading found only in the two Latins Gig. Beat.: *biberunt*.[209] This provides the methodological justification for interpreting the textual history of 18:3 differently than is usually done. πεπτωχαν, whose correction again is πεπτωχασιν, does not originate from an original πεπωχαν that completely disappears from the tradition. But, as Charles alone correctly observes, the previous επεσεν επεσεν influenced πεπτωχαν, and πεπωχεν (Aν) is best understood as a correction in light of 14:8. New Testament textual critics increasingly distance themselves from the belief that they can establish the New Testament text beyond the middle of the second century with any certainty. While Lachmann was content to restore it to the form in which it was read toward the end of the fourth century (leaving the pursuit of prior developments and the identification of the *Urtext* to conjectural critics), research since Lachmann's time continues to reach back to the second century. However, another gap remains between that date and the originals for which our knowledge is in an almost complete vacuum since it is clear that Westcott-Hort's "neutral" text is not really

---

208. Charles—alone among modern textual critics—also recognizes this: "πεποτιχεν is also required by the context: otherwise Rome is represented only as passively evil" (*Critical and Exegetical Commentary on the Revelation*, 2:96).

209. Not Tyc.² = Pseudo-Augustine, *Homiliae*, as Hoskier erroneously indicates.

neutral at all. The present case illustrates that the tradition's original reading has been entirely lost and can only be recovered by examining the Apocalypse's linguistic style, which can help recover the original with all desirable certainty.

In the third place, we will discuss 18:2. The textual tradition is as follows:

και εγενετο κατοικητηριον δαιμονιων (δαιμονων Αν Κ)

1. και φυλακη παντος πνευματος ακαθαρτου [+ και μεμισημενου A f^{336} 2080 Gig. Syr.² Arm.⁴]

2. και φυλακη παντος ορνεου ακαθαρτου [+ και μεμισημενου Gig.]

3. και φυλακη παντος θηριου ακαθαρτου και μεμισημενου

[144] First we must provide the most complete and accurate representation of the tradition. The three lines are numbered beginning with και φυλακη in order to make these readings clearer in their bewildering complexity. Incidentally, 18:2 is missing from three important textual witnesses: C P⁴⁷ and 2344.

1. om. $f^{205} f^{18}$ 1611 2019 Ps.-Aug.

2. om. A Αν f^{104} Syr.¹·² Arm.² Hipp

3. om. S Αν Κ $f^{104/336}$ 2053 – 2062ᵗˣᵗ· Vulg. Ps.-Aug. contra A 1611 2329 $f^{172/250}$ Hipp Oec Gig. Sah. Aeth.

Prim. rearranges lines 2 and 3 (besides και φυλακη¹ already after κατοικητηριον): *et facta est habitatio et refugium daemoniorum et omnis spiritus immundi et omnis bestiae immundae et omnis avis immundae et odibilis.*

The modern critical editions omit line 3 και φυλακη παντος θηριου ακαθαρτου without exception. Bousset[210] believes that the insertion of the line with θηριου might be due to the LXX's influence. Or, one can suppose that A replaces ορνεου with θηριου[211] and that those textual witnesses that have 2 and 3 side by side provide a mixed text from the original and the text of A. In fact, however, the grouping of witnesses requires a different interpretation. Line 3 is so strongly attested by A Hipp Oec Sah. Gig. 1611 2329 and the layer of old readings preserved in $f^{172/250}$ that its status as the original demands serious consideration. Only R. Bentley[212] speaks out

---

210. Bousset, *Die Offenbarung Johannis*, 418 n. 6.

211. Tischendorf writes in his apparatus to 19:21: ορνεα] θηρια A*? A already has a correction here from the first hand, and the word that the scribe himself corrects is apparently unreadable. One cannot therefore construct an analogous case to 18:2 from this passage and say that A replaces ορνυ with θηριον both times.

212. Arthur Ayers Ellis, ed., *Bentleii Critica Sacra: Notes on the Greek and Latin*

confidently for the fact that line 3 is original. Charles[213] considers the text uncertain. Possibly θηριου should be read instead of πνευματος in line 1 or και φυλακη παντος θηριου ακαθαρτου should be added in line 3. Under the hypothesis that line 3 was original in the form above, it provides the following explanation of the overall tradition:

Line 1 is skipped in a few of the subordinate groups as a result of homoioteleuton. For the same reason, A Syr.[1.2] Arm.[2] omit line 2, Aν f[104] omit lines 2 and 3 (bis ακαθαρτου[3]), and S K f[336] Vulg. omit line 3. [145] Only Oecumenius's commentary[214] f[172/250] 2329 Sah. Gig. Aeth., then, offer the complete text. Of these, Oec Sah. belong to the witnesses of the best class. That the coincidence of several homoioteleuton errors in the various text forms corrupts the tradition here is a regular occurrence in transmission. This phenomenon also surfaces elsewhere:

In A: 3:15 (ζεστος$^{1⌢2}$); 4:11 (om. και εκτισθησαν); 5:3 (βλεπειν απο$^{1⌢2}$); 17:17 (γνωμην$^{1⌢2}$); 19:16 (επι$^{1⌢2}$); 21:10–11 (θεου$^{1⌢2}$); 21:12 (δωδεκα$^{1⌢2}$); 22:11 (ετι$^{1⌢2}$); in Aν: 9:19 (om. και εν ταις ουραις αυτων); 11:7 (αυτους$^{1⌢2}$); 12:9 (αυτου$^{1⌢2}$); in K: 3:3 (και$^{1⌢3}$); 21:15 (αυτης$^{1⌢2}$); in Aν K together: 4:2–3 (καθημενος$^{1⌢2}$).

The same is true in C and P[47]. Such errors are most frequent in the extremely carelessly copied Codex S.[215] And, of course, there are countless such examples in the army of minuscules. Particularly important are the following two:

13:7   και εδοθη$^{1⌢2}$ AC P[47] Aν Sah. Arm.

An entire sentence is missing in the whole Greek tradition, except S and K. The greatest confusion occurs in 18:22–23, where five similar constructions that begin with και and close with ετι follow each other. Of them, lines 1–3 are skipped in a series of minuscules, as well as in Syr.[1] and Arm.;

Text of the New Testament, Extracted from the Bentley Mss. in Trinity College Library (Cambridge: Deighton, Bell, 1862), 91.

213. Charles, *Critical and Exegetical Commentary on the Revelation*, 2:343.

214. The text of the Oecumenius commentary can only be reconstructed here from the apparatus of Hoskier's edition. Oecumenius's words would then read: γίνεται λοιπὸν κατοικητήριον δαιμονίων καὶ φυλακὴ παντὸς πνεύματος ἀκαθάρτου διαφυλάττοντος τοῦ τόπου τὴν μεθ' ἡδονῆς ἐν αὐτῇ διαγωγὴν τῶν δαιμόνων. καὶ φυλακή, φησί, παντὸς ὀρνέου ἀκαθάρτου καὶ παντὸς θηρίου ἀκαθάρτου.

The largely authoritative Oecumenius codex (2053) has two homoioteleuton errors one after another here, but these are just prominent features of this manuscript (i.e., not the Oec text).

215. See Weiss, *Die Johannes-Apokalypse*, 86–87.

lines 2–3 are missing in S and many minuscules, Syr. Aeth.; lines 2–4 are omitted in Hipp; line 4 is omitted in A (non C) f^{172} 2329; lines 4–5 are omitted in f^{2014} in 1773. f^{205} has the order 3 5 1 2 4. Furthermore, AC omits πασης τεχνης after πας τεχνιτης.

These examples are meant to demonstrate that such an increase of homoioteleuton errors—conditions also present in 18:2—suggests that line 3 (in 18:2) should belong to the original text and that it is neither impossible nor improbable. But these parallel examples do not prove that the longer text form from 18:2 is original. They only raise the possibility that it is. We gain an additional argument for its status as original if [146] we use the Old Testament *Vorbilder* that the text of Rev 18:2 follows.

Isa 13:21 και αναπαυσονται εκει θηρια και εμπλησθησονται αι οικιαι ηχου, και αναπαυσονται εκει σειρηνες, και δαιμονια εκει ορχησονται, και ονοκενταυροι εκει κατοικησουσιν, και νοσσοποιησουσιν εχινοι εν τοις οικοις αυτου.

Isa 34:11, 14 και κατοικησουσιν εν αυτη ορνεα και εχινοι και ιβεις και κορακες ... και συναντησουσιν δαιμονια ονοκενταυροις.

Two points are important here: (1) The Apocalypse's citation is not a citation of Isaiah but is loosely based on it. Therefore, the Apocalypse's text cannot be restored in light of the LXX. (2) Line 3 in particular, whose authenticity is in question and which speaks of θηρία, has its *Vorbilder* in the Old Testament. Rather than assume A replaces ορνεου with θηριου, it is at least most likely that line 3 also forms a part of the original text.

It can hardly be determined, however, whether και μεμισημενου in line 1 also belongs to the original text. Since these words are attested inadequately in line 2, it is not possible to arrange all three lines evenly, and with that the main criterion for deciding that question vanishes.

2.5. Results

We can summarize the results briefly. They consist partly of clear and certain conclusions and partly of problems for which a particular solution is not available.

(1) The entire Greek tradition of the Apocalypse's text divides into four stems: AC, P^{47} S, Aν, and K.

(2) Αν and K are two markedly distinct recensions. Their unique readings consist overwhelmingly of corrections.

(3) Αν and K are not completely independent of each other, as Bousset and von Soden allege, but they have a common stem, which, though not extensive, is clearly recognizable in a number of common corrections. In several places, Αν and K preserve the original text against A (C) (P⁴⁷) S.[216] But it follows from this that they are not simply later forms of the "older" extant text in AC and P⁴⁷ S.

[147] (4) The "older" text divides again into two clearly distinguishable text forms, AC and P⁴⁷ S. Of these, P⁴⁷ S already contains a considerable number of corrections, while these are almost entirely missing in AC's archetype. P⁴⁷ S preserve the original text alone in one single reading.[217]

(5) AC, with which Oecumenius's text is identical throughout (and closely related to the Vulgate), surpass the remaining text forms in their value as witnesses.[218] In a significant number of places, AC alone preserve the *Urtext*. Their excellent value as witnesses is based on the fact that their common text hardly contains any deliberate corrections. In this way, AC's text stands closer to the *Urtext* than all other text forms.

AC's text is, nonetheless, still not identical with the *Urtext*. In some places at least, the staunchest defenders of AC's text, Westcott-Hort and Charles, abandon it. Furthermore, this same text continues to preserve a number of serious violations against Greek grammar. Views differ in its assessment. Whether these linguistic violations can or should be traced back to the original needs to be examined in every case. Such an examination would be carried out by a systematic study of the Apocalypse's linguistic style. Where AC alone exhibit serious linguistic violations—which are without analogies elsewhere in the tradition—it would no longer be methodologically justifiable to exaggerate AC's authority in those places and to explain the readings of the "neutral" text as the *Urtext*.

---

216. 1:11 (Λαοδικειαν); 3:14 (Λαοδικεια); 4:3 (ιρις); 4:4 (επι τους θρονους εικοσι τεσσαρας πρεσβυτερους); 6:8 (ο θανατος); 9:10 (ομοιας); 19:18 (επ αυτους); 21:12 (τοις πυλωσι). In some places, either Αν or K has alone preserved the *Urtext*. In Αν, see 3:4 (α] οι ?); 5:3 (ουδε ter ?); 5:13 (και τα εν αυτοις παντα ηκουσα λεγοντας); 18:20 (επ αυτην?); 20:9 (εκ του θεου απο του ουρανου). In K: 5:4 (και εγω); 19:6 (λεγοντες); 19:11(καλουμενος πιστος); 19:14 (στρατευματα] + τα); 21:3 (λαος); 22:18 (ο θεος επ αυτον).

217. 9:20 (ουδε).

218. Even von Soden cannot help but abandon, at least in some places, his principle that the majority of textual witnesses are decisive and to recognize the H text (= AC S) as the *Urtext*.

(6) Each of the four text forms preserves the *Urtext* in some places partly alone, in others partly with other text forms, while the rest of the tradition is faulty or revised. This observation leads to a conclusion of fundamental importance: the texts standing furthest from the original in [148] text form are not to be understood as later, revised forms of those texts that are closer to the original. For example, AC's unique readings preclude the possibility that P^{47} S, Aν, and K derive from AC. And it is equally impossible to interpret Aν and K or their possible common foundation as later forms of P^{47} S because P^{47} S, Aν, and K have the same corrections in some places. The unique errors of P^{47} S, as well as those places where Aν K or Aν or K alone preserve the original text, rule out this conclusion. The real problem of the Apocalypse's textual tradition resides in the mutual relationship of the various text forms to each other. All possible alliances appear together side by side here. AC have (though rarely) the same errors with P^{47} S against Aν K. On the other hand, P^{47} S share the same corrections with Aν K or simply one of these later text forms against AC or AC Aν or AC K. Aν has various errors together with A.

(7) The fact that A and C, as well as P^{47} and S, also often diverge and have differences that derive from the other text forms on their side in each case further complicates the problem described above. Of the AC type, C is clearly influenced by other texts. Those places where A alone, or A with one of the other text forms, offers the older text supports this conclusion. In addition, in a few places, A has common errors with S or with Aν.

Barring those purely unique readings that S so richly preserves, P^{47} and S diverge from one another with greater frequency than A and C. S shares a significant number of corrections with Aν and with K, while the list of corrections of P^{47} Aν and P^{47} K offer significantly less conclusive evidence. A few places can be identified where K clearly influences S. Among the S-K readings, however, some readings also surface that lay claim to the original (against AC P^{47} Aν), especially the important passage in 13:7, where a whole sentence drops out due to a homoioteleuton error in AC P^{47} Aν.

It follows from all of this that it is not possible to determine the mutual relationships of the old major stems of the Greek text of the Apocalypse tradition completely and to classify them accurately all together in a stemma. The four text [149] forms are clearly not related to each other exclusively by the original. The common corrections between P^{47} S and Aν K cannot all be understood as purely coincidental, just like those between Aν and K cannot.

Von Soden's claim that three texts (H = AC + P[47] S, Aν, and K) stand independently of one another and without interrelationships[219] fails to correspond to the facts. The problem concerning the mutual relationships of the various major stems forbids such a simple solution. Furthermore, von Soden's principle was misguided:[220] "There is no reason to doubt that every time only one of the three texts preserves a unique reading it is secondary in character."[221] The complicated result that emerges from a careful examination of the nature of the different text forms and their mutual relationships corresponds, however, exactly to what we observe in the New Testament's other books and, for this reason—as analogous situations—should also be expected in the Apocalypse.

At the very beginning of the Apocalypse's textual history stood a text that was handled with little piety and as a result possessed little uniformity. In its various forms, this text was the foundation upon which the later recensions would be made, of which the "neutral" text is the oldest. If textual critics today no longer dispute that, of the extant text forms available for the New Testament's other books, it is the "Western" rather than the "neutral" text that is to be placed at the beginning, then [150] the "neutral" text cannot be placed at the apex of the Apocalypse's textual history either. The Apocalypse's textual history should not be separated from that of the other New Testament writings without reason. Therefore, we should also look for the existence of a "Western" text in the Apocalypse

---

219. Von Soden, *Die Schriften des Neuen Testaments*, 1:2075.

220. He does not conduct the rest consistently.

221. Von Soden, *Die Schriften des Neuen Testaments*, 1:2075. But also the way Weiss solves all available genealogical problems here is not only far too confident but also methodologically disputable. Not only is his "revised" text purely hypothetical and burdened with significant problems, but also the certainty with which Weiss is able to determine what revisions bear the character of the revised text in every case and could therefore only have infiltrated into the witnesses of the older text from the revised one is an illusion. His statistical errors give a false impression because he makes no distinction between orthographic (especially itacistic errors) and serious violations. And just like the errors, the corrections that are present in several texts should not merely be counted but also weighed. Corrections such as μαχαιρης] -ας, απηλθα] -ον, εθαυμασθη] -σεν should not be placed next to variants, for example 15:3 εθνων] αιωνων or 22:14 πλυνοντες τας στολας αυτων] ποιουντες τας εντολας αυτου. The conclusions Weiss (*Die Johannes-Apokalypse*, 102–3, 138–42) draws from his statistical errors are therefore quite problematic.

as well as search for the proper text-historical place of AC's "neutral" text in the book.[222]

Finally, one of the important results of this investigation is the demonstration of the great age of all the text forms discussed. The two latest text forms from a text-historical perspective, Aν and K, are demonstrably older than Codex S and reach at least as far back as the fourth century and are therefore older than A and C. Their value for the reconstruction of the *Urtext* is not negligible. It is clear that some 240 (Aν) or 300 (K) of their corrections produce significantly less depreciation in their textual value, when one considers that A, C, P[47], and especially S hardly have a smaller or even greater number of readings that are evidently wrong. Further, those corrections of Aν and K can, with rare exceptions, be ruled out as candidates for the *Urtext* just like obvious errors in the old majuscules. And in this respect, the corrections in Aν and K have no text-historical or methodological bearing on the recovery of the *Urtext*.

(8) The previous judgment about the four oldest textual witnesses remains unchanged. A is still the most important of all the witnesses of the Apocalypse's text by far. The number of places where A alone or A accompanied by a few minuscules preserve the *Urtext* is the strongest proof of that. C lags significantly behind A, despite being carefully copied.[223] Above all, the fact that C is incomplete in many places where the [151] tradition varies greatly is a serious deficiency. But the damage would be much greater if A were incomplete instead of C. P[47] is preserved even more fragmentarily than C. And although P[47] is much older than the rest of the Apocalypse's manuscripts, it is far less valuable for establishing the text than AC. P[47]'s real significance lies in the fact that it alone allows us to distinguish the P[47] S text form from that of AC Oec with clarity and cer-

---

222. What needs to be said about the Western text, however, can be done in a few words. What we know about it in other New Testament books—namely, that it was the most common text form in the second century—forces us to postulate its existence for the Apocalypse as well. But it has left no obvious trace in the extant manuscript tradition. None of the four ancient Greek text forms presented above come into consideration. Bousset's (*Die Offenbarung Johannis*, 156–57) attempt to prove Hippolytus of Rome is a Greek witness to the Western text is a failure. Hippolytus's text is in the main identical to AC Oec, and where it deviates from this text, it does not agree with the Latin versions (Lagrange, *Critique Textuelle*, 589, 591–93; Westcott and Hort, *New Testament in the Original Greek*, 2:260).

223. C preserves the *Urtext* with Oec 1854 2344 against A P[47] S Aν K (13:8 οὗ ου … αυτου) only in one place.

2. The Major Stems of the Greek Text of the Apocalypse 159

tainty.[224] Where S stands alone as a witness of this text (which is for about two thirds of the Apocalypse), we are often unable to distinguish between the wording of the archetype of the P[47] S form itself and the wording that stems from a later corruption.[225]

2.6. Citations of the Apocalypse in Greek Ecclesiastical Writers and Ancient Papyrus and Parchment Fragments

Irenaeus, Clement of Alexandria, Hippolytus of Rome, Origen, Eusebius, and Methodius of Olympus preserve valuable citations of the Apocalypse for textual criticism that are not mere allusions.[226] Their special value derives from their great antiquity. [152] That they are not strictly verbatim—even if they are real citations—is a quality they share with the biblical citations of the church fathers. All the citations useful for the textual criticism of the Apocalypse are presented below. The Greek citations come

---

224. P[47] does not preserve the *Urtext* alone; P[47] S preserve it together in a single place (9:20 ουδε). The places where S preserves the *Urtext* alone (see 122 n. 165) are invariably missing in P[47].

225. Textual criticism would suffer far less damage if S instead of P[47] were incomplete. In S's text, the following layers lie one upon the other: (1) as a foundation, a good old text, which repeatedly comes to the fore, where S with AC and P[47] have the *Urtext*; (2) a layer of corrections, which S has in common with P[47], but which cannot be confirmed in the missing parts of P[47]; (3) one or two layers of corrections infiltrated from Av and K. Their numbers will be low; (4) as the uppermost layer of debris, there are a lot of random corrections, thoughtless transcription mistakes, omissions, and spelling errors. The degree to which S's scribes are responsible for this last layer and the degree to which it already comes from its *Vorlage* must remain undetermined.

The fact that some corrections that are not in P[47] occur in some of the minuscules with an old text proves that they are older than S (provided they are not purely orthographic errors).

226. According to the collections of Burgon (in Frederick G. Kenyon, *Handbook to the Textual Criticism of the New Testament*, vol. 2 [London: Macmillan, 1912], 224), the number of the Apocalypse's citations amounts to 3 in Justin, 65 in Irenaeus, 11 in Clement of Alexandria, 188 in Hippolytus of Rome, 165 in Origen, 27 in Eusebius. In addition, Methodius, which Burgon does not mention, can also be added. These numbers, however, are misleading in that the "citations" are largely reminiscences that are useless for textual criticism. We will not discuss the text of the Apocalypse in the three commentators, Oecumenius, Andreas, and Arethas here. Arethas's text is the K text. Andreas's text has already been discussed above. And Oecumenius's text deserves its own investigation.

from the critical editions of the Berlin corpus (GCS); the Latin of Irenaeus is from Harvey[227] and Sanday and Turner's[228] collection of material.

2.6.1. Clement of Alexandria

I found two of Clement of Alexandria's citations that deserve to be included:

Stählin 1:222,7–9 = Rev 6:9, 11: καὶ ἡ Ἀποκάλυψίς φησιν· »εἶδον τὰς ψυχὰς τῶν μεμαρτυρηκότων ὑποκάτω τοῦ θυσιαστηρίου. καὶ ἐδόθη ἑκάστῳ στολὴ λευκή«.[229]

Since Clement cites freely, we can only conclude that he probably did not read των ανθρωπων for εσφαγμενων (S Aν) and μαρτυριαν] + του αρνιου (K).

Stählin 2:503,32–33 = Rev 21:6: οὕτως καὶ αὐτὸς εἴρηται ὁ κύριος ἄλφα καὶ ὦ, ἀρχὴ καὶ τέλος.
This reading is not useful for textual criticism.[230]

2.6.2. Origen[231]

1:5	+ εκ ante των νεκρων cum Aν Compl.
1:6	βασιλειαν cum rel. contra βασιλεις και Aν
1:7	videbit = οψεται cum AC K
	οψονται S Aν^{part.}
1:8	+ αρχη και τελος Ωρ, + η αρχη και το τελος S Aν (article om. *f*[2014] 1773 2019 2081** 2329).

227. W. Wigan Harvey, ed., *Sancti Irenaei Episcopi Lugdunensis: Libros quinque adversus Haereses*, 2 vols. (Cambridge: Typis Academicis, 1857).

228. William Sandy, C. H. Turner, and Alexander Souter, eds., *Novum Testamentum sancti Irenaei episcopi Lugdunensis*, OLBT 7 (Oxford: Clarendon, 1923).

229. Citations from Otto Stählin, ed., *Des Clemens von Alexandreia ausgewählte Schriften aus dem Griechischen übersetzt*, 5 vols., BK 2.7, 8, 17, 19, 20 (Munich: Kosel-Pustet, 1934–1938).

230. Touilleux's arguments (*L'Apocalypse et les Cultes de Domitien et de Cybèle*, 21) for the importance of further readings are useless for textual criticism.

231. See also Bousset, *Die Offenbarung Johannis*, 157–58. Furthermore, Origen does not always use the same manuscript for the Apocalypse (see 5:1, 3; 19:13), just as in the rest of the New Testament.

The agreement with the Aν groups possesses no evidential value because Origen does not cite in a literal manner and because he also omits the article before αλφα.

1:9 συγκοινωνος cum AC S Aν, κοινωνος
     om. εν τη ante βασιλεια cum AC S K contra Aν
     εν ιησου cum C S P f^1678 al. pc., εν χριστω A, εν χριστω ιησου K, ιησου χριστου Aν

[153] 2:7 θεου] + μου cum K

2:10 αχρι] μεχρι cum f^1678 f^2065 792

2:14 (twice cited) om. και ante φαγειν contra K

2:19 om. σου post υπομονην cum S 792 2329

3:4 αλλα] αλλ cum K, om. Aν
     ~ ονοματα ολιγα Ωρ sol., without evidential value
     α] ατινα Ωρ, οι Aν

3:7 ο εχων την κλειν [κλειδα Aν] του [om. AC f^1678 1611 1854 2053] δαυιδ και ανοιγων cum S [ο ανοιγων sine και rel.] και ουδεις κλεισει, και κλειων και ουδεις ανοιξει with S, while all others partly deviate. With the exception of the *Commentary on John* (ed. Preuschen 103,31–32),[232] this passage is cited twice in the Philocalia (ed. Robinson 37 and 46)[233] and in the following textual form:
     ο αγιος και αληθινος cum C Aν K
     ~ ο αληθινος και αγιος A S sol.
     κλειν as above
     + του ante δαυιδ cum S Aν K as above, and everything else, also as above. All three citations are identical in wording.

3:8 ανεωγμενην] ηνεωγμενην cum S sol.
     ην ... αυτην cum plural, αυτην om. S al. pc.

3:12 only the beginning freely cited, habet εν contra S*

3:20 + εγω ante εστηκα cum Prim. sol.
     om. ακουση της φωνης και (cited 3x: 4:437,32–33; and Lommatzsch 13:252 and 14:178, 206)[234]

---

232. Erwin Preuschen, ed., *Der Johanneskommentar*, GCS 10 (Leipzig: Hinrichs, 1903).

233. J. Armitage Robinson, ed., *The Philocalia of Origen* (Cambridge: Cambridge University Press, 1893).

234. Karl Heinrich Eduard Lommatzsch, ed., *Opera omnia quae Graece vel Latine tantum existant*, 25 vols. (Berlin: Haude & Spener, 1831–1848).

ανοιξη] + μοι Ωρ sol.

om. και ante εισελευσομαι cum A (hiat C) Αν contra S K

5:1　　του θρονου] τον θρονον Ωρ sol.

εσωθεν και εξωθεν cum Αν K (*Philoc.* 37)

εσωθεν και οπισθεν cum A (hiat C) (*Sel. Ezech.*)

εμπροσθεν και οπισθεν cum S (*Philoc.* 46)

5:2　　om. εν ante φωνη *Sel. Ps.* cum Αν, habet *Philoc.* 37

om. εστιν cum rel. contra K

5:3　　ουρανω] + ανω cum K *Sel. Ps.*

on the contrary om. *Sel. Ezech.* (ed. Lommatzsch, p. 14:412)
and *Philoc.* 37

ουτε ter cum K (*Philoc.*)

ουτε$^{1.3}$ S (om. ουτε υποκατω της γης)

5:4　　om. εγω cum S Αν (on the contrary ego in the Lat. versions)

ευρεθη cum rel., ευρεθησεται S*

[154] 5:5　　om. εκ^1 *Philoc.*

om. ο^2 cum S f^{1006} f^{1678} 1611 2053 2329

ανοιξαι cum rel. plur., ο ανοιγων K

om. λυσαι ante τας σφραγιδας cum rel. contra S f^{2051} Vulg.

5:6　　(αρνιον) εστηκος cum A K

εστηκως S Αν

5:8　　habet αι ante προσευχαι (bis) cum A (hiat C) Αν, om. S* K

6:8　　(not a literal citation) ο θανατος και ο αδης ακολουθει αυτοις, as
well as a second time, but without αυτοις. We cannot conclude
from the presence of αυτοις that Origen definitely reads αυτω
with S K instead of μετ αυτου with AC Αν.

7:2　　ανατολης (bis) cum C S Αν K, ανατολων A f^{18}

εκεκραξεν Ωρ sol., εκραξεν C S Αν K

εκραζεν A P 2053

7:3　　+ μητε ante την γην Ωρ 1st loco, om. 2nd loco

μητε bis Ωρ, μηδε bis S al. pc., μητε^1] και A

αχρι cum AC al. pc. (bis), αχρις S, αχρις ου Αν K

7:4　　om. και post εκατον cum A S Αν contra C K

τεσσαρακοντα cum A Αν K, τεσσερακοντα C S

εσφραγισμενοι 1st loco cum plural

εσφραγισμενων 2nd loco cum K

κελευσθεις σιωπησαι μη γραψαι

7:5　　εσφραγισμενοι cum rel. plur., -αι K

10:4 Free citation; presupposes the reading μη αυτα γραψης (against μετα ταυτα γραφεις Αν).

11:8 om. και ante ο κυριος cum Sᵃ Αν; it is however without evidential value because it is a free citation.

ο κυριος αυτων cum AC Αν K, αυτων om. P⁴⁷ S*

14:1 το αρνιον cum rel. plur., το om. P⁴⁷ Αν

(αρνιον) εστως cum P⁴⁷ Αν, εστος AC S, εστηκος K

+ και ante εκατον Ωρ sol.

om. αριθμος ante εκατον cum rel. plur. contra K

τεσσαρακοντα Ωρ, τεσσερακοντα AC S, ρ̅μ̅δ P⁴⁷ Αν K, likewise 14:3

14:2 η φωνη ην cum rel. plur., φωνην P⁴⁷ Αν

habet ως ante κιθαρωδων contra Αν

14:3 om. ως ante ωδην¹ cum P⁴⁷ S K

ουδεις cum rel. plur., ουδε εις K

εδυνατο cum rel. plur., ηδυνατο Αν

habet αι ante εκατον cum rel. contra Sᵃ al. pc

[155] 14:4 om. εισιν post ουτοι² contra K

αν] εαν cum K

ηγορασθησαν cum rel. plur., + υπο ιησου ante ηγορασθησαν K

απαρχη bis cum rel. plur., απ αρχης S f³³⁶ Prim. Beat.

14:5 habet γαρ (bis) cum P⁴⁷ S K Meth. Sah. Boh.

14:6 om. αλλον cum P⁴⁷ S* Αν K

πετομενον cum rel. plur.

ευαγγελισαι] -σασθαι cum P⁴⁷ S Compl. f¹⁷²/²⁵⁰ f¹⁶⁷⁸ f²⁰¹⁴ f²⁰³¹ al. pc.

+ επι ante τους cum AC P⁴⁷ S contra Αν K

καθημενους cum C P⁴⁷ S K, κατοικουντας A (Αν)

+ επι ante παν cum rel. plur., om. Αν

14:7 λεγων] λεγοντα cum P⁴⁷ 1611 al. pc., om. S

θεον cum rel. plur., κυριον K

τω ποιησαντι] τον ποιησαντα Ωρ

αυτον τον ποιησαντα K

+ την ante θαλασσαν cum P⁴⁷ S K

15:6 (free citation) λινουν λαμπρον και καθαρον : λινουν cum P⁴⁷ 61 – 69 f²⁰³¹ 94 al. pc.

καθαρους λινους λαμπρους S sol.

19:11 om. τον ante ουρανον Ωρ sol.

ανεωγμενον cum rel. plur., ηνεωγμενον A (hiat C) S P al. pc.

καλουμενος πιστος cum K, ~ S, καλουμενος om. A (hiat C) Αν

19:12   habet ως ante φλοξ cum A (hiat C) *f*[1006] *f*[1678] *f*[2029] *f*[172/250] *f*[2065]
multiple versions (bis)

εχων ονομα γεγραμμενον cum A (hiat C) Αν

+ ονοματα γεγραμμενα και ante ονομα K (hiat S)

19:13   βεβαμμενον] ρεραντισμενον 1st loco cum P 2019 2065 2329 al.

ρεραμμενον 2nd loco cum (S) 1611 pc. Hipp (bis)

καλειται] εκεκλητο Ωρ sol., κεκληται A (hiat C) Sᵃ K, κεκλητο S*

om. ο ante λογος cum min. pc.

19:14   στρατευματα] + αυτου cum 2017 Sah. Boh., + τα K

ηκολουθει cum rel. plur., ηκολουθουν Αν

εφ] επι cum K

ενδεδυμενοι] -οις cum S* *f*[1678] Syr.[1]

om. λευκον Ωρ 1st loco cum Boh. Aeth. Arm.[2.3]

habet 2nd loco

λευκον] + και Ωρ 2nd loco cum S Αν[part.]

[156] 19:15   οξεια cum rel. plur., διστομος οξεια K

παταξη cum rel. plur., -ξει S al. pc.

~ της οργης του θυμου cum S 2329 Sah.

20:6a   om. και αγιος cum 61 – 69

22:11   (*Comm. Jo.* 441, 87): ὡς Ἰωάννης φησί· καί ὁ καθαρὸς καθαρισθήτω
ἔτι καὶ ὁ ἅγιος ἁγιασθήτω in the place of: και ο δικαιος δικαιοσυνην
ποιησατω ετι και ο αγιος αγιασθητω

ο ρυπαρος ρυπανθητω ετι (bis) cum S 94 1854 2017

22:13   or 21:6 γεγονα εγω το ā και το ō και ο πρωτος και ο εσχατος, η
αρχη και το τελος

εγω ειμι το ā και το ō, η αρχη και το τελος, ο πρωτος και ο εσχατος

εγω ειμι η αρχη και το τελος, το ā και το ō, ο πρωτος και ο εσχατος

Origen conflates 22:13 and 21:6. 22:13 is cited in the second and third
locations because ο πρωτος και ο εσχατος occurs only in this verse (not in
21:6). However, ειμι, which Origen has, surfaces only in 469 1852ᴮ 2073
and the versions. The order η αρχη και το τελος ο πρωτος και ο εσχατος,
which Origen has in the second location, agrees with Αν (where the article
that should accompany αρχη and τελος is missing) against A (hiat C) S
K. In the first location, και ο πρωτος και ο εσχατος is inserted from 22:13,
where 21:6 is first cited and γεγονα is read with S Αν K but where εγω is
read with A (hiat C) *f*[1006] 2053 – 2062 *f*[2065] 469 against S Αν K. Origen
omits the και before η αρχη with K.

This list provides very important results. The text Origen used is on the whole identical with the text of P⁴⁷ S; see 2:19; 3:7; 5:1 (εμπροσθεν και οπισθεν); 5:4 (om. εγω cum S Αν); 5:5 (om. ο²); 14:3 (om. ως ante ωδην cum P⁴⁷ S K); 14:5 (habet γαρ cum P⁴⁷ S K Meth.); 14:6 (om. αλλον cum P⁴⁷ S* Αν K; ευαγγελισασθαι cum P⁴⁷ S); 14:7 (λεγοντα cum P⁴⁷; + την ante θαλασσαν cum P⁴⁷ S K); 15:6 (λινουν cum P⁴⁷); 19:13 (ρεραντισμενον cum S; [ε]κεκλητο cum S*); 19:14 (ενδεδυμενοις cum S; + και ante καθαρον cum S Ανᵖᵃʳᵗ·); 19:15 (~ της οργης του θυμου cum S); 21:6 (γεγονα cum S Αν K); 22:11 (ρυπανθητω cum S, hiant AC).

With K: 14:4 (αν] εαν); 14:7 (τον ποιησαντα); 19:11 (καλουμενος πιστος); 19:14 (εφ] επι).

With A: 3:20 (om. και ante εισελευσομαι cum A Αν, hiat C); 5:6 (εστηκος); 19:12 (habet ως ante φλοξ).

[157] The majority of Origen's unique readings presuppose no *Vorlage*, since Origen often cites freely from memory. That many unique readings of P⁴⁷ and S also surface alongside the common readings of P⁴⁷ S Orig. needs no explanation. Many of S's unique readings were confirmed as such by Origen (who does not cite them) and P⁴⁷ (which does not preserve them).

2.6.3. Hippolytus of Rome

Among the patristic witnesses, Hippolytus is the most important alongside Origen because of his age (third century), his Western origins, and the scope of his citations. Indeed, the yield of Hippolytus's citations for textual criticism surpasses Origen's considerably because a section of continuous, coherent text in literal citations is extant in a full two chapters (17–18).[235]

---

235. The Apocalypse's accurate and continuously cited sections are 11:2–7 (more accurately 11:4–7); 12:1–6, 13–17; 13:11–18; 17:1–18:24; 20:6; 22:15 in the commentary on Dan 5:1–10. The most important references are in *De Christo et antichristo*. The latter work, edited by Achelis (in Bonwetsch and Achelis, *Exegetische und homiletische Schriften*), comes down to us in three manuscripts: E (= Ebroicensis 1), R (= Remensis 78), and H (= Hierosolymitanus s. sepulchri 1), of which H is the authoritative one. E and R, which are closely related to each other, essentially have the Αν text, as Bousset already observed (*Die Offenbarung Johannis*, 153 n. 4). Since E and R's text cannot be regarded as Hippolytus's, we will ignore them in the present context. Hoskier's information about Hippolytus's text of the Apocalypse is not based upon Achelis's critical edition but upon Tischendorf's outdated text and is, therefore, wrong for the most part. It only offers the text of E R. According to tradition, Hippolytus also

11:3 περιβεβλημενοι cum C Sᵃ Αν^plur. K

      -ους A S* Αν^part. (hiat P⁴⁷)

11:4 habet αι² cum rel. plur.

    om. S* *f*²⁰⁵⁽⁻²⁰⁴⁵⁾ 1854 (et E R)

    κυριου cum rel. plur., θεου Αν

    της γης om. H sol.

    εστωσαι cum Sᵃ Αν, εστωτες rel.

11:5 ει τις bis] ητις H (scribal error)

    θελει¹] θελησει Hipp cum P⁴⁷

    του ante στοματος om. H sol

    αυτους θελει²] θελει αυτους H cum C K

              θεληση (-σει E R) αυτους A (E R)

        ~ θεληση (-σει P⁴⁷) αδικησαι αυτους P⁴⁷ S

[158] 11:6 υετος βρεξη τας ημερας της προφητειας αυτων Hipp, βρεξη cum
*f*¹⁶⁷⁸ 2053 2344

    habet εν ante παση cum rel. plur. contra P⁴⁷ al. pc.

    εαν] αν cum C 1854 2053

11:7 και οταν τελεσωσι om. H sol cum *f*⁹²⁰

    ~ μετ αυτων πολεμον cum rel. contra Αν

12:1 σημειον μεγα ωφθη … γυνη περιβεβλημενη] ειδον σημειον μεγα
γυναικα περιβεβλημενην Hipp sol.

    μεγα] + και θαυμαστον (see 15:1) et om. εν τω ουρανω Hipp sol.

12:2 om. και ante κραζει (bis) cum Αν K

    + του ante τεκειν H (et ed. Achelis) cum *f*¹⁰⁰⁶

12:3–4a missing

12:4b cum TR

    (οταν] οτε H sol.)

12:5 αρρενα] αρσενα bis H cum Αν *f*¹⁰⁰⁶ 1611 1854 2053 Meth.

    (αρρενα E R cum P⁴⁷ S K, αρσεν AC)

    om. εν ραβδω σιδηρα bis Hipp

    om. και ante ηρπασθη H sol (non ed. Achelis)

    ηρπασθη H bis cum rel. plur., ηρπαγη E R cum S Compl. al. pc.

    + προς ante τον θρονον H cum rel. contra Αν (+ εις E R)

12:6 εχει] + εκει H cum rel. plur. (om. C Αν^part.)

    τρεφωσιν] εκτρεφωσιν cum K

---

wrote a commentary on the Apocalypse, but no Greek author familiar with his other
writings mentions it. Should we consider this a coincidence?

12:13 om. οτι — γην Hipp sol.
       αρρενα] αρσενα H bis cum (A) C S
12:14 om. αι ante δυο 1st loco cum P⁴⁷ S K, habet 2nd loco
       πετηται bis cum rel. plur., πεταται Αν
       om. εις τον τοπον αυτης Hipp bis
12:15 ~ εκ του στοματος αυτου οπισω της γυναικος H cum rel. fere omn.
       (στοματος αυτου¹⌒² E R)
       ταυτην] αυτην cum rel. contra Αν
12:16 cum TR H (om. E R; see 12:15), om. η γη² P⁴⁷ al. pc.
12:17 επι τη γυναικι cum rel. plur., επι om. C P⁴⁷
       ιησου E R ed. Achelis cum rel. plur.] του θεου H cum S
13:11 cum TR
13:12 ~ τους εν αυτη κατοικουντας cum rel. fere omn. 13:12 in a later
       place again, there κατοικουντας] οικουντας H, το θηριον] τω θηριω
       H, in the rest as before
[159] 13:13 ποιη καταβαινειν] καταβαινη H sol.
       ενωπιον] και ενωπιον H, κατενωπιον E R
13:14 πλανα] επλανα H contra E R Slav.
       ος εχει cum AC P⁴⁷ Αν
13:15 om. ινα ante οσοι cum rel. plur. contra A al. pc. H
       αν H cum C S Αν, εαν E R cum A P⁴⁷ K
       την εικονα] τη εικονι cum rel. plur.
       om. ινα ante αποκτανθωσι cum rel. plur.
13:16 δωση] δωσιν H cum rel. plur., δωσωσιν K
       (δωση R, δωσει E)
       των μετωπων] το μετωπον cum rel. plur. contra P⁴⁷ Αν
13:17 om. και 2nd loco cum C S* 1611 al. pc.
       1st loco om. E R Slav. (contra H et ed. Achelis)
       om. η ante το ονομα cum A Αν K contra P⁴⁷ S
       (του ονοματος C)
13:18 ~ εστιν ανθρωπου H bis cum f²⁰⁵ 2429 (non ed. Achelis)
       αυτου] + εστιν bis cum C Αν
17:1   om. εκ H (et ed. Achelis) cum S f¹⁰⁰⁶ f²⁰¹⁴ f²⁰⁶⁵
       (μετ εμου] μοι E R Slav., non ed. Achelis)
       om. μοι post λεγων cum rel. contra Αν
       των υδατων των] υδατων cum A S Αν contra (P⁴⁷) K
17:2   ~ οι κατοικουντες την γην εκ της πορνειας αυτης cum rel. fere
       omn.

17:3   ειδον] ειδα H et ed. Achelis, ιδα A (on the other hand 17:6 ειδον Hipp)

γεμον ονοματων] γεμοντα ονοματα H (γέμον τὰ ὀνόματα ed. Achelis) cum A (hiat C) S P Oec 2329

γεμον ονοματων E R cum Αν

βλασφημιας om. H sol. (non ed. Achelis)

17:4   ἡ²] ην cum rel. fere omn.

πορφυρα και κοκκινω] πορφυρουν (-αν A) και κοκκινον cum rel. plur.

om. και ante κεχρυσωμενη cum Αν K

~ ποτηριον χρυσουν cum rel. contra Αν

(γεμον] -ων E R cum S al. pc.)

ακαθαρτητος] τη ακαθαρτητι cum rel. fere omn.

αυτης] της γης cum K, + και της γης S

17:5   πορνῶν cum TR

17:6   om. εκ H ed. Achelis cum K

17:7   ~ ερω σοι cum A (hiat C) K

17:8   + το ante θηριον¹ cum rel. omn.

[160]   υπαγει H ed. Achelis cum A (hiat C) al. pc.

υπαγειν E R cum S Αν K

θαυμασθησονται] -μαζουσιν H ed. Achelis sol.

                  -μασουσιν E R 792 sol.

τα ονοματα] το ονομα cum A (hiat C) K

επι το βιβλιον H ed. Achelis cum rel., επι του βιβλιου K

εν βιβλω E R cum f²⁰¹⁴

βλεποντων] βλεποντες Hipp cum 792 1854 2019 al. pc.

και παρεσται cum rel. omn.

17:9   επτα ορη εισιν H cum rel. fere omn.

(επτα¹ om. E R, επτα²] επι τα E R)

+ αι ante επτα³ H ed. Achelis sol.

17:10   om. και ante ο εις cum rel. omn.

επεσαν cum rel. plur. (επεσον R cum K)

αυτον δει cum rel. plur., ~ δει αυτον K

17:11   αυτος cum A (hiat C), ουτος S K

εστιν²⌢³ H (non ed. Achelis)

17:12   ~ τα κερατα τα δεκα H ed. Achelis sol.

αλλ] αλλα H ed. Achelis cum A (hiat C) S f¹⁰⁰⁶ 61 – 69 2329

17:13   om. ουτοι H ed. Achelis sol. et iungunt μιαν γνωμην εχουσι cum praecedent. cum al. pc.

habet την² cum S Αν, om. A (hiat C) K

εαυτων] αυτω H sol. ed. Achelis

        αυτων E R cum rel. omn.

διαδιδοασιν] διδοασιν cum rel. omn.

17:14   cum TR

17:15   ~ καθηται η πορνη Hipp sol.

17:16   επι] και cum rel. omn.

μισησουσι] μισουσι H sol. (non ed. Achelis) cum ƒ²⁰¹⁴ 2053 – 2062 (the ποιησουσι that follows shows μισουσι to be a scribal error)

om. τας ante σαρκας H sol. (non ed. Achelis)

και γυμνην cum A (hiat C) S, om. Αν, + ποιησουσιν αυτην K

17:17   τας καρδιας] την καρδιαν Hipp sol.

μιαν γνωμην H ed. Achelis cum rel. plur., ~ E R cum K

τελεσθη τα ρηματα] τελεσθησονται οι λογοι του θεου cum rel. plur., τελεσθωσιν οι λογοι τ. θ. K

17:18   cum TR, + επι ante της γης K

18:1   om. και ante μετα cum rel. contra Αν

+ αλλον ante αγγελον cum rel. fere omn.

[161] 18:2   εν ισχυι φωνη μεγαλη H ed. Achelis cum TR

εν om. S K (E R)

    om. μεγαλη A S K contra Αν

    επεσεν bis cum A Αν contra S K

δαιμονιων H cum A S al. pc., δαιμονων E R cum Αν K

ακαθαρτου] + και μεμισημενου cum A ƒ³³⁶ 2080

ορνεου] θηριου cum A al. pc.

18:3   θυμου του οινου cum Αν, ~ S K, του οινου om. AC 1611 2053

πεπωκε] πεπτωκασι H Slav. ed. Achelis cum S K

        πεπτωκαν AC, πεπτωκεν E R

om. του ante στρηνους H (error, not ed. Achelis)

18:4   του ουρανου] των ουρανων Hipp sol.

εξελθετε] -θατε cum A S

~ ο λαος μου εξ αυτης cum C S P ƒ¹⁶⁷⁸ contra A K

εξ αυτης om. Αν

συγκοινωνησητε] συνκοινωνησης H (non ed. Achelis)

ινα² — αυτης²] εκ των πληγων αυτης ινα μη λαβητε cum rel. plur. contra Αν

18:5   ηκολουθησαν] εκολληθησαν cum rel. fere omn.

~ αι αμαρτιαι αυτης H ed. Achelis cum al. pc.

(αχρι] εως E R cum P sol.)

εμνημονευσεν cum rel. plur., + αυτης K

18:6　om. υμιν cum rel. contra Aν

om. αὐτῇ² cum rel. contra Aν

+ τα ante διπλα E R et ed. Achelis cum C S K contra A Aν

ποτηριω cum AC Aν, + αυτης S K

18:7　εαυτην] αυτην H ed. Achelis cum rel. contra S Aν E R

+ οτι ante καθημαι cum rel. plur.

(καθημαι] καθως Kplur.)

18:8　κρινων] -νας cum rel. plur. contra Sᵃ al. pc.

18:9　κλαυσονται] -σουσι H ed. Achelis cum C Aν K

om. αυτην cum rel. contra Aν

επ αυτη] επ αυτην cum C S K

18:10　om. εν ante μια cum rel. plur.

εν μια ωρα] μιαν ωραν A al. pc.

18:11　κλαιουσι και πενθουσι] κλαυσουσι και πενθησουσι cum K

επ αυτη] επ αυτην cum C S P

18:12　χρυσου ed. Achelis cum TR, χρυσιου E R, om. H

(αργυρου] -ριου E R cum al. pc.)

μαργαριτου] -τας cum C P (A)

[162]　βυσσου] -ους Hipp sol. (all three manuscripts), βυσσινου AC K

πορφυρας cum TR, -ρου K

σηρικου] σιρικου H ed. Achelis

om. και ante χαλκου H (non ed. Achelis)

18:13　κινναμωμον] -μου cum S* K

+ και αμωμον E R (non ed. Achelis) cum rel. contra K

θυμιαματα] θυμιαμα Hipp cum Aνpart. ƒ¹⁰⁰⁶ versions

18:14　~ σου της επιθυμιας της ψυχης cum AC S ƒ¹⁰⁰⁶ 1854

απο σου¹⌢² H (non ed. Achelis)

απηλθεν²] απωλετο E R (hiat H) cum rel. plur. contra Aν

ου μη ευρης αυτα] αυτα ου μη ευρησουσιν H cum AC S P ƒ¹⁶⁷⁸

1611 ƒ¹⁷², ου μη αυτα ευρης E R cum ƒ¹⁰⁰⁶

18:15　τουτων] σου H et ed. Achelis sol. (but it is difficult to acknowl-
edge that Achelis is correct here)

18:16　om. και ante λεγοντες H cum rel. fere omn.

ουαι bis cum rel. contra K

om. και ante κεχρυσωμενη H cum Aνpart. (non ed. Achelis)

om. εν ante χρυσω H (non ed. Achelis) cum A K

χρυσω] -σιω E R cum A K (non ed. Achelis)

μαργαριταις] -τη H (et ed. Achelis) cum AC S P *f*[1006] 1611 2053 – 2062 2329

18:17 ηρημωθη om. H sol. errore
των πλοιων ο ομιλος TR
[ο] επι των πλοιων πλεων Aν
om. ο ομιλος Hipp A (των πλοιων Hipp)
ο επι [+ τον S al. pc.] τοπον πλεων AC S K

18:18 εκραζον] -ξαν cum AC al. pc.
ορωντες] βλεποντες cum rel. fere omn.

18:19 εβαλον] -λαν H et ed. Achelis cum C
om. και ante εκραξαν H (error)
εκραζον] -ξαν cum AC 2329
λεγοντες cum rel. plur., και λεγοντες K

18:20 επ αυτην H et ed. Achelis cum Aν, επ αυτη E R cum C S K
+ και οι ante αποστολοι cum rel. contra C Aν
om. οι ante προφηται H (error)

18:21 cum TR (μυλον)

18:22 om. και πας τεχνιτης — 23 φανη εν σοι ετι H E R contra Slav. cum S al. pc.
σοι²⌒³ et ετι³ om. Slav.

18:23 + φωνη ante νυμφης H cum C 2329 Syr.[1]

[163] ετι post ακουσθη om. H (error)

18:24 αιμα cum rel. plur., αιματα K

20:6a τουτων] τουτον H E R contra Slav., rejected by Achelis as an error
~ ο δευτερος θανατος cum rel. contra Aν

22:15 om. δε cum rel. omn.
και²⌒³ H (error)
om. ο ante φιλων cum rel. plur.

Hippolytus's other writings are far less useful. The commentary on Daniel contains a long continuous section (5:1–10) that is not cited in *De Christo et antichristo*.

3:7 κλειει¹ cum Aν, κλεισει rel.
κλειει²] κλειων cum AC S Aν (aliter K)
ανοιγει cum AC Aν, ανοιξει S K

5:1 του θρονου] τον θρονον Hipp sol.
οπισθεν] εξωθεν cum Aν K
κατεσφραγισμενον] εσφραγισμενον Hipp sol.

5:2 + εν ante φωνη Hipp^A cum AC S K, om. rel. cum Aν

ισχυρον om. Hipp sol.

om. εστιν cum rel. contra K

5:3   ηδυνατο cum TR, εδυνατο rel.

ουδε ter] ουτε

5:4   om. εγω cum S Aν

πολυ] πολλοι cum al. pc.

om. και αναγνωναι cum plur. contra Aν

5:5   om. ων cum cod. plur.

ριζα] + και το γενος Hipp sol.

habet λυσαι cum S Vulg. Syr.[1] al. pc.

5:6   om. και ιδου cum cod. fere omn.

των$^{1 \frown 2}$ Hipp sol.

εστηκος Hipp$^{plur.}$ cum plur., -κως S Aν

om. ως cum al. pc.

οι εισιν] α εστιν Hipp, α εισιν K

~ επτα πνευματα του θεου cum cod. fere omn.

τα απεσταλμονα cum Aν, τα om. rel.

5:7   ειληφε] ελαβε Hipp sol.

habet το βιβλιον cum f^{1006} $f^{104/336}$ $f^{205(-2054)}$ f^{2051} 2019 – 2429

5:8   κιθαραν cum cod. plur., -ας Aν

[164]   αι^{1}] α cum S f^{1006} f^{2065} al. pc.

om. αι^{2} cum S* K

5:9   ~ ημας τω θεω cum $f^{104/336}$ $f^{172/250}$ 2050 al. pc., ημας om. A sol.

5:10   om. αυτους Hipp sol.

βασιλεις] βασιλειαν cum A (hiat C) S f^{1678} 1611 1854 2050

βασιλευσομεν] -σουσιν cum S Aν

-ουσιν A K

6:9–10 are entirely freely cited. In 6:10, απο ante των κατοικουντων cum Aν, εκ rel.

6:11   εδοθη ... στολη λευκη] εδοθησαν ... στολαι λευκαι Hipp cum Latt.

εκαστοις] αυτοις (et om. εκαστω) cum K

αναπαυσωνται] περιμεινωσιν Hipp sol.

~ χρονον ετι μικρον cum A (non C) f^{1006}

εως — αυτων^{2}] οπως [και] οι συνδουλοι αυτων πληρωσωσιν την μαρτυριαν αυτων

9:13–14   free citation, entirely unproductive for textual criticism

11:3   cum TR (περιβεβλημενοι cum C K)

The first of two of Hippolytus's sermons published by Eduard Schwartz contains two verbatim citations from the Apocalypse.[236]

1:8b   ο ων και ο ην κτλ.

        + ο θεος ante ο παντοκρατωρ Hipp sol.

19:11 ειδον] -εν Hipp sol.

        ανεωγμενον] ηνεωγμενον cum A S P al. pc.

        επ αυτον] επ αυτου cum 2053 – 2062

        om. καλουμενος cum A Aν

19:12 om. ως cum plur. contra A al. pc.

        om. και Hipp sol.

        ~ διαδηματα πολλα επι την κεφαλην αυτου Hipp sol.

19:13 βεβαμμενον] ρεραντισμενον cum P 2019 (S Orig.) al.

        καλειται] κεκληται cum A (hiat C) S K

Hippolytus's other extant writings preserve no text-critically useful citations for the Apocalypse.

Overall, Hippolytus's text confirms the text of the old majuscules, agreeing with S or P[47] S in the following places:

[165] 5:4   om. εγω cum S Aν

    5:5   habet λυσαι cum S Vulg. Syr.[1]

    5:8   αι[1]] α cum S; om. αι[2] cum S K

    5:10 βασιλευσουσιν cum S Aν

    11:5 θελει[1]] θελησει cum P[47]

    18:4 ~ ο λαος μου εξ αυτης cum C S P

    18:9 επ αυτην cum C S K; likewise 18:11 cum C S P

    19:13 ρεραντισμενον cum P 2019 (S Orig.) al.

Just a few of the many corrections of Aν and K surface in Hippolytus:

    3:7   κλειει[1] cum Aν

    5:1   οπισθεν] εξωθεν cum Aν K

    5:6   οι] α cum K; + τα ante απεσταλμενα cum Aν

    6:11 om. εκαστω cum K

    11:3 περιβεβλημενοι cum C K

    11:4 εστωσαι cum S[a] Aν

    11:5 θελει αυτους cum C K

---

236. Eduard Schwartz, *Zwei Predigten Hippolyts*, SBAW 3 (Munich: Bayerische Akademie der Wissenschaften, 1936).

12:2   om. και ante κραζει cum Αν K

12:5   αρσενα cum Αν

12:6   εκτρεφωσιν cum K

13:18   αυτου] + εστιν cum C Αν

17:4   om. και ante κεχρυσωμενη cum Αν K; αυτης] της γης cum K

17:6   om. εκ cum K

18:3   ~ θυμου του οινου cum Αν

18:9   κλαυσουσι cum C Αν K

18:17   τον τοπον] των πλοιων cum Αν

The relatively frequent agreements with C are remarkable.

2.6.4. Eusebius of Caesarea

Most of Eusebius's citations of the Apocalypse stem from older sources that Eusebius (in his *Church History*) cites literally.[237]

1:1–4: Schwartz 694,2–5, from Dion

1:1   om. ο θεος et α δει γενεσθαι Dion sol.

1:2   ιησου χριστου] αυτου cum 2329

        om. τε cum cod. fere omn.

1:4   (bis ειρηνην) cum TR

Schwartz 428,16–17, from Letter of the Gallic Communities

[166] 1:5   om. εκ ante των νεκρων cum rel. contra Αν

Schwartz 694,18–19, from Dion

1:9   om. και ante αδελφος cum rel. omn.

        συγκοινωνος cum rel. plur., κοινωνος K

        om. εν τη ante βασιλεια cum rel. contra Αν

        + εν ante υπομονη cum 1854

        ι. χριστου] ιησου Dion sol., all others read differently

        om. δια ante την μαρτυριαν cum AC al. pc.

        om. χριστου AC S* Αν

---

237. Eusebius citations below are from Eduard Schwartz, ed. *Die Kirchenge-schichte*, vol. 2 of *Eusebius Werke*, GCS 9 (Leipzig: Hinrichs, 1908).

Schwartz 648,25–26, from Dion

13:5 εδοθη] + γαρ Dion sol.

βλασφημιας] -αν cum Aν K

ποιησαι μηνας] και μηνες sol.

Schwartz 406.6, from Letter of the Gallic Communities

14:4 αν cum rel. plur., εαν K Orig.

υπαγη cum rel. plur., υπαγει AC al. pc.

Schwartz 692,14–17, 694,22–24, from Dion

22:7 cum TR

22:8 καγω (bis) cum A S K, και εγω Aν

ο βλεπων και ακουων ταυτα (bis) cum S Aν, ~ A K

Schwartz 424, 24–25, from Letter of the Gallic Communities

22:11 δικαιωθητω cum TR $f^{1678(-2080)}$ f^{2014}

δικαιοσυνην ποιησατω rel.

Heikel 372,12–13, *Dem. ev.* 8.2.30d[238]

5:5a habet o^2 cum rel. plur., om. S al. pc.

2.6.5. Methodius of Olympus[239]

Only two longer sections (12:1–6 and 14:1–5) are quoted verbatim.

7:9 (not strictly literal) habet αυτο cum rel. plur., om. K

ηδυνατο cum TR, εδυνατο rel. plur.

12:1 ~ ωφθη μεγα σημειον Meth. sol.

δωδεκα] δεκαδυο cum Aν[part.] 2329

12:2 cum TR (om. και ante κραζει)

12:3 ~ πυρρος μεγας cum rel. plur. contra A Aν

~ επτα διαδηματα cum rel. fere omn.

[167] 12:4 τριτον] + μερος Meth. sol.

τεκειν] εκτεχειν Meth. sol.

12:5 αρρενα] αρσενα cum Aν

---

238. Ivar A. Heikel, ed., *Demonstratio evangelica*, vol. 6 of *Eusebius Werke*, GCS 23 (Leipzig: Hinrichs, 1913).

239. Hoskier's data are also unreliable here and probably taken from an out-dated edition.

habet εν ante ραβδω cum rel. contra Αν
ηρπασθη cum rel. plur., ηρπαγη S Compl.
+ προς ante τον θρονον cum rel. contra Αν
12:6   εχει] + εχει cum rel. contra C Αν
απο] υπο cum K
τρεφωσιν cum TR, εκτρεφωσιν K
14:1   + το ante αρνιον cum rel. contra Αν
εστηκος] εστως cum AC S P al. pc.
ονομα] + αυτου και το ονομα cum rel. plur.
14:2   φωνην ηκουσα] η φωνη ην ηκουσα ως φωνην cum rel. contra Αν,
sed φωνην cum 2019 254 Beat. Arm., + Arab. (om. rel.)
14:3   om. ως ante ωδην cum P47 S K
ηδυνατο cum TR, εδυνατο rel. plur.
14:4   om. εισιν ante οι ακολουθουντες cum rel. contra K
ακολουθουντες] -θησαντες cum f920
οπου αν cum TR, οπου εαν al.
απαρχη cum TR, απ αρχης S al. pc.
14:5   δολος] ψευδος cum rel. fere omn.
om. γαρ cum AC K
om. ενωπιον του θρονου του θεου cum rel. omn.
20:13   ~ τους νεκρους τους εν αυτη cum rel. contra Αν
~ τους νεκρους τους εν αυτοις cum rel. contra Αν

Methodius also confirms the text of the old majuscules, although he does not have και before κραζει in 12:2. The agreements with Αν (12:5 αρσενα) and K (12:6 υπο) can also be from an independent correction, assessed similarly to the agreements with f920 (14:4) and with some Αν groups (12:1). The few verses preserved in Methodius's text of the Apocalypse, however, are insufficient for reliably assessing the variants mentioned above. His text shares the omission of ως 14:3 with P47 S K. Methodius does not preserve AC's reading in 14:4 οπου αν υπαγει (instead of -η), which only WHort and Charles regard as the *Urtext*.

2.6.6. Irenaeus

The number of Irenaeus's citations of the Apocalypse is numerous,[240] but most are transmitted only in Latin and [168] survive partially in the Arme-

---

240. See the compilation in William Sanday and Cuthbert Hamilton Turner, eds.,

nian tradition. The reliability of these versions, especially in the Scripture citations, is problematic in certain respects. That the translators of the biblical text had also translated Irenaeus's text and did not insert the text of the Latin or Armenian Bible with which they were familiar is clear today. However, we must also consider that sometimes they harmonize their translation (whether consciously or unconsciously) to the biblical text with which they are familiar.

1:12   om. εχει contra K
      loquebatur = ελαλει, ελαλησεν Aν

1:13   om. επτα cum AC Aν (against other Latins)
      ομοιωμα υιω (or υιου) Arm. with A Syr.[1]

1:14   cum TR Lat.
      om. λευκον Arm. cum al. pc.

1:15   πεπυρωμενοι] -νω Lat. and Arm. cum S 2050 2053 – 2062
      om. πολλων in one place

1:16   εχων] habet Lat. and Arm., habebat the other Latins
      χειρι Lat. and Arm. against Latins

1:17   partially preserved in Irenaeus and an unimportant reading

1:18   om. αμην Lat. and Arm. cum AC S* contra Aν K
      ~ του θανατου και του αδου Lat. and Arm. cum AC S K contra Aν

2:6   cum TR

3:7b   *aperiet, et nemo claudet; claudet, et nemo aperiet.* The rendering is too free to facilitate a conclusion about the Greek *Vorlage.*

4:7   Also Greek in Anastasios Sinaites το δε τριτον εχων προσωπον ανθρωπου cum K, ως ανθρωπου A, ως ανθρωπος Aν
      Lat.: *habens faciem quasi humanam* seems to come closest to A's text

5:6   literally translated, but without Greek attestation

5:8   only the last words, and not useful for text-critical purposes. Also in Greek: habet αι ante προσευχαι cum A (hiat C) Aν contra S* K

6:2   *exivit vincens ut vinceret* with other Latins: om. και ante ινα

11:19 only the beginning; useless for text-critical purposes

Novum Testamentum sancti Irenaei Lugdunensis, OLBT 7 (Oxford: Clarendon, 1923), 193–203.

[169] 12:4   only free usage. *tertiam partem* does not prove that τριτον] +
μερος stood in the *Vorlage*.

13:2   habet ην contra P⁴⁷ Aν
leonis with most witnesses, λεοντων S al. pc.

13:3   om. ειδον cum rel. fere omn.
habet εκ contra Aν
et admirata est universa terra against Aν (but strikingly identical with Vulg. here)

13:4   οτι (= quoniam) εδωκεν cum rel. plur., τω δεδωκοτι K
θηριω] + τουτω Ir. Syr.¹
και τις δυναται cum rel. plur., τις δυνατος (sine και) K

13:5   βλασφημιαν Arm. cum Aν K
et blasphemia Lat. This is a neuter plural, as 13:6 (*ad blasphemium*) confirms, thus assuming βλασφημιας (with C P⁴⁷ S) or
possibly βλασφημα (with A).
om. ποιησαι Lat.(?), habet Arm.
om. πολεμον contra K

13:6   *ad blasphemium* = εις βλασφημιαν cum Aν K
habet καιᵘˡᵗ· cum Aν (but also Vulg.)

13:7a om. cum AC P⁴⁷ Aν (Lat. and Arm.)
habet και λαον contra Aν

13:8   *cuius non est scriptum nomen* = οὗ ου γεγραπται το ονομα αυτου
Lat. and Arm. (against Vulg.) cum AC
nomen = το ονομα cum AC K, τα ονοματα P⁴⁷ S Aν

13:9   *aures* with many translations, also Latins, and the Greeks unanimously ους

13:10 *si quis in captivitatem duxerit, in captivitatem ibit*
si quis gladio occiderit, oportet eum gladio occidi against Arm.
υπαγει¹⌢² cum C P⁴⁷ S Aν
The identical text of the other Latins somewhat undermines the
Latin reading *duxerit*.

13:12 ποιει² = facit cum rel. plur., εποιει K
cuius ... eius = οὗ ... αυτου cum rel. plur.

13:13 ποιει] faciet with *f*¹⁷²/²⁵⁰ *f*²⁰⁶⁰ and many translations ινα και πυρ
ποιη εκ του ουρανου καταβ. accurately translated against K

13:14 πλανα] *seducet* (see 13:13)
homines (sine τους εμους contra K)

13:15 useless for textual criticism

13:16b likewise

[170] 13:17 om. και¹ cum C S* *f*²⁰¹⁴ al. pc. (and other Latins)

το ονομα] *nominis* cum C al. pc.

13:18 quite free; only the number 666 is given exactly

17:8 only one part is cited clearly

in perditionem vadit = υπαγει cum A al. pc. versions, υπαγειν rel.

17:12 *cum bestia* = μετα του θηριου

(other Latins post bestiam = μετα το θηριον)

17:13 none of the Greek text's variants are visible

17:14 practically identical with Vulg.

19:11 *vocabatur fidelis*, assumes καλουμενος, which AC Aν omit

Conybeare retroverts the Armenian text: εκαλειτο πιστος και αληθινος

19:12 *sicut flamma* = ως φλοξ cum A al. pc., however, thus also Vulg.

Conybeare retroverts Armenian: εις φλογα πυρος

ονομα γεγραμμενον against K (and S)

19:13 βεβαμμενον] *aspersum* = ρεραντισμενον, likewise Gig. Prisc.

Arm. according to Conybeare περιρεραμμενον (= S*)

19:14 *in equis albis* against Aν εφιπποι πολλοι

om. και ante καθαρον contra Aν

19:15 om. διστομος contra K

om. και ante της οργης

19:16 habet επι² (Lat. and Arm.) contra S

19:20 εβληθησαν] βληθησονται Lat. and Arm. cum Aν

20:6a literally identical with Vulg.; no variant of recognizable importance

20:11 *locus non est eis* (instead of ευρεθη)

20:12 habet τους μεγαλους και τους μικρους contra K

20:13a, 13b, 14a, 15 no recognizable variants

21:1 απηλθαν (-ον) plural Lat. and Arm. (singular Aν)

21:2 om. απο του θεου cum *f*²⁰⁶⁵

21:3 *de throno* cum A S Latt., εκ του ουρανου rel.

λαοι cum A S Aν, λαος K Vulg.

habet αυτων θεος cum A (Aν) contra S K

21:4 om. θεος (Lat. and Arm.) cum S Aνᵖˡᵘʳ· K

habet οτι (Lat. and Arm.) cum S K Latt.ᵖˡᵘʳ·

21:5 om. μοι cum A K

~ πιστοι και αληθινοι contra Aν

[171] 21:6   *facta sunt* (= γεγοναν cum A al. pc.?, γεγονα S* Aν K) Lat. and
          Arm.; likewise the Syrian fragment in this location
     The readings from the above list should be highlighted:
     1:15 (πεπυρωμενω with S); 4:7 (*quasi humanam* = ως ανθρωπου with
A; Anastasios Sinaites's Greek text is less reliable); 13:6 βλασφημιας with
C P[47] S; 13:7a (om. cum AC P[47] Aν; confirms the great antiquity of this
error); 13:8 (*Urtext* with [A]C); 13:17 (του ονοματος with C); 17:8 (υπαγει
with A); 19:12 (ως φλοξ with A, however, also Vulg.); 21:3 (θρονου with A
S, however, also Vulg. and other Latins; habet αυτων θεος with A [Aν]; cf.
other Latins). With Aν K only 13:6 (βλασφημιαν, habet και[ult.] cum Aν);
19:20 (βληθησονται).
     Irenaeus is one of the oldest witnesses to the "Western" text in other
New Testament writings. Here, however, Irenaeus's text does not seem to
have differed greatly from the "neutral."

2.6.7. Old Manuscript Fragments

Six old manuscript fragments are extant: P[18] (third/fourth century); P[24]
(early fourth century); P[43], 0163 (fifth century); 0169 (fourth century); and
0207 (fourth century). On 0207, see my "Der Apokalypse-Text des Kodex
0207," 187–89. With the exception of P[43], the four that remain are printed
and discussed by Charles.[241]
     Here is a summary of the results:
     P[18] (1:4–7) consistently agrees (as far as it is legible and apart from a
unique reading in 1:6) with AC. P[18] shares the omission of των αιωνων in
1:6 with A and some minuscule groups, an omission that can only be an
error. P[18] does not preserve any of the unique readings of S, Aν, and K.
     P[24] (5:5–8; 6:5–8). P[24]'s very damaged text is identical to A's, except for
the spelling of εμμεσω in 5:6. P[24] reads εχων (K εχον) in 5:6 with A S Aν, and
φωνην in 6:7 with A S Aν, which C K omits.
     P[43] is only a small, almost useless scrap of papyrus sheet from the sec-
tion of a roll, most likely from the seventh century. The leaf is an opis-
tograph, with the text of each side written by a different hand. The roll
clearly only contained extracts from the Apocalypse because the two sides
preserve parts of widely separated chapters of the Apocalypse. The text's
scanty remains do not belong to either Aν or K.

---

241. Charles, *Critical and Exegetical Commentary on the Revelation*, 2:447–51.

[172] 2:13   om. τα εργα σου και (deduced from the existing space) cum AC
S al. pc. contra Aν K

om. εν αις cum AC al. pc. (on the basis of the space)

15:8   habet επτα^2 with all against Aν

16:1   τη εικονι] την εικονα cum S al. pc.

0163 (16:17–19) also agrees literally with A (hiat C), even in the read-ing αστραπαι και φωναι και βρονται (A f^{1006} 1611 1854 2053 – 2062 f^{2014} f^{2065}). 0163 does not contain any of the corrections of P^{47} S and Aν K.

0169 (3:19–4:2) is most closely related to S. 0169 or 0169^c reads 3:20 + και ante εισελευσομαι with S K (*Urtext*), 3:19 ζηλευε] ζηλωσον 0169^c with S Aν. 0169 reads with A (hiat C) S: 4:2 om. και^1 0169* A S* K. 4:3 + και ο καθημενος 0169 A S; further 4:1 ηνεωγμενη] ανεωγμενη 0169 Aν$^{plur.}$ K; 4:2 + και ante ευθεως 0169^c S^a Aν; καθημενος] -ον 0169 2329 Prim.

0169 does not confirm the unique readings of A 4:1 αναβα] αναβηθι and α] οσα. Also, none of Aν and K's unique readings surface in 0169.

0207 (9:2–15) reads εσκοτωθη in 9:2 with A (hiat C), om. τεσσαρων in 9:13 with A P^{47} S^a and the versions, which, in both cases, is undoubtedly the *Urtext*, but not ειχαν in 9:8 with A S. Only the omission of εκτω in 9:14 with A is a common error. In contrast to the other old fragments, 0207 shares several corrections with Aν and K: 0207 shares with Aν the two stylistic improvements in 9:12 ερχεται] ερχονται and 9:14 (φωνην) λεγοντα] λεγουσαν (likewise P^{47}), as well as the omission of και^3 in 9:10. 0207 shares the following readings with K alone:

9:4 μετωπων] + αυτων; 9:5 αυτοις] αυταις; 9:6 ευρωσιν] ευρησουσιν (like-wise S); 9:7 ομοιοι χρυσω] χρυσοι; 9:11 the relationship of μετα ταυτα to what follows.

0207 differs greatly from to the Origen text of P^{47} S.

These older manuscript fragments confirm A's outstanding value as the Apocalypse's best manuscript once again.

Second Section
3. The Linguistic Style of the Apocalypse

As with the edition of any text, the author's linguistic style should be used systematically alongside the manuscript tradition to establish the Apocalypse's text. Paying attention to the author's linguistic style in textual criticism is particularly important and fruitful because the Apocalypse's mode of expression often contradicts acceptable Greek parlance and showcases many stereotypical repetitions. Among modern textual critics, Bousset[1] and Charles apply this principle. The description of the Apocalypse's grammar that follows was drawn up in order to derive the most reliable criteria possible for making text-critical decisions and assessing the tradition's individual stems. This description focuses solely on what is important for textual criticism.

3.1. Morphology

We should first discuss the "Ionic" genitive and dative ending in μαχαιρα.
  13:10 μαχαιρη bis AC P⁴⁷ 2351
         μαχαιρα S Aν K
  13:14 μαχαιρης AC (dub. P⁴⁷) S 2351 (2329)
         μαχαιρας Aν K

---

1. "Textual criticism can only be pursued in close connection with research into grammar and linguistic style. This is all the more applicable in regard to the Apocalypse, since its language is extraordinarily stable. This fact leads to the principle that readings that bear witness to uniform usage in Apocalypse are generally preferable, although some caution must be practiced. Conformation of one reading by way of a parallel should only be adopted where such a harmonization makes sense in the process of transcription." (Bousset, *Die Offenbarung Johannis*, 158).

All modern critical editions[2] (with the exception of von Soden's) regard μαχαιρης the *Urtext* because the manuscripts considered the best witnesses, including the Apocalypse's oldest manuscript (P[47]), preserve this form. [174] We need to examine first whether this is truly justified. In particular, we note that even outside of the Apocalypse the genitive and dative forms of μαχαιρα occur with -η in certain manuscripts:

Matt 26:52   μαχαιρη S B A C L
Luke 21:24   μαχαιρης B* Δ
      22:49   μαχαιρη S B* D L T
Acts 12:2   μαχαιρη S B* D* 61
Heb 11:34   μαχαιρης P[46] S (hiat B) A D*
      11:37   μαχαιρης P[46] S (hiat B) D*

Even in the LXX, μαχαιρης is written with -η in all these same manuscripts.[3] Because these forms already surface in papyri of the Ptolemaic period, where the majority preserve Attic forms,[4] the "Ionic" could be the *Urtext*. It is impossible to be certain here.[5]

---

2. Likewise Blass, *Grammatik des neutestamentlichen Griechisch*, §43.

3. See Thackeray, *Introduction, Orthography and Accidence*, 140–42.

4. See Mayser, *Grammatik der griechischen Papyri*, 1.1:12. Also, the ca. 300 CE papyrus of the apocryphal Acts of Paul (Univ.-Bibl. Hamburg) has two analoguous examples of ημερης.

5. That there is no real tradition in orthographica is recognized. See, e.g., James Hope Moulton, *Prolegomena*, vol. 1 of *A Grammar of New Testament Greek* (Edinburgh: T&T Clark, 1908), 35; and the judgment of J. Wackernagel (review of *Grammatik der griechischen Papyri aus der Ptolemäerzeit*, by Edwin Mayser, *TLZ* 33 [1908]: 36) "that even the best tradition of the Septuagint has not been able to preserve the orthography of its time of origin," and Paul Maas (review of *Ephraem Syri Opera*, edited by Sylvio G. Mercati, *ByzZ* 23 [1914–1919]: 264): "In these cases [for Orthographica], there are probably grammarian rules and scribal habits, but no tradition." That here even the best of the manuscripts are unreliable proves that the vulgar accusative form often occurs as -αν in the third declension: 9:4 σφραγιδαν S; 9:14 σαλπιγγαν P[47]; 10:5 χειραν P[47]; 12:13 γυναικαν P[47]; 12:13 αρσεναν A; 13:14 εικοναν A; 22:2 μηναν A. For the LXX, see Thackeray, *Introduction, Orthography and Accidence*, 146–45; Joseph Ziegler, *Isaias*, Septuaginta 14 (Göttingen: Vandenhoeck & Ruprecht, 1939), 102; Ziegler, *Duodecim prophetae*, Septuaginta 13 (Göttingen: Vandenhoeck & Ruprecht, 1943), 119; Ziegler, *Susanna, Daniel, Bel et Draco*, Septuaginta 16.2 (Göttingen: Vandenhoeck & Ruprecht, 1954), 74; for the rest of the New Testament, von Soden, *Die Schriften des Neuen Testaments*, 1:1388. For S, see the remark of Milne and Skeat, *Scribes and Correctors of the Codex Sinaiticus*, 54.

Conversely, AC S* read χρυσαν for χρυσην in 1:13. Except for von Soden, all modern editions consider this form a harmonization to αργυραν rather than the *Urtext*. Although the word surfaces in a fourth/fifth-century CE papyrus and even in later times, neither the LXX nor the rest of the New Testament offers an analogy.[6] Only the weight of the three oldest manuscripts and the fact that Aν and K are, on the whole, heavily corrected argue for its inclusion in the text in 1:13.

Most modern editions since Lachmann consider the vowel weakening α < ε in τεσσαρα – τεσσερα (in nominative and [175] accusative) the *Urtext* in the Apocalypse. The details are as follows:

4:6   τεσσερα A (hiat C)
4:8   τεσσερα A (hiat C) S
5:8   τεσσερα A (hiat C) S 2020
5:14   τεσσερα A (hiat C) 2020 628
19:4   τεσσερα AC S 616
τεσσερακοντα: 7:4 C S (non A); 11:2 A (hiat C) S; 13:5 AC S; 14:1 AC S; 14:3 AC S; 21:17 A (hiat C); S compendium, as always P⁴⁷.[7]

Only von Soden selects the α form consistently. Bousset and Merk select the α form of τεσσαρα in 4:6; 5:8, 14 and the ε form in 4:8 and 19:4, besides always using τεσσαρακοντα.

The testimony of the three ancient majuscules (P⁴⁷ is lacunose here) once again provides the basis for the decision of the modern critical editions. In the LXX, the facts are of particular methodological importance for evaluating the two forms. Also, the two forms with ε are common in the majuscules, although the forms are unattested in papyri before the first century CE and only gain currency in the second century CE (i.e., they could not have been in the LXX's original text).[8] But we must conclude that only the scribes of the majuscules that have come down to us insert the corresponding forms of the dominant language of their

---

6. See Blass, *Grammatik des neutestamentlichen Griechisch*, §45.

7. Otherwise in the New Testament, John 19:23 τεσσερα S A L M (non-B) (so also Tisch WHort against Sod Vog Merk).

8. See Thackeray, *Introduction, Orthography and Accidence*, 73–74, 62–63. Also, Moulton (*Prolegomena*, 457) draws attention to this tension between New Testament majuscules and papyri; see James Hope Moulton and Wilbert Francis Howard, *Accidence and Word-Formation*, vol. 2 of *A Grammar of New Testament Greek* (Edinburgh: T&T Clark, 1919), 172, where the ε form is rejected as spurious.

time. And these are the same manuscripts that also have these Hellenistic forms in the New Testament.

The spelling ημισου = ημισυ is generally rejected. It surfaces in 11:9 in A (non C), 11:11 in A S* (non C P⁴⁷), 12:14 in P⁴⁷ S*. It also emerges in the LXX (3 Kgdms 3:25; Isa 44:16) in Codex B.[9]

The tradition is divided between the older κολλυριον in C S Aᵥᵖᵃʳᵗ· K and κολλουριον in A Aᵥᵖᵃʳᵗ· Compl. (κουλλουριον Aᵥᵖᵃʳᵗ·) in 3:18, as well as the LXX. Because both forms are common elsewhere, a decision is not possible.

[176] The tradition is divided between μαστοις C Aᵥ K (and most modern editions), μασθοις S 2050 f¹⁰⁴ f²⁰⁶⁰ (Tisch), and μαζοις A f¹⁰⁰⁶ f²⁰¹⁴ Compl. (Weiss) in 1:13. The fact that μαστος is the best or unanimously testified form in the LXX[10] and the rest of New Testament[11] indicates that A makes a correction here.[12]

Only Compl. and a small number of other minuscules have the classic αρκτος in 13:2 instead of the later, albeit already attested by the LXX, αρκος.

Αρρην – αρσην

12:5   αρσεν AC
         αρσενα Aᵥ f¹⁰⁰⁶ 1611 2053 Hipp. Meth.
         αρρενα P⁴⁷ S K
12:13   αρσενα AC S f¹⁰⁰⁶ 1611 1854 2053 2351 al. pc.
         αρρενα P⁴⁷ Aᵥ K

In addition to the Attic αρρην, the Koine also preserves the Ionian αρσην.[13] The LXX attests the form with ρσ almost exclusively and, consistent with this, it is preserved everywhere the word appears in the New Testament outside the Apocalypse. The form with ρσ is certain in: Matt 19:4; Mark 10:6; Luke 2:23; Gal 3:28 (αρρεν S); also 1 Cor 6:9 and 1 Tim 1:10. Also, Rom 1:27, where the tradition is very divided, maintains the ρσ form pre-

---

9. See Thackeray, *Introduction, Orthography and Accidence*, 180.

10. See also ibid., 104 (μασθος weakly attested as a variant).

11. Luke 11:27; 23:29; where both times D F G reads μασθος.

12. That μαστος and μασθος are usually used in the feminine and μαζος in the masculine (according to the testimony of the lexicon of "Suidas") only confirms that A's reading is a subsequent improvement. In line with this conclusion, Andreas also writes μαζοι in the commentary (not in the text).

13. See Albert Thumb, *Die griechische Sprache im Zeitalter des Hellenismus: Beiträge zur Kenntnis und Beurteilung der Κοινή* (Strassburg: Trübner, 1901), 77–78; Mayser, *Grammatik der griechischen Papyri*, 1.1:220.

dominantly.[14] The same is also true in the Apocalypse, and all the more so since S A (and C) preserve the form with ρρ in Rom 1:27.

The dative of τεσσαρες (7:2; 20:8), τεσσαρσι, is not in question. Only S reads the later τετρασι in 20:8.[15]

The occurrence of πυρος in place of πυρρος in 6:4 (A P Q Av^part. Kpart.) and 12:3 (C Av^part. Kplur.) is probably due to simple scribal carelessness. A few minuscules, however, write βορας for βορρας (21:13).

[177] υαλος – υελος, υαλινος – υελινος

ερευναω – ερευναω

These two words should be discussed together since they display the same vowel weakening α < ε.

Beside the Ionian-Hellenistic υελος, the Koine also preserves the Attic υαλος.[16] The Apocalypse also has the α form like the LXX.[17] And the majority of textual witnesses consistently support the α form. Only the K text and its mixed texts advance υελος, υελινος, so that in one place (21:21) υελος garners the majority of witnesses for K.[18]

2:23   εραυναω AC

ερευναω S Av K

Because the AC stem alone has the α form here, other occurrences of the two forms should be examined carefully. Both forms commonly occur side by side and even vary within the same manuscript in the LXX.[19] The findings are as follows in the New Testament (outside of the Apocalypse):

The α form surfaces:

---

14. In the first place, only B D* G al. pc. αρσενες; in the second, B S^c D E GK L P against S* A C; in the third, αρσεσιν all except S* A and some minuscules.

15. Likewise, Acts 10:11 E; 11:5 D; 12:4 H; in the LXX Judg 9:34 B.

16. See Thumb, *Die griechische Sprache*, cit. 18:75 (γυαλί in modern Greek).

17. Only the Apocalypse uses the word within the New Testament.

18. See, in addition, Schmid, "Untersuchungen zur Geschichte des griechischen Apokalypsetextes," 446. The facts are the following: 4:6 υελινη a minority of Av and K. 15:2 υελινην P^47 Compl and a minority of Av and K; 21:18 υελω Compl *f*^1006 1854 2050 and a minority of Av and K; 21:21 υελος K Compl *f*^1006 1611 1854 2050 and some manuscripts from Av. The strange thing is that the number of K witnesses for the ε form increases towards the end of the Apocalypse.

19. See the compilation for the LXX in Thackeray, *Introduction, Orthography and Accidence*, 79 n. 1; and Ziegler, *Duodecim prophetae*, 110. The papyri of the Ptolemaic period only have ερευναω. εραυναω appears in the papyri only after Christ (Mayser, *Grammatik der griechischen Papyri*, 1.1:113); see also Thumb, *Die griechische Sprache*, supra 176–77; Gerhard Delling, "ἐρευνάω," *TWNT* 2:653.

John 5:39 S B*; 7:52 S B D T Orig.; Rom 8:27 S P⁴⁶; 11:33 S B A (hiat P⁴⁶); 1 Cor 2:10 S B* A C P⁴⁶; 1 Pet 1:10 S B* A; 1:11 S B*

This testimony, alongside the facts of the LXX in the same manuscripts, leads to a conclusion similar to the one reached about τεσσαρα – τεσσερα, namely, that one should doubt that a real tradition is present here.

Contracted and uncontracted forms:

χρυσους regularly occurs in a contracted form, as almost always in the LXX[20] and as in the rest of the New Testament (2 Tim 2:20; Heb 9:4 bis). All modern critical editions, therefore, correctly reject the uncontracted form [178] in 2:1, where AC read χρυσεων. The same preference for the uncontracted forms also appears in S and P⁴⁷: cf. 9:20 χρυσα] -σεα P⁴⁷ S 2351; αργυρα] -ρεα P⁴⁷ 2351; χαλκα] -κεα S, χαλκα P⁴⁷; see also 4:4 χρυσους] -σεας S; 5:8 χρυσας] -σεας S (contrast 15:6, 7 χρυσας). Moreover, 21:17 πηχεων S 1611 2030 2329.

The uncontracted form of πυλων also surfaces, although strongly attested only in the dative plural. The tradition is closed throughout so that the original form is not in doubt. Only in 22:14 does the dative form of the Aν text (πυλεωσι) prevail over πυλωσι. In 21:25, however, one will also have to read πυλωνες rather than πυλεωνες in Aν.

3.1.1. Assimilation of Consonants[21]

In general, the tendency to isolate syllables is stronger than their assimilation in Koine Greek. While the older papyri assimilate prepositions with their objects, later witnesses frequently preserve εν and συν without assimilation. Similarly, the oldest LXX manuscripts fail to assimilate εν and συν before the gutturals. Also, the failure to assimilate συν is the rule in the Apocalypse's ancient manuscripts, whereas the opposite is true for εν, and also across the boundary between the preposition and its object.

    1:9   συνκοινωνος C S P 2329 al. pc. against A Aν (and Sod Vog Merk)
            (κοινωνος K)

---

20. See Thackeray, *Introduction, Orthography and Accidence*, 172–73. Except, e.g., Sir 6:30 χρυσεος S B A C; 4 Macc 9:26, 28 σιδηρεας S*.

21. See also generally Mayser, *Grammatik der griechischen Papyri*, 1.1:233–36; for the LXX, 132–33; for the New Testament, Blass, *Grammatik des neutestamentlichen Griechisch*, §19; Westcott and Hort, *New Testament in the Original Greek*, 2:149–50.

18:4   συνκοινωνησητε AC S 2329 against Aν K (and Sod Vog Merk)

On the other hand:

4:6   εμπροσθεν] ενπροσθεν S P Q (hiat C) (Tisch)

19:10 and 22:8   εμπροσθεν all

18:3, 11, 15   εμποροι all

18:23   ενποροι Q sol.

11:13   εμφοβοι all except C

3:18   εγχρισ- most, ενχρισαι S 2329

AC consistently disregard the boundary between the preposition and its object in the case of εμμεσω (which AC always write). Weiss alone explains it as the *Urtext*. See 1:13; 2:1; 4:6 (A [hiat C] cum 1854 2329); 5:6 (bis A [hiat C] cum 2329; 1st loco 1854); 6:6 (AC 2329); 22:2 (A [hiat C] 2050).[22] [179] 12:2   εγγαστρι Q sol.[23]

The LXX portions of these same manuscripts, however, follow the opposite tendency. Joseph Ziegler consistently uses the assimilated forms with συγ- in his editions of Isaiah and the Twelve Minor Prophets. Since the lack of assimilation in the LXX has only been common since the second century BCE,[24] the scribes who prefer συν- must be following contemporary trends. We can only say with a certain level of probability that the Apocalypse's original text follows this trend.

3.1.2. Declension

Only the Hellenistic form of κλεις in the accusative (κλειδα and κλειδας) occurs in the LXX. This is also certain in Matt 16:19 (S* B* L W Θ Orig., κλεις rel.) and Luke 11:52 (κλειδα the majority, κλειν D). The majority of the Apocalypse's textual witnesses, however, have the Attic form in the singular and plural.

1:18   κλεις AC Aν
         κλειδας S K

3:7   κλειν] κλειδα Aν

---

22. Likewise, A always in the LXX; see Ziegler, *Duodecim prophetae*, 117; Ziegler, *Susanna, Daniel, Bel et Draco*, 74.

23. Likewise, A – 534 Hos 14:1; Amos 1:3, 13.

24. The same manuscripts generally omit the assimilation in the other New Testament writings; Eph 5:11 συνκοιν. S A B* P[46] D* F G L; Phil 4:14 S B* D* E F G (hiat P[46]); Rom 11:17 S A B* P[46] D* F G; 1 Cor 9:23 S B* P[46] D* F G; Phil 1:7 S B* A D E F G.

20:1   κλειν] κλειδα only a few minuscule groups of Aν and *f*[104]. Because the Attic form is also in the rest of New Testament in AC and the later tradition, this form's prevalence in the Apocalypse is not as certain as it seems at first glance.

3.1.3. Verb

Turning to verbs, we will primarily discuss augmentation and conjugation.
    The tradition varies between different forms in a few verbs:
    σκοτοω – σκοτιζω
    8:12   ινα σκοτισθη unanimously attested
    9:2   εσκοτωθη A (hiat C) 0207 *f*[1006] 61 – 69
            εσκοτισθη S Aν K (Bousset Sod Vog)
[180] 16:10 εσκοτωμενη AC P[47] S* Aν[plur.] K
            εσκοτισμενη S[a] Q Aν[pc.]
Only in 9:2 is the original reading uncertain from the outset. The tradition also wavers in Eph 4:18, where P[46] S A B read εσκοτωμενοι and D F G and the K text reads εσκοτισμενοι. The form σκοτοω has the weightier witnesses here, which confirms the decision for the same form in Rev 9:2.
    6:11   αποκτεννεσθαι AC S K[aliqui]
            αποκτενεσθαι K[plur.] Compl.
            αποκτεινεσθαι Aν
The form αποκτεννειν, which the rest of the New Testament also knows[25] but where the tradition regularly varies, is overwhelmingly attested. But it occurs only in the infinitive.[26] The present subjunctive always reads αποκτεινω.
    The frequent transition from the μι form to the ω form in Koine Greek surfaces in the two following cases:
    3:9   διδω AC (all modern editions except Sod)
            διδωμι Aν K (δεδωκα S)
    22:2   αποδιδουν A (hiat C) Oec Aν[part.]
            αποδιδους S Aν[plur.] K[plur.]

---

25. See Blass, *Grammatik des neutestamentlichen Griechisch*, §73.
    26. And in 13:10, like 13:1, the future αποκτενει surfaces in some minuscules. But here a likely textual corruption should be assumed. See also pp. 147–49.

3. The Linguistic Style of the Apocalypse

The only appropriate reading αποδιδουν in 22:2, which comes from αποδιδοω, confirms the authenticity of AC's text in 3:9.[27] In contrast, all read διδοασιν (from διδωμι) in 17:13.

22:8   δεικνυοντος A (hiat C) S Αν
       δεικνυντος S K

The Attic form is otherwise dominant in the New Testament. The Hellenistic form, however, also surfaces in Matt 16:21 (here only B δεικνυναι) and John 2:18. The Hellenistic form in the active voice prevails over the Attic in the LXX.[28]

απολλυων is unanimously attested in 9:11.

αφιω is decisively and strongly attested twice instead of αφιημι:

2:20   αφεις (= αφιεις[29]) S* AC K, αφηκας Sᵃ Ανᵖᵃʳᵗ·

11:9   αφιουσιν S* AC Αν, αφησουσιν Sᵃ K

[181] See also Friedrich Blass, *Grammatik des neutestamentlichen Griechisch*, §94.2; for the LXX, see Thackeray, *Introduction, Orthography and Accidence*, 251.

Instead of πετομαι, Αν only preserves the late reading πεταμαι in 12:14,[30] although it also surfaces in the LXX.[31] In addition to this reading, a small number of manuscripts preserve ω instead of ο (πετωμενος) four times (4:7; 8:13; 14:6; 19:17). This testimony, however, is insufficient to conclude that πεταομαι undergirds a part of the tradition.

Conversely, δυνη (δυνασαι 2053ᵗˣᵗ·-ᶜᵒᵐᵐ· al. pc.) in 2:2 presupposes δυνομαι, which is attested as an Old Testament variant[32] and surfaces primarily in Mark 9:22–23 and Luke 16:2.

AC read πειν (C πιν) and P⁴⁷⁽ᵛⁱᵈ·⁾ S Αν K read πιειν in 16:6 as an aorist infinitive form from πινειν.

In the rest of the New Testament, the oldest majuscules[33] usually preserve the later πειν, which also surfaces in the LXX of the same manuscripts.[34] On the other hand, πειν is unattested in the papyri of the Ptol-

---

27. The LXX already knows this form; see Thackeray, *Introduction, Orthography and Accidence*, 249–50.

28. See ibid., 245.

29. See Blass, *Grammatik des neutestamentlichen Griechisch*, §31.2.

30. Likewise, 14:6 S πεταμενον.

31. See Thackeray, *Introduction, Orthography and Accidence*, 281–82.

32. See ibid., 249.

33. But never A, thus, as rarely as in the LXX (see the following note).

34. According to Thackeray (*Introduction, Orthography and Accidence*, 64), B reads πειν 12x among 45 cases, S reads it 9x among 23 cases, and A never reads it

emaic period.[35] This fact proves that Rev 16:6 πειν (πιν C) is not a simple scribal error of AC. On the other hand, as in the case of τεσσερα and εραυναω, an actual tradition cannot be spoken of here.

2:17   νικωντι] νικουντι AC
2:7   likewise A (non C)
15:2   νικουντας C
(See Rom 12:21 νικου A.)

The influence of the ε conjugation on the α conjugation[36] explains these errors.

Against the rest of the New Testament, the Apocalypse uses the active ευαγγελιζω[37] instead of the middle ευαγγελιζομαι (10:7; 14:6). Part of the tradition preserves the middle in both places: in 10:7 it is preserved in Compl. f^{2014} f^{2031} f^{2051} 1611 1854 2344 2351 94; in 14:6 it is preserved in P[47] S Compl. f^{2014} f^{2031} f^{1678} $f^{172/250}$ 2029 2329.

[182] The Apocalypse's linguistic style, manifest in its use of θαυμαζειν, is strange and inconsequential. While the active form stands in 17:6 (εθαυμασα) and 17:7 (εθαυμασας), the word surfaces as a deponent in 13:3 (in the aorist tense) and in 17:8 (in the future tense).[38] In 13:3, S K preserve εθαυμασεν once again, while Aν understands the grammatical form εθαυμασθη as a passive and changes ολη η γη into εν ολη τη γη. The reading in 17:8 takes the form θαυμασθησονται only in A (hiat C) P 1611. S Aν K have the middle form θαυμασονται.

3.1.4. Augment Formation

We cannot speak of an actual textual tradition in the case of δυναμαι, μελλω, and ανοιγω.

The data for δυναμαι are as follows:

---

among 50 cases. In the New Testament, outside of the Apocalypse, the exact findings are as follows: Matt 27:34 πειν bis S* D; Mark 15:23 D (om. S B); John 4:7, 9, 10 S* B* C* D L; Acts 23:12, 21 B*; Rom 14:21 D*; 1 Cor 9:4 S* B* D* F G; 10:7 S B* D* F G.

35. See Mayser, *Grammatik der griechischen Papyri*, 1.2:138.

36. Similar examples in the LXX tradition in Thackeray, *Introduction, Orthography and Accidence*, 241–42; Robert Helbing, *Grammatik der Septuaginta, Laut- und Wortlehre* (Göttingen: Vandenhoeck & Ruprecht, 1907), 111.

37. See also Blass, *Grammatik des neutestamentlichen Griechisch*, §309.1.

38. For the linguistic-historical understanding of this development, see ibid., §78 and §307.

ηδυνατο 5:3 A (hiat C) Aν; 7:9 and 14:3 Aν; 15:8 S Aν. εδυνατο 5:3 S
K; 7:9 AC S K; 14:3 AC P[47] S K; 15:8 AC P[47] K.

A comprehensive assessment of the individual textual witnesses is not available. A and S vary.

An actual textual tradition is even less apparent in the case of μελλω.

3:2 εμελλον AC S Aν[plur.]

εμελλες K[plur.], ημελλες K[part.]

10:4 εμελλον S K[plur.]

ημελλον AC P[47] Aν[plur.] K[part.]

Bousset, von Soden, Vogels, and Merk harmonize 10:4 to 3:2. However, the case for a harmonization is no better than its opposite. The authority of the manuscripts should be followed, and the two unabalanced forms should be allowed to stand side by side.

The augment of ανοιγω should be considered in conjunction with the different formations of the aorist in the passive voice. The aorist active form ηνοιξα (not ανεῳξα) is attested unanimously in all places (6:1, 3, 5, etc.). Also, the various textual stems generally agree in their preservation of ηνοιχθη or ηνοιγη in the aorist passive form with the augment. That is to say, the augment occurs in the prefix of the aorist passive form as it does in the aorist active form. This is unanimously the case in 11:19 and 15:5. However, [183] the tradition is far more mixed in 20:12: the late Compl. group writes ανεῳχθη(σαν) in both halves of the verse, the plurality of Aν writes ανεῳχθη(σαν) in 20:12a, and S[a] and K (in 20:12b) offer the form ηνεῳχθη(σαν) with the double augment in 20:12b. In the perfect passive, however, the two forms of ανεῳγμενος and ηνεῳγμενος stand alongside each other with equally strong attestation:

3:8 ανεῳγμενην AC Aν K

ηνεῳγμενην S P 1611 2050 2053[txt.-comm.] 2329 𝑓[205] 𝑓[2051] 2059 81 al. pc.

4:1 ανεῳγμενη Aν[part.] K

ηνεῳγμενη A (hiat C) S Aν[part.]

10:2 ανεῳγμενον K

ηνεῳγμενον C (om. A) P[47] S Aν[plur.]

10:8 ανεῳγμενον P[47] K

ηνεῳγμενον AC Aν[plur.]

19:11 ανεῳγμενον Aν K

ηνεῳγμενον A (hiat C) S P 1611 𝑓[2051]

Only K consistently has the simple augment, while all other textual witnesses vary, showing again that we cannot speak of an actual tradition here.[39] We consider two forms of the aorist passive below.

The tradition is unanimous regarding ευρισκω: the aorist (ευρεθη 5:4; 12:8) has no augment in keeping with later Greek.

On the other hand, in the case of ερημοω, the form with the augment is dominant in the tradition:[40]

17:16 ηρημωμενην] ερημωμενην Aν^{part.} K^{aliqui}
18:17, 19 ερημωθη Aν^{aliqui}

3.1.5. Reduplication of ρ

19:13 περιρεραμμενον S*
		ρεραντισμενον P 2019 2329 Hipp. Orig.
		ρεραμμενον 1611
		ερραμμενον Oec
		ερ(ρ)αντισμενον 1678 – 1778^{mg.} ƒ¹⁰⁰⁶ 792 ƒ¹⁷²
		(see Heb 10:22 ρεραντισμενοι P⁴⁶ S* AC D)

[184] 3.1.6. Formation of Aorists

Throughout its development, Koine Greek tends to replace the second-aorist with the first. πιπτω is the most important example of this. The details are as follows:

First-Person Singular
		1:17 επεσα AC S Aν K^{part.}
				επεσον K^{plur.}
		19:10 επεσον Aν^{pc.} K^{plur.}
		22:8 επεσον K^{omn.}

Third-Person Plural
		5:8 επεσαν] -σον Aν^{part.} K^{plur.} and exactly the same in 5:14; 6:13; 7:11; 11:16; 16:19; 17:10; 19:4.

---

39. On the whole, the facts correspond to that of the LXX (cf. Thackeray, *Introduction, Orthography and Accidence*, 202–3), the rest of the New Testament (see von Soden, *Die Schriften des Neuen Testaments*, 1:1387–88), and Koine Greek in general.

40. Even in the LXX, only individual manuscripts omit the augment here, particularly B.

Imperative Aorist

6:16 πεσατε A P 2329 2351 f^{104} al. pc. (WHort Weiss Charles)

πεσετε C S Αν K (Tisch Bousset Sod Vog Merk)

In Luke 23:30, where the same citation from Hos 10:8 is used as in Rev 6:16, πεσετε is better attested: S* A B D K M Π al. contra πεσατε C L N Q W X Δ al. Ziegler adopts πεσατε (with B Q min.) in his edition of the Twelve Minor Prophets.

The first- and second-aorist forms also oscillate among the following verbs:

10:9 απηλθα A P^{47} 2329 2351 f^{336} al. pc.

απηλθον C S Αν K

15:6 εξηλθαν C sol.

εξηλθον A P^{47} S Αν K

21:1 απηλθαν A (hiat C) S 2329

απηλθον K, παρηλθεν Αν

21:4 απηλθαν A (hiat C) sol.

απηλθον Αν, απηλθεν S K

On the other hand, ηλθαν occurs only in 2329 in 7:13; εξηλθον occurs in all witnesses in 9:13.

In the imperative:

18:4 εξελθατε A S al. pc.

εξελθετε Αν

εξελθε C K

Significantly, no manuscript or group is consistent.[41]

[185] 9:8 ειχαν A (hiat C) S 792 (Tisch WHort Charles)

ειχον Αν K

In contrast, ειχον is consistent in all witnesses in 9:9 (only WHort and Charles place ειχαν in the text for consistency's sake).[42]

17:3 ιδα A (hiat C), ειδα Hipp.

17:6 ιδα A (hiat C), ειδα S 2329 (non Hipp.)

This form occurs only in these two places (and not only in A), while ειδον is always attested unanimously in many other places. In one place, C alone inserts this form in the text:

---

41. In the rest of the New Testament, see Matt 22:22 απηλθαν B D al. pc.; Mark 1:29 ηλθαν L; John 18:6 απηλθαν S B D; Matt 10:13 ελθατω S C 33 al. pc.; 25:36 ηλθατε S B A D E F G L al. pc.

42. 9:10 ειχαν (in place of εχουσιν) 2329.

19:3   ειρηκαν] ειπαν C sol., ειπον f¹⁶⁷⁸
18:19   εβαλαν C sol.
16:6   εξεχεαν all
16:1   εκχεατε Aν K
        εκχεετε AC S (hiat P⁴⁷) f¹⁰⁰⁶ 1611 f¹⁶⁷⁸ 2053 al. pc. (and all
        modern editions against Blass)⁴³
2:4   αφηκας A Sᶜ Aν K
        αφηκες C S* (WHort)

The α form infiltrates a few places in some late minuscules where γινεσθαι occurs:

1:9   εγεναμην f²⁸¹⁴ 2059* 2019ᶜᵒʳʳ· 2919
1:10   εγεναμην f²⁸¹⁴ 2059* – 2081 2919
(not in 1:18; 4:2)

The perfect tense -ες surfaces a few times:

2:3   ου κεκοπιακες AC (and most modern editions; -κας Bousset
        Merk), ουκ εκοπιασας S Aν K
2:5   πεπτωκας AC K (Aν)
        πεπτωκες S (Tisch WHort Sod Vog)
11:17   ειληφας] -φες C sol. (WHort)

The third-person ending of the first-aorist surfaces in the perfect:

18:3   πεπτωκαν AC
        πεπτωκασιν S K, πεπωκεν Aν
19:3   ειρηκαν A S Aνᵖˡᵘʳ·
        ειρηκασιν f¹⁰⁰⁶ 2053 – 2062 al. pc.
        ειρηκεν K, ειπαν C, ειπον f¹⁶⁷⁸
21:6   γεγοναν A (hiat C) 1678 – 1778
        γεγονασιν f¹⁰⁰⁶ 2020 – 2080 2053 – 2062 al. pc.
        γεγονα S* Aν K

[186] All these forms should be evaluated in light of each other and in light of analogous cases in the rest of New Testament, the LXX, and general Koine Greek usage. That the same manuscripts contain non-Attic forms is immediately apparent. First and foremost, this is true of AC. This is usually also true of P⁴⁷'s extant portions, as well as of S's, for the most part. We

---

43. Blass, *Grammatik des neutestamentlichen Griechisch*, §73.

also observe that the same or analogous forms surface in the rest of New Testament [44] and the LXX[45] of the same manuscripts. Most of these forms had currency when the Apocalypse was written. Nevertheless, we cannot evaluate all of the preceding examples in the same way. Though επεσα must be regarded the *Urtext* due to its strong attestation and prevalence in the LXX, the other analogous aorist formations must be evaluated differently. Moreover, the partial harmonizations of the scribe to the more common forms of his day should be considered. We observe this in the LXX of the same manuscripts, which makes it impossible to determine whether the author or later scribes are responsible for these forms.

Scribal activity must be assumed in the case of αφηκας] -κες, ειδα, and ειχα. It is unlikely that the author himself writes ειδα twice after writing ειδον in nearly fifty places and that he juxtaposes the two forms of ειχαν and ειχον in 9:8, 9. εβαλαν in 18:19 should already be rejected because of its testimony.

Imperative aorist of βαινω:
4:1   αναβα S Aν K (and all modern editions)
        αναβηθι A (hiat C) Oec[comm. semel]
11:12   αναβατε AC P[47] S P 792 2329 2351 al. pc.
        αναβητε Aν K
The LXX attests the classical form -βηθι (of αναβαινω), but the later form αναστα also surfaces alongside αναστηθι. For βαινω, the rest of the New Testament uses both forms side by side.[46]

First- and Second-Aorist Passive
12:5   ηρπασθη AC P[47] Aν K
        ηρπαγη S Compl. al. pc. (like 2 Cor 12:2, 4; 1 Thess 4:17)
        ηρπαχθη Q
[187] In the case of ανοιγω, the reading drops from the tradition in 20:12. And while K alone preserves ηνοιχθη (the rest have the second-aorist ηνοιγη) in 11:19 and only f[920] (one of the K groups) reads ηνοιχθη in 15:5,

---

44. See ibid., §§81–83; von Soden, *Die Schriften des Neuen Testaments*, 1:1382–83.
45. See Thackeray, *Introduction, Orthography and Accidence*, 210–12.
46. See ibid., §23.8; Blass, *Grammatik des neutestamentlichen Griechisch*, §95.3. Matt 17:20 μεταβα S B al., μεταβηθι C D al. On the other hand, Matt 27:40 καταβηθι; Luke 14:10 προσαναβηθι; John 7:3 μεταβηθι.

nearly the entire tradition preserves the first-aorist form in 20:12. Only f^{2051} offers ηνοιγη here.

In 2:10, πειραζω is attested almost unanimously in the non-Attic form of the aorist passive with σ: πειρασθητε. f^{2814} 2060 – 2286 1611 attest πειραθητε. In the case of βασταζω, the correct Attic form of the aorist βαστασαι is attested unanimously in 2:3 as in the rest of the New Testament. Αν provides the Hellenistic βασταξαι in 2:2. Conversely, regarding σαλπιζειν, the aorist εσαλπισα (6:1, etc.) is always read as in the LXX and in the rest of the New Testament. As for στηριζω, the tradition varies in 3:2, again, as in the LXX[47] and in the the rest of New Testament,[48] between the Attic στηριξον (S Αν) and the Koine form στηρισον (AC K$^{part.}$, τηρησον K$^{rel.}$).

ερρεθη has, against the Attic, a short vowel in the aorist indicative:[49]

> 6:11   ερρηθη only f^{2051} 2595 2045 $f^{172/250}$ 1854
> 9:4   ερρηθη Q f^{2028} $f^{172/250}$ 1854
> 7:11   ειστηκεισαν Α Κ, εστηκισαν C, ιστηκισαν S, εστηκεσαν Αν$^{plur.}$

The form -εισαν is the rule in the LXX and in the rest of the New Testament.

3.1.7. Elision

We should also discuss elision in this context. απο, επι, and υπο always undergo elision before pronouns. Only in 19:14 does it occur before a noun (εφ ιπποις Α [hiat C] S, επι ιπποις Κ, εφιπποι πολλοι Αν). On the other hand, απο ανατολης is always attested (7:2; 16:12; 21:13). In 21:10, επι ορος is attested by A (hiat C) S al. pc. and επ ορος by Αν Κ. With αλλα, however, finding a firm principle is difficult since the tradition varies greatly here.

> 2:4   αλλα εχω S Κ, αλλ εχω AC Αν
> 2:14   αλλα εχω Κ, αλλ εχω AC S Αν
> 2:20   αλλα εχω Α Κ, αλλ εχω C S Αν

---

47. See Thackeray, *Introduction, Orthography and Accidence*, 223.

48. The Koine form has the better witness in Luke: 9:51 εστηρισεν P^{45} B C L 33; εστηριξεν S A D W al.; 22:32 στηρισον S B A K L al.; στηριξον D Γ Δ. In the letters, however (Rom 16:25; 1 Thess 3:2, 13; 2 Thess 2:17; 3:3 [στηρισειν B]; Jas 5:8; 1 Pet 5:10), the Attic form with ξ is always attested virtually unanimously.

49. Likewise in the LXX (Thackeray, *Introduction, Orthography and Accidence*, 219) and in the New Testament, Rom 9:12, 26; Gal 3:16 respectively in their important manuscripts. On the other hand, Matt 5:21, 27, etc., ερρηθη B D E V Γ al.

3:4   αλλα εχεις AC S al. pc., ~ αλλ ολιγα εχεις K, αλλα om. Av[plur.]

[188] 10:9   αλλα εν S 1611, αλλ εν AC Av K (on the other hand, 10:7 αλλ εν all, except a few minuscules)

17:12   αλλα εξουσιαν A (hiat C) S f[1006] 2329 61 – 69 Hipp.

αλλ εξουσιαν Av K

20:6   αλλα εσονται S 1854 2053[txt.]

αλλ εσονται A (hiat C) Av K

9:5   αλλ ινα all.

Only Av consistently displays elision. The remaining text forms vary and the *Urtext* is unrecognizable in a few places (2:4, 20).

Both Av K, like A, eliminate the hiatus in 2:25:

αχρι οὗ C S

αχρις οὗ Av K

εως οὗ A

In nearly all the places discussed so far, the text of the old manuscripts AC P[47] S is under consideration. Usually the discussion revolves around linguistic phenomena generally in currency in Koine Greek at the time of the Apocalypse's formation. The possibility that some of the old majuscules' readings also represent the *Urtext* is therefore present as a rule. The fact that the same linguistic phenomena also surface in the LXX of those same manuscripts, including those that were even anomalous to the Greek language at the time of the LXX's formation,[50] prevents us from declaring such readings original with absolute certainty. Clearly, we can no longer produce the Apocalypse's original text at the level of orthography with any certainty.

---

50. The same results surface, as expected, in the tradition of the biblical texts as in other ancient literature, such as the Shepherd of Hermas. About a papyrus fragment published by Campbell Bonner in 1934, the editor notes: "The papyrus preserves many peculiarities of the vulgar idiom, which do not appear in the Athos text. In this respect the difference between the two manuscripts is so marked that we can scarcely doubt that the Athos MS [fourteenth/fifteenth century] represents a text deliberately revised (however incompletely) in the effort to conform it to accepted literary standard" ("A Papyrus Codex of the Shepherd of Hermas," *HTR* 18 [1925]: 123–24). The same phenomenon is stated by Oscar von Gebhardt (*Die Psalmen Salomos*, TU 13.2 [Leipzig: Hinrichs, 1895], 30–32) in regard to one of the manuscripts of the Psalms of Solomon.

3.1.8. Proper Names

A (hiat C) S Αν K[plur.] attest Μωυσεως in 15:3; P[47] writes Μω[υ]σεως. Only Compl. ƒ[1678] and a smaller number of other minuscules preserve Μωσεως.

[189] Some problems emerge with the spelling of city names in chapters 1–3.

1:11   Σμυρναν the majority
          Σμυρνην ƒ[2051]

Μυρναν in A and some minuscules is only a scribal error, as 2:8 shows. The Σ has fallen out due to the preceding εις. S writes (with Vulg. and Syr.[1]) Ζμυρνα both times and is not considered the *Urtext*,[51] despite being spelled that way in coins until Trajan's time (and also in inscriptions).

Regarding Thyatira, where we disregard the spelling with ει or ι for the moment, AC Q 1611 1854 2050 2351 ƒ[1678] ƒ[172/250] al. pc. preserve the accusative form Θυατ(ε)ιραν in 1:11, constructing the noun as feminine. In 2:18, 24, however, the masculine Θυατ(ε)ιροις[52] is read with the rest. WHort (against Charles) correctly rejects the feminine form as an error. Not only is the feminine form unprecedented in the inscriptions and in the literature, but 2:18 also stands against it. Weiss[53] correctly speaks of a thoughtless harmonization of the adjacent feminine forms here.

In the place of Λαοδικεια, which is attested in the inscriptions, Strabo, and elsewhere, the following witnesses read:

1:11   Λαοδικιαν AC S min. pc.

3:14   Λαοδικια AC S min. pc.

Because of this, all modern critical editions except von Soden and Merk adopt the incorrect spelling above. The witness of AC S, however, is of no value in this case because it is precisely these manuscripts that teem with itacistic errors and exhibit the aforementioned tendency for monophthongal spelling.[54] It is therefore [190] methodologically correct to spell

---

51. Against James Hope Moulton and George Milligan, *The Vocabulary of the Greek Testament* (London: Hodder & Stoughton, 1914–1929), 274.

52. From (τα) θυατειρα.

53. Weiss, *Die Johannes-Apokalypse*, 135.

54. A full list of documents would be a waste of space. I have therefore limited myself to a few words and the remark that the number of examples could significantly increase.

♦   κλεις: 1:18 κλις AC; 3:7 κλιν AC S; 9:1 κλις A (hiat C) S; 20:1 κλιν A (hiat C) S.

♦   κλειω: 3:7 κλισει AC, κλισαι S; 11:6 κλισαι AC; 20:3 εκλισεν S; 21:25 κλισθωσιν A (hiat C).

Λαοδίκεια orthographically with Αν K.[55] Similarly, Φιλαδέλφεια rather than Φιλαδελφία should be written (against AC S and a large part of Αν manuscripts), just as Θυατειροις in 2:18, 24 is also spelled correctly (against AC[56]) in all modern editions.

3.2. The Use of the Article

This section is of considerable importance for textual criticism. Here we will discuss a wealth of details that needs to be examined closely.

(1) The article is routinely missing before proper names, including

---

- χειρ: 1:16 χιρει (= χειρι) C; 6:5 χιρι C; 9:20 χιρων S; 10:2 χιρει C; 10:5, 8, 10; and 13:16 none; 14:14 χιρι C; 17:4; 20:1, 4 none.
- εικων: 13:14 ικονα C; 13:15a ικονι C; 13:15b; 14:9, 11; 15:2; 16:2; 20:4 none.
- σεισμος: 6:12 σισμος AC S; 8:5 σισμος A (hiat C); 11:13 σισμος AC S; σισμω AC S; 11:19 σισμος AC; 16:18 σισμος A (hiat C) S bis.
- θειον: 9:7 θιον AC S; 9:18 AC 2329; 19:20 θιω S (hiat C); 20:10 θιου A (hiat C) S; 21:8 θιω S (hiat C) 2329.
- δεικνυω: 1:1 none; 4:1; 17:1; and 21:9 διξω S (hiat C); 21:10 εδιξεν A (hiat C) S; likewise 22:1 S (hiat C); 22:6 διξαι S (hiat C); 22:8 διγνυοντος A (hiat C), διχνυντος S.
- τειχος: 21:12 τιχος A (hiat C) (likewise in all the following places) S; 21:14 S; 21:15 none; 21:17 χιλος (!) S; 21:18 τιχους S; likewise 21:19 S.
- σημειον: 12:1, 3 σημιον C S; 13:13 C S P; 13:14 C; 15:1 C S; 16:14 none; 19:20 S.
- τρεις: τρις 6:6 C S; 11:9 AC; 11:11 A C S al. pc.; 21:13 none.
- δει: δι 4:1 S; 10:11 S; 11:5 A (non 13:10); 20:3 S; 22:6 S. Likewise δειπνον] διπνον, πορνεια] πορνια, etc.
- Reversed cases are rare (e.g., 3:16 χλειαρος A; 10:10 μελι] μελλει C S 4:3 ιρις] ιερεις A [hiat C] S.

The preference for the recurring forms ιδον, ιδες, ιδε in this list stems from the preference of these manuscripts for the monophthongal spelling of the ι sound in A C S Q ƒ[104/336] and a few other minuscules with minor fluctuations. These readings have nothing to do with tradition. Therefore, ελεεινος should also be written in 3:17 (WHort ελεινος with AC); 9:21 φαρμακειων and not φαρμακιων; 18:23 φαρμακεια and not φαρμακια.

55. The same applies, of course, also for Col 2:1; 4:13, 15, where 2:1 P[46] and 4:13, 15 B have the form of ει.

56. Accordingly, Θυατειρα in 1:11. By contrast, in the two OT names Νεφθαλιμ (7:6) and Βενιαμιν (7:8), the spelling -ειμ (C Αν K[plur.] against A Q al. pc., Νεφθαλι S with the LXX) or -ειν (A P al. pc.) should be rejected. Similarly, in 7:5 Ρουβην should be written with the LXX and the old majuscules against the army of minuscules. The minuscules have partly Ρουβιν or Ρουβειν or Ρουβειμ or (as the larger number) Ρουβιμ. On the displacement of -ιν through -ιμ in the Greek tradition, see G. R. Driver, review of *Traité de Grammaire Hébraïque*, by Mayer Lambert, *JTS* 40 (1939): 178.

Jesus, while it regularly accompanies θεος. See 1:1, 9, 11; 2:13; 2:20;[57] 5:5; 2:14; 7:4; 21:12;[58] 7:5–8; 11:8; 14:1; [191] 15:3; 16:16; τω ποταμω τω μεγαλω Ευφρατη in 9:14. Correspondingly, the τον before Ευφρατην in 16:12 should be rejected (τον ποταμον τον μεγαν [+ τον AC P[47] 792 f^{1006} 1611 2329 f^{2014} $f^{172/250}$] Ευφρατην).[59] Furthermore, Βαβυλων η μεγαλη is written in 14:8; 16:19; 17:5; 18:2. Only Q 1611 and a few other minuscules insert the article before Βαβυλων in 18:2. Likewise, η πολις η μεγαλη [+ η $f^{172/250}$ and a few others] Βαβυλων is written in 18:10. In 18:21, Βαβυλων η μεγαλη πολις surfaces. In 21:2, την πολιν την αγιαν Ιερουσαλημ καινην is attested. In contrast to Βαβυλων η μεγαλη, the article is missing in the attributive καινην, apparently because την πολιν την αγιαν already functions attributively. The article is also missing before indeclinable nouns, even in the case of a genitive; note την διδαχην Βαλααμ in 2:14. Only some minuscules insert it here: η ριζα [+ του f^{205} f^{2014} f^{2031}] Δαυιδ in 5:5. το γενος Δαυιδ is read (unanimously) in 22:16; thus την κλειν [+ του S Αν K against AC 1611 f^{1678} 1854 Oec] Δαυιδ in 3:7 is a later correction.

τω Βαλακ in 2:14 usually drops out, which Bousset and Charles correctly trace to the indeclinability of the noun.[60]

The following case is difficult to assess:

2:6   τα εργα των Νικολαιτων
2:15   την διδαχην [+ των S Αν] Νικολαιτων

The problem does not lie in the unanimously attested article in 2:6 (since Νικολαιται is not an actual proper name but a designation for a class of people) but in the article's absence in AC K in 2:15 (which should not be understood as a subsequent correction). The subsequent insertion in S Αν, on the other hand, is easier to explain.[61] No decision is possible in this case without authoritative intervention.

---

57. την γυναικα [+ σου A K, + την A] Ιεζαβελ. The article's omission is natural here (exactly like 1:1 τω δουλω αυτου Ιωαννη and 14:1 το ορος Σιων).

58. These three places belong together because of the same change υιοι Ισραηλ. Αν corrects υιων Ισραηλ to του Ισραηλ in 21:12.

59. In fact, of the modern editions, only WHort and von Soden keep the article; Charles puts it in brackets; Tisch Weiss Bousset Vogels Merk omit it. Bousset omits the article by appealing to the lack of articles with proper names. The subsequent insertion, however, is more difficult to explain than a later omission.

60. Indeed, την διδαχην Βαλααμ precedes it in the same verse. But here the article's absence is less egregious than would be the case with ος εδιδασκεν Βαλακ.

61. Of the modern editions, only WHort and Charles omit the article on the basis of their general evaluation of AC's text.

[192] 20:8 τον [om. S*] Γωγ και [+ τον K] Μαγωγ. The fact that Γωγ is not the name of an individual but the name of a people probably accounts for the article.

Ιησους never has the article (1:9; 12:17; 14:12; 17:6; 19:10 [bis];[62] 20:4). The combination Ιησους Χριστος also never has it (see 1:1, 2, 5). But the article usually always accompanies Χριστος (11:15; 12:10; 20:4, 6). The article consistently accompanies θεος, except in 21:7, where it is a predicate noun, and in 7:2, where the anarthrous governing noun (σφραγιδα θεου ζωντος) best accounts for the omission.[63] We need to make clear distinctions in the case of (ο) κυριος. The article is missing in the stereotypical expression κυριος (κυριε) (11:17; 15:3) ο θεος (1:8; 4:8; 11:17; 15:3; 16:7; 18:8; 19:6;[64] 22:5), except in 4:11 (ο κυριος και ο θεος ημων), where ο κυριος represents the vocative case,[65] and in 21:22 (ο γαρ κυριος ο θεος), where the γαρ probably prompts the article's inclusion. Moreover, the article is omitted in εν κυριω (14:13) and κυριος κυριων (predicate noun in 17:14). On the other hand, the article always surfaces whenever a word or a phrase further qualifies κυριος: 11:4 του [om. A Q f^{1006}] κυριου της γης; 11:8 ο [om. f^{2060}] κυριος αυτων; 11:15 του κυριου ημων; 22:21 του κυριου Ιησου. We should also consider ο [om. Aν K contra A S 1611 Oec 2329] κυριος ο θεος των πνευματων των προφητων in 22:6, where the article's omission in Aν K is a harmonization with the preceding verse.

(2) The Apocalypse regularly uses the (generic) article for ηλιος, σεληνη, γη, θαλασσα, and ουρανος. Only two (or three) exceptions should be mentioned. The article's absence in both cases is clearly justified. The formulaic Old Testament expression απο ανατολης ηλιου (7:2; 16:12) calls for the anarthrous ανατολης, which also explains the anarthrous ηλιου. In 22:5 (ουκ εχουσι χρειαν φωτος λυχνου και φωτος ηλιου), however, the article's omission in ηλιου is caused by its absence in the parallel λυχνου.

(3) In other cases (mostly formulaic prepositional phrases with the genitive) the governing noun's article is missing in line with Semitic usage:[66]

---

62. The K text inserts the article in its second occurrence in 19:10; the Compl. text inserts it with a few others in 14:12; only f^{1006} f^{2065} in 17:6; 1st loco in 19:10 and only a few minuscules in 20:4.

63. Thus, also Bousset, *Textkritische Studien*, 173.

64. κυριος om. Aν.

65. See also p. 216.

66. Yet see Blass, *Grammatik des neutestamentlichen Griechisch*, §259.1.

[193] 6:16 απο [+ του 2429] προσωπου του καθημενου; likewise, 12:14 απο
προσωπου του οφεως. In contrast, 20:11 οὗ απο του [om. Αν K contra A S P
792 *f*[1006] 1611 2050 2329] προσωπου. The previous relative pronoun may
have led to the addition of the article. The omission in Αν K would then be
a harmonization to the common expression. This is more likely than the
assumption that Αν K preserve the *Urtext*.[67]

The article is also missing in other prepositional phrases:

2:23 εν θανατω; 6:8 εν ρομφαια και εν λιμω και εν θανατω; 14:10 εν πυρι
και θειω; 13:3 εις θανατον; 2:22 εις κλινην; 13:10 εις αιχμαλωσιαν; 2:10 εις
φυλακην; 2:10 and 12:11 αχρι θανατου; 9:7, 9 εις πολεμον. In contrast, 20:8
εις τον [om. Αν] πολεμον; 16:14 εις τον [om. P[47] Αν] πολεμον της ημερας.
Only 20:8 departs from the rule if we maintain that the article is original.
In 16:14, the article is used because the genitive that follows is also definite.
Despite that, the article is missing in εκ χειρος του αγγελου in 8:4 and in εις
θεραπειαν των [om. S 2053 – 2062[txt.]] εθνων in 22:2. The absence of the article in the phrases εκ πασης φυλης υιων Ισραηλ in 7:4 and των δωδεκα φυλων
υιων Ισραηλ in 21:12 (contrast ενωπιον των υιων Ισραηλ in 2:14) should be
considered idiosyncratic. The article's omission in the governing noun
υιων may have led to the use of the anarthrous proper name Ισραηλ. Only
a few unimportant minuscules add it both times. Αν changes υιων Ισραηλ
into του Ισραηλ in 21:12. The three following cases are also idiosyncratic:

7:2 εχοντα σφραγιδα θεου ζωντος,[68] 14:10 ενωπιον αγγελων αγιων
[των αγγελων A, των αγιων αγγελων K], and 21:14 δωδεκα ονοματα
των δωδεκα αποστολων.

(4) The repetition of the article is the rule in several juxtaposed nouns
(see, e.g., 6:15; 13:16; on the other hand, 1:9; 5:12; 9:15; 11:9; 21:8).

Conversely, the article is not repeated when the same person is called
by more than one name.[69]

There are exceptions to both rules, as well as [194] several text-critically
uncertain cases, which are of primary importance here.

1:9   εν τη θλιψει και [+ εν τη Αν] βασιλεια και υπομονη.
3:17   ο ταλαιπωρος και [+ ο A K] ελεεινος και πτωχος και τυφλος και
       γυμνος.

---

67. Charles (*Critical and Exegetical Commentary on the Revelation*, 1:cxx n. 2)
argues that the article is from the hand of the Apocalypse's assumed redactor.

68. See also p. 203.

69. See 1:5b, 6, 9; 3:14 (also below); 3:17 (see below); 6:10 (likewise); 12:17; 22:8.

5:12 την δυναμιν και [+ τον K] πλουτον και [+ την min. pc.] σοφιαν και
[+ την 1611 2057] ισχυν και [+ την 1611 2057] τιμην και [+ την
1611] δοξαν και [+ την 1611] ευλογιαν.

9:15 εις την ωραν και [+ εις την K] ημεραν και μηνα και ενιαυτον.

11:9 των λαων και [+ των Q] φυλων και γλωσσων και εθνων.

The tradition tends to repeat the article in these lists of three or more items. However, as a rule, the article is not repeated before the third item.[70] Moreover, the article before the second item should also be deleted as spurious in 3:17.[71]

Text-critical decisions are difficult in the following cases where the two sole items stand side by side:

3:14   ο πιστος και [+ ο C S] αληθινος

6:10   ο αγιος και [+ ο min. pc.] αληθινος

17:13 την δυναμιν και [+ την S Aν] εξουσιαν

18:14 τα λιπαρα και τα [om. C S 1611 2053 2329 al. pc.] λαμπρα

20:8   τον Γωγ και [+ τον K] Μαγωγ

20:10 του πυρος και [+ του S f^{1006} 1611 f^{1678} 2329 f^{2014} $f^{104/336}$ $f^{172/250}$
al. pc.] θειου

Modern editions unanimously reject the articles in question not only in 6:10 but also in 3:14; 20:8, 10, and rightly so. Also, S's text in 2:10 is an obvious correction, just like the K text in 20:8, since the subsequent deletion of the material is more difficult to explain than its insertion. 6:10 confirms that 3:14 o^2 is spurious. Conversely, the omission of $\tau\alpha^2$ in 18:14 is a stylistic improvement. A clear decision is only possible in 17:13. A subsequent insertion, however, is easier to understand than a later omission.

(5) Apocalyptic style typically introduces images and concepts with the article the first time they occur.[72] [195] Beyond this rule, the tradition should be examined in the following passages:

10:1   η [om. Aν] ιρις

10:3   αι [om. S* al. pc] επτα βρονται

11:3   τοις δυσι μαρτυσι μου unanimously

12:14 αι [om. P^{47} S K] δυο πτερυγες του [om. S 1854] αετου του μεγαλου

---

70. However, S often omits the article carelessly in such lists; see 4:11; 6:15; 11:18; 13:16; 20:12. Likewise, 4:11 om. την^3 A; likewise in 9:20 a few minuscule groups.

71. Of the modern editions, only Charles's preserves the latter reading. It is a marginal reading in WHort.

72. See Bousset, *Die Offenbarung Johannis*, 174.

On the other hand, 17:1 υδατων πολλων] των υδατων των πολλων K is a correction in light of 17:15.

In other cases, a concept or a thing is initially introduced without the article and only provided with the article subsequently.

4:6   τεσσαρα ζωα—4:8, 9; 5:6, 8, 11, 14, etc., τα (τεσσαρα) ζωα. 4:8 om. τα Αν K.

5:6   αρνιον—5:8 and so from then on always το αρνιον. 14:1 om. το Αν.

13:16   χαραγμα—13:17 passim το χαραγμα.

15:1   αγγελους επτα—reference is made to it in 21:9.

20:2   χιλια ετη—appears as τα [om. Αν] χιλια ετη in 20:3, as well as in 20:5, 7 (unanimously). However, only K in 20:4 and S 1611 f^{1678} 2329 Oec f^{149} f^{920} in 20:6 keep the article, which cannot be original in both cases due to insufficient testimony.

4:4   εικοσι τεσσαρας πρεσβυτερους, 4:10 and from then on always with article, accordingly also 11:16 οι [om. A S*] κδ πρεσβυτεροι. Since 11:11 refers to 11:9, the reading μετα τας [om. A S Compl.] τρεις ημερας και ημισυ, which WHort designates as doubtful, is undoubtedly original. Likewise, την [om. (S) K] πληγην in 13:14 is original (according to 13:3).

In light of the above, we can also expect the article in επι το θηριον (which 13:10 described) to stand in 17:3 (γυναικα καθημενην επι θηριον).[73] However, the omission of the article in 17:3 is due to the form of presentation: the seer initially only sees the female figure sitting on a beast. The article's omission in 14:1 (the 144,000, which stand with the Lamb on Zion) should be understood in the exact same way (primarily a description of the vision) and has no exegetical significance.[74]

[196] (6) The repetition of the article in the attributive position— whether it is placed after the noun, or is an adjective, a pronoun, an ordinal, or a participle—corresponds to the general grammatical rule. The tradition varies several times, however, with participles.

---

73. The K text reads επι θηριον το κοκκινον, and only a few groups of K write επι το θηριον το κοκκινον.

74. Are the 144,000 of the 7:4–8 described differently? Charles wrongly infers that 21:6 (του υδατος της ζωης δωρεαν) should be compared with 22:17 (υδωρ ζωης δωρεαν) because 22:17 should be placed before 21:6. The anarthrous and therefore indefinite sounding υδωρ ζωης is in the best order after 21:6.

8:6   οι επτα αγγελοι οι [om. S f^{336} al. pc.] εχοντες

9:15   οι τεσσαρες αγγελοι οι [om. S al. pc.] ητοιμασμενοι

15:6   οι επτα αγγελοι οι [om. S Aν$^{part.}$ al. pc.] εχοντες

5:6   τα επτα πνευματα του θεου τα απεσταλμενα Aν

        απεσταλμενοι A (hiat C) 2053

        απεσταλμενα S al. pc.

        αποστελλομενα K

11:4   αι δυο ελαιαι και αι δυο λυχνιαι αι [om. S Aν$^{part.}$ al. pc.] ... εστωτες

14:13   οι νεκροι οι [om. P^{47} 1746 2042] εν κυριω αποθνησκοντες

17:18   η πολις η μεγαλη η [om. S al. pc.] εχουσα

21:9   τας επτα φιαλας των γεμοντων [γεμουσας sine τας K]

Bousset[75] believes that the Aν reading in 5:6 should certainly be considered the *Urtext* because S omits the article consistently in all the places cited and A 2053 have a singular reading there.

19:9   ουτοι οι λογοι [+ οι A, hiat C] αληθινοι του θεου εισι

The second οι can hardly be dismissed, since it may have fallen out after λογοι in S Aν K due to negligence.

This rule (i.e., about the repetition of articles with words in the attributive position) is text-critically important in cases of prepositional phrases whose objects are definite in the same way.

1:4   ταις επτα εκκλησιαις ταις εν τη Ασια unanimously

2:24   τοις λοιποις τοις εν Θυατειροις unanimously

5:5   ο λεων ο [om. S f^{1006} 1611 f^{1678} 2329 Orig.] ων εκ της φυλης

8:3   το θυσιαστηριον το χρυσουν το [om. S 2329] ενωπιον του θρονου

11:16   οι [om. A S^{a}] $\overline{κδ}$ πρεσβυτεροι οι [om. A P^{47} Aν] ενωπιον του θεου καθημενοι. Here the tradition is very uneven; see p. 109.

11:19   ο ναος του θεου ο [om. P^{47} S Aν K contra AC f^{1006} f^{1678} 2329 $f^{172/250}$ 2351 61 – 69] εν τω ουρανω

8:9   των κτισματων των [om. Aν$^{part.}$ K] εν τη θαλασση

[197] 16:3   πασα ψυχη ζωης απεθανεν τα [om. P^{47} S Aν K contra AC 1611 al. pc.; των f^{1006} 2019] εν τη θαλασση

16:12   των βασιλεων των απο ανατολης unanimously

19:14   τα στρατευματα τα [om. A S Aν contra K, hiat C (om. Tisch Sod)] εν τω ουρανω

20:8   τα εθνη τα [om. S 1854 2329 2053 – 2062 61 – 69 f^{172} al. pc.] εν ταις $\overline{δ}$ γωνιαις

---

75. Bousset, *Textkritische Studien*, 174.

14:17 εκ του ναου του [αυτου P⁴⁷ Aᵛᵖᵃʳᵗ·] εν τω ουρανω
20:13 τους νεκρους τους εν αυτη
       ~ τους εν αυτη νεκρους Aν
       τους νεκρους τους εν αυτοις
       ~ τους εν αυτοις νεκρους Aν

Although the article's repetition is original in all the places previously listed (with the possible exception of 5:6), the two examples that follow depart from the rule.

2:9   την βλασφημιαν [+ την S Syr.¹·² (1611)] εκ [om. Aν] των λεγοντων

Aν deletes εκ and thereby eliminates the linguistic tendency to repeat the article. Bousset[76] attempts to explain S's reading (την) as original because otherwise S almost always omits the article.[77] See, however, p. 210 on 17:11 and p. 225.

15:5   ο ναος της σκηνης του μαρτυριου εν τω ουρανω

While Charles considers the text corrupt, Bousset[78] accounts for the article's absence before εν as a result of the distance of εν τω ουρανω from the governing noun (contrarily, see 11:19 above). This is the most satisfactory explanation.

Charles[79] concludes that the introductions to the seven letters should read τω αγγελω τω εν … εκκλησιας instead of τω αγγελω της εν … εκκλησιας on the grounds of stylistic consistency.

They actually read:
2:1   της] τω AC 1854
2:8   της] τω A
2:18   της] τω A, om. C
3:1   της] τω Q

On the other hand, της is attested unanimously in 2:12; 3:7, 14. The real reason for the rejection of της as a later correction [198] is that otherwise a prepositional phrase never comes between the article and its correspond-

---

76. Ibid., 174.

77. Charles suggests another explanation (*Critical and Exegetical Commentary on the Revelation*, 1:cxx n. 1).

78. Bousset, *Textkritische Studien*, 174.

79. Charles, *Critical and Exegetical Commentary on the Revelation*, 1:cxx and clvi, especially clx–clxi. Conversely, Johann Jakob Griesbach, *Novum Testamentum Graece*, 2nd ed., 2 vols. (London: Elmsly, 1796–1806); and Lachmann, *Novum Testamentum Graece*. See especially Westcott and Hort, *New Testament in the Original Greek*, 2:137; also Bousset, *Die Offenbarung Johannis*, 176, 202 n. 1; Lagrange, *Critique Textuelle*, 582–83; conversely, Weiss, *Die Johannes-Apokalypse*, 64 n. 2.

ing noun (in keeping with the Apocalypse's linguistic style),[80] while an anarthrous noun can precede a prepositional phrase. This argument nevertheless remains unpersuasive because the article before εκκλησιας is far more difficult to dispense with than its repetition in τω αγγελω. Had the author not written τω της εν Εφεσω εκκλησιας αγγελω, then this cumbersome formulation would have resulted: τω αγγελω τω της εν Εφεσω εκκλησιας. Because of this, the author omits τω^2 as an expendable article.

(7) The article regularly accompanies the predicate noun when a certain trait or function is being highlighted as characteristic for the relevant subject; see 1:8, 17; 2:23; 3:17; 7:14; 11:4; 18:23; 20:5, 14; 21:6; 22:13, 16. The article should thus be kept as original in the following places where the tradition varies:

4:5   α εισι τα [om. K] επτα πνευματα

5:8   αι εισιν αι [om. S* K] προσευχαι των αγιων

21:12   α εστι τα [om. K] ονοματα [τα ονοματα om. S Αν] των ιδ̄ φυλων

21:22   ο γαρ κυριος ... ο [om. S Αν K contra A 1678 – 1778 1773, hiat C] ναος αυτης εστιν.

In contrast, the article is correctly omitted in 14:4 (παρθενοι γαρ εισιν); 16:14; 17:9, 12, 15; 19:10 = 22:9.

But it is expected in the following locations:

1:20   αγγελοι (= "the angels") των επτα εκκλησιων εισιν και αι λυχνιαι αι επτα επτα εκκλησιαι (= "the seven congregations") εισιν[81]

2:9   ουκ εισιν, αλλα συναγωγη του σατανα

Here, however, "a synagogue of Satan" is analogous to αγγελοι των επτα εκκλησιων in 1:20.

13:18   αριθμος γαρ ανθρωπου εστιν

The article may be missing before αριθμος because ανθρωπου is anarthrous. Its omission is analogous with αγγελοι των επτα εκκλησιων in 1:20.

---

80. Therefore, not η εν Εφεσω εκκλησια but η εκκλησια η εν Εφεσω.

81. Westcott and Hort (*New Testament in the Original Greek*, 2:136) and Charles (*Critical and Exegetical Commentary on the Revelation*, 1:cliv–clv) see an old textual corruption here. The article's absence before the second επτα can easily be understood as a scribal error but probably also as an intentional change. The linguistic oddity of placing αι επτα one after another should be avoided. Also, the similarly anarthrous αγγελοι in the same verse presents a perfectly analogous case. Αν eliminates the oddity, which lies in the combination of two επτας (even without an article in the second), by inserting ας ειδες.

[199] 17:11 και αυτος [+ ο S al. pc.] ογδοος (= "the eighth") εστιν

For a correct reading of S, see p. 208 on 2:9 and below on 20:2.

17:14 κυριος κυριων εστι και βασιλευς βασιλεων

See also 19:16, where the article is also missing.

21:3 αυτοι λαοι αυτου εσονται

(8) The addition of the article to words in the predicate (which occurs only with proper nouns) is strange, since they occur opposite anarthrous proper nouns, as shown above.

6:8 ονομα αυτω ο [om. C S f^{1006} 1611 1854 2053 1773 f^{2031} Compl.] θανατος ([WHort] Tisch [Vog])

8:11 το ονομα του αστερος λεγεται ο [om. S Aν$^{part.}$ f^{1678} 2053 2329] αψινθος

19:13 καλειται το ονομα αυτου ο [om. min. pc.] λογος του θεου

On the other hand, again:

9:11 ονομα αυτω Εβραιστι Αβαδδων και εν τη Ελληνικη ονομα εχει [+ ο min. pc.] Απολλυων

17:5 ονομα γεγραμμενον ... Βαβυλων η μεγαλη, η μητηρ

19:16 το ονομα γεγραμμενον˙ βασιλευς βασιλεων και κυριος κυριων (see 17:14 above)

Entirely conflicting are the following:

12:9 ο καλουμενος διαβολος και ο [om. P^{47} K] σατανας

The anarthrous διαβολος causes the article's omission before σατανας in P^{47} K.

20:2 ος εστιν [+ ο S 1611 f^{1678} 2053 – 2062 2329 f^{2014}] διαβολος και ο [om. Aν al. pc.] σατανας

(9) Nothing is peculiar about the article's use with πας. The article always occurs in the plural, other than in 19:18 (παντων ελευθερων και δουλων), where Bousset's proposal that παντων ελευθερων τε και δουλων should be written hardly comes into consideration. The article, however, is omitted in the singular (in the sense of "everyone") if it is linked to a noun. The article is added in connection with a substantival participle. See also:

18:17 πας κυβερνητης και πας ο [om. Aν] επι τον τοπον πλεων

21:27 παν κοινον και ο ποιων S* K f^{1006} 2050 2329 al. pc.

　　　ποιων (sine ο) A (hiat C) S^a

　　　ποιουν Aν

22:18 παντι τω [om. Aν] ακουοντι

However, 22:15 πας [+ ο Aν] φιλων και ποιων.

[200] 3.3. The Use of the Case

Some important idiosyncracies for textual criticism should be mentioned here. First, we refer to two verbs that are constructed differently.

The accusative case usually follows ακουειν (as in the rest of the New Testament) when it refers to things (1:3; 7:4; 9:16; 22:8, 18); the genitive follows when it refers to people (6:1, 3, 5; 8:13; 16:5, 7). However, sometimes the accusative occurs "in irregular changes"[82] with φωνη (1:10; 4:1; 5:11; 6:6–7; 9:13; 10:4, 8; 12:10; 14:2; 18:4; 19:1, 6) and sometimes the genitive (3:20; 14:13; 16:1; 21:3). The reason for the distinction is not clear. The textual tradition produces almost no variation in these places. The Αν group *f*[2051] and the lone manuscript 469 regularly place φωνη in the genitive for the accusative.[83] This is similar to other witnesses in some places (4:1 and 5:11 *f*[2044]; 9:13 S[a]; 18:4 C; vice versa 6:7 C 2053; 14:13 several minuscules). The authoritative textual witnesses are divided in only one place:

    11:12 φωνην μεγαλην A K

           φωνης μεγαλης C P[47] S Αν

In 5:13, παν κτισμα ... ηκουσα λεγοντας [λεγοντων *f*[172/250] *f*[2031]] emerges outside of the usual rule.

The facts are more complicated with προσκυνειν, which is constructed with the dative and the accusative.

(1) Dative

    4:10   προσκ. τω ζωντι εις τους αιωνας

    7:11   πρ. τω θεω

    11:16 πρ. τω θεω

    13:4   πρ. τω δρακοντι

           πρ. τω θηριω C S K (hiant P[47] Αν; however, Αν presupposes the reading τω θηριω)

              το θηριον A *f*[2014] [84]

---

82. Bousset, *Textkritische Studien*. See also Charles, *Critical and Exegetical Commentary on the Revelation*, 1:xcl. In the LXX, φωνη occurs about 80x in the accusative and 50x in genitive. See Robert Helbing, *Die Kasussyntax der Verba bei den Septuaginta: Ein Beitrag zur Hebraismenfrage und zur Syntax der Κοινή* (Göttingen: Vandenhoeck & Ruprecht, 1928), 150–53.

83. See the exact details in Schmid, "Untersuchungen zur Geschichte des griechischen Apokalypsetextes," 435 n. 2.

84. So from the modern editions WHort[mg.] Weiss Bousset Charles[txt.].

13:15 πρ. τη εικονι S Αν K

τὴν εικονα A Αν^{pc.} (hiant C P⁴⁷ 2053⁸⁵)

[201] 14:7 πρ. τω ποιησαντι τον ουρανον

αυτον τον ποιησαντα τον ουρανον K

16:2 τους προσκυνουντας τη εικονι

τὴν εικονα S Αν^{pc.} (see 19:20⁸⁶)

19:4 πρ. τω θεω (see 22:9)

19:10 πρ. αυτω (sc. τω αγγελω)

τω θεω προσκυνησον

19:20 πρ. τη εικονι

τὴν εικονα S* ƒ¹⁶⁷⁸ 2053 – 2062 ƒ⁹²⁰ (see 16:2⁸⁷)

22:9 πρ. τω θεω (= 19:4)

(2) Accusative

9:20 τα δαιμονια (τω δαιμονι ƒ¹⁶⁷⁸)

13:8 αυτον (sc. το θηριον)

αυτω S Αν ƒ¹⁰⁰⁶ 1611 1854 2053 792

13:12 το θηριον το πρωτον [τω θηριω τω πρ. ƒ¹⁰⁰⁶ ƒ¹⁷²/²⁵⁰] (13:15, see the dative section above)

14:9 το θηριον [τω θηριω C ƒ¹⁰⁰⁶] και την εικονα [τη εικονι ƒ¹⁰⁰⁶ ƒ¹⁰⁴/³³⁶] αυτου

14:11 το θηριον και την εικονα αυτου

τω θηριω και τη εικονι αυτου ƒ¹⁰⁰⁶ al. pc.

το θηριον και τη εικονι ƒ¹⁰⁴/³³⁶

20:4 το θηριον ουδε την εικονα αυτου

τω θηριω Αν Compl. ƒ¹⁰⁴/³³⁶ ƒ¹⁰⁰⁶ 2053 ƒ²⁵⁰

τη εικονι Αν^{part.} Compl. ƒ¹⁰⁴/³³⁶ ƒ¹⁰⁰⁶ 1611

In comparison, the absolute use of προσκυνειν:

3:9 (ενωπιον); 5:14; 15:4; 22:8 (εμπροσθεν); 11:1 τους προσκυνουντας εν αυτω (sc. τω ναω)

A semantic distinction is usually sought between the two constructions of προσκυνειν: προσκυνειν with the dative (or with ενωπιον) means "worship" (God or the dragon), while προσκυνειν with the accusative means "bow down" (before the beast and his image).[88] The distinction

_____

85. So WHort^{mg.} Bousset Charles.

86. So Bousset.

87. So Bousset, Charles.

88. Thus Ernst Lohmeyer (*Die Offenbarung des Johannes*, HNT 16 [Tübingen:

is not between God (or a pseudo-God) and between beings that are not divine, but between worship (divine honors) and external prostration (which can also apply to a divine being). J. Horst[89] rejects [202] this distinction as groundless, correctly, as we will see. The dative construction relates to God (4:10; 7:11; 11:16; 14:7; 19:4, 10; 22:9) and the dragon (13:4), while the accusative construction relates to το θηριον (13:8;[90] 13:12; 14:9, 11) and τα δαιμονια (9:20).

εικων occurs in the accusative case only in the combination το θηριον και την εικονα αυτου (14:9, 11; 20:4). Otherwise, it is in the dative case (16:2; 19:20).[91] Accordingly, the dative should also be read in 13:15 (with S Aν K against A; dub. P[47]).[92] A's correction in this passage weakens its value as a witness in 13:4, where Aν presupposes the dative τω θηριω, since it can be understood as a homoioteleuton error (θηριω$^1 \frown ^2$).[93] Because the dative τω θηριω should be read in 13:4, we should also note that θηριον fluctuates grammatically between the dative and accusative cases. If the dative construction is used consistently only with God and the dragon (unlike εικων, where the dative occurs only if εικων stands alone; or θηριον, where the dative occurs only once and elsewhere in the accusative, going so far as to influence the accompanying objects: και [ουδε] την εικονα αυτου), then the attempt to use case to distinquish between worship and purely outward

---

Mohr, 1926], 14:7), following Bousset (*Textkritische Studien*, 163). Basically also Weiss (*Die Johannes-Apokalypse*, 64 n. 1), Charles (*Critical and Exegetical Commentary on the Revelation*, 1:cxli, 211–12), Allo (*Saint Jean, L'Apocalypse*), and others.

89. Johannes Horst, *Proskynein: Zur Anbetung im Urchristentum nach ihrer religionsgeschichtlichen Eigenart* (Gütersloh: Bertelsmann, 1932), 33–43.

90. AC P[47] K against S Aν.

91. Only S has the accusative in both of these cases. P[47] now shows this is a correction in 16:2.

92. The crucial words are missing in C: θηριου$^1 \frown ^3$.

93. P[47] θηριου$^1 \frown ^3$. It is a premature and mindless explanation when Weiss (*Die Johannes-Apokalypse*, 194; see also 64 n. 1 and 109) also states: "The dragon is worshiped, the beast is honored." It is a mere illusion that the dative τω θηριω is harmonized to the previous τω δρακοντι; A alone preserves the *Urtext*. Although the dative is likely a later correction, the accusative cannot be understood in that way. Thus, it should be countered at once that, according to the same methodological principle, both 14:9 (with C τω θηριω και την εικονα αυτου) and 20:4 (with Aν τω θηριω ουδε την εικονα αυτου) must also be explained as the *Urtext*. The real situation, however, is this: that A, due to its explicit preference for the accusative with προσκυνειν (see the supporting examples from the LXX in Horst, *Proskynein*, 38 n. 2), indicates that 13:4 and 13:15 are corrections and do not have the *Urtext*.

acts of homage (always[94] an expression of divine worship) proves unworkable.[95] But the adopted distinction is also groundless because—with the exception of 3:9—divine honors [203] are in view in all cases.[96] Conversely, this distinction should not be used to establish the original reading where the tradition is not uniform, since the Apocalypse's linguistic style fails to support the distinction.[97]

19:5 αινειτε τω θεω AC S P Q al. pc. [τον θεον Aν K] is only singular in the New Testament; see in the LXX 1 Chr 16:36; 23:5; 2 Chr 20:19; 2 Esd 3:10–11; Jer 4:2; 20:13; Pss. Sol. 5:1; 10:5.

2:14 εδιδασκε τω Βαλαχ (τον Βαλαχ K)[98] is unusual but attested elsewhere.[99]

ευαγγελιζειν in 10:7, as in the rest of the New Testament (not in the LXX), has the accusative of personal object, which only a few minuscules replace with the dative case (f^{2014} 94 al. pc.). In 14:6, επι occurs with accusative (AC P[47] S P 1611 f^{1678} 1854 2053 2329 $f^{172/250}$). The two later recensions Aν and K delete the επι.[100] The finding for φωτιζειν is exactly analogous: 21:23 showcases the use of the accusative. However, in 22:5, which is almost identical to 21:23, επ αυτους should be read with A (hiat C) S f^{1006} f^{1678} 2050 2329 94 $f^{172/250}$, which in Aν K is changed again (om. επ).

The accusative usually accompanies περιβαλλεσθαι (10x). In 3:5 and 4:4, εν follows περιβαλλεσθαι in the phrase εν ιματιοις λευκοις. 3:5 proves

---

94. Only 3:9 (προσκυνησουσιν ενωπιον των ποδων σου) is an exception.

95. Bousset carries out his principle with text-critical coercion, though he not only reads 13:15 with A την εικονα, but he also explains the reading την εικονα of S in 16:2 and 19:20 as the *Urtext*.

96. This is not to deny that, in a case of worship, the "proskynesis" can be first thought of elsewhere as the outward act. Cf., in addition, 19:10 επεσα εμπροσθεν των ποδων αυτου προσκυνησαι αυτω (= worship) and 22:8 επεσα προσκυνησαι εμπροσθεν των ποδων του αγγελου, in which the latter case εμπροσθεν των ποδων must not be drawn to επεσα.

97. In the rest of the New Testament, except John, Rev, and Matt 4:10//Luke 4:8, the Attic accusative is preserved. However, it is dative in the LXX almost without exception (only 6 of the 123 occurrences).

98. εν τω Βαλαχ Aν is probably a simple scribal error (dittography).

99. See Walter Bauer, *Griechisch-Deutsches Wörterbuch zu den Schriften des Neuen Testaments und der übrigen urchristlichen Literatur* (Giessen: Töpelmann, 1928).

100. It is not correct to cite 10:7 (with Bousset, *Textkritische Studien*, 163) as evidence that the Aν-K reading is original at 14:6.

that εν in 4:4, which is unattested in A (hiat C) P 1854 f^{2014} f^{2031},[101] is the *Urtext* and that this group of manuscripts only deletes it.

The Apocalypse's linguistic style exhibits the following in the case of γραφειν: alongside γεγραμμενον εν τω βιβλιω (1:3; 13:8; 20:12; 21:27; 22:18, 19)—otherwise γραψον εις βιβλιον (1:11), but also επι την ψηφον (2:17) επ αυτον (3:12, επ αυτω Aν^part.), επι των μετωπων (14:1) and επι το μετωπον (17:5),[102] επι τον μηρον (19:16)—επι το βιβλιον surfaces (17:8; against 13:8; 21:27), [204] which only K (επι του βιβλιου), 792 f^{1006} 2329 (εν τω βιβλιω) and f^{2014} (εν βιβλιω) correct.

In the case of ουαι, the unusual construction gives rise to corrections with the accusative, so that the tradition varies greatly.

8:13   ουαι ουαι ουαι τους κατοικουντας S K

              τοις κατοικουσι A (hiat C) Aν (WHort^mg. Charles[103])

12:12   ουαι την γην και την θαλασσαν AC Aν

              τη γη και τη θαλασση P^47 K

              εις την γην και την θαλασσαν S

12:12 proves that the accusative is original in 8:13 and that A Aν make corrections.[104]

Apart from the stock phrase ημερας και νυκτος (4:8; 7:15; 12:10; 14:11; 20:10; correspondingly 21:25 ημερας, ημερα S*), the Apocalypse uses the accusative (of χρονος, ωρα, ημερα, μην, ετος) to indicate various lengths of time. In 2:10, on the other hand (θλιψιν ημερων δεκα), where only the K text preserves θλιψιν ημερας δεκα, ημερων δεκα qualifies θλιψιν. The classical accusative is almost unanimously attested in 3:3 (ποιαν ωραν [ποια ωρα f^{1678} 2050]) to indicate when an event occurs. Instead of the usual expression (εν ταις ημεραις εκειναις and the like), and again in ωρα, the dative is used to indicate time.

---

101. This is why WHort^txt. also omits it. Its absence in Syr.[1] does not prove that it was not in the Greek *Vorlage*.

102. See p. 223.

103. The decision of Charles, who considers the accusative in 12:12 the *Urtext*, is to be understood only from his overestimation of A.

104. In 12:12, Aν f^{2814} f^{2028} corrects the reading to τοις κατοικουσι την γην. In 18:10, 16, 19 ουαι ουαι η πολις η μεγαλη occurs 3x, to which the LXX provides several models (see Isa 5:8, 11, 18–22; Amos 5:18; Hab 2:6, 12, 19; Zeph 2:5). The nominative here apparently represents the vocative (see also p. 216).

18:10   μιᾷ ωρα S C Aνᵖˡᵘʳ· K

    εν μια ωρα Aνᵖᶜ· f¹⁶⁷⁸ 2329

    μιαν ωραν A f¹⁰⁰⁶ 1611 2053 f²⁰⁶⁵ al. pc. (WHortᵐᵍ·)

18:16   μιᾷ ωρα unanimously, 18:19 almost all (εν μια ωρα f²⁰²⁸)

The instrumental dative is heavily suppressed in the Apocalypse. Above all the instrumental εν replaces it, even if incompletely (see p. 227). Most unusual is the unanimously attested τοις πυλωσιν εισελθωσιν in 22:14. In addition to εν, εκ and απο occur with the passive voice in place of the dative case (see p. 226). Twice even δια with the accusative occurs: 4:11 (δια το θελημα σου εισιν) [205] and 12:11 (ενικησαν αυτον δια το αιμα [του αιματος 61 – 69 792 2019 2073] … και δια τον λογον).¹⁰⁵

The vocative, which the New Testament increasingly replaces with the nominative,¹⁰⁶ surfaces only a few times in the Apocalypse. Otherwise, the nominative with the article is used. It occurs relatively frequently with κυριος (cf. 7:14; 15:4; 22:20 κυριε Ιησου), especially in the phrase κυριε ο θεος (11:17; 15:3; 16:7).

On the other hand, see 4:11:

    ο κυριος και ο θεος ημων A (hiat C) K

    κυριε ο θεος ημων Aν

    κυριε ο κυριος και θεος ημων S

15:3   ο βασιλευς των εθνων (βασιλευ S* Kᵖᶜ· f²⁰⁵¹)

18:20 ουρανε και οι αγιοι is especially significant. On the other hand, note 12:12:

    ευφραινεσθε οι ουρανοι και οι εν αυτοις σκηνουντες A Aν f¹⁰⁰⁶ 1611 2344 2351 (WHortᵐᵍ· Bousset Charles)

    om. οι ante ουρανοι C S K (hiat P⁴⁷)

The Apocalypse's linguistic style and 18:20, where the vocative ουρανε is not changed, support the article's authenticity. It is highly unlikely that it is a thoughtless harmonization to the οι σκηνουντες¹⁰⁷ that follows.

3.4. Pronouns

Only the most important text-critical details are listed below.

---

105. See also Mayser, *Grammatik der griechischen Papyri*, 2.2:368, 426.

106. See also Blass, *Grammatik des neutestamentlichen Griechisch*, §147; Charles, *Critical and Exegetical Commentary on the Revelation*, 1:cxxxix–cxl.

107. Thus Weiss, *Die Johannes-Apokalypse*, 111.

(1) The Reflexive

εαυτ- is attested with certainty in the following passages:

2:2   τους λεγοντας εαυτους [om. f^{2051}] αποστολους

2:9   των λεγοντων Ιουδαιους ειναι εαυτους [αυτους min. pc., om. f^{336}]

3:9   των λεγοντων εαυτους Ιουδαιους ειναι

6:15   εκρυψαν εαυτους

10:3   ελαλησαν ... τας εαυτων

19:7   η γυνη αυτου ητοιμασεν εαυτην [αυτην f^{18} f^{1678} f^{2044}]

2:20   (η λεγουσα εαυτην προφητιν) reads S* Q $f^{104/336}$ (also Tisch)
       αυτην

[206] In 10:7 (τους εαυτου δουλους AC P^{47} S Αν, τους δουλους αυτου K)
εαυτου is also attested with certainty. The opposite is true of 18:7 and αυτην
should be read with AC S* K rather than εαυτην (thus Weiss) with S^a Αν
(εδοξασεν). As a result, ητοιμασαν αυτους (A [hiat C] S* 2351), rather than
ητοιμασαν εαυτους Αν K (Weiss Sod Vog Merk), should also be considered
the *Urtext* in 8:6.

The spelling αὑτ- (e.g., 8:6 WHort Bousset Charles; 18:7 WHort
Vog Charles) should also be rejected because it is completely alien to the
Apocalypse,[108] as 9:11 proves (εχουσιν επ αυτων, only a few minuscules εφ
εαυτων).[109]

(2) The indefinite pronoun τις only surfaces in the combinations ει τις,
εαν τις, and ινα

μη τις (the latter in 13:17). Otherwise, εἷς is deployed.[110] This confirms
that παν δενδρον (S Αν, om. παν A), rather than τι δενδρον (C K), is the
Urtext in 7:1.[111]

(3) The relative pronoun's classic attraction to the case of the antecedent occurs only in 18:6 (εν τω ποτηριω ᾧ). K alone produces it in 1:20 (των
αστερων ους AC Αν, ὧν K).

---

108. Blass (*Grammatik des neutestamentlichen Griechisch*, §64.1) explains it as un-
Hellenistic. See also the important statements by Mayser, *Grammatik der griechischen
Papyri*, 1.2:65 n. 1.

109. Elsewhere, all modern editions recognize the personal pronoun instead of
the reflexive; cf. 11:11 εστησαν επι τους ποδας αὐτων [εαυτων f^{1006}]; 11:16 οι καθημενοι
επι τους θρονους αὐτων; 12:3 εχων ... επι τας κεφαλας αὐτου; likewise 13:1; 14:9; 17:13
(αὐτων) εαυτων f^{2814}); 13:16 (δωσιν αυτοις); 18:19 (αὐτων) εαυτων C); 19:16; 20:1, 4.

110. We note the following corrections: 8:13 ενος om. S; 15:7 ἓν om. P^{47} S Αν
(probably a thoughtless error); 17:1 εις] τις f^{104}; 18:21 εις om. 1678 – 1778; 19:17 ενα
om. K; 22:2 + ενα ante εκαστον Αν.

111. See also pp. 106–7.

(4) If a predicate noun stands in a relative clause, the ruling noun determines the gender of the relative pronoun.

4:5   λαμπαδες ... αι εισι τα επτα πνευματα K (Bousset)

             α εισι Aν (and most modern editions)

             α εστι A (hiant C S) (Weiss)

5:6   κερατα επτα και οφθαλμους επτα, οι εισι τα επτα πνευματα A (hiat C) S Aν (and all modern editions)

             α εισι K

5:8   φιαλας ... γεμουσας θυμιαματων, αι εισιν αι προσευχαι A (hiat C) Aν K

             α εισιν S Q 792 f^{1006} 2050 (Tisch WHort[mg.])

21:8   τη λιμνη τη καιομενη ... ο εστιν ο θανατος

[207] Therefore, 4:5 and 21:8 belong together, as do 5:6 and 5:8. See p. 254 for the Hebraizing repetition of the relative pronoun through the use of the personal pronoun (3:8 ην ουδεις δυναται ... αυτην, etc.) and for the *constructio ad sensum* (3:4 ονοματα οι).

3.5. The Verb

The random use of different verb tenses, narrative (aorist) and description (present), description and prophecy (future), is characteristic of the Apocalypse's style.[112] Numerous variants have been introduced into the textual tradition because of this. Those that are relevant for textual criticism are presented here.

Several times, a perfect tense stands in the place of the aorist, immediately adjacent to it.

2:3   υπομονην εχεις και εβαστασας ... και ου κεκοπιακες AC

                   ουκ εκοπιασας S Aν K

16:6   εξεχεαν και ... δεδωκας AC 1611 2329

             εδωκας P[47] S Aν K

The Apocalypse uses the aorist and perfect of διδωμι side by side, preventing a clear decision in this passage.[113] Apart from this example, there are no corrections to the perfect tense in the Apocalypse. Therefore, the aorist, which already seems logical, is a later harmonization to the previous εξεχεαν.

---

112. See also Bousset, *Textkritische Studien*, 168–71; Charles, *Critical and Exegetical Commentary on the Revelation*, 1:cxxiii–cxxvii.

113. See the aorist in 1:1; 2:21; 11:13; 20:13 beside the perfect in 3:8.

As the author almost always writes ειληφα (2:27; 3:3; 5:7; 8:5; 11:17; the aorist only in 10:10; 17:12; and 5:8; 20:4 in the subordinate clause), his use of the perfect with λεγειν twice (7:14 ειρηκα, ειπον K; 19:3 ειρηκαν, ειπαν C, ειπον f[1678]) prompted corrections in the textual tradition in both places.

The difference between the present and the aorist, both in the infinitive and the imperative, is completely blurred.[114] The aorist is much better attested than the present, more so in the infinitive than in the imperative.

Present and aorist imperatives occurring alongside one another include:

2:5   μνημονευε [-νευσον f[1678] 1854 2329 2595] και μετανοησον

3:3   μνημονευε [-νευσον 1854 sol.] και μετανοησον

3:19   ζηλευε [ζηλωσον Αν, ζηλου Αρ] και μετανοησον

[208] The juxtaposition of the present and aorist infinitive emerges in a particularly striking way after μελλειν.

- μελλω with the present infinitive: 2:10 (πασχειν, παθειν K; βαλλειν, βαλειν K, βαλλειν βαλειν S); 3:10; 6:11; 8:13; 10:4, 7; 12:5; 17:8.
- μελλω with the aorist infinitive: 3:2 (εμελλον αποθανειν, αποθνησκειν f[2014], ημελλες αποβαλλειν K, ημελλες αποβαλειν Compl. f[2065]); 3:16 (εμεσαι, εμειν S); 12:4 (τεκειν, τικτειν Compl. f[1678] 1854).

This finding precludes an unequivocal decision at 1:19, where A S[a] Αν read μελλει γινεσθαι, and C S* K read μ. γενεσθαι.

Imperfect and aorist

The introduction of the imperfect in place of the aorist should once again be noted.

Not only is the aorist completely absent in the case of δυναμαι, but it is also avoided with βλεπειν, even in the infinitive.

Also, the aorist should be rejected as most likely a harmonization to the previous ηκουσα in 22:8 (οτε ηκουσα και εβλεπον A [hiat C] Oec [thus also WHort[mg.] Weiss Bousset Charles[txt.]], εβλεψα S Αν, ειδον K).

Also, a part of the tradition replaces the imperfect with the aorist in the two following passages:

1:12   ελαλει] ελαλησεν Αν (λαλει A)

2:14   εδιδασκεν] εδιδαξεν K

---

114. See 2:25 ο εχετε κρατησατε and 3:11 κρατει ο εχεις side by side.

The tradition fluctuates between the imperfect and aorist in the case of κραζειν.

6:10   εκραξαν AC S K, εκραζον Aν
7:2   εκραξε(ν) C S Aν K, εκραζεν A P 2053^txt.
10:3   εκραξεν bis omn.
12:2   κραζει A P^47 S Aν, εκραζεν C K^plur., εκραξεν K^part.
18:2   εκραξεν (εκεκραξεν A) omn.
18:18 εκραξαν AC f^1006 1611 f^1678 2329 P f^172
       εκραζον S Aν K
18:19 εκραξαν AC 2329
       εκραζον S Aν K
19:17 εκραξεν A S Aν K (hiat C)
       εκραζεν Q al. pc.

The aorist tense is firmly the *Urtext* in 6:10; 10:3; 18:2; and 19:17, as is the present tense in 12:2 (and 7:10). Questionable examples include 7:2 and 18:18, 19. 7:2 is probably a simple scribal error in A P. Regarding 18:18–19, see p. 98.

[209] The *consectio temporum* with the subjunctive in the subordinate clause surfaces neither in the original text nor in the later tradition.[115]

(1) Present indicative in the main clause, subjunctive in subordinate clause:
    11:6   εχουσιν εξουσιαν, ινα μη ... βρεχη [βρεξη f^1678 2053^txt. 2329 Hipp.]
    12:6   οπου εχει..., ινα ... τρεφωσιν [τρεφουσιν C S]
    13:13 ποιει ... ινα ποιη [ποιηση P^47 1678 – 2080 1773 f^172/250 (2329)]
    21:23 ου χρειαν εχει ... ινα φαινωσιν [φανωσιν 2065, 2432]
    7:1   ειδον κρατουντας ... ινα μη πνεη [πνευση S 1854 f^205 f^172/250 al. pc.]

(2) Indicative aorist—subjunctive aorist:
    20:3   εσφραγισεν ... ινα μη πλανηση [πλανα K]

(3) Indicative and imperative present—subjunctive aorist:
    2:10   μελλει βαλλειν ... ινα πειρασθητε
    3:11   κρατει ... ινα μηδεις λαβη

---

115. The rule Bousset establishes (*Textkritische Studien*, 170) does not correspond to the facts.

Later witnesses supplement the frequently missing copula several times,[116] even in relative clauses.

1:4   των επτα πνευματων α ενωπιον του θρονου C K
        α] των A S *f*[2014], + εστιν Aν; likewise 5:13
        θρονου] + εστιν Aν
5:2   τις αξιος] + εστιν K
1:16   η οψις αυτου, ως ο ηλιος φαινει
        ~ η οψις αυτου φαινει ως ο ηλιος S

3.6. Prepositions

Only what is important for textual criticism is discussed here.[117]

First we identify a few characteristic peculiarities in the use of επι. It has long been noted that the case that follows επι in the expression ο καθημενος επι τ. θρον. (occurring 28x) depends upon the case of the previous [210] participle ο καθημενος. If the participle is in the nominative or accusative case, the accusative follows επι. If the participle stands in the genitive or dative case, the genitive or dative follows επι. This principle is often breached, however, in the entire tradition or in a part of it.

(1) Nominative and Accusative
    4:2   επι τον θρονον καθημενος A (hiat C) S K
            του θρονου Aν
    4:4   επι τους θρονους ... καθημενους all
            likewise 6:5 all except *f*[2814] *f*[2051] (επ αυτω)
            (6:8 ο καθημενος επανω αυτου [αυτου om. C Aν])
    7:15   ο καθημενος επι του θρονου A (hiat C) S Aν
            τω θρονω K
    9:17   τους καθημενους επ αυτων AC Aν K
                    επανω αυτων P[47] S (likewise 20:11 S *f*[1678])
    11:16   οι καθημενοι [καθηνται C P[47] S K] επι τους θρονους αυτων all
    14:6   τους καθημενους [κατοικουντας] επι της γης all
    14:14   επι την νεφελην καθημενον [-ος Aν] all

---

116. See also ibid., 170.

117. See also the detailed descriptions in ibid., 165–68; and Charles, *Critical and Exegetical Commentary on the Revelation*, 1:cxxvii–cxxxiv.

14:16 ο καθημενος επι την νεφελην C Aν

    της νεφελης A P⁴⁷ S

    τη νεφελη K

17:3 καθημενην επι θηριον all

19:11 ο καθημενος επ αυτον

    επ αυτου Hipp. Oec

20:11 τον καθημενον επ αυτον Aν K

    επ αυτου A (hiat C) f^{1006} f^{1678} 1611 2053 2329 al. pc.

    επανω αυτου S (see 9:17 above)

21:5 ο καθημενος επι τω θρονω all

(2) Genitive

4:10; 5:1, 7   του καθημενου επι του θρονου all

6:16   του καθημενου επι του θρονου AC Aν

    τω θρονω S K (see 7:15 above)

17:1   της καθημενης επι υδατων all

19:18   των καθημενων επ αυτων Aν K

    επ αυτους A (hiat C) 61 – 69

    επ αυτοις S

19:19, 21   του καθημενου επι του ιππου all

[211] (3) Dative

4:9   τω καθημενω επι τω θρονω A (hiat C) S 1854 2050 2080

    του θρονου Aν K

5:13   τω καθημενω επι τω θρονω A (hiat C) K

    του θρονου S Aν

6:4   τω καθημενω επ αυτον AC S K

    αυτω Aνⁿᵃʳᵗ· 2329

7:10   τω καθημενω επι τω θρονω plur.

    του θρονου Kᵖᵃʳᵗ· al. pc.

14:15   τω καθημενω επι της νεφελης all

19:4   τω καθημενω επι τω θρονω AC S K

    του θρονου Aν

Thus, the aforementioned rule is clearly maintained overall, although it is broken here and there, namely, in (1) 7:15; 9:17; 14:6; 21:5; in (2) never; in (3) 6:4 (in the vast majority of textual witnesses); 14:15. While Charles assumes textual corruption or the final redactor's errors in these cases, the facts, properly interpreted, show that the author does not follow his rule rigidly, a rule that is not important for its own sake. Because the rule is nevertheless maintained everywhere, the regular form should be taken as the *Urtext* where it is ignored in a part of the tradition (thus in 14:16,[118] 20:11, and 19:18). None of the main text forms are free of violations. Αν seems to prefer the genitive case (see 4:2, 9; 5:13; 19:4), and K seems to prefer the dative (see 7:15; 14:16; 6:15).

It is nonetheless methodologically unjustifiable to follow[119] A's text blindly as the best exemplar of the tradition. Nothing indicates that later scribes and correctors were aware of the rule and altered noncompliant passages accordingly.

Whether the accusative singular or dative plural of μετωπον occurs after επι should not be attributed to some objective reason but merely to the author's inclination or linguistic intuition.

[212] 13:16 επι το μετωπον A S K

                   του μετωπου C

                   των μετωπων P⁴⁷ Αν

       17:5   επι το μετωπον all

       20:4   επι το μετωπον the majority

                   των μετωπων Αν^Part.

On the other hand: επι των μετωπων 7:3; 9:4; 14:1; 22:4. But again, the rule is broken in 14:9 (επι του μετωπου [τω μετωπω S] αυτου η επι την χειρα αυτου), which may be all the more surprising, as the second object of επι occurs in the accusative case.

επι with χειρ:

14:9   επι την χειρα [της χειρος P⁴⁷ 1611 2329 f²⁰⁵¹ 94 1773 is a harmonization to the previous επι του μετωπου]

20:1   επι την χειρα [εν τη χειρι S 1611 f¹⁶⁷⁸]

Conversely, 13:16 επι της χειρος αυτων της δεξιας and 1:20 επι της δεξιας μου [επι τη δεξια μου 2053 – 2062, εν τη δεξια μου A 1611 2595].

The accusative always occurs in the plural with κεφαλη. The tradition varies with the singular but so does the linguistic style:

επι τας κεφαλας 4:4; 9:7; 12:3; 13:1 (επι ταις κεφαλαις 1854; επι της κεφαλης f¹¹⁰ 2053); 18:19 (επι της κεφαλης S 2053 – 2062 2057).

---

118. την νεφελην with C Αν (WHort^mg· Bousset) against της νεφελης A P⁴⁷ S (and all the rest of the modern editions).

119. This includes 14:16 (see previous note); 19:18 (WHort^txt·); and 20:11 (WHort^txt· Charles Merk).

Conversely:

10:1   επι την κεφαλην AC sol.

         της κεφαλης P[47] S Aν K (Sod Vog Merk)

14:14   επι την κεφαλην A (non C) 1611 1854 *f*[1678] *f*[2014] 2344 K[pc.] (Bousset Charles)

         της κεφαλης C P[47] S Aν K[plur.]

19:12   επι την κεφαλην [εν τη κεφαλη 61 – 69]

12:1   επι της κεφαλης all

The accusative την κεφαλην (in the singular) is only certain in 19:12. The accusative in 14:14 is probably a harmonization to the previous επι την νεφελην. Conversely, the preceding genitive υποκατω των ποδων may have occasioned the use of the genitive in 12:1. But this is unlikely. And it remains the case that the genitive and accusative cases surface side by side with κεφαλη in the singular after επι.

The author, furthermore, writes επι της γης and επι της θαλασσης or εις την γην and εις την θαλασσαν without any real difference between the two modes of expression. For επι, see 5:3, 10, 13; 7:1; 10:2, 5, 8; 16:18; 18:24.

The two exceptions to this rule, 14:16 (εβαλεν ... επι [213] την γην) and 15:2 (εστωτας επι την θαλασσαν), are understandable insofar as in the case of βαλλειν (cf. 2:24; 18:19; otherwise always εις with the accusative) and ισταναι (cf. 3:20; 7:1; 11:11; 12:18; 14:1; 15:2; otherwise, only 19:17) επι is otherwise followed by the accusative.[120]

For εις: 5:6; 6:13 (επι την γην S 792 1854 2329 2344 al. pc.); 8:5, 7; 9:1, 3; 12:4, 9, 13; 13:13 (επι την γην P[47] K); 14:19 (επι την γην P[47] 1611; επι της γης S *f*[1678]); 16:1, 2 (επι την γην Aν).[121]

οι κατοικουντες επι της γης (never εν τη γη) occurs consistently (3:10; 6:10; 8:13; 11:10 bis; 13:8, 14 bis; 17:8), except in 13:12 τους εν αυτη κατοικουντας (here the word order is also different) and in 17:2 οι κατοικουντες την γην

---

120. Conversely, 10:5, 8 εστωτα (-τος) επι της θαλασσης. Two linguistic rules that the author employs conflict here. In 14:16 and 15:2, one is decisive; in 10:5, 8, the other is decisive. The loyalty and unity of the tradition in both classes is noteworthy. An exception is 8:3 εσταθη επι το θυσιαστηριον A Aν [του θυσιαστηριον (!) C], του θυσιαστηριου S K; επι το θυσιαστηριον[2] all. Also, the text of A Aν is more likely the original here, since it corresponds to the Apocalypse's linguistic style. This argument is stronger than the assumption that the accusative was only harmonized with το θυσιαστηριον.

121. All corrections that occur here are obvious at first glance, as they almost always construct επι with the accusative.

3. The Linguistic Style of the Apocalypse

(likewise 17:8 K). Accordingly, in 14:6 τους καθημενους [κατοικουντας Α (Αν)] επι της γης.

The accusative case occurs with verbs of mourning in 1:7 (κοψονται επ [om. S 792 2050 2351] αυτον); 18:9 (κοψονται επ αυτην C S K, επ αυτη Α Αν f¹⁰⁰⁶ 1611 2053 2329); and 18:11 (πενθουσιν επ αυτην C S P 1854 f³³⁶, επ αυτη K, εφ εαυτους Αν, εν αυτη Α 2329). The dative, however, occurs with χαιρειν (11:10 επ αυτοις unanimously), ευφραινεσθαι (18:20 επ αυτη C S K, επ αυτην Αν, εν αυτη Α¹²²), and οργιζεσθαι (12:17).

The Apocalypse has a marked preference for εκ.¹²³

εκ is used in place of the partitive genitive once in the phrase εἷς (μία, ἓν) εκ: 5:5; 6:1 bis; 7:13 (εκ om. S 1611 1854); 13:3 (εκ om. A Q* 1854 2053); 17:1 (εκ om. S f¹⁰⁰⁶ f²⁰¹⁴); 21:9 (εκ om. Αν f¹⁷²).¹²⁴ See also 2:10; 3:9; 5:9 (+ ημας S Αν K, hiat C); 11:9. Accordingly, 2:9 την βλασφημιαν εκ [om. Αν] των λεγοντων is also to be interpreted in this way.

The use of εκ with verbs of filling and fullness corresponds to classical linguistic style:¹²⁵ γεμιζειν 8:5; μεθυσκεσθαι [214] 17:2; μεθυειν 17:6 (εκ¹ om. Sᵃ K 1854 2329 for it dative S* f¹⁶⁷⁸). In 15:8 (εγεμισθη ο ναος καπνου εκ της δοξης), where only P⁴⁷ K write εκ του καπνου, εκ is omitted in the original text because of the εκ της δοξης that follows.

Furthermore, εκ is preferred over απο.

- εξερχομαι εκ 9:3; 14:15, 17, 18, 20; 15:6; 16:17 (απο K); 18:4; 19:21. Conversely, εξερχομαι απο in 19:5 (AC K, εκ S Αν Tisch)—identical with 16:17; εκπορευομαι εκ 1:16; 4:5; 9:17, 18 (απο K); 11:5; 19:15; 22:1.
- ερχεσθαι εκ (απο A [hiat C]) 7:14.
- εκδικειν εκ 6:10 (απο Αν); 19:2.
- κρινειν εκ 18:20.
- εξαλειφειν εκ 3:5; 7:17 (απο S f¹⁶⁷⁸ f²⁰¹⁴ f²⁰⁵¹ al. pc.); 21:4 (εκ A [hiat C] S, απο Αν K).
- λαβειν εκ 5:7; 6:4 (om. A Αν f¹⁰⁴/³³⁶ [WHort] [Charles]); 10:10; 18:4.
- λυειν εκ 1:5 (απο K).
- μετανοειν εκ 2:21, 22; 9:20, 21; 16:11.

---

122. A has the same correction in 18:11 and 18:20.
123. See Blass, *Grammatik des neutestamentlichen Griechisch*, §212.
124. 1:5 conversely + εκ ante των νεκρων Αν; influenced by Col 1:18.
125. See Blass, *Grammatik des neutestamentlichen Griechisch*, §172.

In the passive (rather than the instrumental dative): 2:11; 3:18; 8:11 (εκ] επι A, hiat C); 9:2, 18; 18:1.

The linguistic style varies between εκ and απο in the two following cases:

5:9   αγοραζειν εκ, 14:3, 4 απο.

18:3, 19   πλουτειν εκ, 18:5 απο (εκ *f*^2044).

Bousset[126] talks about the constant exchange of the preposition in the phrase εκ του ουρανου απο του θεου.

The exact details are as follows:

3:12   εκ του ουρανου απο του θεου
         εκ] απο K

20:9   εκ του ουρανου απο του θεου K
         εκ του θεου απο του ουρανου Aν
         εκ του ουρανου A (hiant C S) *f*^1678 *f*^2014

21:2   εκ του ουρανου απο του θεου A (hiat C) S K
         απο του θεου εκ του ουρανου Aν

21:10 εκ του ουρανου απο του θεου A (hiat C) S Aν
         εκ του ουρανου εκ του θεου K
         απο του ουρανου εκ του θεου Aρ *f*^250
         See also 16:17 εκ του ναου απο του θρονου A (hiat C) P^47 *f*^1006
         1611 *f*^1678 2053 – 2062 61 – 69.
         εκ του ουρανου απο του θρονου Aν

[215]   απο του ναου του ουρανου απο του θρονου K
         απο του ναου του θεου S

In reality, as the list demonstrates, the linguistic style is consistent. This consistency, however, proves precisely that Aν and K do not supplement the text of 20:9 with parallel passages[127] but rather that A commits a thoughtless error of omission. Only the overrating of A prevents many modern editors from recognizing that the longer text is original without hesitation. And since Aν, which is one of the two witnesses of the longer text, also makes a change in 21:2, the K text, which literally matches with 3:12; 21:2, 10, claims the original. In 16:17, the correction ναου] ουρανου in Aν has both A and P^47 S has against it. K, however, combines the Aν text with the original text.

This review of the use of εκ discloses, in general, K's tendency to replace εκ with απο.

---

126. Bousset, *Textkritische Studien*, 167.
127. Thus Weiss, *Die Johannes-Apokalypse*, 7.

We do not observe much of text-critical importance in those cases where εκ heavily represses απο. απο occurs (1) with the passive: 9:18 (υπο *f*²⁸¹⁴); 12:6 (υπο K); conversely, 6:13 υπο] απο S 1678ᶜᵒʳʳ· (2) in the Hebraism απο προσωπου 6:16; 12:14; 20:11 οὗ απο του προσωπου A (hiat C) S P 792 *f*¹⁰⁰⁶ 1611 2050 2329, του om. Αν K. Here the article, which Αν K eliminate in order to adjust to the common phraseology, is prompted by the previous relative οὗ.

In the case of εν, its frequent use in place of the heavily repressed instrumental dative,[128] which nonetheless asserts itself alongside εν, even with the same noun, is notable. The tradition is particularly unstable here. We present the evidence for (εν) φωνη first.

    5:2   κηρυσσοντα εν [om. Αν] φωνη μεγαλη

    14:7   λεγων εν [om. A] φωνη μεγαλη

    14:9   λεγων εν [om. *f*²⁰⁶⁰] φωνη μεγαλη

    14:15 κραζων εν [om. P⁴⁷ 1773 2329] φωνη μεγαλη

    19:17 εκραξεν εν [om. A Αν, hiat C] φωνη μεγαλη

    18:2   εκραξεν εν [om. S Ανᵖˡᵘʳ· Kᵖˡᵘʳ·, hiat C) ισχυρα φωνη (+ μεγαλη Αν)

               ισχυραν φωνην Kᵖᵃʳᵗ· *f*³³⁶ (see 6:10 below)

[216] On the other hand:

    5:12   λεγοντες φωνη μεγαλη

    6:10   εκραξαν φωνη μεγαλη

             φωνην μεγαλην K

    7:2   εκραξε φωνη μεγαλη

    7:10   κραζουσι φωνη μεγαλη

    8:13   λεγοντος φωνη μεγαλη

    10:3   εκραξε φωνη μεγαλη

    14:18 εφωνησε κραυγη μεγαλη C P⁴⁷ Αν 1006 1854 2329

             φωνη μεγαλη A S *f*¹⁰⁰⁶ *f*¹⁶⁷⁸ 2053ᵗˣᵗ· al. pc.

             εν κραυγη μεγαλη K

If we consider that εν is missing after κραζειν (6:10; 7:2, 10; 10:3) and φωνειν (14:18), a certain order emerges in the available evidence. εν then should likely also be discarded in 18:2 (εν A Ανᵖᶜ·) and 19:17 (S K), leaving only 14:15, where only P⁴⁷ 1773 2329 lack εν, to stand in contrast to the general rule. On the other hand, we discern no rule with λεγειν.

---

128. See also Charles, *Critical and Exegetical Commentary on the Revelation*, 1:cxxxix.

The evidence with (εν) πυρι is similar.

εν πυρι 16:18 (εν om. S 2595); 17:16 (εν om. S P f^{172/250} al. pc.); 18:8 (om. 2329).

On the other hand, πυρι 8:8; 21:8 (+ εν 1854 2030).

8:7   μεμιγμενα εν (om. Αν) αιματι

18:16 κεχρυσωμενη εν (om. Α Κ) χρυσ(ι)ω

Contrastingly, 17:4 κεχρυσωμενη χρυσ(ι)ω unanimously.

λυειν, αγοραζειν, λευκαινειν εν (τω) αιματι 1:5; 5:9; 7:14 unanimously with εν.

ποιμαινειν εν ραβδω 2:27 (εν om. Q); 12:5 (εν om. Αν Oec); 19:15

πατασσειν εν 11:6 (εν om. P⁴⁷ Q al. pc.); 19:15 (εν]) επ f²⁰⁵).

αποκτεινειν εν 2:23 (om. 61 – 69 al. pc.); 6:8; 9:20; 11:13; 13:10.

21:16 εμετρησεν (+ εν Αν)

19:13 βεβαμμενον (+ εν Αρ)

Usage in the passive:

περιβαλλεσθαι εν occurs in 3:5 (εν om. 2329) and 4:4 (εν om. A [hiat C] P 1854 f²⁰¹⁴ f²⁰³¹ 2065, 2432; likewise WHort). Otherwise, the phrase occurs ten times with the accusative. Correspondingly, ενδυεσθαι occurs with the accusative (1:13; 15:6; 19:14).

The tradition in the old main stems tends to eliminate εν. Subsequent insertion is rare. The later minuscules offer nothing noteworthy about this tendency.

[217] εις and εν.

εν = εις only in 11:11 (εισηλθεν εν αυτοις A Αν^{part.}; om. εν C Αν^{rel.}, εις αυτους P⁴⁷ S K).

If multiple nouns follow a preposition, these are usually repeated.[129] See, for example, 6:8 (εν² om. S, εν³ om. S min. pc.); 12:11 (δια² om. P⁴⁷ al. pc.); 15:2 (εκ² om. P⁴⁷ S f^{104/336} 2329); 16:13; 17:6.

Exceptions are:

1:9   εν τη θλιψει και [+ εν τη Αν] βασιλεια και υπομονη
       δια τον λογον του θεου και [+ δια S Αν K] την μαρτυριαν Ιησου

6:9   δια τον λογον του θεου και [+ δια C S Αν K contra A 1854 Sah.^{1/2}
       Boh. Latt.] την μαρτυριαν

9:15   εις την ωραν και [+ εις την K] ημεραν και μηνα και ενιαυτον

9:18   εκ του πυρος και [+ εκ Αν] του καπνου και [+ εκ Αν] του θειου

---

129. Similar to the article; see pp. 204–5.

16:4   εις [επι P⁴⁷ S 94] τους ποταμους και [+ εις K, + επι P⁴⁷ 94] τας
         πηγας

See also the sequence of nouns in 5:9 εκ πασης φυλης και γλωσσης και λαου
και εθνους.

10:11   επι λαοις και [+ επι K] εθνεσι και [+ επι f²⁰¹⁴] γλωσσαις και
           βασιλευσι πολλοις

14:6   επι της γης και επι [om. Aν] παν εθνος και φυλην και γλωσσαν και
         λαον.

3.7. Conjunctions and Particles

3.7.1. εαν

The aorist subjunctive always accompanies εαν in conditional sentences.
Exceptions to this rule are weakly attested and should be considered
simple scribal errors.

2:5   εαν μη μετανοησης] -σεις f¹⁰⁴ 2050
2:22   εαν μη μετανοησωσιν] -σουσιν A (non C) S
3:3   εαν μη γρηρορησης] -σεις f¹⁰⁴ al. pc.
3:20   εαν μη ακουση και ανοιξη] ακουσει min. pc., ανοιξει min. aliqui
22:18   εαν τις επιθη] επιθηση f²⁰¹⁴ f²⁰²⁹ f¹⁶⁷⁸(⁻¹⁷⁷⁸), επιθησει min. pc.
22:19   εαν τις αφελη] αφελει min. pc., αφεληται f²⁰²⁹, αφελειται Q sol.

[218] Tisch WHort Charles Merk consider the indicative form in 2:22 original. The text of A S with Weiss Bousset Sod Vog, however, should also be
rejected (see the similar error in C S in 12:6 and also ινα p. 1233) because
the indicative after εαν is otherwise an anomaly in the Apocalypse.

As in the rest of the New Testament, εαν instead of αν repeatedly
surfaces in combination with other conjunctions and relative pronouns.
The tradition's strong fluctuation between αν and εαν should therefore be
emphasized, making a complete overview of the data necessary.

2:25   αχρι αν C S 2329 al. pc.
          αχρις οὗ αν Aν (εως οὗ αν A)
          αχρι οὗ εαν 1611 2053
3:19   οσους αν S 2050 2053 al. pc.
          οσους εαν A (hiat C) Aν K
11:6   οσακις αν C 1611 f¹⁶⁷⁸ 1854 2053 2329 al. pc.
          οσακις εαν A P⁴⁷ S Aν K
13:15   οσοι αν C S Aν
          οσοι εαν A P⁴⁷ K

14:4   οπου αν AC (hiat P⁴⁷) Aν

οπου εαν K Orig.

The tradition's strong fluctuation is paralleled in the rest of New Testament and in the LXX.[130] Modern critical editions unanimously adopt the first reading in 2:25 and 14:4, as well as the form attested in the second reading in 3:19; 11:16; 13:15.

A second question that needs to be addressed pertains to the mood of the verb that occurs in these passages. Nothing should be made about the forms in 2:25 (ηξω) and 3:19 (φιλω).

11:6   θελησωσιν A S Aν K (and all modern editions)

θελησουσιν C

θελωσιν P⁴⁷ 61 – 69 2329 al. pc.

13:15   προσκυνησωσιν AC P⁴⁷ Aν^part. K

-σουσιν S Aν^part. (Tisch)

14:4   υπαγη S (hiat P⁴⁷) Aν K

υπαγει AC f¹⁰⁴/³³⁶ 2329 al. pc. (WHort Charles)

The present indicative is impossible;[131] υπαγει should therefore be considered a purely itacistic error.

[219] 3.7.2. οταν

The aorist subjunctive regularly accompanies οταν.[132] This rule is important for assessing several places where the tradition varies.

4:9   οταν δωσωσιν S Aν^plur. (Bousset)

δωσουσιν A (hiat C) P Aν^part. (and most modern editions)

δωσιν K al. pc.

8:1   οταν ηνοιξε ACf¹⁰⁰⁶ 1611 (and modern editions outside Bousset)

οτε ηνοιξε S Aν K (Bousset)

9:5   οταν παιση [πεση A S al.] all

10:7   οταν μελλη most

μελλει P⁴⁷ Aν^part. al. pc. (orthographic error)

11:7   οταν τελεσωσιν AC S K (τελωσιν P⁴⁷)

οτε τελεσουσιν Aν^pc.

οτε τελεσωσιν 2059 – 2081 2595

---

130. See Blass, *Grammatik des neutestamentlichen Griechisch*, §107; Westcott and Hort, *New Testament in the Original Greek*, 2:173; von Soden, *Die Schriften des Neuen Testaments*, 1:1385–86; Thackeray, *Introduction, Orthography and Accidence*, 65ff.

131. See Blass, *Grammatik des neutestamentlichen Griechisch*, §380.3.

132. Not always (so Bousset, *Textkritische Studien*, 170).

12:4 οταν τεχη the vast majority
     τεχει f[104] al. pc.
17:10 οταν ελθη practically all
     ελθει only two minuscules
18:9 οταν βλεπωσιν (ιδωσιν S f[1678]) almost all
     βλεπουσιν min. pc.
20:7 οταν τελεσθη most
     οτε τελεσθη f[2051] f[1678]
     οτε ετελεσθη 2059 2081
     οτε ετελεσθησαν f[2814] f[2028]

The aorist subjunctive accompanies οταν five times, the present subjunctive accompanies it twice (10:7; 18:9), and the aorist (8:1) and the future indicative (4:9) respectively accompany it once.[133] One is tempted to reject οταν and read οτε in 8:1 with S Aν K, since οτε surfaces in the previous six seals. Why οταν is used with the aorist indicative in the seventh seal, which, despite being linguistically correct, occurs only once in the Apocalypse, remains inexplicable.[134] οτε, however, is obviously a harmonization to the text of the first six seals.

3.7.3. ινα

ινα with the subjunctive is unanimously [220] or virtually unanimously attested in most places. However, we need to represent the evidence precisely in the following passages.

3:9 ποιησω αυτους ινα ηξουσιν και προσκυνησουσιν ... και γνωσιν AC
    S Aν[part.] K[pc.]
    ηξωσιν και προσκυνησωσιν Aν[plur.] K[plur.] (Sod)
6:4 εδοθη ... και ινα σφαξουσιν AC 2019 2329
    σφαξωσιν S Aν K (Sod)
6:11 ερρεθη αυτοις ινα αναπαυσονται A S Aν[part.] K[part.] (WHort Bousset
    Charles)
    αναπαυσωνται C Aν[part.] K[part.] (see 14:13)
8:3 εδοθη αυτω ... ινα δωσει AC S Aν[part.]
    δωση Aν[plur.] K (Sod)
    δω 61 – 69 f[1006] 2053

---

133. See Blass, *Grammatik des neutestamentlichen Griechisch*, §382.4.

134. I can only describe what Weiss (*Die Johannes-Apokalypse*, 177–78) says about this as meaningless.

9:4   ερρεθη αυταις ινα αδικησουσιν A (hiat C) 2019 2329 2351
                      αδικησωσιν S Aν K (Weiss Bousset 1st loco
                      Vog [non Sod])
9:5   εδοθη … ινα μη αποκτεινωσιν (-νουσιν 2019) αλλ ινα βασανισθη-
        σονται A (hiat C) S Aνplur.
        βασανισθωσιν K (Sod 2nd loco)
9:20 ου μετενοησαν … ινα μη προσκυνησουσιν AC P47 S f104 2019
                      προσκυνησωσιν Aν K (Sod)
13:12 ποιει … ινα προσκυνησουσιν AC P47 f104 2019 2053 al. pc.
                      προσκυνησωσιν Aν K (Sod Vog)
                      προσκυνειν (sine ινα) S
14:13 ινα αναπαησονται A P47 S sol.
        αναπαυσονται C Aν (Bousset 2nd loco)
        αναπαυσωνται K (Sod)
22:14 μακαριοι, ινα εσται … και εισελθωσιν both unanimously

But for 9:4, where C is lacunose, the indicative is the most strongly attested
reading in all these passages. Now we should note that ινα has no final
meaning in all these passages, but, as Weiss emphasizes, the ινα is para-
phrasing the infinitive. Weiss rejects this point in 6:11 and 9:4 but without
reason. In the last two passages (14:13 and 22:14) ινα = οτι.[135] Thus, the
indicative should be taken as the *Urtext* in all these passages. Once again,
AC's exceptional value emerges in an impressive way.

As something of a cross-check to this language usage, we need to
examine whether ινα with the future indicative is also used consistently as
a substitute for the infinitive in the Apocalypse.

[221] Assuming the tradition is trustworthy, two passages fail to fit the
norm.

13:16 ποιει … ινα δωσιν αυτοις AC P47 S* Aν
                      δωσωσιν Kplur., δωσουσιν Krel.
                      δωσει al. pc.
19:8 εδοθη … ινα περιβαληται almost all
                      περιβαλληται pc., περιβαλειται 051 792

The meaning of ινα is not final in both cases.[136] In 9:5 and 22:12, the future
indicative occurs alongside the present subjunctive or the aorist subjunc-

---

135. Blass, *Grammatik des neutestamentlichen Griechisch*, §369.2; in contrast,
Charles, *Critical and Exegetical Commentary on the Revelation*, cxxxv n. 2.

136. At 13:16, however, Westcott and Hort (*New Testament in the Original Greek*,
2:158–59) and Blass (*Grammatik des neutestamentlichen Griechisch*, §369.2) want the

tive in the most striking way. Obviously, the use of the future indicative after ινα, which in the New Testament (just as in the Apocalypse) surfaces relatively frequently,[137] has not been implemented consistently.

In other passages, where the final meaning of ινα is clear,[138] the subjunctive is usually attested unanimously or virtually unanimously, as noted above. What is certain is that slightly varying minuscules or minuscule groups (such as f^{104}, 2060, 2286, also 2329, 4x [12:6; 13:15; 19:15; 20:3]) and S frequently write -ει instead of -η in particular places. We must surely consider these instances simple itacistic errors because the same vacillation fails to occur in the plural forms (-ωσιν, -ουσιν).[139] Only the following places will be discussed:

12:6   ινα εχει τρεφωσιν [εκτρεφωσιν K Hipp.] αυτην A Aν K

τρεφουσιν C (dub. P^{47}) S al. pc. (Tisch WHort[mg.] Charles[txt.])

We should definitely reject the indicative as spurious here because the Apocalypse otherwise consistently uses the subjunctive with the final ινα, and the present indicative (rather than future tense) is absolutely singular here.[140] 16:15 (ινα) βλεπωσι] βλεπουσι P^{47} Aν should be assessed similarly. [222] 12:14 ινα πετηται

πεταται Aν

As in 16:15, Aν uses the present indicative here.[141]

13:15   ινα και λαληση ... και ποιηση

λαλησει f^{104} al. min. pc.

ποιησει S $f^{104/336}$ 2329 al. min. pc. (WHort[mg.] Weiss)

και ποιηση] ποιησαι P^{47}

---

best attested reading δωσιν to go back to an ancient itacistic error (δωσιν = δωσι = δωση). The conjecture is paleographically possible but should be rejected on exegetical grounds. Not only the context but also the other previously listed examples of this construction (3:9; 13:12) require that the subject of δουναι be different than that of ποιειν. αὐτοῖς = ἑαυτοῖς does not speak against it (see p. 217).

137. See Blass, *Grammatik des neutestamentlichen Griechisch*, §369.2.

138. 2:10, 21; 3:11, 18; 6:2; 7:1; 8:6, 12; 9:15; 11:6; 12:4, 6, 14, 15; 13:13, 15, 17; 16:12, 15; 18:4; 19:15, 18; 20:3; 21:15, 23.

139. Only 2019, a very poorly copied manuscript, repeatedly writes -ουσιν instead of -ωσιν against Aν (the group to which it belongs). There can, of course, be no discussion of "tradition" in such a case.

140. Thus also Blass, *Grammatik des neutestamentlichen Griechisch*, §369.6. See the discussion on this reading also in Weiss, *Die Johannes-Apokalypse*, 100.

141. For the form α, see p. 191.

Here is a real problem, which Weiss and Charles identify.[142] και ποιηση, ινα ... αποκτανθωσιν presupposes that the image of the (first) beast is acting as the subject. But the οσοι εαν μη προσκυνησωσιν τη εικονι του θηριου that follows seems to presuppose that the subject of ποιηση is not the image of the (first) beast but the second beast. ποιηση, then, is grammatically inadmissible, "an entirely mechanical harmonization to λαληση" (Weiss). But if we accept this explanation, we cannot solve the problem with the very inadequately attested ποιησει from an orthographically unreliable codex like S, but ποιησαι must be required.[143]

13:17   ινα μη τις δυνηται AC P[47] S

δυναται Αν K (WHort[mg.] Weiss)

This verse resumes the previous discussion of 13:16 (p. 232), where the aorist subjunctive was not assessed according to the otherwise respected rule. After the overwhelming and strong attestation of the subjunctive in 13:16, the occurrence of the present indicative here in the two later recensions is surprising. Weiss[144] considers the Αν-K reading the *Urtext* and the subjunctive δυνηται an obvious harmonization to the previous δωσιν. Since, according to Weiss, the ινα in 13:17 is probably a circumlocution for the infinitive (not however the infinitive in 13:16), the change from the subjunctive to the indicative would be intentional and correct. In reality, however, the presumed difference between the two ινας does not exist and the two verses form a logical unit. The present indicative δυναται, however, must be rejected since it is contrary to the Apocalypse's linguistic style: it must have the future indicative.[145]

[223] 19:15 ινα παταξη

παταξει S f[104/336] 2329 al. pc.

In all these cases, we observe the indicative's infiltration into the terrain of the subjunctive in the individual text forms.[146] In none of them, however, does the error go back to the Apocalypse's original text.

---

142. Weiss, *Die Johannes-Apokalypse*, 131; Charles, *Critical and Exegetical Commentary on the Revelation*, 2:420 n. 5.

143. The sentence construction would then read as follows: εδοθη αυτω δουναι πνευμα ... και ποιησαι. ποιησαι is then parallel to δουναι in the sentence structure.

144. Weiss, *Die Johannes-Apokalypse*, 103, 195–96.

145. See p. 233 for 12:6.

146. Compare to Georgios N. Hatzidakis, *Einleitung in die neugriechische Grammatik* (Leipzig: Breitkopf, 1892), 216–17.

3.7.4. αχρι

αχρι (αχρις οὗ), as a conjunction, is usually accompanied by the aorist subjunctive.

2:25   αχρι (εως A, αχρις Aν) οὗ αν ηξω
                      ανοιξω K
     ηξω is not a future indicative here but an aorist subjunctive from ηξα.

7:3   αχρι [αχρις οὗ K] σφραγισωμεν
                    σφραγισομεν f²⁸¹⁴ f²⁰²⁸ 2053 al. pc.

15:8   αχρι τελεσθωσιν all

17:17 αχρι τελεσθησονται AC S Aν
         τελεσθωσιν K

20:3, 5 αχρι τελεσθη

Analogous is 6:11 εως [+ οὗ Aν] πληρωθωσι AC 2344
                    πληρωσωσιν S Aν K

Only 17:17 breaks the rule. Even without the departure, the idea differs from that of 15:8; 20:3, 5.

3.7.5. ου μη

The findings are similar in the case of ου μη (usually aorist subjunctive[147]); cf. 2:11; 3:5, 12; 7:16 (ουδε μη); 18:7, 21, 22 (ter), 23 (bis); 21:25, 27.

The tradition is divided only in the following passages:

3:3   ου μη γνως] γνωση S K (Tisch WHort[mg.] Charles[mg.])
     The future tense is a harmonization to the two occurrences of the future ηξω before and after the verb.

9:6   ου μη ευρωσιν AC Aν
     ευρησουσιν S K 0207 (Tisch WHort[txt.] Sod Vog Charles[txt.] Merk)
     This example should be evaluated exactly like 3:3.

18:14 ου μη αυτα ευρησουσιν A S f¹⁶⁷⁸ f¹⁷² Hipp.
     αυτα ου μη ευρησουσιν C P 1611 f¹⁸
     ου μη ευρησεις αυτα Aν
     αυτα ου μη ευρης K (Bousset)
     [224] K alone keeps the form of the corresponding rule. This

---

147. See Blass, *Grammatik des neutestamentlichen Griechisch*, §364.

cannot be the *Urtext*, however, because the second-person singular is a clear correction, not the impersonal plural.

15:4   τις ου μη φοβηθη κυριε και δοξασει AC P⁴⁷ Aν
       δοξαση S K (Sod)

The S-K reading is an umistakable harmonization to φοβηθη.

3.7.6. ουδε – ουτε

Not only should the tradition's strong fluctuation be recognized, but ουτε
often takes the place of ουδε even in the original text.[148] An overview of all
the available evidence is once again necessary.

(1) ουτε – ουτε = "neither – nor"
     3:15, 16 (ουτε¹] ου K); 9:20; (21:4).

(2) ου – ουτε
    9:21 ου – ουτε – ουτε – ουτε. Likewise 21:4; however here ου – ουδε –
           ουδε – ουδε 2050.

(3) 5:3 ουδεις – ουτε – ουτε – ουτε K (Tisch WHortᵐᵍ· Sod Charlesᵐᵍ·)
          ουδεις – ουτε¹ – ουτε³ S al. pc.[149]
          ουδεις – ουδε – ουδε – ουτε A (hiat C) *f*¹⁰⁴ (WHortᵗˣᵗ· Weiss Vog
          Merk)
          ουδεις – ουδε – ουδε – ουδε Aν (Bousset Charlesᵗˣᵗ·)
    5:4 ουδεις – ουτε [ουδε *f*²⁰¹⁴]

(4) 7:16 ου – ουδε [+ μη A 1611 61 – 69 23 2351] – ουδε [ουδ' ου K] – ουδε
    9:4 μη – ουδε – ουδε
          μη – μηδε – μηδε *f*¹⁶⁷⁸ 1854 2329
    9:20 ουτε ante μετενοησαν A Aν (WHortᵐᵍ·¹ Bousset 2nd loco Sod
          Vog Charlesᵐᵍ·¹)
          ουδε P⁴⁷ S 61 – 69 *f*¹⁶⁷⁸ 2053 (Tisch WHortᵗˣᵗ· Weiss Bousset 1st
          loco Charlesᵐᵍ·)
          ου C K (WHortᵗˣᵗ· Charlesᵐᵍ·² Merk)

---

148. See also ibid., §445.1; Mayser, *Grammatik der Griechischen Papyri*, 1.1:177
and 2.3:171ff.
149. om. ουτε υποκατω της γης (γης¹⌒²).

12:8 ουκ – ουδε
      ουτε Αν
20:4 ουκ – ουτε – και ουκ Αν
      ουτε] ουδε A (hiat C) S K (and all modern editions)
      και ουκ] ουδε 1611
21:23 ου – ουδε
      ουτε *f*¹⁶⁷⁸ 2050
[225] 7:1 μητε – μητε
7:3   μη – μητε – μητε
      μη – μηδε – μηδε S *f*³³⁶ 1854 *f*²⁰⁶¹ al. pc.
      μη – και – μητε A (non C) *f*¹⁶⁷⁸ 2351 (WHort^mg· Weiss Charles^mg·)

In 5:4; 7:1, 3; 9:21; and 21:4, ουτε or μητε is made certain by the textual tradition. The situation is reversed in 7:16; 9:4; 12:8; and 21:23, where the textual tradition makes ουδε certain. The infiltration of ουτε into the terrain of ουδε in the original text, however, makes it difficult to determine the original reading in the other places. ουτε will certainly have to be discarded in 20:4 because of Αν's insufficient testimony. And P⁴⁷ S probably preserve the original reading in 9:20. A decision based on hard evidence is impossible in 5:3.

3.7.7. ως

The Apocalypse uses ως (ωσπερ only 10:3, never καθως¹⁵⁰) in a peculiar way. Part of the tradition omits the particle, where ως is used in a unique way in various places.¹⁵¹

4:6 om. Αν^pc·
4:7 ως ανθρωπου A (hiat C)
     ως ανθρωπος Αν
       ανθρωπου K
     ως ομοιον ανθρωπω S
5:1 om. *f*¹⁸ *f*⁹²⁰ Hipp. al. pc.

---

150. The form ωσει surfaces in various places in some of the witnesses to the text, so 1:14 in C Αν; 16:13 in P⁴⁷ S *f*¹⁶⁷⁸ *f*²⁰⁵¹; 1:17; 16:3 in S; 13:3 and 20:8 (ως η] ωσει) in K. In other places, ωσει surfaces in individual minuscule groups. This reading does not come into question as the *Urtext*.

151. See also Charles, *Critical and Exegetical Commentary on the Revelation*, 1:357; Charles, *Studies in the Apocalypse*, 95–96.

5:11   ως φωνην S K, ως om. A (hiat C) Aν (habent Tisch WHort$^{mg.}$ Bousset)

6:6   om. ως ante φωνην K

6:12   om. 1854 Sah. Boh. Arm.^{3} Gig. Vict. Beat.

9:7   om. ως^{1} f^{1678} al. pc.

14:2   om. ως ante κιθαρωδων Aν

14:3   om. ως ante ωδην P^{47} S K contra AC Aν (om. Tisch Weiss [Sod])

16:3   om. f^{2814}, 2059 – 2081 2595

    ~ ως αιμα Aν$^{rel. plur.}$ f$^{104/336}$

[226] 16:21 om. S 94 141 – 1719

19:1   om. ως ante φωνην Aν

19:6   om. ως^{1} Aν

    om. ως^{2} A (hiat C) f^{149} 2057

19:12 om. ως ante φλοξ S Aν K contra A (hiat C) f^{1006} f^{1678} f^{2029} verses (see 1:14 ως φλοξ)

    (habent ως WHort$^{mg.}$ [Bousset] Charles)

    Conversely, 21:21 + ως ante ην S

                  + ως ante εξ ενος P Q 1611 f^{2014} (Bousset)

The general tendency is restricted to the "mannered use" of ως. And indeed, all important textual witnesses except C are involved in it, even A in one place (19:6). Nevertheless, this observation does not allow us to declare ως original retrospectively in 5:11; 14:3, and possibly also in 19:12. None of the reasons adduced for or against the authenticity of ως in these places are clearly decisive. Thus, in the case of 19:12, the parallel passage of 1:14 can be cited both as proof of the authenticity of ως as well as accepted as a subsequent harmonization at A.

3.8. Stereotypical Expressions

The Apocalypse receives its peculiar linguistic flavor through its many stereotypical phrases. These also have some significance for textual criticism. We shall only consider the text-critically important cases.[152]

(1) The double name Ιησους Χριστος is only used in the introductory verses (1:1, 2, 5). Afterwards, the simple Ιησους occurs alone, making certain the

---

152. Comprehensive compilation of material in Bousset, *Textkritische Studien*, 176–77.

inauthenticity of the accompanying Χριστος that follows in 1:9 (εν Ιησου C
S P 1611 *f*¹⁶⁷⁸ 2050 2344, εν Χριστω A, εν Χριστω Ιησου K, Ιησου Χριστου
Aν; Ιησου²] + Χριστου K); 14:12 (+ Χριστου *f*²⁰¹⁴); 22:20 (+ Χριστου Sᵃ Aν
Aρ); and 22:21 (+ Χριστου Aν K). Otherwise ο Χριστος itself (+ αυτου 11:15;
12:10) occurs four times (11:15; 12:10; 20:4, 6), each with the article, which
only Aν 20:4 deletes.

(2) The phrase δια τον λογον του θεου και την μαρτυριαν Ιησου has a formulaic character.
    1:2   Ιησου] + Χριστου (see above)
    1:9   + δια ante την μαρτυριαν S Aνᵖˡᵘʳ· K, Ιησου] + Χριστου K
    6:9   + δια ante την μαρτυριαν C S Aν K against A 1854 Sah.¹ᐟ² Boh.
           Latt.
[227] 20:4   ~ δια την μαρτυριαν Ιησου και τον λογον του θεου all
Minor variations surface repeatedly in these frequently used phrases; thus,
two different forms stand side by side here: one with δια² (6:9; 20:4) and the
other (1:2, 9) without it.

(3) εκ του οινου…:
    14:8   εκ του οινου του θυμου της πορνειας αυτης
Likewise 18:3, though with the following variants in the textual tradition:
           του οινου om. AC 2053 – 2062
           ~ του θυμου του οινου Aν (see also p. 146)
    On the other hand, 17:2 εκ του οινου της πορνειας αυτης
    Notably, no single manuscript harmonizes this passage to 14:8 or 18:3.
    Similarly: 16:19 εκ του οινου του θυμου της οργης αυτου
    Likewise, 19:15 του οινου του θυμου [+ και Aν] της οργης του θεου
    On the other hand, 14:10 εκ του οινου του θυμου του θεου

(4) The tradition also preserves the stereotypical combination οι μικροι και
οι μεγαλοι without deviation in 11:18; 13:16; 19:5, 18.
    Only 20:12 ~ οι μεγαλοι και οι μικροι, where Q Aρ *f*²⁵⁰ restore the other
form.

(5) Exactly analogous are 3:14; 19:11; 21:5 (~Aν); 22:6 πιστος και αληθινος.

(6) The tradition of the phrase αστραπαι και φωναι και βρονται (και σεισμος),
which surfaces four times, is problematic.

4:5   αστραπαι και φωναι και βρονται

αστραπαι και βρονται και φωναι Aν[part.]

11:19 αστραπαι και φωναι και βρονται

αστραπαι και βρονται και φωναι f[172/250] f[2014] al. pc.

16:18 αστραπαι και φωναι και βρονται A (hiat C) Aν[part.] f[1006]

αστραπαι και βρονται και φωναι P[47] K

βρονται και αστραπαι και φωναι και βρονται S*

(και βρονται[2] om. S[a])

και φωναι om. Aν[part.]

8:5   βρονται και αστραπαι και φωναι A (hiat C) f[1678] 2329 Syr.[2]
       (WHort[mg.] Weiss Charles)

βρονται και φωναι και αστραπαι S K Sah. Boh. Syr.[1] Latt. (so
most of the modern critical editions)

φωναι και βρονται και αστραπαι Aν

[228] 4:5 and 11:19 confirm that A Aν[part.] preserve the original text in 16:18. In all three passages, 4:5; 11:19; and 16:18 have a part of the tradition that changes the order to βρονται και φωναι. The expected order[153] is not handed down in any particular textual group in 8:5. This suggests that it was not present in the original text. S K and Aν agree that αστραπαι stands in the third position, A and S K agree that βρονται precedes αστραπαι, and A and Aν agree that the βρονται and αστραπαι similarly follow one another. Weiss[154] regards the text of S K secondary to that of A because the arrangement of the similar βρονται and φωναι betrays itself as a correction. This, however, is unconvincing and also improbable because the transposition of αστραπαι to the third position is an obvious corruption. Considering Aν a subsequent correction of S K if the text of S K is not simultaneously the *Urtext* is also questionable. Aν cannot be understood, however, as a correction of A. More likely, A is a half correction of S K, which improves the misplaced position of αστραπαι in the last place. The text of S K then maintains the stronger claim to being the original text, which the most important versions also support. We cannot do more in this case.

(7) Contrary to the rest of the New Testament (Matt 2:1; 8:11 = Luke 13:29) and the LXX's linguistic style, the Apocalypse writes απο ανατολης (in the

---

153. Normally the lightning is mentioned before the thunder, as occurs in the three other places. But Exod 19:16 preserves εγενοντο φωναι και αστραπαι.

154. Weiss, *Die Johannes-Apokalypse*, 108.

singular) three times (7:2; 16:12; 21:13). A (against C) has the reading in the first passage, A Aν (against C P^{47} S K) have it in the second, and K has it in the third, which is a harmonization to the commonly used plural απο ανατολων.

(8) The Apocalypse writes η βιβλος (3:5; 20:15 [το βιβλιον K]) της ζωης and (17:8; 20:12; 21:27 [η βιβλος f^{1678} 2060, 2286 2050] το βιβλιον της ζωης next to each other. The tradition varies more strongly in 13:8:

τω [om. C] βιβλιω AC Aν K

τη βιβλω P^{47} f^{2814} f^{1678}

βιβλω (anarthrous) S 1611 1854 f^{2060} 2019 2057

However, τω βιβλιω is attested strongly and decisively.

The tradition surrounding the Greek word for the "book" in the angel's hand in Rev 10 is very mixed.

[229] 10:2	βιβλαριδιον	AC^c S* Aν$^{plur.}$
	βιβλιδαριον	C* Aν$^{rel.}$ Compl.
	βιβλιον	P$^{47vid.}$ K 792 1854
10:8	βιβλαριδιον	S Aν$^{plur.}$ (hiat P^{47})
	βιβλιδαριον	Aν$^{rel.}$ K Compl. $f^{104/336}$ $f^{172/250}$
	βιβλιον	AC f^{1006} 1611 61 – 69
10:9	βιβλαριδιον	C Aν$^{plur.}$, βιβλαριον A 2329
	βιβλιδαριον	Aν$^{rel.}$ K Compl. $f^{104/336}$ $f^{172/250}$
	βιβλιον	P^{47} S f^{1006} f^{1678} 1854 2053$^{txt.}$
10:10	βιβλαριδιον	A (hiat C) Aν$^{plur.}$ Syr.^{1} Prim.
	βιβλιδιον	P^{47}
	βιβλιδαριον	Aν$^{rel.}$ Compl. al. pc.
	βιβλιον	S K $f^{104/336}$ $f^{172/336}$ 792 1854

Of all the textual groups, only Aν has a consistently attested form (βιβλαριδιον or βιβλιδαριον, although we cannot ascertain which of these is the original Aν text). The remaining textual groups fluctuate: AC read βιβλιον in 10:8; P^{47} reads it in 10:2, 9; S in 10:9, 10; and K in 10:2, 10. C* replaces the more unusual βιβλαριδιον with βιβλιδαριον in 10:2, and K does it in 10:8, 9.

All modern critical editions correctly reject βιβλιδαριον in every passage because of its inadequate attestation. Of these readings, WHort Weiss Charles Merk adopt βιβλιον into the text of 10:8, apparently on the authority of AC. In contrast, Tisch (because of S) Bousset Sod Vog adopt βιβλαριδιον. In addition to the authority of AC (as the best textual stem of the Apocalypse's entire Greek textual tradition by far), βιβλιον in 10:8 can be defended on the grounds that βιβλαριδιον is more easily understood as a harmonization to 10:2, 9, 10, rather than as the only subsequent intrusion to the uniform expression that disturbs βιβλιον.[155] Just how problematic the evidential value of this consideration is, however, is manifest by the fact that βιβλιον is read in 10:2 (P[47] K); 10:9 (P[47] S); and 10:10 (S K). Why should not βιβλιον in 10:8 be the same correction in AC?[156] The versions fail to settle the issue in this case, as the details in the aforementioned places show, since they blur further the distinction between βιβλιον and βιβλαριδιον.[157] [230] Thus, the reading βιβλαριδιον in 10:8 has an equally founded claim to the status of original as does AC's text. We cannot decide unequivocally what the *Urtext* is without decisive evidence.

3.9. Singular and Plural *Constructio ad sensum*

(1) With the noun: The *constructio ad sensum* usually occurs with nouns if it refers to one thing as belonging to a plurality, the plural, e.g., αι κεφαλαι αυτων.

Exceptions:

13:16 επι το μετωπον αυτων AC S K
       επι των μετωπων αυτων P[47] Αν

20:4 επι το μετωπον [των μετωπων min. pc.] η επι την χειρα αυτων

11:8 το πτωμα αυτων AC K
       τα πτωματα αυτων P[47] S Αν

11:9 το πτωμα αυτων[1] AC P[47] S K (plural Αν)
       on the other hand, in the second location: τα πτωματα αυτων all

17:17 τας καρδιας αυτων
       την καρδιαν αυτων 1854 Hipp.

(2) Only A (hiat C) with Αρ[1] *f*[104] 1773 departs from the consistently followed rule that verbs related to several singular subjects are in the sin-

---

155. As always, Weiss is certain about entirely too much here (ibid., 105, 184), when he simply asserts that βιβλαριδιον stands in the narrative, while the worthy βιβλιον was used in the mouth of the angel (108).

156. Unfortunately, a gap exists at this place in P[47].

157. Thus, the Latins Prim. and Vulg. offer *libellus* in 10:2, *liber* in the other locations; Vict. offers *librum* in 10:2, *libellum* in 10:10; and Gig. Tyc. Cass. consistently offer *liber*.

gular if it precedes them and in the plural if it follows them[158] in 20:13: εδωκαν] -κεν (probably a thoughtless harmonization to the previous εδωκεν). Accordingly, εγενετο χαλαζα και πυρ μεμιγμενα (with A [hiat C] K, μεμιγμενον S Aν) should be read in 8:7. εγενετο is in the singular because it precedes the subject; μεμιγμενα is in the plural because it refers to both nouns.

(3) With a neuter plural, the verb is usually in the plural and in some exceptional cases only in the singular:

1:19   α μελλει [μελλουσι 2051, 2064, 2067]
13:14 α εδοθη [εδοθησαν f²⁰⁵]
14:13 τα εργα ακολουθει (unanimously)
16:14 α εκπορευεται [εκπορευονται Q f¹⁰⁴, εκπορευεσθαι sine α P⁴⁷ S* Aν]
18:14 τα λιπαρα ... απωλετο [απηλθεν Aν, απωλοντο S f¹⁰⁴ Compl., likewise Tisch Bousset 1st loco]
[231] 19:14 τα στρατευματα ηκολουθει [ηκολουθουν Aν]
20:3   τελεσθη [τελεσθωσι f²⁰¹⁴ f¹⁴⁹ 1611] τα χιλια ετη
20:5   τελεσθη [τελεσθωσι f²⁰¹⁴ 792 2070, 2305]
20:7   τελεσθη [τελεσθωσι 792; οτε ετελεσθησαν f²⁸¹⁴ f²⁰²⁸]

The plural can generally be understood as a *constructio ad sensum*, as Bousset[159] and Charles[160] note.[161] But this understanding cannot apply everywhere, since 19:14 has the singular with τα στρατευματα (plural only Aν). On the other hand, the plural also occurs with impersonal subjects (1:19; 8:11; 15:4; 16:20; 20:12; 21:4); α εισι και α μελλει in 1:19 is especially characteristic. The finding is not surprising; it fits within the parameters of language development.[162] Notably, corrections occur in both directions within textual transmission.[163]

---

158. Supporting evidence in Bousset (*Textkritische Studien*, 164) and Charles (*Critical and Exegetical Commentary on the Revelation*, 1:cxli).

159. Bousset, *Textkritische Studien*, 164–65.

160. Charles, *Critical and Exegetical Commentary on the Revelation*, 1:cxli.

161. See, above all, 3:4; 4:8, 9; 5:14; 11:2, 13, 18; 15:4; 21:24.

162. See Blass, *Grammatik des neutestamentlichen Griechisch*, §133; and for the Byzantine era, Fritz Hörmann, "Beiträge zur Syntax des Johannes Kinnamos" (diss., Münich, 1938), 4–5.

163. See above for examples of the plural instead of the singular. For the singular instead of the plural, see the following places: 3:2 εμελλον] -εν f¹⁰⁴/³³⁶; 4:5 α εισιν Sᵃ Aν, α εστιν A (hiat C) (likewise Weiss and Charles), αι εισιν K; 9:18 απεκτανθησαν] -θη P⁴⁷

(4) The *constructio ad sensum* surfaces frequently in collective nouns:

7:9   οχλος πολυς … εστωτες [-ας K, εστωτων C f^{1678} f^{2028} 284]

13:3–4 εθαυμασθη ολη η γη και προσεκυνησαν

προσεκυνησεν P^{47} 2019

18:4   εξελθατε [-θετε Aν] … ο λαος μου A S Aν Hipp.

εξελθε C K 1611 2053 – 2062

19:1   οχλου πολλου λεγοντων nearly unanimously (by contrast, 19:6 does not belong here)

In addition, the two following similar passages:

8:9   το τριτον των πλοιων διεφθαρησαν A (hiat C) S Aν

διεφθαρη K

9:18   απεκτανθησαν το τριτον των ανθρωπων AC S Aν K

απεκτανθη P^{47} f^{1678} 94 f^{498} 2019

The details are as follows for εκαστος:

2:23   δωσω υμιν εκαστω κατα τα εργα υμων

υμων] αυτου Q 2050 2329

5:8   εχοντες εκαστος κιθαραν [-ας Aν]

[232] 6:11   εδοθη αυτοις εκαστω στολη

εκαστω αυτων f^{2014}, om. εκαστω K

20:13   εκριθησαν εκαστος κατα τα εργα αυτων

αυτων] αυτου K

On the other hand, 21:21 εις εκαστος … ην, 22:12 εκαστω ως το εργον αυτου εσται

See also 4:8 τα τεσσαρα ζωα εν καθ εν εχον

εχοντα P f^{1678} 1611 2050 al. pc.

Constructio ad sensum also occurs in those cases where natural rather than grammatical gender is used in relative pronouns and the like in the attibutive position.

(1) with αρνιον, θηριον, and ζωον

5:6   αρνιον εστηκως ως εσφαγμενον εχων

εστηκως S Aν$^{part.}$ al. pc., εχων AC S Aν$^{part.}$ f^{104}

εστηκος AC Aν K pc., εχον Aν$^{plur.}$ K

---

94 f^{1678} al. pc.; 9:20 δυνανται] -ναται P^{47} K; 11:18 ωργισθησαν] -θη P^{47} S*; 15:4 εφανηρω-
θησαν] -θη P^{47}; 16:20 ευρεθησαν] -θη P^{47}; 21:4 απηλθαν] -θεν K.

Of the modern critical editions, von Soden alone reads εστηκος and εχον. All others read εχων, but only Tisch WHort[mg.] Bousset Charles[mg.] read εστηκως.

Everyone abandons εστηκως except Tischendorf, who as always swears by his prized Codex Sinaiticus, and Bousset abandons it with reservations. On the other hand, von Soden alone rejects εχων.

5:12   αξιον ... το αρνιον
      αξιος A (hiat C) (WHort[mg.] Weiss Bousset 1st loco Charles[mg.])

14:1   αρνιον εστος AC S (all modern editions)
      εστως P[47] Αν
      εστηκος K
      εστηκως f[104] al. pc.

11:7   το θηριον το αναβαινον
      το αναβαινων A (non C) f[104] 2060, 2286

13:1   θηριον αναβαινον
      αναβαινων f[104] 2060, 2286 al. pc.

13:8   αυτον (sc. το θηριον) AC P[47] K, αυτω S Αν

13:11   θηριον αναβαινον
      αναβαινων P[47] f[104] 2060 – 2286

13:14   τω θηριω ος εχει AC P[47] Αν
      ο εχει S K (Sod sol.)
      (In contrast, 13:2 το θηριον ο ειδον all; 17:11 το θηριον ο ην all)

17:3   θηριον ... γεμοντα ... εχοντα
      γεμοντα A (hiat C) S* P 2053 – 2062 2329

[233]   εχοντα S P sol.
      γεμων f[104] f[2060] al. pc.
      εχων A (hiat C) f[2814] f[2060] f[104] al. pc.
      γεμον Αν K
      εχον Αν[plur.] K

Modern critical editions are very divided here. Sod Vog Merk read γεμον; Weiss alone reads γεμον τα; Tisch WHort Bousset Charles read γεμοντα. Weiss Sod Vog Merk read εχον; WHort[txt.] Bousset 1st loco Charles[mg.] read εχων; Tisch WHort[mg.] Bousset 2nd loco Charles[mg.] read εχοντα.

17:11   το θηριον ... αυτος A (hiat C) Αν
      ουτος S K

4:7   ζωον ... εχων A (hiat C) f[104/336] al. pc.
      εχον S Αν[plur.] K[plur.] (WHort[mg.] Sod Vog)

4:8   (ζωον) εν καθ εν εχων A (hiat C) Av^part. f^104/336

εχον S Av^rel. K (Weiss Sod Vog)

17:16   τα δεκα κερατα ... και το θηριον ... ουτοι

These passages should be discussed together because of their similarities. First, το θηριον in 17:11, 16 should obviously be understood as a masculine. In both cases, however, the masculine form is selected only with αυτος or ουτοι, and it precedes the neuter relative pronoun (ο ην και ουκ εστι 17:11; α ειδες 17:16). Likewise, the masculine is chosen only in a newly inserted sentence in 4:8 (και αναπαυσιν ουκ εχουσιν ... λεγοντες). Therefore, the question at hand is whether a relative pronoun linked to a neuter noun or participle could be construed as a masculine. The textual tradition's diverse inventory at individual places appears to suggest that here, as in other cases, a singular principle is not carried out consistently. Decisions must be made on a case-by-case basis depending on the available testimony. That the tradition undergoes changes here, not only through conscious corrections but also through purely orthographic violations, is not difficult to recognize. The neuter participle or neuter relative pronoun is unanimously attested in 13:1, 2 and 17:11[164] so that its authenticity is not in doubt. Furthermore, [234] the neuter participle in 11:7 and 13:11 should obviously be considered the original reading, and A or P[47] simply have an orthographic error, especially in 11:7 (το αναβαινων A). And we can likewise make definitive judgments about 4:7, 8, despite the contrary judgment of all modern critical editions except Sod Vog (and in 4:8 also Weiss). That a few Av and some K manuscripts are also added in these two places to A and f^104/336 as apparent witnesses for the masculine implies nothing and apparently has not been decisive for the modern editions. For if the neuter here can be understood as an obvious correction of the rest of the text's witnesses, we should nonetheless emphasize to the contrary that a masculine εχων among the three neuter forms of ομοιον (4:7) must be considered an impossibility for the Apocalypse's language. And it is not tolerable when the masculine stands immediately next to εν καθ εν αυτων in 4:8. In both cases, only the prevailing tendency to overrate A's authority (C is missing both times) since WHort explains why almost all modern critical editions adopt the masculine form and reject the neuter

---

164. There are only the same orthographically inferior minuscule groups f^104/336 and f^2060—the same ones that repeatedly write -ει instead of -η, as has been noted (p. 233)—and a constantly changing small number of other minuscules that out of sheer orthographic ignorance write ω for ο.

as a correction.[165] The high regard for this best of the Apocalypse manuscripts, however, must not be uncritically extended to orthography. The
same judgment is also true for 5:12, where A alone (C is missing again)
provides αξιος εστι το αρνιον.[166] Indeed, this is the more difficult reading
because neither the distant εχων of 5:6 nor the masculine αξιος ει (5:9)
supports it. Thus, it is only A's mistake.[167]

Two passages with identical wording, 5:6 and 14:1, should now be discussed. Only Bousset considers the masculine εστως in 14:1 the *Urtext*.
The others do not because P reads with AC S εστος. Meanwhile, P[47] joins
Αν as a "witness" for εστως, so that now this reading's manuscript testimony seems even stronger than the testimony for εστηκως in 5:6 (S Αν[part.]).

[235] However, the two passages discussed above, 11:7 and 13:11, prove
that the old witnesses, and all the more the carelessly copied S, may have
replaced ο with ω through a simple scribal error.[168] Weiss[169] judges quite
correctly here: "On no account is εστως authentic, since it could not have
occurred before the neuter εσφαγμενον constr. ad syn." The two following
passages can be cited as confirmation of the claim that the old majuscules
cannot be followed without caution and criticism in orthographic matters
where it is beyond question that the *constructio ad sensum* occurs.

17:4 ποτηριον χρυσουν ... γεμων S* *f*[104] al. pc. (Tisch WHort[mg.]
Charles[mg.]). In addition to S, the particularly orthographically bad *f*[104]
again offers the obviously erroneous γεμων.

Not to be judged any differently, despite the contrary opinion of the
modern critical editions[170] (except Weiss Sod Vog), is 21:14: το τειχος ...
εχων A (hiat C, om. S) P 1 2059, 2081 *f*[104] min. al. against Αν[plur.] K. Again,
A's authority explains why most modern critical editions attribute this
orthographic error to the original text itself.

---

165. For Weiss to reject the masculine εχων in 4:8 as a simple scribal error and yet
to state with the usual certainty that εχων is the *Urtext* in 4:7 is entirely methodologically inconsistent. As always, Weiss is not at a loss for an explanation in these places
(*Die Johannes-Apokalypse*, 122, 169): "The creature with human eyes is personified
and therefore the εχων ad syn is presented in masculine."

166. Against Weiss on this verse.

167. Even the most determined defenders of AC's text and particularly of A,
WHort and Charles, present αξιος only as a marginal reading.

168. Conversely, P[47] 11:18 οργισθη instead of ωργισθη.

169. Weiss, *Die Johannes-Apokalypse*, 56.

170. See also Blass, *Grammatik des neutestamentlichen Griechisch*, §136.4.

In 13:14, the masculine ος is undoubtedly the *Urtext* due to its strong
testimony. Similarly, the masculine εχων in 4:8 (about which more will be
said below) is so well attested that it is certainly original.

17:3, where the tradition is obscure at first glance, requires careful discussion.[171] A (C and P[47] missing) first reads γεμοντα with S* P 2053 – 2062
2329, continuing with the orthographically inferior minuscule groups *f*[104]
and *f*[2060] and several other minuscules with the nominative. The same
minuscules, however, also write γεμων before this, which is simply an
orthographic variant for γεμον (thus Aν K), simultaneously demonstrat-
ing that εχων is a simple scribal error for εχον (thus Aν[plur.] K). Thus only
A remains as a "witness" for εχων again, and therefore the adoption of a
simple scribal error (instead of εχον) is also probable here as in the passages discussed above: 4:7, 8; 11:7; and 21:14. A Aν[plur.] K, then, attest the
grammatically correct εχον, and only S P read εχοντα, which is nothing
more than [236] a harmonization to the previous γεμοντα. But if εχοντα is
abandoned, then γεμοντα[172] stands in a different text-historical light. Its
testimony by A S P 2053 – 2062 2329 is certainly much stronger than that
of εχοντα. But its status as the original remains uncertain. The assumption
that γεμον (Aν K) should be a later correction is obvious, but it remains
possible that γεμοντα is a simple error caused by a thoughtless harmonization to ονοματα, just like the rejected readings of all or nearly all modern
editions: 9:10 ομοιοις (A [hiat C] S); 2:9 Ιουδαιων (C S* 2050 2329); 11:3
περιβεβλημενους (A [non C] S* P *f*[104]); 19:20 της καιομενης (A [hiat C] S
P); and 21:9 των γεμοντων (A [hiat C] S A).

That two participles standing so closely together in the *Urtext* would
have different genders is without analogy in the Apocalypse. (The first is
the masculine, standing nearer to the neuter noun θηριον, and the second
is the grammatically correct neuter.) This is the basic reason for the rejection of γεμοντα: it is a thoughtless harmonization to ονοματα, and εχοντα in
S P is a conscious, subsequent harmonization to γεμοντα.

In summary, the *constructio ad sensum* surfaces only in some of the
cases presented in this section. A careful deliberative critique of the textual
tradition will eliminate the rest.

---

171. See already p. 82.

172. The spelling γεμον τα is impossible (Weiss). Not only does the subsequent
εχοντα speak against it, but also the fact that the βλασφημιας, which is dependent upon
τα ονοματα, should have the article.

(2) A number of other places must be examined for the existence of this construction.

Three times it occurs with φωνη:

4:1 η φωνη η πρωτη … λεγων A (hiat C) S* K
λεγουσα Aν

9:13 φωνην μιαν … λεγοντα A (hiat C) S*
λεγουσαν P⁴⁷ Aν, λεγοντος K

11:15 φωναι μεγαλαι … λεγοντες A K
λεγουσαι C P⁴⁷ S Aν (Sod Vog)

In all three cases,[173] the masculine form of the participle λεγων is still considered the *Urtext*, correctly so, by all or most modern critical editions.

[237] We need to make an important observation here: the masculine participle never follows the feminine noun to which it refers immediately but is always separated by several intervening words. The attribute standing adjacent to the noun, on the other hand, always retains the noun's gender. The same observation applies to the cases discussed above. Thus, εστηκος and εσφαγμενον keep the neuter gender of αρνιον in 5:6, and only εχων is masculine. In 13:14, the relative pronoun ος occurs immediately adjacent to τω θηριω, but the logical connection between the two remains far from clear, as ος introduces a new clause, albeit a relative clause.

The tradition's imbalance encumbers the following case regarding αυτος.

9:3 εξηλθον ακριδες … και εδοθη αυταις A (hiat C) Aν K [al. pc.
αυτοις S Q f²⁰⁶⁰ f¹⁰⁴ 2329

9:4 και ερρηθη αυταις A (hiat C) Aν K
αυτοις S Q 61 – 69 f¹⁷²/²⁵⁰ f¹⁸ f²⁰⁶⁵ 2329

9:5 και εδοθη αυταις Aνᵖᵃʳᵗ· K f¹⁰⁴ 1611 2053
αυτοις A (hiat C) S Aνʳᵉˡ·

Of the modern critical editions, WHortᵗˣᵗ· Vog Charles Merk read αυταις three times; Tisch (with S) Weiss Bousset read αυτοις three times; and WHortᵐᵍ· Sod[174] read αυταις¹·², αυτοις³ (with A). S's testimony[175] for αυτοις in 9:3 and 9:4 is quite inadequate and should be rejected. In 9:5, αυτοις

---

173. For 4:1 and 11:15, see again p. 252. 9:13–14 departs from the rule discussed there, as the accusative λεγοντα stands here.

174. And Charles *Critical and Exegetical Commentary on the Revelation*, 1:cxlii and 242–43; on the other hand, 1:289–90.

175. Q's testimony is useless because K, to which Q otherwise belongs, always reads αυταις.

may be a simple careless error in A. At the very least, αυτοις is not certain in 9:5. This reading is therefore not adopted with certainty in any verse in the text.

3:4   ονοματα … α

οι Αν (Bousset 2nd loco)

The modern critical editions ignore the Αν reading because P reads ᾶ. The Αν reading should probably be abandoned, since Αν otherwise never preserves the *Urtext* alone when all other text forms have a different reading. However, Αν is not inferior to S in its value as a witness.

9:7   τα ομοιωματα … ομοια

ομοιοι S 792 2057 (Tisch WHort[mg.] Weiss Charles[mg.])

[238] If we abandon S's reading in 9:3–5, we cannot render a different judgment in 5:6.

5:6   πνευματα του θεου απεσταλμενοι A (hiat C) 2053

απεσταλμενα S *f*[1678] 1854 2050 (WHort[mg.] Charles[mg.])

τα απεσταλμενα Αν[plur.] (Bousset 2nd loco)

αποστελλομενα K (Bousset 1st loco)

That the remaining text forms diverge and the neuter can be understood as an obvious correction give the text of A 2053 the balance of probability. The support of 2053 shows that A's reading is not simply a careless error.

5:13   παν κτισμα και τα εν αυτοις παντα ηκουσα λεγοντας Αν

λεγοντα A (hiat C) *f*[2814] *f*[2051] 2057 2595 (WHort[mg.] Charles[mg.])

… και τα εν αυτοις˙ παντας ηκουσα λεγοντας K

+ και ante ηκουσα S *f*[172/250] *f*[2031] al. pc.

A makes a correction here. Αν alone preserves the *Urtext*.

7:4   χιλιαδες εσφραγισμενοι [-ων K]

14:3–4 αι [om. *f*[104/336]] ρμδ̄ χιλιαδες οι ηγορασμενοι. ουτοι (unanimously)
On the other hand, 14:1 ρμδ̄ χιλιαδες εχουσαι.

11:4   ουτοι εισιν αι δυο ελαιαι και αι δυο λυχνιαι αι [om. S Αν *f*[172/250], al. pc., οι *f*[149]] … εστωτες [εστωσαι Αν Hipp.]

The linking of the feminine article (which only WHort place in brackets) with a masculine participle in the examples below constitutes the most egregious violation of Greek grammar. The prepositional phrase that separates the article from the participle, however, tempers the incongruity.

19:14   στρατευματα … ενδεδυμενοι A (hiat C) Αν K

-οις

19:4   οι πρεσβυτεροι οι κ̄δ̄ και τα τεσσαρα ζωα ... λεγοντες

There is no longer an actual *constructio ad sensum* here, since λεγοντες also refers to οι πρεσβυτεροι.

The numerous cases where a participle's natural gender replaces its grammatical one are a serious anomaly for the Greek language (and are also unusual in the rest of the New Testament). However, the Apocalypse also commits additional infractions against the Greek language. Of these, we mention the following, divided into two classes: [239] (1) Hebraisms and (2) other linguistic irregularities.

These features give the Apocalypse its peculiar linguistic flavor.

3.10. Hebraism

Charles[176] attempts to attribute the Apocalypse's "solecisms" almost entirely to its "Hebrew" style, which was far more Hebrew than the LXX. In order to properly assess the tradition, we must arbitrate between Hebraisms that can be ascribed to the author himself and those that are simple scribal errors of a later tradent.

(1) The apposition to a noun standing in an oblique case occurs in the nominative case.[177] This serious violation of the Greek language repeatedly causes corrections in part of the tradition.

1:5   απο Ιησου Χριστου ο μαρτυς ο πιστος

                         ος μαρτυς πιστος εστιν *f*[172/250]

2:13   εν ταις ημεραις Αντιπας ο μαρτυς μου ο πιστος, ος απεκτανθη

          ημεραις] + αις Κ, + εν αις Αν, + εν ταις S*

If we do not accept Lachmann's conjecture—that Αντιπα should be read— then the nominative Αντιπας is in apposition to ο μαρτυς ... K, Αν, and S have made unsuccessful attempts to clarify the text.

2:20   την γυναικα Ιεζαβελ η λεγουσα AC S* 2053 2329

                             την λεγουσαν Αν, ἡ λεγει Κ

3:12   της καινης Ιερουσαλημ η καταβαινουσα

                         ἡ καταβαινει Κ

---

176. Charles, *Critical and Exegetical Commentary on the Revelation*, 1:cxlii–clii.

177. Indeed, the nominative always has the article with it, except for λεγων. The article is missing, so the case of the preceding noun is maintained; cf. 9:14 τω αγγελω ο εχων next to 7:2 αγγελον εχοντα (ibid., 1:cl).

8:9   το τριτον των κτισματων τα εχοντα

                           των εχοντων f^{2028} 2031 – 2056

9:14   τω εκτω αγγελω ο εχων

                           τω εχοντι $f^{172/250}$ 1611 2329

20:2   τον δρακοντα ο οφις ο αρχαιος A (hiat C) f^{1678}

                           τον οφιν τον αρχαιον S Aν K

        A f^{1678} have the original text.

[240] 6:1 may also be added here:

        ηκουσα ενος … λεγοντος ως φωνη βροντης

                           φωνη] φωνης Aν, φωνην S al. pc.

The proposed spelling of φωνῇ by WHort Weiss Sod Vog Merk should be rejected and the nominative read (with Tisch Bousset Charles), following the parallels in 9:9; 14:2 (bis); 19:6 (see Charles).[178] The "unprecedented construction" (Weiss) must be tolerated, and the parallel to 5:12 is entirely inappropriate.

(2) The participle λεγων (λεγοντες) is repeatedly treated as indeclinable.[179]

4:1   η φωνη η πρωτη … λεγων

                           λεγουσα Aν

5:11–12   ο αριθμος αυτων … λεγοντες

                           λεγοντων f^{498} f^{920} 2065, 2432

                           λεγουσαι f^{2028}

11:1   εδοθη μοι καλαμος … λεγων

        Part of the tradition (S^c Q $f^{172/250}$ Compl. 1854 2329 2351 61 – 69 versions)—admittedly of no importance for determining the *Urtext*—attempts to bring order to the construction by inserting και ειστηκει ο αγγελος before λεγων. The original text contains an entirely intolerable difficulty. Instead of the passive voice, the reading should be: εδωκεν μοι καλαμον … λεγων.[180]

11:15   εγενοντο φωναι … λεγοντες A K

                           λεγουσαι C P^{47} S Aν

14:6–7 ειδον αλλον … εχοντα … λεγων

                           λεγοντα P^{47} (om. S) f^{2814} f^{2031} 1611

                           2053 254

---

178. Ibid., 1:161.

179. Blass, *Grammatik des neutestamentlichen Griechisch*, §136.4; he also offers several analogous examples from the LXX.

180. For additional, analogous cases from the LXX, see Charles, *Critical and Exegetical Commentary on the Revelation*, 1:374.

19:6   ηκουσα ως φωνην ... και ως φωνην ... και ως φωνην ...
λεγοντες K (WHort^mg· Weiss Bousset)[181]
    λεγοντων A (hiat C) P Ap² f¹⁷² f¹⁰⁰⁶ 1611 2053 – 2062 2329
f²⁰¹⁴ f²⁰⁶⁵
    λεγοντας Αν, λεγουσων S

The λεγοντων adopted by most modern editions, which A's authority supports and S confirms, can be considered [241] the most appropriate reading. However, A's reading does not explain the origin of either the K or the Αν reading.

Blass and Charles adopt the same approach for εχων as they do for λεγων.[182] Of the passages to be considered, 4:7, 8; 17:3; and 21:14 should be eliminated since εχων is a scribal error for εχον in every case (on this see p. 245). Only in 5:6 (see above) and in 14:14 (καθημενον ομοιον υιον ανθρωπου εχων] εχοντα P⁴⁷ S* min.) is this construction likely or certainly present.

(3) *Nominativus pendens*
    2:26; 3:21   ο νικων ... δωσω αυτω
    3:12   ο νικων ... ποιησω αυτον
        (On the other hand, 2:7, 17 τω νικωντι δωσω αυτω; see below 4.)
    6:8   ο καθημενος επανω αυτου, ονομα αυτου ο θανατος
        ονομα αυτου om. 141 – 1719 2329
Related to this is 9:11 εχουσιν ... τον αγγελον της αβυσσου, ονομα αυτω.
    ονομα αυτω] ω ονομα P⁴⁷ 94, ω ονομα αυτω S
Similarly also 1:20 το μυστηριον των επτα αστερων ... και τας επτα λυχνιας...,
οι επτα αστερες αγγελοι ... εισιν.

(4) Pleonastic insertion of the demonstrative or personal pronoun in relative clauses:
    2:7   τω νικωντι δωσω αυτω
                αυτω om. S Compl. f²⁰⁵ f²⁰³¹
    2:17   τω νικωντι δωσω αυτω
                αυτω om. S sol.

---

181. Charles also originally explains this reading as the *Urtext* (*Studies in the Apocalypse*, 85) but prefers λεγοντων later in his commentary.
182. Blass, *Grammatik des neutestamentlichen Griechisch*, §136.4; Charles, *Critical and Exegetical Commentary on the Revelation*, 1:cl.

The *nominativus pendens* used in 2:26 and 3:21 with the following αυτω or αυτον is somewhat corrected in 2:7 and 2:17.

3:8　ην ουδεις δυναται κλεισαι αυτην
　　　ην] και f²⁸¹⁴ f²⁰²⁸, αυτην om. S f²⁰³¹ al. pc.

6:4　τω καθημενω επ αυτον εδοθη αυτω
　　　　　　　　　　αυτω om. A Sᶜ

7:2　οις εδοθη αυτοις
　　　　　αυτοις om. f¹⁷⁷ 1854 f²⁰¹⁴ f²⁰³¹ 2329

[242] 7:9　ον αριθμησαι αυτον ουδεις εδυνατο
　　　　　αυτον om. K

12:6　οπου εχει εκει τοπον
　　　　εκει om. C Aνᵖᵃʳᵗ· (but cf. 2:12; 11:8; 20:10)

12:14　οπου τρεφεται εκει
　　　　οπως τρεφηται εκει K

13:8　οὗ ου γεγραπται το ονομα αυτου (A) C f¹⁶⁷⁸ 1854 2053 2344
　　　　ων ου γεγραπται … αυτων P⁴⁷ S f¹⁰⁰⁶ 1611 2329
　　　　ων ου γεγραπται Aν K
　　　　However, 17:8 ων ου γεγραπται το ονομα [+ αυτου 2919 792]

13:12　οὗ εθεραπευθη … αυτου
　　　　　　　αυτου om. P 61 – 69 1006 sol. 2329

17:9　οπου η γυνη καθηται επ αυτων (all)

20:8　ὧν ο αριθμος αυτων
　　　　　　αυτων om. Aν

20:11　ου απο του προσωπου] + αυτου f¹⁰⁰⁶ 2053 – 2062 2329 2031 – 2056 f²⁰⁶⁰ al. pc.

21:6　εγω τω διψωντι δωσω [+ αυτω K, Tisch]

21:7　ο νικων κληρονομησει ταυτα
　　　　ο νικων δωσω αυτω ταυτα K

　　　K harmonizes these two verses to 2:7, 17.

Part of the tradition makes corrections in almost every place on this short list: A makes corrections in 6:4; C in 12:6; S in 2:7, 17; 3:8; Aν in 12:6; 13:8; 20:8; K in 7:9; 12:14; 13:8; and some unimportant witnesses make corrections in several places.

(5) Participle instead of finite verb:

10:2　εχων] ειχεν Aνᵖᵃʳᵗ·, εχει Aνʳᵉˡ·

12:2　εν γαστρι εχουσα

19:12　εχων

21:12　εχουσα

21:14 εχων A (hiat C) Αυ[part.] f[104]

εχον S Αυ[rel.] K (see p. 248)

(6) Resumption of the participle through the finite verb:

1:5–6 τω αγαπωντι ... και λυσαντι ... και εποιησεν

εποιησεν] ποιησαντι Q** f[42/325] 61 – 69 1854 2019 2429

1:17–18 εγω ειμι ο πρωτος ... και ο ζων και εγενομην νεκρος [= και
γενομενος νεκρος]

2:2 τους λεγοντας εαυτους αποστολους [+ ειναι Αυ K] και ουκ εισιν [=
οντας] all

[243] 2:9 των λεγοντων Ιουδαιους ειναι εαυτους και ουκ εισιν all

2:20 την γυναικα Ιεζαβελ, η λεγουσα ... και διδασκει και πλανα [=
διδασκουσα και πλανωσα], ἣ λεγει ... και διδασκει K

3:9 των λεγοντων εαυτους Ιουδαιους ειναι και ουκ εισιν αλλα ψευδονται
[= και ουκ οντων αλλα ψευδομενων]

7:14 οι ερχομενοι ... και επλυναν ... και ελευκαναν [= οι ερχομενοι ...
και πλυναντες ... και λευκαναντες]

12:2 εν γαστρι εχουσα και κραζει C P[47] S f[1006] Oec 2020 – 2080
~ κραζει και A, και om. Αυ K

14:2–3 φωνην ηκουσα κιθαρωδων ... και αδουσιν [και αδοντων f[2051]]

15:2–3 ειδον ... εστωτας ... εχοντας ... και αδουσιν [και αδοντας S (non
P[47]) f[2051] multiple versions]

See also 4:8 and 3:7: ο ανοιγων και ουδεις κλειει, και κλειων και ουδεις ανοιξει.

For these verses, the K text reads: ο ανοιγων και ουδεις κλεισει αυτην ει
μη ο ανοιγων και ουδεις ανοιξει.

How seldom later correctors make changes to the text in these places
is striking. They appear to have been at a loss about what to do.

(7) και for the introduction of the concluding clause:[183]

3:20 εαν τις ακουσῃ..., και εισελευσομαι S K

και om. A Αυ

Some modern critical editions erroneously reject και (WHort[txt.]
Weiss Sod Vog Merk) because they overrate A's authority.

6:12 και ειδον οτε ηνοιξε ... και σεισμος μεγας εγενετο

και[2] om. f[2051] 2019

___

183. For its presence in the rest of New Testament, see Blass, *Grammatik des neutestamentlichen Griechisch*, §442.7. The και corresponds to the Hebrew *waw consecutivum*.

10:7   εν ταις ημεραις εκειναις..., και ετελεσθη
       Misunderstanding the sense of the passage, the Aν text con-
       nects the subordinate clause και τελεσθῇ Aν with οταν μελλη
       σαλπιζειν so that the main clause is missing in this verse.

14:9–10   ει τις προσκυνει..., και αυτος πιεται all

(8) The difficult infinitive in place of the *verbum finitum* is also an explicit
Hebraism:[184]

12:7   Μιχαηλ και οι αγγελοι αυτου του πολεμησαι AC *f*[1006] 1611 Compl.
       f[2031] *f*[2065] 2019, om. του P[47] S Aν K

[244] We must also consider 13:10b alongside this passage. The interpretation of 13:10b is taken up here because of its relationship to the conclusion that A alone preserves the original text, or at least comes close to
it.[185]

    ει τις εν μαχαιρη αποκτανθηναι, αυτον εν μαχαιρη αποκτανθηναι
For the Hebraism απο προσωπου and for the instrumental εν, see further
p. 227.

3.11. Other Linguistic Irregularities

Even Charles, who, in addition to Bousset, investigates the Apocalypse's
language and textual tradition most accurately, acknowledges that a remnant of difficult linguistic incongruities remain. Although he demonstrates
that a number of changes (which Bousset dubs grammatical violations) are
actually Hebraisms, he also cites several examples which neither Greek
nor Hebrew grammar "explains," that is to say, justifies. "The bulk of these
solecisms though not all, are simply slips of our author which a subsequent
revision would have removed, if the opportunity of such a revision had
offered itself."[186]

Explaining this class of linguistic errors poses a particularly serious
problem for textual criticism—a formal dilemma. Because they generally
occur only in part of the tradition, usually in AC, and because the later

---

184. See also Charles, *Critical and Exegetical Commentary on the Revelation*,
1:cxlvi, 322; ibid., 315.

185. On this see pp. 147–49.

186. Charles, *Critical and Exegetical Commentary on the Revelation*, 1:cliii. Weiss
wrongly maintains (*Die Johannes-Apokalypse*, 56): "Nowhere in the Apocalypse are
pure grammatical blunders present with reason."

texts Aν K correct the same text of the Apocalypse, there is no specific criterion for deciding definitively in some places whether AC's erroneous text is the original and the other text groups have made corrections or, conversely, whether AC's text is corrupt and the original reading resides in the other textual witnesses. It is nonetheless methodologically unjustifiable for Hort and even for Charles to consider the text of AC (S) absolutely "neutral" and to adopt its clear errors in many places. Textual criticism will have to accept a *non liquet* in some places.

We mention the following solecisms here:

1:10   ηκουσα φωνην ... ως σαλπιγγος λεγουσης (instead of λεγουσαν Sᶜ)

[245] 1:15   οι ποδες αυτου ομοιοι χαλκολιβανω ως εν καμινω πεπυρωμενης AC
πεπυρωμενω S 2050 2053 – 2062ᵗˣᵗ· ƒ³³⁶ Sah. Syr.¹·² Vulg. Vict. Aeth.

πεπυρωμενοι Aν K (see on this already p. 74)

We cannot deny the fact that AC's text is linguistically incorrect.[187] If we assume that πεπυρωμενω is the *Urtext* and the text of AC is a scribal error, the reading -οι of Aν K can be understood as a misguided correction. But AC's error may go back to the original.

1:20   το μυστηριον των επτα αστερων ... και τας επτα λυχνιας τας χρυσας

Both the absolute accusative (which is then completed by a newly inserted main clause) and the new accusative τας επτα λυχνιας (instead of a dependent genitive from το μυστηριον, which only ƒ⁴⁹⁸ Sah. Boh. Prim. Arab. Aeth. produce) disrupt the sentence. The tradition's uniformity proves that the difficulty goes back to the original or at least to the entire tradition's archetype.

4:4 The accusatives attested by A (hiat C) S ƒ¹⁶⁷⁸ 2053 ƒ²⁵⁰ θρονους¹ ... πρεσβυτερους καθημενους περιβεβλημενους ... στεφανους χρυσους represent a breach of the construction. Such is also present in Aν K, which read θρονους¹] θρονοι, but which also retain the accusatives that follow. If we add ειδον, the reading θρονους of A S claims the right to the status of the original.[188]

---

187. Weiss (comment on this verse) gives an utterly incredible explanation and justification of the genitive (here and 17:8).

188. See the comment on this verse on p. 76.

A similar disturbance surfaces in 13:3 and 14:14 (see below) as well as in

7:9   εστωτες ... περιβεβλημενους ... φοινικες A
        εστωτας   -ους ... φοινικας K
        εστωτες   -οι ... φοινικες Aν
        εστωτων C al. pc., φοινικας with K as well as S*.

Weiss reads εστωτας but not φοινικας and allows an independent sentence to begin with και φοινικες. Tischendorf, following S*, reads φοινικας. Aν and K eliminate the ruptured sentence structure in two different ways. Only Aν corresponds to the [246] Apocalypse's other type of representation (cf. 4:2; 19:11). However, it is clearly a subsequent correction here.[189]

9:7   τα ομοιωματα ... ομοιοι S 792 2026
        ομοιωματα A (hiat C)
        ομοια Aν K

Despite Tischendorf (who here as always swears upon S) and Weiss, ομοιοι is in all probability a simple scribal error of S's careless scribe and does not go back to the original. The error ομοιωματα of A is more easily explained as deriving from ομοια than ομοιοι.

9:12   ερχεται ετι δυο ουαι A (hiat C) P⁴⁷ S K
        ερχονται Sᵃ Aν

The immediately preceding η ουαι η μια disproves Weiss's assertion[190] that the singular surfaces because the author thought ουαι was neuter. The incongruity in number as such must be allowed to persist.

10:8   η φωνη, ην ηκουσα, λαλουσαν ... και λεγουσαν AC S Aν
        λαλουσαν ... λεγουσαν] -σα bis K (brings the text in order)
        η φωνη ην] φωνην f¹⁰⁰⁶ 1854 2053 2329 2344 f¹⁰⁴ (another correction with the same result)

11:3   προφητευσουσιν ... περιβεβλημενους σακκους A S* (hiat P⁴⁷)
        Aνᵖᵃʳᵗ· f¹⁰⁴ al. pc.
        περιβεβλημενοι C Aνᵖˡᵘʳ· K Hipp.

Only WHort and Charles track the error of A S* Aνᵖᵃʳᵗ· (based on a thoughtless harmonization to σακκους) to the original. Because A S also have common errors in other places, such as the ομοιοις (instead of ομοιας)

---

189. Blass (*Grammatik des neutestamentlichen Griechisch*, §136.2) understands the sentence structure as follows: The accusative περιβεβλημενους is dependent upon the ειδον at the beginning of the sentence over και ιδου with nominative. The continuation και φοινικες must then be understood as a new sentence.

190. Weiss, *Die Johannes-Apokalypse*, 181.

σκορπιοις in 9:10,[191] which all modern editions reject, or the senseless and therefore undoubtedly spurious ιερεις (instead of ιρις) in 4:3, it is not possible to attribute the error (περιβεβλημενους) to the original without being partial to the "neutral" text.

13:3   μιαν ... ως εσφαγμενην..., και η πληγη ... εθεραπευθη

The addition of ειδον in front of μιαν in f[1006] f[2065] 203 – 506 is probably analagous (cf. 4:4).

[247] 14:14 νεφελη λευκη, και ... καθημενον ομοιον ... εχων

καθημενος ομοιος Αν

ο ... καθημενος ομοιον P[47]

Αν's correction brings order to the text. P[47] S* min. instead change εχων into εχοντα. But εχων appears to be treated as indeclinable here (see p. 253) and then to be understood as accusative. In that case, και επι την νεφελην should be thought of as depedent upon ειδον over και ιδου νεφελη λευκη. The four similar cases in 4:4; 7:9; 13:3; and 14:14 should also be explained in the same way.

The following readings contain a difficult incongruity in gender:

14:19   την ληνον ... τον μεγαν AC Αν [part.] K[plur.]

τον ληνον ... τον μεγαν Αν[pc.]

την ληνον ... την μεγαλην S f[1006] f[172/250] f[104/336] f[1678] Αν[part.]

την ληνον ... του μεγαλου P[47] 2019 – 2429

16:13   και ειδον ... πνευματα ... ως βατραχοι A (hiat C) Αν K

ωσει βατραχους P[47] S*

The decisively and well-attested nominative βατραχοι shows that πνευματα is in the nominative case. The vision's content is thus described in an independent sentence, similar to (as 6:2, 5, 8; 7:9; 14:1, 14) και ειδον και ιδου.[192]

17:4   γεμον βδελυγματων και τα ακαθαρτα (unanimously attested)

Eliminating the incongruity in 17:4 by following Weiss (see his comment on this verse) and perhaps Charles in allowing τα ακαθαρτα to be dependent on εχουσα is not possible. "The impurities of her fornication" are rather to be understood beside the abominations as the content of the cup, which the Whore of Babylon has in her hand. The difficulty of the genitive and accusative in relation to one another must be tolerated. The fact is that the author constructs γεμειν both with the accusative (see the preceding

191. See p. 78.

192. So correctly Weiss in his comment on this verse.

verse 17:3: γεμον ονοματα βλασφημιας) and with the genitive (cf. 4:5, 8; 5:8; 15:7; 21:9).

17:8   θαυμασθησονται οι κατοικουντες…, ων ου γεγραπται…, βλεποντων
          βλεποντες Aᵛᵖᶜ· Compl. 792 1854 2019 Hipp.

The incorrect genitive should not be understood as a genitive absolute (with complementary αυτων)[193] but rather as a byproduct of the influence of the relative ὧν.

[248] 19:20 την λιμνην του πυρος της καιομενης A (hiat C) S P f⁰⁵¹ 2595 2057
                    την καιομενην Aν K

Because της καιομενης (or την καιομενην) is not the attributive to του πυρος but (cf. 21:8 τη λιμνη τη καιομενη πυρι και θειω) to την λιμνην, the error does not lie in the word's gender but in its case. The intervening genitive του πυρος appears to be the cause. But whether the correct την καιομενην of Aν K is the *Urtext* or only a correction cannot be decided.

21:9   των αγγελων των εχοντων τας επτα φιαλας των γεμοντων των επτα
          πληγων A (hiat C) S* Aν
          των γεμοντων] γεμουσας K

Weiss sees no other possibility here than to assume a thoughtless error of the older text. The linguistically correct reading τας γεμουσας, which Weiss adopts into his text, is only present in a few minuscules (f²⁸¹⁴ f²⁰²⁸ f¹⁰⁴ f¹⁰⁰⁶) and is explicable only as a correction because of its weak attestation. Since errors also surface elsewhere with very strong attestation that do not go back to the original,[194] the strong witness to the error is not indisputable proof here that it goes back to the author. But this possibility should be acknowledged.

22:2   ξυλον ζωης ποιων … αποδιδουν
          ποιων A (hiat C) 2080, αποδιδουν A Aνᵖᵃʳᵗ· al.
          ποιουν S Aν K,   αποδιδους S Aνᵖˡᵘʳ· K

The textual tradition's inventory is contradictory here insofar as A juxtaposes the masculine ποιων and the neuter αποδιδουν, and, conversely, S Aν K place the masculine αποδιδους beside the correct ποιουν. Indeed, Tisch WHortᵐᵍ· Bousset 1st loco Charlesᵐᵍ· read ποιων and (the latter also Sod) αποδιδους. But neither one is justified. ποιων is masculine only in appearance. In reality, as the nearby neuter αποδιδουν proves, it is a simple scribal error that does not go back to the original. That A preserves αποδιδουν with

_____

193. So Weiss in his comment on this verse.

194. See in particular 13:7 εδοθη¹⌒² AC P⁴⁷ Aν against S K; 13:10 ει τις εν μαχαιρα αποκτεινει δει αυτον εν μαχ. αποκτανθηναι all except A; 18:3 πεπωκαν or πεπτωκαν.

some minuscules as the original here (as enigmatic as the emergence of the masculine αποδιδους remains) must be concluded from the fact [249] that the form -διδουν comes from διδοω, which the AC stem also attests in 3:9. With this decision, any linguistic violation in this location disappears.

The phrase ομοιον υιον ανθρωπου surfaces twice:

1:13   ομοιον υιον ανθρωπου S K
          υιω ανθρωπου AC Aν
14:14 ομοιον υιον ανθρωπου A S K
          υιω ανθρωπου P⁴⁷ C Aν

In both places only a part of the tradition, namely, S K, retain these difficulties, which seem to be violations of the language based on a thoughtless harmonization to the accusative ομοιον. That it surfaces twice, however, suggests that it goes back to the original[195] and that the linguistically correct text is a subsequent correction.

Finally, the designation for God appears as a rigid, indeclinable formula: ο ων και ο ην και ο ερχομενος 1:4, 8; 4:8 (~ ο ην και ο ων και ο ερχ.), also 11:17; 16:5 ο ων και ο ην, linked with απο in 1:4. Only the K text mitigates the difficulty here, which lies in the combination απο ο ων, by inserting the genitive θεου after απο.

3.12. Results

As with any author, a precise examination of the Apocalypse's linguistic style is very important for textual criticism. The tradition is afforded a consistent cross-check in this manner. This is particularly important in the Apocalypse because of the nature of its linguistic form, its idiosyncrasies, and violations of Greek grammar, which precipitate repeated corrections in the tradition. The frequent stereotypical formulations that give the Apocalypse's language a certain rigidity and liturgical solemnity are especially important for textual criticism because they offer the possibility of looking into the value of each of the tradition's stems. Moreover, two insights emerge. Again and again, the study of the book's linguistic style shows that the seer repeats certain stereotypical phrases. Time and again, moreover, exceptions also surface where the [250] rule is broken. These exceptions surface in various kinds of linguistic phenomena. There-

---

195. Of the modern editions, only Weiss rejects it. Charles judges it properly (*Critical and Exegetical Commentary on the Revelation*, 1:36–37): The seer uses ὅμοιος with the meaning of ὡς and constructs it in these two places also as ὡς.

fore, we must conclude that they go back to the author himself and cannot be attributed to a redactor or to the tradition. The demonstrable rules of the Apocalypse's linguistic style are not rigid laws, to which the author is bound with absolute rigor, but are linguistic habits, which the author occasionally disregards.[196] It is methodologically unjustified to see a later hand wherever the rules are broken.[197] With that, however, we do not abandon the other methodological principle: that where the tradition is divided, the reading that corresponds to the rule claims the right to be considered the original.

The second insight obtained from a study of linguistic style refers to the value of the textual tradition's individual forms or stems. The linguistic style confirms what has already been shown in other ways regarding the outstanding value of AC's text. But this rating of AC's text was also qualified. AC's text is generally "neutral" in ways that P[47] S, Aν, and K are not, but this judgment should not be extended to orthography. Furthermore, real corrections are not entirely missing in the individual witnesses of AC's text, not even in A. However, the respective grammatical errors of AC in particular require a careful consideration of whether these go back to the original itself. We cannot always arrive at clear results, but it is methodologically unfounded for WHort and Charles to prefer this text almost without limitations.[198]

Working through the Apocalypse's textual tradition from the ground up, as was done here, does not achieve revolutionary results but, on the contrary, confirms that the textual arrangement of the newer editions to appear since Tischendorf and Tregelles are in principle [251] correct.[199] The current study is justified, in the first place, in the fully standardized usage of the manuscript tradition. We now really know how the archetype of Aν and of K read. The subordinate value of these two recensions, however,

---

196. The description of the occurrence of the Apocalypse's four horsemen is a particularly clear example of this in 6:1ff.; pp. 136–37.

197. Therefore, we dismiss Charles's list (*Critical and Exegetical Commentary on the Revelation*, 1:cliv–clv) of collected "primitive corruptions," like the following in §14.

198. This prejudice for AC is the counterpart of Tischendorf's preference for his discovery, Codex Sinaiticus.

199. In line with this, a judgment is also pronounced over Touilleux's otherwise stated opinion. His radical rejection of the previous criticism of the Apocalypse's text and its methods lacks the necessary expertise. The study of the linguistic style itself leads to results that confirm the results of the use of the textual tradition.

has been confirmed anew, especially through the study of the Apocalypse's linguistic style. Also, the inflated estimates of their common witnesses by Bousset and all the more von Soden must be corrected because although the two recensions share a recognizable but narrow common basis, they are not completely independent of each other.

The "older text" has been split into two clearly distinguishable text forms since P[47]'s discovery: AC and P[47] S. Also, P[47], which is now the oldest manuscript of the Apocalypse by far, confirms the outstanding value of AC's text again.

The number of places where the modern editions diverge, as one can see most conveniently in Nestle's edition, is not small. By methodically using the tradition and considering the author's linguistic style, the number of uncertain places can be significantly reduced.[200] There remain, however, a small number of places where careful, deliberative criticism of the tradition will not eliminate a *non liquet* and the choice between two competing readings for the *Urtext* cannot be settled. Future text-critical studies will hardly be able to remove this remnant of uncertainty. But on the whole, it is correct to say that by using the textual tradition fully we have greater certainty, even in those places where agreement already existed about the text's reconstruction, and the initially quoted judgment that the Apocalypse's text was "extremely uncertain" or "very poorly transmitted" can no longer be justified.

---

200. In particular, many of S's separate unique readings, which Tischendorf includes in his text, should be deleted. But also many readings that von Soden accepts on his theory that H I K are three independently juxtaposed texts are definitely to be rejected.

Appendix: Errata

Errata Pertaining to Codex Sinaiticus's Correctors

Sigla Use

49, 53 n. 113, 75	18:7	εαυτην S^a	S^a (= C^a)	> C^{c*}
128 n. 247	12:6	+ πεντε S^a	S^a (= C^a)	> C^{c*}
180	16:10	εσκοτισμενη S^a	S^a (= C^a)	> C^{c*}
227	16:18	om. και βρονται^2 S^a	S^a (= C^a)	> C^{c*}
70	21:27	και ποιων S^c	S^c (= C^c)	> C^a
241	6:4	αυτω [om. A S^c]	S^c (= C^c)	> C^a

Notes

14	Schmid claims that C^a corrects the first two leaves of Codex Sinaiticus and that C^c begins with his corrections at σκηνωσει in 7:16. This is incorrect. C^a made corrections throughout the Apocalypse; C^c corrects the first two pages; and C^{c*} begins at 7:16.
127–29	Schmid's attribution of the corrections of S^c to scribes A and D is erroneous. The corrections of A and D were made in the scriptorium (fourth century). S^c are *post*-scriptorium corrections (ca. seventh century). Schmid's claims about the fourth century origins of S^c's corrections, and their implications for the dating of the Andreas Text Type, are therefore problematic.

Errata Pertaining to Readings in Greek Manuscripts

57, 128 n. 247, 180	11:9	αφησουσιν S^a	> S^a correction is incomplete
172	4:2	και ευθεως S^a	> ευθεως δε S^a
196	11:16	οι [om. A S^a]	> οι [om. A]
226	22:20	+ Χριστου S^a	> + Χριστε S^a

Other Errata

Updated Manuscript Designations in the Translation

1	>	2814		1140	>	2922
94	>	2917		1352	>	2824
180	>	2918		1857	>	2923
181	>	2919		1894	>	2926
205^A	>	2886		2036^A	>	2891
209	>	2920		2040	>	911
429	>	2921		2062^A	>	1824
598	>	2595		2062^B	>	2350

Additional Updates

15	Under Q (046), Gregory of Nyssa is crossed out in Schmid's personally annotated copy of the *Studien*.
15, 31	P is dated to the ninth (not the tenth) century.
15, 31, 171	0163 is dated to the seventh century, not the fifth.
27	Regarding 18 – 2039 – 2138 919 2004 2200, elsewhere Schmid explains that 18 – 2039 – 2138 together form the subgroup f^{18}. The manuscripts 919 2004 2200 that follow are closely related to this subgroup but do not belong to it. This explains why only the first three manuscripts are connected with hyphens. See J. Schmid, "Untersuchungen zur Geschichte des griechischen Apokalypsetextes. Der *K*-Text," *Bib* 17 (1936): 11–44, 167–201, 273–93, 429-60.
31	Schmid's original listing of third and fourth century papyri that preserve the book of Revelation has expanded to include P^{85} (fourth/fifth), P^{98} (second?), and P^{115} (third/fourth).

34	2351 has two hands, not one.
39	Schmid's claim that the Andreas Commentary is not originally included in any manuscript with other New Testament writings is incorrect (e.g., 82 94 250 254 424 632 743 911 1678 1862). See Ulrich Schmid, "Die Apokalypse, überliefert mit anderen neutestamentlichen Schriften – eapr-Handschriften," in *Studien zum Text der Apokalypse*, ed. Marcus Sigismund, Martin Karrer, and Ulrich Schmid; ANTF (Berlin: de Gruyter, 2015), 421–41.
86	1611 is crossed out in Schmid's personally annotated copy of the *Studien*.
111	81–86 corrected to 81–108 (for Byz.-Ngr. Jb 11 [1934]) in Schmid's personally annotated copy of the *Studien*.
218	C is removed as a witness for οσοι αν in 13:15 from Schmid's personally annotated copy of the *Studien*.
223	C is removed as a witness for ου μη ευρωσιν in 9:6 from Schmid's personally annotated copy of the *Studien*.
235	In the penultimate paragraph, 6:8 is corrected to 4:8 in Schmid's personally annotated copy of the *Studien*.
251; cf. 14, 173	P[47] is no longer the oldest manuscript of the Apocalypse.

Typos Corrected in the Translation

18 n. 45	F.H.A.A.	> F.H.A.
48	κατσικουντας	> κατοικουντας
102	πρσεβυτοι	> πρεσβυτεροι
111	81–86	> 81–108
143	βσβυλων	> βαβυλων
128	(4)	> (44)
131	wav	> waw
159	105	> 205
195	κδ	> $\overline{κδ}$

212	εις της γην and εις της γην θαλασσαν	> εις την γην and εις την θαλασσαν
235	6:8	> 4:8
240	11:9	> 11:19

Bibliography

Aland, Kurt. "Zur Liste der griechischen neutestamentliche Hand-schriften." *TLZ* 78 (1953): 465–96.

Aland, Kurt, and Barbara Aland. *The Text of the New Testament: An Introduction to the Critical Editions and to the Theory and Practice of Modern Textual Criticism.* Translated by Erroll F. Rhodes. 2nd ed. Grand Rapids: Eerdmans, 1986.

Allen, Garrick V. "Exegetical Reasoning and Singular Readings in the New Testament Manuscript Tradition: The Apocalypse in Codex Alexandrinus." *JBL* 135 (2016): 859–80.

Allo, E. Bernard. *Saint Jean, L'Apocalypse.* 3rd ed. Paris: Gabalda, 1933.

Bauer, Walter. *Griechisch-Deutsches Wörterbuch zu den Schriften des Neuen Testaments und der übrigen urchristlichen Literatur.* Giessen: Töpelmann, 1928.

Bees, Nikos A. "Χειρόγραφον τῆς μονῆς Πετριτζονιτίσσης-Μπασκόβου: Πρακτικά Χριστιανικῆς Ἀρχαιολογικῆς Ἑταιρείας" [Manuscript of the Monastery of Petrizontissis-Mpaskobo: Proceedings of the Christian Archaeological Society]. *BNJ* 14 (1937–1938): 457.

Birdsall, J. Neville. "The Text of the Revelation of Saint John: A Review of Its Materials and Problems with Especial Reference to the Work of Josef Schmid." *EvQ* 33 (1961): 228–37.

Blass, Friedrich. *Grammatik des neutestamentlichen Griechisch.* Edited by Albert Debrunner. 9th ed. Göttingen: Vandenhoeck & Ruprecht, 1954.

Bludau, A. "Die Apokalypse und Theodotions Danielübersetzung." *TQ* 79 (1897): 1–26.

Bonner, Campbell. "A Papyrus Codex of the Shepherd of Hermas." *HTR* 18 (1925): 115–27.

Bonwetsch, G. Nathanael, and Hans Achelis, eds. *Exegetische und homiletische Schriften.* Vol. 1 of *Hippolytus Werke.* GCS 1.2. Leipzig: Hinrichs, 1897.

Bousset, Wilhelm. *Die Offenbarung Johannis*. Göttingen : Vandenhoeck & Ruprecht, 1896.

———. "Neues Testament: Textkritik." *TRu* 17 (1914): 187–206.

———. *Textkritische Studien zum Neuen Testament*. TU 11.4. Leipzig: Hinrichs, 1894.

———. "Zur Textkritik der Apokalypse." Pages 1–44 in *Textkritische Studien zum Neuen Testament*. TU 11.4. Leipzig: Hinrichs, 1894.

Bover, José María. "¿El códice 1841 (= 127) es el mejor representante del Apocalipsis?" *EstEcl* 18 (1944): 165–85.

———. *Novi Testamenti Biblia graeca et Latina*. Madrid: Consejo Superior de Investigaciones Científicas, 1943.

Burgon, John William. *The Revision Revised: Three Articles Reprinted from the Quarterly Review*. London: Murray, 1883.

Chapman, John. "The Order of the Gospels in the Parent of Codex Bezae." *ZNW* 6 (1905): 339–46.

———. "The Original Contents of Codex Bezae." *Expositor* 6/12 (1905): 46–53.

Charles, R. H. *A Critical and Exegetical Commentary on the Revelation of St. John*. 2 vols. Edinburgh: T&T Clark, 1920.

———. *Studies in the Apocalypse*. 2nd ed. Edinburgh: T&T Clark, 1915.

Clark, Kenneth W. *A Descriptive Catalogue of Greek New Testament Manuscripts in America*. Chicago: University of Chicago Press, 1937.

Colwell, Ernest C. "Method in Establishing the Nature of Text-Types of New Testament Manuscripts." Pages 45–55 in *Studies in Methodology in Textual Criticism of the New Testament*. NTTS 9. Grand Rapids: Eerdmans, 1969.

Conybeare, Fred C. *The Armenian Version of Revelation and Cyril of Alexandria's Scholia on the Incarnation and Epistle on Easter*. London: Text and Translation Society, 1907.

Cramer, John Anthony. *In Epistolas Catholicas et Apocalypsin*. Vol. 8 of *Catenae Graecorum Patrum in Novum Testamentum*. Oxford: Typographeo Academico, 1844.

Crum, W. E., and H. J. Bell, eds. *Wadi Sarga: Coptic and Greek Texts from the Excavations Undertaken by the Byzantine Research Account*. With an introduction by R. Campbell Thompson. Coptica 3. Hauniae: Gyldenalske Boghandel-Nordisk, 1922.

Deissmann, Adolf. "Handschriften aus Anatolien in Ankara und Izmit." *ZNW* 34 (1935): 262–84.

Delling, Gerhard. "ἐρευνάω." *TWNT* 2:653–54.

Dobschütz, Ernst von, ed. *Eberhard Nestle's Einführung in das griechische Neue Testament*. 4th ed. Göttingen: Vandenhoeck & Ruprecht 1923.

———. "Zur Liste der NTlichen Handschriften." *ZNW* 32 (1933): 185–206.

Driver, G. R. Review of *Traité de Grammaire Hébraïque*, by Mayer Lambert. *JTS* 40 (1939): 177–79.

Ehrhard, Albert. *Überlieferung und Bestand der hagiographischen und homiletischen Literatur der griechischen Kirche von den Anfangen bis zum Ende des 16. Jahrhunderts*. 3 vols. TU 50–52. Leipzig: Hinrichs, 1937–1952.

Elliott, J. K. "Recent Work on the Greek Manuscripts of Revelation and Their Consequences for the *Kurzgefasste Liste*." *JTS* 66 (2015): 574–84.

Ellis, Arthur Ayers, ed., *Bentleii Critica Sacra: Notes on the Greek and Latin Text of the New Testament, Extracted from the Bentley Mss. in Trinity College Library*. Cambridge: Deighton, Bell, 1862.

Estienne, Robert. *Novum Testamentum*. 2 vols. Paris: n.p., 1546.

Gebhardt, Oscar von. *Die Psalmen Salomos*. TU 13.2. Leipzig: Hinrichs, 1895.

Green, Thomas Sheldon. *A Course of Developed Criticism on Passages of the New Testament Materially Affected by Various Readings*. London: Bagster, 1856.

Gregory, Caspar René. *Prolegomena*. Vol. 3 of *Novum Testamentum Graece: Editio octava critica maior*. Edited by Constantin von Tischendorf. Leipzig: Hinrichs, 1894.

———. *Textkritik des Neuen Testamentes*. Leipzig: Hinrichs, 1900.

Grenfell, Bernard P., and A. S. Hunt, eds. *The Oxyrhynchus Papyri: Part VI*. London: Egypt Exploration Society, 1908.

———, eds. *The Oxyrhynchus Papyri: Part X*. London: Egypt Exploration Fund, 1914.

Griesbach, Johann Jakob. *Novum Testamentum Graece*. 2nd ed. 2 vols. London: Elmsly, 1796–1806.

Gurry, Peter J. "How Your Greek NT Is Changing: A Simple Introduction to the Coherence-Based Genealogical Method (CBGM)." *JETS* 59 (2016): 675–89.

Gwynn, John. *The Apocalypse of John in a Syriac Version Hitherto Unknown*. Dublin: Academy House, 1897.

Hagedorn, Dieter. "P.IFAO II 31: Johannesappokalypse 1,13–20." *ZPE* 92 (1992): 243–47.

Harvey, W. Wigan, ed. *Sancti Irenaei Episcopi Lugdunensis: Libros quinque adversus Haereses*. 2 vols. Cambridge: Typis Academicis, 1857.

Hatch, William H. P. *Facsimiles and Descriptions of Minuscule Manuscripts of the New Testament.* Cambridge: Harvard University Press, 1951.

Hatzidakis, Georgios N. *Einleitung in die neugriechische Grammatik.* Leipzig: Breitkopf, 1892.

Haussleiter, Johannis. *Victorini Episcopi Petavionensis Opera.* CSEL 49. Vienna: Tempsky, 1916.

Heikel, Ivar A., ed. *Demonstratio evangelica.* Vol. 6 of *Eusebius Werke.* GCS 23. Leipzig: Hinrichs, 1913.

Helbing, Robert. *Die Kasussyntax der Verba bei den Septuaginta: Ein Beitrag zur Hebraismenfrage und zur Syntax der Κοινή.* Göttingen: Vandenhoeck & Ruprecht, 1928.

———. *Grammatik der Septuaginta, Laut- und Wortlehre.* Göttingen: Vandenhoeck & Ruprecht, 1907.

Hernández, Juan, Jr. "The Creation of a Fourth-Century Witness to the Andreas Text Type: A Misreading in the Apocalypse's Textual History." *NTS* 60 (2014): 106–20.

———. "The Legacy of Wilhelm Bousset for the Apocalypse's Textual History: The Identification of the Andreas Text." Pages 19–32 in *Studien zum Text der Apokalypse.* Edited by Marcus Sigismund, Martin Karrer, and Ulrich Schmid. ANTF 47. Berlin: de Gruyter, 2015.

———. "Nestle-Aland 28 and the Revision of the Apocalypse's Textual History." Pages 71–81 in *Studies on the Text of the New Testament and Early Christianity: Essays in Honour of Michael W. Holmes.* Edited by Daniel M. Gurtner, Juan Hernández Jr., and Paul Foster. NTTSD 50. Leiden: Brill, 2015.

Holmes, Michael W. "Working with an Open Textual Tradition: Challenges in Theory and Practice." Pages 65–78 in *The Textual History of the Greek New Testament: Changing Views in Contemporary Research.* Edited by Klaus Wachtel and Michael W. Holmes. TCS 8. Atlanta: Society of Biblical Literature, 2011.

Hörmann, Fritz. "Beiträge zur Syntax des Johannes Kinnamos." Diss., Münich, 1938.

Horner, George William. *The Coptic Version of the New Testament in the Northern Dialect.* 4 vols. Oxford: Clarendon, 1898.

———. *The Coptic Version of the New Testament in the Southern Dialect.* 7 vols. Oxford: Clarendon, 1911.

Hoskier, H. C. *Concerning the Date of the Bohairic Version.* London: Quaritch, 1911.

———. *Concerning the Text of the Apocalypse.* 2 vols. London: Quaritch, 1929.

Hunt, Arthur S. *The Oxyrhynchus Papyri: Part VIII.* London: Egypt Exploration Society, 1911.

Jacquier, Eugène. *Le Nouveau Testament dans l'Eglise chrétienne.* 2nd ed. 2 vols. Paris: Gabalda, 1911.

Jülicher, Adolf. *Einleitung in das Neue Testament.* 7th ed. GTW 3.1. Tübingen: Mohr, 1931.

———. Review of *The Armenian Version of Revelation and Cyril of Alexandria's Scholia on the Incarnation and Epistle on Easter,* by Fred C. Conybeare. *TLZ* 33 (1908): 78–80.

Karrer, Martin. "Der Text der Apokalypse—Textkritik und Theologiegeschichte." Pages 207–43 in *Revelation, Colloquium Biblicum Louvaniense.* Edited by Adela Yarbro Collins. BETL 291. Leuven: Peeters, 2017.

———. "Der Text der Johannesapokalypse." Pages 43–78 in *Die Johannesapokalypse: Kontexte—Konzepte—Rezeption / The Revelation of John: Contexts—Concepts—Reception.* Edited by Jörg Frey, James A. Kelhoffer, and Franz Tóth. WUNT 287. Tübingen: Mohr Siebeck, 2012.

———. *Johannesoffenbarung (Offb.1,1–5,14).* EKKNT 24.1. Göttingen: Vandenhoeck & Ruprecht, 2017.

Kelley, William. *Revelation of John: Edited in Greek with a New English Version, and a Statement of the Chief Authorities and Various Readings.* London: Williams & Norgate, 1860.

Kenyon, Frederick G., ed., *The Chester Beatty Biblical Papyri: Descriptions and Texts of Twelve Manuscripts on Papyrus of the Greek Bible.* London: Walker, 1934. Facsimile ed., 1936.

———. *Handbook to the Textual Criticism of the New Testament.* Vol. 2. London: Macmillan, 1912.

Kilpatrick, G. D. "Professor J. Schmid on the Greek Text of the Apocalypse." *VC* 13 (1959): 1–13.

Labahn, Michael, and Martin Karrer, eds. *Die Johannesoffenbarung: Ihr Text und ihre Auslegung.* ABG 38. Leipzig: Evangelische Verlagsanstalt, 2012.

Lachmann, Karl. *Novum Testamentum Graece.* Berlin: Reimer, 1831.

Lagrange, Marie-Joseph. *Critique Textuelle.* Vol. 2 of *Introduction à l'étude du Nouveau Testament.* Paris: Gabalda, 1935.

Lembke, Markus. "Die Apokalypse-Handschrift 2846: Beschreibung, Kollation und Textwertbestimmung eines wichtigen neuen Zeugen." *NovT* 54 (2012): 369–95.

Lembke, Markus, Darius Müller, and Ulrich B. Schmid with Martin Karrer, eds. *Text und Textwert der griechischen Handschriften des Neuen Testaments VI: Die Apokalypse; Teststellenkollation und Auswertungen.* ANTF 49. Berlin: de Gruyter, 2017.

Lohmeyer, Ernst. *Die Offenbarung des Johannes.* HNT 16. Tübingen: Mohr, 1926.

Lommatzsch, Karl Heinrich Eduard, ed. *Opera omnia quae Graece vel Latine tantum existant.* 25 vols. Berlin: Haude & Spener, 1831–1848.

Maas, Paul. Review of *Ephraem Syri Opera.* Edited by Sylvio G. Mercati. *ByzZ* 23 (1914–1919): 264.

———. *Textual Criticism.* Translated by Barbara Flower. Oxford: Clarendon, 1958.

Malik, Peter. "Another Look at P.IFAO II 31 (P⁹⁸): An Updated Transcription and Textual Analysis." *NovT* 58 (2016): 204–17.

———. "Corrections of Codex Sinaiticus and the Textual Transmission of Revelation: Josef Schmid Revisited." *NTS* 61 (2015): 595–614.

———. "The Earliest Corrections in Codex Sinaiticus: Further Evidence from the Apocalypse." *TC* 20 (2015): 1–12.

Mayser, Edwin. *Grammatik der griechischen Papyri aus der Ptolemäerzeit.* 2 vols. Berlin: de Gruyter, 1923–1938.

Merk, Augustinus. "Nova editio Novi Testamenti graece et latine." *Bib* 24 (1943): 182–84.

———. *Novum Testamentum Graece et Latine.* Rome: Sumptibus Pontificii Instituti Biblici, 1933.

Metzger, Bruce M. Review of *Studien zur Geschichte des griechischen Apokalypse-Textes,* by Josef Schmid. *Gn* 29 (1957): 285–89.

Mill, John. *Novum Testamentum Graecum.* Oxford: n.p., 1707.

Milligan, George. *The New Testament Documents: Their Origin and Early History.* London: Macmillan, 1913.

Milne, H. J. M., and T. C. Skeat. *Scribes and Correctors of the Codex Sinaiticus.* London: British Museum, 1938.

Mink, Gerd. "Contamination, Coherence, and Coincidence in Textual Transmission: The Coherence-Based Genealogical Method (CBGM) as a Complement and Corrective to Existing Approaches." Pages 141–216 in *The Textual History of the Greek New Testament: Changing Views in Contemporary Research.* Edited by Klaus Wachtel and Michael W. Holmes. TCS 8. Atlanta: Society of Biblical Literature, 2011.

———. "Problems of a Highly Contaminated Tradition: The New Testament; Stemmata of Variants as a Source of Genealogy for Witnesses."

Pages 13–85 in *Studies in Stemmatology II*. Edited by Pieter van Reenen, August de Hollander, and Margot van Mulken. Amsterdam: Benjamins, 2004.

———. "Was verändert sich in der Textkritik durch die Beachtung genealogischer Kohärenz?" Pages 39–68 in *Recent Developments in Textual Criticism: New Testament, Other Early Christian and Jewish Literature; Papers Read at a Noster Conference in Münster, January 4–6, 2001*. Edited by Wim Weren and Dietrich-Alex Koch. STR 8. Assen: Van Gorcum, 2003.

Moulton, James Hope. *Prolegomena*. Vol. 1 of *A Grammar of New Testament Greek*. Edinburgh: T&T Clark, 1908.

Moulton, James Hope, and George Milligan. *The Vocabulary of the Greek Testament*. London: Hodder & Stoughton, 1914–1929.

Moulton, James Hope, and Wilbert Francis Howard. *Accidence and Word-Formation*. Vol. 2 of *A Grammar of New Testament Greek*. Edinburgh: T&T Clark, 1919.

Müller, Darius. "Der griechische Text der Johannesapokalypse und seine Überlieferung: Untersucht an der Teststellenkollation und Auswertungslisten in 'Text und Textwert VI. Die Apokalypse.'" PhD diss., Kirchliche Hochschule Wuppertal/Bethel, 2017.

Neuss, Wilhelm. *Die Apokalypse des hl. Johannes in der altspanischen und altchristlichen Bibel-Illustration*. 2 vols. Münster: Aschendorff, 1931.

Oman, John. *The Text of Revelation: A Revised Theory*. Cambridge: Cambridge University Press, 1928.

———. *The Text of Revelation: Theory of the Text, Rearranged Text and Translation*. Cambridge: Cambridge University Press, 1923.

Pallas, Demetrios I. "Κατάλογος των χειρογράφων του Βυζαντινού Μουσείου Αθηνών" [Catalog of Manuscripts of the Byzantine Museum of Athens]. *BNJ* 11 (1934–1935): α΄–οα΄.

Parker, David C. "A New Oxyrhynchus Papyrus of Revelation: P[115] (P.Oxy 4499)." *NTS* 46 (2000): 159–74.

Politis, L. N. "Τὰ ἐκ Σερρῶν χειρόγραφα ἐν τῇ Ἐθνικῇ Βιβλιοθήκῃ" [Serbian Manuscripts in the National Library]. *Hellēniká* 4 (1931): 525–26.

Preuschen, Erwin, ed. *Der Johanneskommentar*. GCS 10. Leipzig: Hinrichs, 1903.

Radermacher, Ludwig. *Neutestamentliche Grammatik: Das griechisch des Neuen Testaments im Zusammenhang mit der Volkssprache dargestellt*. 2nd. ed. Tübingen: Mohr, 1925.

Richard, Marcel. *Répertoire des Bibliothèques et des Catalogues de Manuscrits Grecs*. Paris: Centre national de la recherche scientifique, 1948.

Robinson, J. Armitage, ed. *The Philocalia of Origen*. Cambridge: Cambridge University Press, 1893.

Sanday, William, and Cuthbert Hamilton Turner, eds. *Novum Testamentum sancti Irenaei Lugdunensis*. OLBT 7. Oxford: Clarendon, 1923.

Sanders, Henry A. *Beati in Apocalipsin libri duodecim*. Rome: American Academy in Rome, 1930.

Schmid, Josef. *Der Apokalypse-Kommentar des Andreas von Kaisareia: Einleitung*. Vol. 1.2 of *Studien zur Geschichte des griechischen Apokalypse-Textes*. MThS 1. Munich: Zink, 1956.

———. *Der Apokalypse-Kommentar des Andreas von Kaisareia: Text*. Vol. 1.1 of *Studien zur Geschichte des griechischen Apokalypse-Textes*. MThS 1. Munich: Zink, 1955.

———. "Der Apokalypse-Text des Kodex 0207 (Papiri della Societa Italiana 1166)." *BZ* 23 (1935–1936): 187–89.

———. "Der Apokalypse-Text des Oikumenios." *Bib* 40 (1959): 935–42.

———. *Der Apokalypsetext des Arethas von Kaisareia und einiger anderer jüngerer Gruppen*. Vol. 1 of *Untersuchungen zur Geschichte des griechischen Apokalypsetextes*. TFBNP 17. Athens: Byzantinische-neugriechischen Jahrbücher, 1936.

———. "Der Apokalypsetext des Chester Beatty 𝔓⁴⁷." *BNJ* 11 (1934–1935): 81–108.

———. *Die alten Stämme*. Vol. 2 of *Studien zur Geschichte des griechischen Apokalypse-Textes*. MThS 2. Munich: Zink, 1955.

———. "Die handschriftliche Überlieferung des Apokalypse-Ausleger und Oikumenios der Bischof von Trikka." *BNJ* 14 (1937–1938): 322–30.

———. "Die handschriftliche Überlieferung des Apokalypse-Kommentar des Arethas von Kaisareia." *BNJ* 17 (1939–1943): 72–81.

———. "Neue griechische Apokalypsehandschriften." *ZNW* 59 (1968): 250–58.

———. "Unbeachtete Apokalypse-Handschriften." *TQ* 117 (1936): 149–87.

———. "Unbeachtete und unbekannte griechische Apokalypsehandschriften." *ZNW* 52 (1961): 82–88.

———. "Untersuchungen zur Geschichte des griechischen Apokalypsetextes: Der *K*-Text." *Bib* 17 (1936): 11–14, 167–201, 273–93, 429–40.

———. "Zur Liste der neutestamentlichen Handschriften." *ZNW* 34 (1935): 308–9.

———. "Zur Textkritik der Apokalypse." *ZNW* 43 (1950–1951): 112–28.

———. "Zur Textüberlieferung des Oikumenios-Kommentars zur Apo-kalypse." *BZ* 19 (1931): 255–56.

Schmid, Ulrich. "Die Apokalypse, überliefert mit anderen neutestamentli-chen Schriften—eapr-Handschriften." Pages 421–41 in *Studien zum Text der Apokalypse.* Edited by Marcus Sigismund, Martin Karrer, and Ulrich Schmid. ANTF 47. Berlin: de Gruyter, 2015.

Scholz, Johann Martin Augustin. *Novum Testamentum Graece.* 2 vols. Leipzig: Fleischer, 1830–1836.

Schwartz, Eduard, ed. *Die Kirchengeschichte.* Vol. 2 of *Eusebius Werke.* GCS 9.1. Leipzig: Hinrichs, 1908.

———. *Zwei Predigten Hippolyts.* SBAW 3. Munich: Bayerische Akademie der Wissenschaften, 1936.

Scrivener, Frederick Henry. *An Exact Transcript of the Codex Augiensis: A Graeco-Latin Manuscript of S. Paul's Epistles.* Cambridge: Deighton, Bell, 1859.

———. *A Full and Exact Collation of About Twenty Greek Manuscripts of the Holy Gospels (Hitherto Unexamined).* Cambridge: Cambridge Uni-versity Press, 1853.

———. *A Plain Introduction to the Criticism of the New Testament.* Cam-bridge: Deighton, Bell, 1861.

———. *A Supplement to the Authorised English Version of the New Testa-ment.* London: Pickering, 1845.

Scrivener, Frederick Henry, and Edward Miller. *A Plain Introduction to the Criticism of the New Testament.* 4th ed. London: Bell, 1894.

Severyn, Albert. *Le codex 239 de Photius.* Vol. 1 of *Recherches sur Chres-tomathie de Proclos.* Liège: Faculté de Philosophie et Lettres, 1938.

Sigismund, Marcus, and Darius Müller, eds. *Studien zum Text der Apo-kalypse II.* ANTF 50. Berlin: de Gruyter, 2017.

Sigismund, Marcus, Martin Karrer, and Ulrich Schmid, eds. *Studien zum Text der Apokalypse.* ANTF 47. Berlin: de Gruyter, 2015.

Soden, Hermann von. *Die Schriften des Neuen Testaments in ihrer ältesten erreichbaren Textgestalt.* 2 vols. Berlin: Duncker, 1902–1913.

Souter, Alexander. *Novum Testamentum Graece.* 2nd ed. Oxford: Claren-don, 1947.

Stählin, Otto, ed. *Des Clemens von Alexandreia ausgewählte Schriften aus dem Griechischen übersetzt.* 5 vols. BK 2.7, 8, 17, 19, 20. Munich: Kosel-Pustet, 1934–1938.

Stampini, Ettore, Gaetano de Sanctis, Carlo Cipolla, and Carlo Frati.

"Inventario dei codici superstiti greci e latini antichi della Biblioteca Nazionale di Torino." *RFIC* 32 (1904): 584.

Streeter, B. H. "The Caesarean Text of the Gospels." *JTS* 26 (1924–1925): 373–78.

———. "The Four Gospels: A Study of Origins." *JTS* 26 (1925): 278–94.

Swete, Henry Barclay. *The Apocalypse of St. John: The Greek Text with Introduction, Notes, and Indices.* 3rd ed. London: Macmillan, 1909.

Tasker, R. V. G. "The Chester Beatty Papyrus of the Apocalypse of John." *JTS* 50 (1949): 60–68.

Thackeray, Henry St. John. *Introduction, Orthography and Accidence.* Vol. 1 of *A Grammar of the Old Testament in Greek: According to the Septuagint.* Cambridge: Cambridge University Press, 1909.

Thumb, Albert. *Die griechische Sprache im Zeitalter des Hellenismus: Beiträge zur Geschichte und Beurteilung der Κοινή.* Strassburg: Trübner, 1901.

Tischendorf, Constantin von. *Monumenta sacra inedita.* Leipzig: Tauchnitz, 1846.

———. *Monumenta sacra inedita: Nova collectio.* Vol. 6. Leipzig: Hinrichs, 1869.

———. *Novum Testamentum Graece.* 3 vols. Leipzig: Köhler, 1841. 2nd ed. Leipzig: Winter, 1849.

———. *Novum Testamentum Graece: Editio octava critica maior.* 2 vols. Leipzig: Hinrichs, 1869–1872.

———. *Novum Testamentum Sinaiticum cum Epistula Barnabae et Fragmentis Pastoris.* 2 vols. Leipzig: Brockhaus, 1863.

Touilleux, Paul. *L'Apocalypse et les Cultes de Domitien et de Cybèle.* Paris: Geunther, 1935.

Tregelles, Samuel Prideaux. *Book of Revelation in Greek Edited from Ancient Authorities.* London: Bagster, 1844.

Tzamolikos, P. *An Ancient Commentary on the Book of Revelation: A Critical Edition of the Scholia in Apocalypsin.* Cambridge: Cambridge University Press, 2013.

Vitelli, Girolamo, ed. *Papiri Greci e Latini.* Vol. 10. Florence: Ariani, 1932.

Vogels, Heinrich Joseph. *Novum Testamentum Graece.* Düsseldorf: Schwann, 1920.

———. *Untersuchungen zur Geschichte der lateinischen Apokalypse-Übersetzung.* Düsseldorf: Schwann, 1920.

Wackernagel, J. Review of *Grammatik der griechischen Papyri aus der Ptolemäerzeit,* by Edwin Mayser. *TLZ* 33 (1908): 34–39.

Walton, Brian. *Biblia sacra polyglotta*. London: Roycroft, 1657.

Weiss, Bernhard. *Die Johannes-Apokalypse: Textkritische Untersuchungen und Textherstellung*. TU 7.1. Leipzig: Hinrichs, 1891.

Westcott, Brooke Foss, and Fenton John Anthony Hort. *Introduction to the New Testament in the Original Greek, with Notes on Selected Readings*. Eugene, OR: Wipf & Stock, 2003.

———. *The New Testament in the Original Greek*. 2 vols. Cambridge: Cambridge University Press, 1881.

Wettstein, Johann Jakob. *Novum Testamentum Graecum*. Vol. 2. Amsterdam: Dommer, 1752.

Willoughby, Harold R., and Ernest Cadman Colwell, eds. *The Elizabeth Day McCormick Apocalypse*. 2 vols. Chicago: University of Chicago Press, 1940.

Woide, Charles Godfrey. *Novum Testamentum Graecum*. London: Nichols, 1786.

Ziegler, Joseph. *Duodecim prophetae*. SVTG 13. Göttingen: Vandenhoeck & Ruprecht, 1943.

———. *Isaias*. SVTG 14. Göttingen: Vandenhoeck & Ruprecht, 1939.

———. *Susanna, Daniel, Bel et Draco*. SVTG 16.2. Göttingen: Vandenhoeck & Ruprecht, 1954.

Biblical References Index

Modern Authors Index

Subject Index

Lightning Source UK Ltd.
Milton Keynes UK
UKHW010035070223
416578UK00002B/302

9 780884 142829